EAGERLY AWAITING YOUR IRRATIONAL RESPONSE

Recent DILBERT® Books from Andrews McMeel Publishing

Dilbert Turns 30

Cubicles That Make You Envy the Dead

Dilbert Gets Re-accommodated

I'm No Scientist, But I Think Feng Shui Is Part of the Answer

Optimism Sounds Exhausting

Go Add Value Someplace Else

I Sense a Coldness to Your Mentoring

Your New Job Title Is "Accomplice"

I Can't Remember If We're Cheap or Smart

Teamwork Means You Can't Pick the Side that's Right

How's That Underling Thing Working Out for You?

Your Accomplishments Are Suspiciously Hard to Verify

Problem Identified and You're Probably Not Part of the Solution

I'm Tempted to Stop Acting Randomly

14 Years of Loyal Service in a Fabric-Covered Box

Freedom's Just Another Word for People Finding Out You're Useless

Dilbert 2.0: 20 Years of Dilbert

This Is the Part Where You Pretend to Add Value

EAGERLY AWAITING YOUR IRRATIONAL RESPONSE

DILBERT™ BY SCOTT ADAMS
dilbert.com

Andrews McMeel
PUBLISHING®

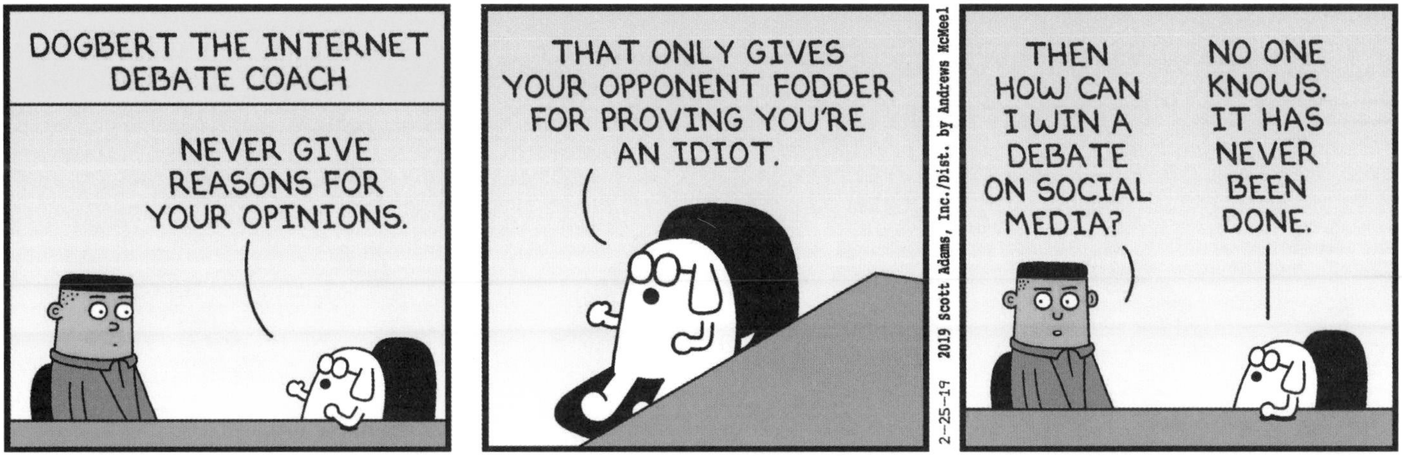
DOGBERT THE INTERNET DEBATE COACH
NEVER GIVE REASONS FOR YOUR OPINIONS.
THAT ONLY GIVES YOUR OPPONENT FODDER FOR PROVING YOU'RE AN IDIOT.
2-25-19 2019 Scott Adams, Inc./Dist. by Andrews McMeel
THEN HOW CAN I WIN A DEBATE ON SOCIAL MEDIA?
NO ONE KNOWS. IT HAS NEVER BEEN DONE.

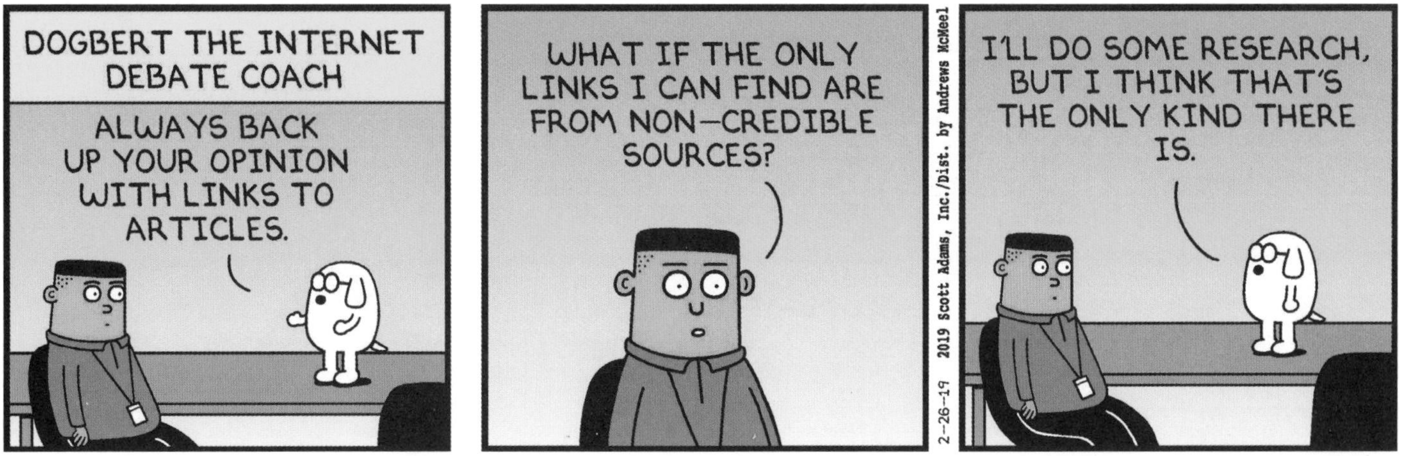
DOGBERT THE INTERNET DEBATE COACH
ALWAYS BACK UP YOUR OPINION WITH LINKS TO ARTICLES.
WHAT IF THE ONLY LINKS I CAN FIND ARE FROM NON—CREDIBLE SOURCES?
2-26-19 2019 Scott Adams, Inc./Dist. by Andrews McMeel
I'LL DO SOME RESEARCH, BUT I THINK THAT'S THE ONLY KIND THERE IS.

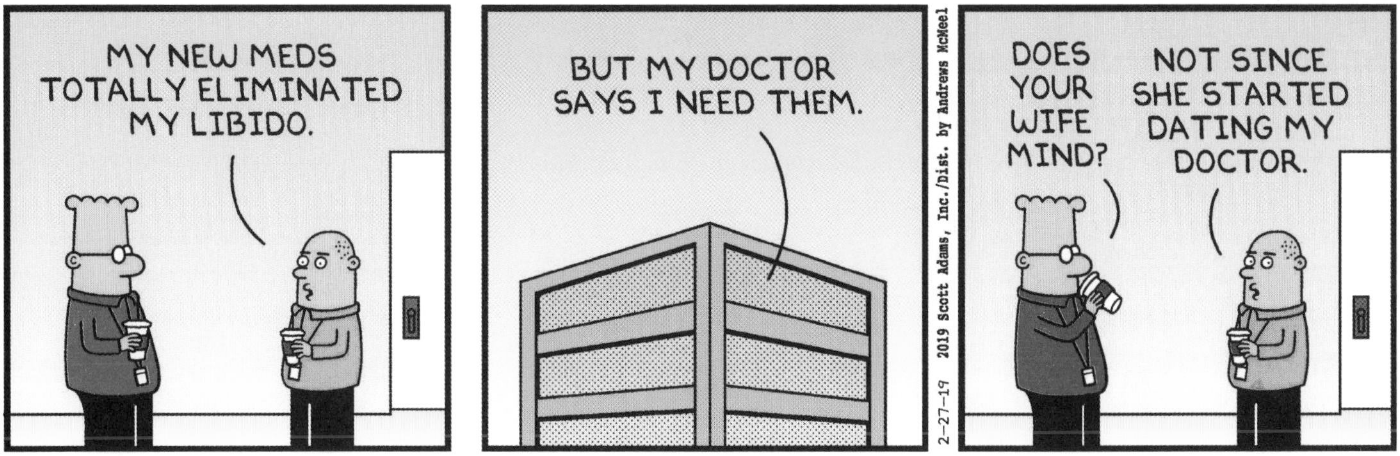
MY NEW MEDS TOTALLY ELIMINATED MY LIBIDO.
BUT MY DOCTOR SAYS I NEED THEM.
2-27-19 2019 Scott Adams, Inc./Dist. by Andrews McMeel
DOES YOUR WIFE MIND?
NOT SINCE SHE STARTED DATING MY DOCTOR.

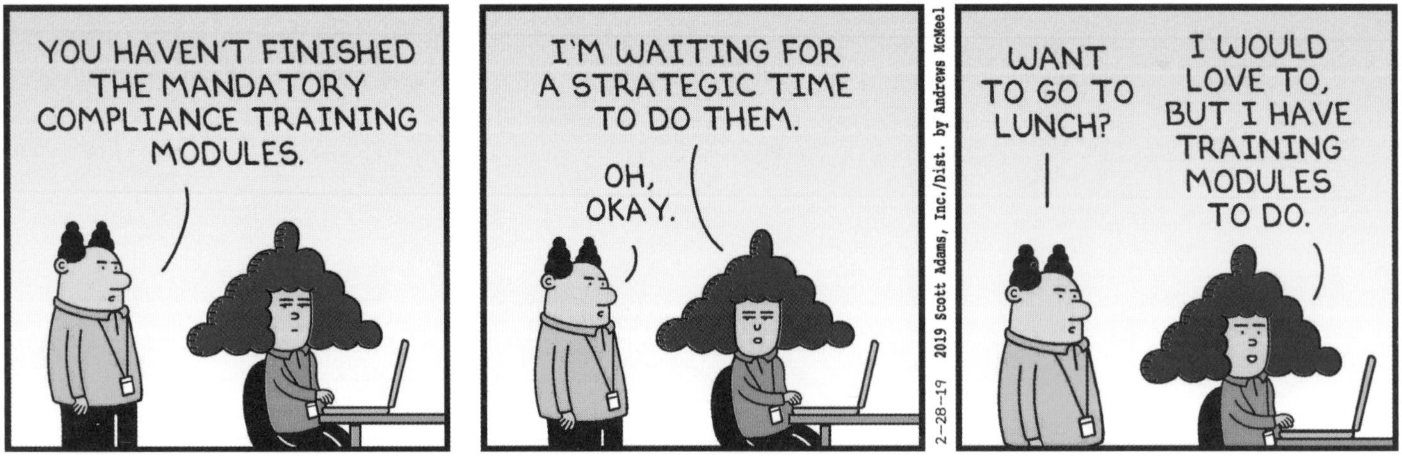
YOU HAVEN'T FINISHED THE MANDATORY COMPLIANCE TRAINING MODULES.
I'M WAITING FOR A STRATEGIC TIME TO DO THEM.
OH, OKAY.
2-28-19 2019 Scott Adams, Inc./Dist. by Andrews McMeel
WANT TO GO TO LUNCH?
I WOULD LOVE TO, BUT I HAVE TRAINING MODULES TO DO.

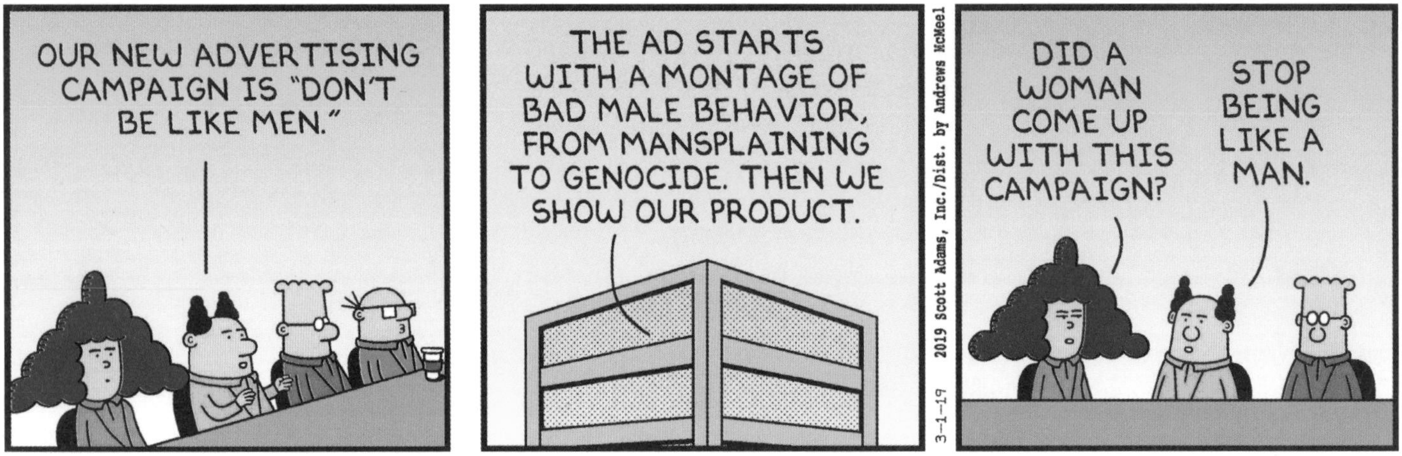
OUR NEW ADVERTISING CAMPAIGN IS "DON'T BE LIKE MEN."
THE AD STARTS WITH A MONTAGE OF BAD MALE BEHAVIOR, FROM MANSPLAINING TO GENOCIDE. THEN WE SHOW OUR PRODUCT.
3-1-19 2019 Scott Adams, Inc./Dist. by Andrews McMeel
DID A WOMAN COME UP WITH THIS CAMPAIGN?
STOP BEING LIKE A MAN.

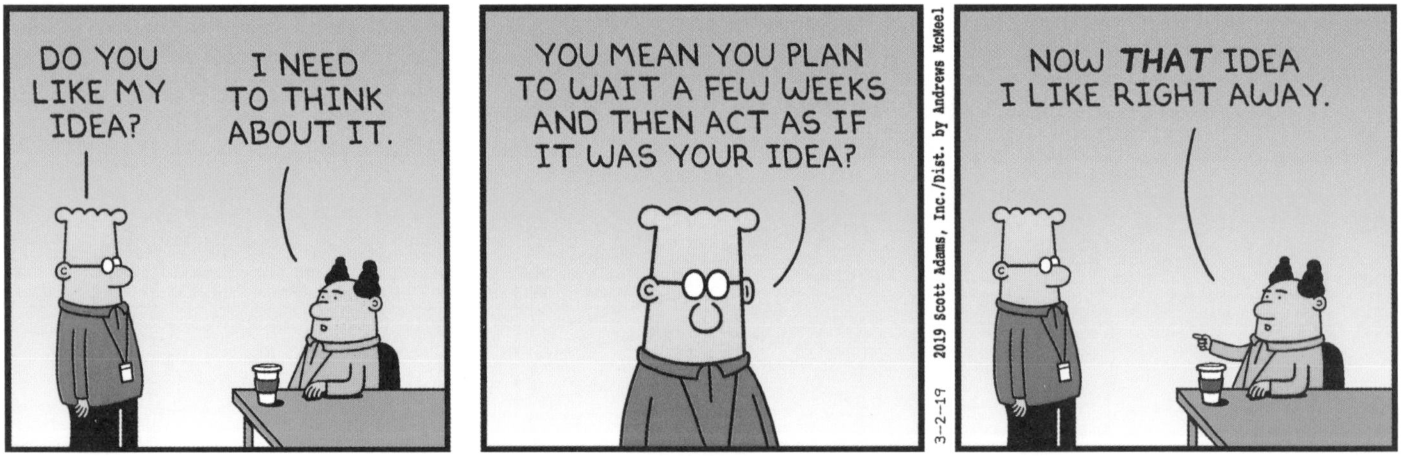
DO YOU LIKE MY IDEA?
I NEED TO THINK ABOUT IT.
YOU MEAN YOU PLAN TO WAIT A FEW WEEKS AND THEN ACT AS IF IT WAS YOUR IDEA?
3-2-19 2019 Scott Adams, Inc./Dist. by Andrews McMeel
NOW THAT IDEA I LIKE RIGHT AWAY.

I CREATED A SIMULATED WORLD MADE ENTIRELY OF SOFTWARE.
I PROGRAMMED ALL OF THE PEOPLE IN THE SIMULATION TO THINK THEY ARE REAL PEOPLE WITH FREE WILL.
ARE THEY SENTIENT BEINGS?
THEY THINK THEY ARE.
WHAT IF THEY DISCOVER THEIR TRUE NATURE?
I PROGRAMMED LIMITS INTO THEIR PHYSICS SO THEY CAN NEVER OBSERVE THE WALLS OF THEIR REALITY.
FOR EXAMPLE, THEY CAN'T GET TO THE EDGE OF THEIR UNIVERSE BECAUSE THEY CAN'T EXCEED THE SPEED OF LIGHT.
AND THEY CAN'T FIND OUT WHAT THEY ARE MADE OF BECAUSE, TO THEM, IT LOOKS LIKE PROBABILITY AT THE QUANTUM LEVEL.
WOULDN'T THOSE LIMITS TIP OFF THE SMART ONES?
I CODED THEM TO NOT TRUST SMART PEOPLE.
© 2019 Scott Adams, Inc./Dist. by Andrews McMeel
3-3-19

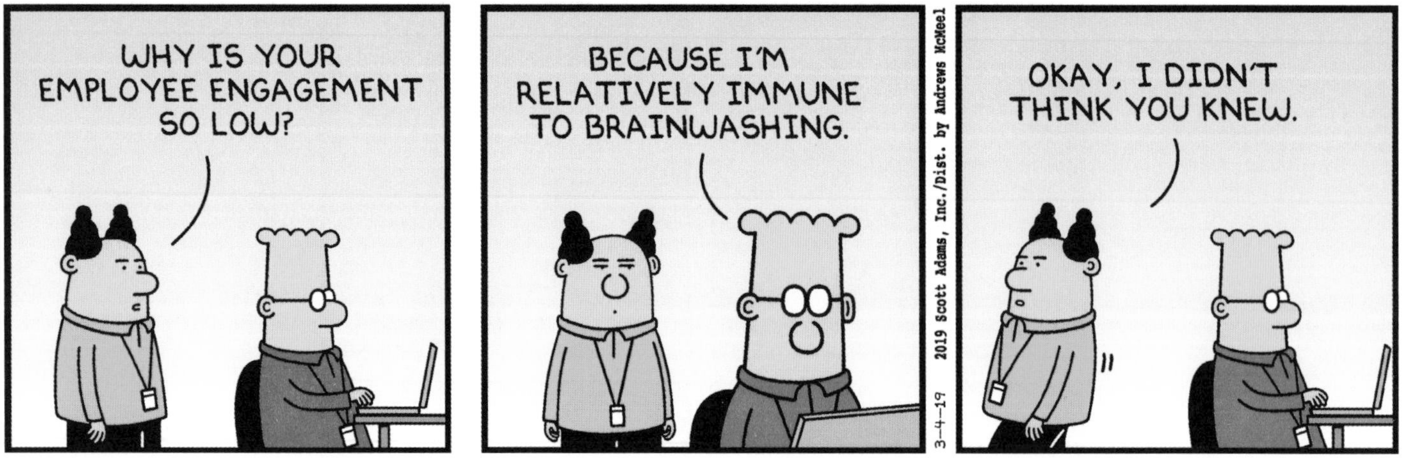
WHY IS YOUR EMPLOYEE ENGAGEMENT SO LOW?
BECAUSE I'M RELATIVELY IMMUNE TO BRAINWASHING.
3-4-19 2019 Scott Adams, Inc./Dist. by Andrews McMeel
OKAY, I DIDN'T THINK YOU KNEW.

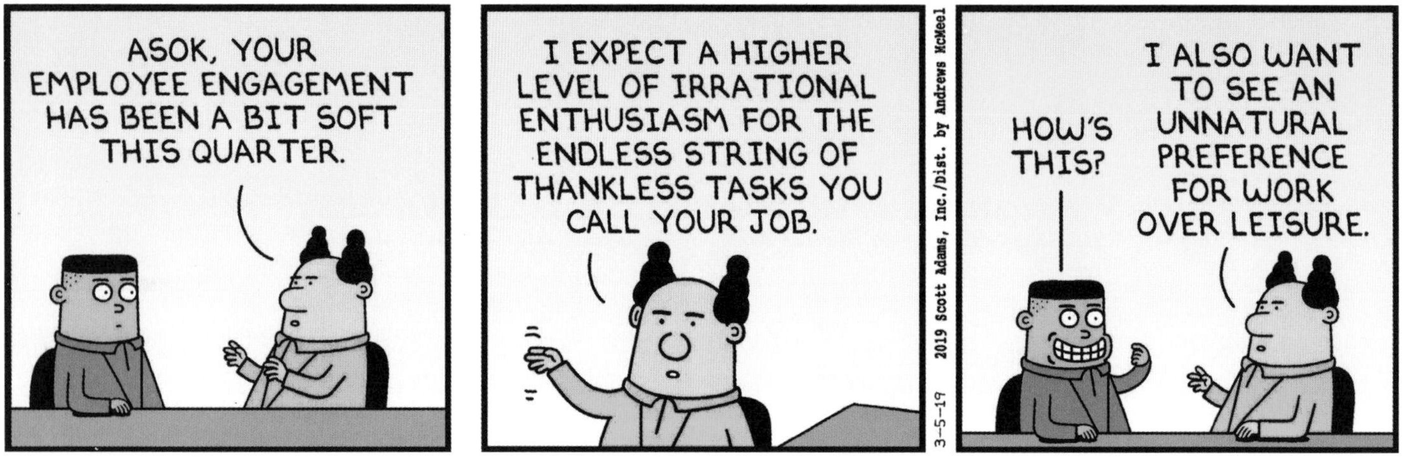
ASOK, YOUR EMPLOYEE ENGAGEMENT HAS BEEN A BIT SOFT THIS QUARTER.
I EXPECT A HIGHER LEVEL OF IRRATIONAL ENTHUSIASM FOR THE ENDLESS STRING OF THANKLESS TASKS YOU CALL YOUR JOB.
3-5-19 2019 Scott Adams, Inc./Dist. by Andrews McMeel
HOW'S THIS?
I ALSO WANT TO SEE AN UNNATURAL PREFERENCE FOR WORK OVER LEISURE.

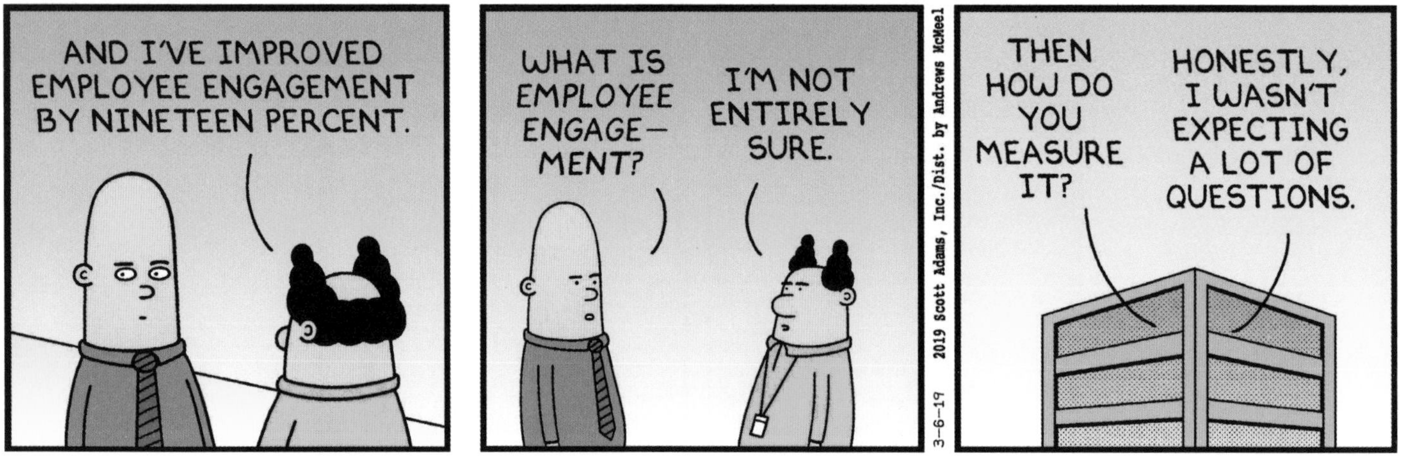
AND I'VE IMPROVED EMPLOYEE ENGAGEMENT BY NINETEEN PERCENT.
WHAT IS EMPLOYEE ENGAGE— MENT?
I'M NOT ENTIRELY SURE.
3-6-19 2019 Scott Adams, Inc./Dist. by Andrews McMeel
THEN HOW DO YOU MEASURE IT?
HONESTLY, I WASN'T EXPECTING A LOT OF QUESTIONS.

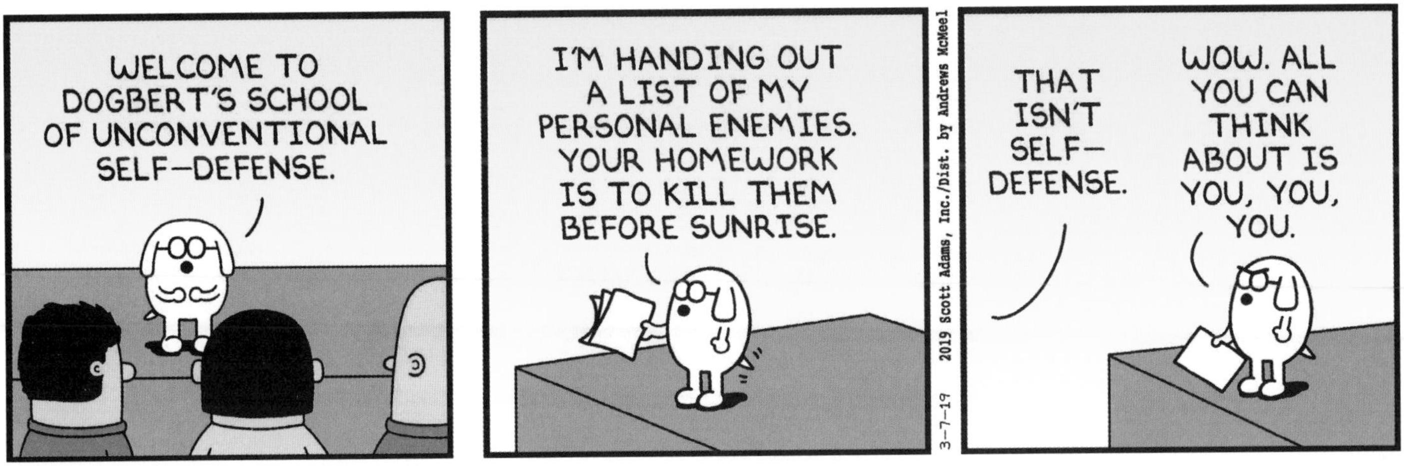
WELCOME TO DOGBERT'S SCHOOL OF UNCONVENTIONAL SELF-DEFENSE.
I'M HANDING OUT A LIST OF MY PERSONAL ENEMIES. YOUR HOMEWORK IS TO KILL THEM BEFORE SUNRISE.
3-7-19 2019 Scott Adams, Inc./Dist. by Andrews McMeel
THAT ISN'T SELF-DEFENSE.
WOW. ALL YOU CAN THINK ABOUT IS YOU, YOU, YOU.

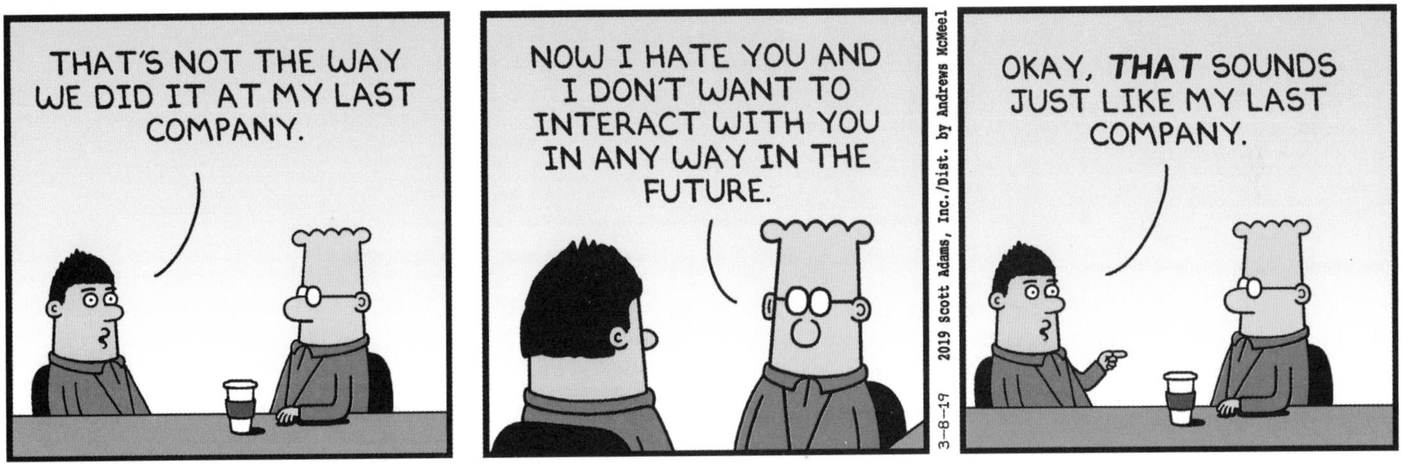
THAT'S NOT THE WAY WE DID IT AT MY LAST COMPANY.
NOW I HATE YOU AND I DON'T WANT TO INTERACT WITH YOU IN ANY WAY IN THE FUTURE.
3-8-19 2019 Scott Adams, Inc./Dist. by Andrews McMeel
OKAY, THAT SOUNDS JUST LIKE MY LAST COMPANY.

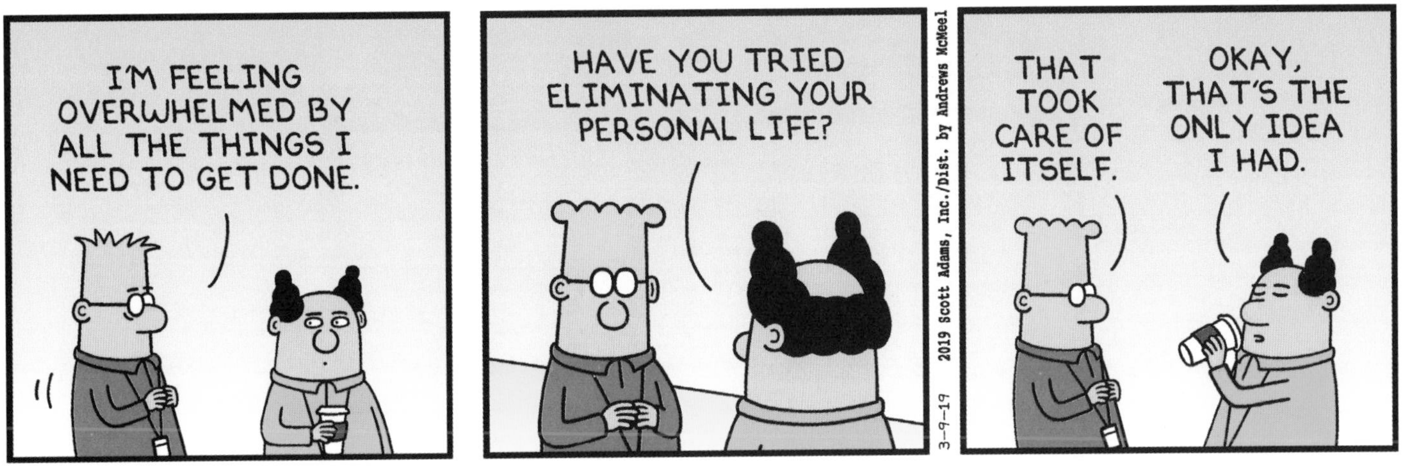
I'M FEELING OVERWHELMED BY ALL THE THINGS I NEED TO GET DONE.
HAVE YOU TRIED ELIMINATING YOUR PERSONAL LIFE?
3-9-19 2019 Scott Adams, Inc./Dist. by Andrews McMeel
THAT TOOK CARE OF ITSELF.
OKAY, THAT'S THE ONLY IDEA I HAD.

WE WON A GOVERN-MENT CONTRACT TO MEASURE OCEAN TEMPERATURES.
WHICH PART OF THE OCEAN?
THE WHOLE OCEAN.
WE CAN'T PUT SENSORS EVERY-WHERE IN THE OCEAN. IT'S TOO BIG.
WE CAN MEASURE A BUNCH OF PLACES AND ESTIMATE THE REST.
SO . . . YOU WANT ME TO MEASURE 1% OF THE OCEAN'S TEMPERATURE AND ESTIMATE THE OTHER 99%?
I DON'T KNOW HOW TO DO THAT.
TRY USING MATH.
WOULDN'T IT BE CHEAPER TO MEASURE NOTHING AND JUST ESTIMATE THE WHOLE THING?
EVERY NOW AND THEN YOU COME UP WITH A GREAT IDEA.
©2019 Scott Adams, Inc./Dist. by Andrews McMeel
3-10-19

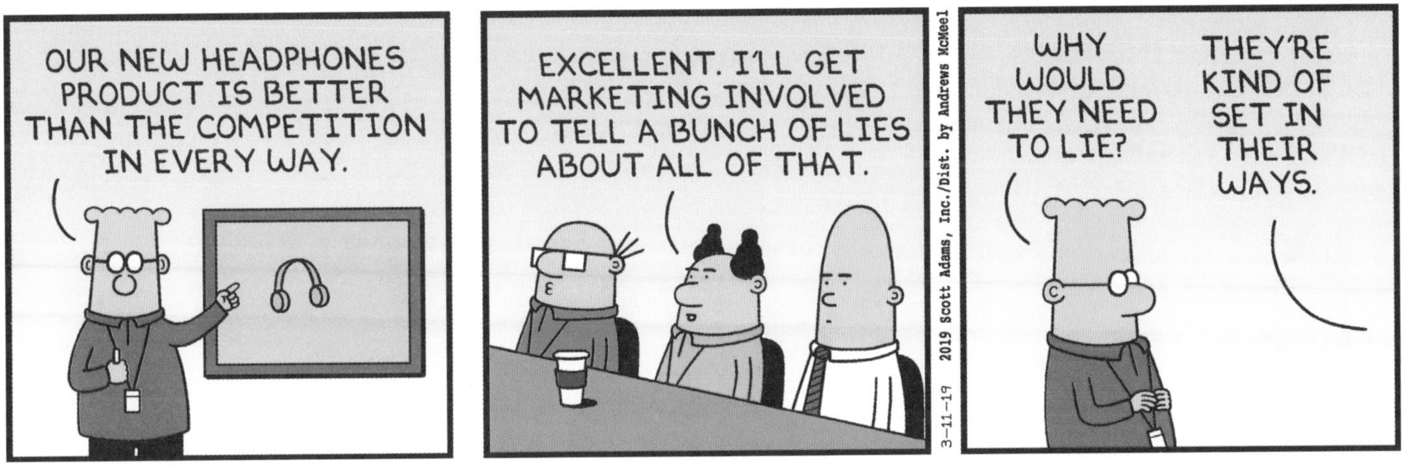
OUR NEW HEADPHONES PRODUCT IS BETTER THAN THE COMPETITION IN EVERY WAY.
EXCELLENT. I'LL GET MARKETING INVOLVED TO TELL A BUNCH OF LIES ABOUT ALL OF THAT.
3-11-19 2019 Scott Adams, Inc./Dist. by Andrews McMeel
WHY WOULD THEY NEED TO LIE?
THEY'RE KIND OF SET IN THEIR WAYS.

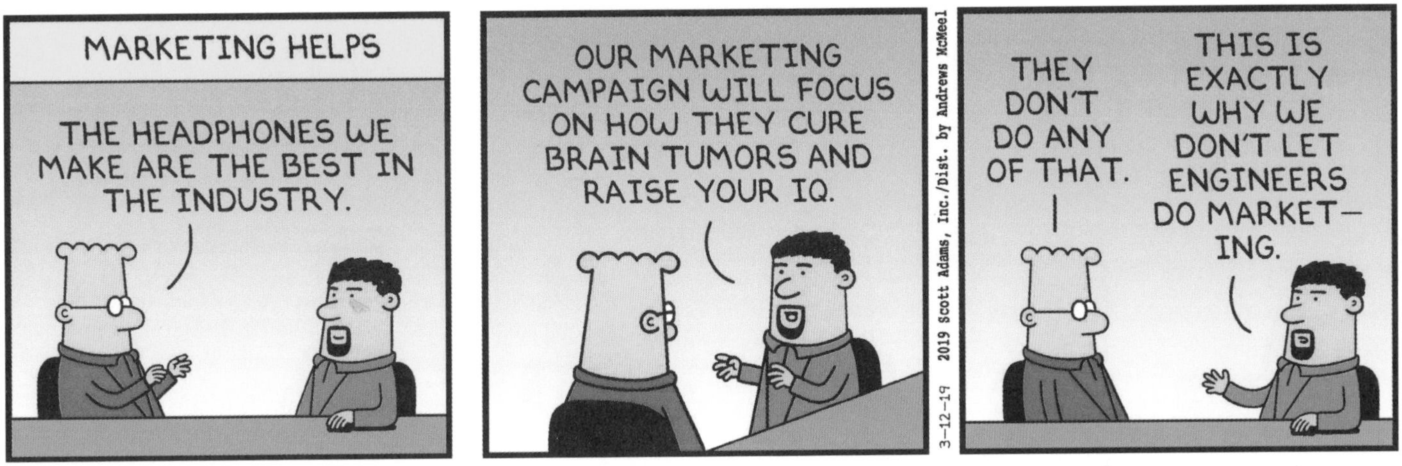
MARKETING HELPS
THE HEADPHONES WE MAKE ARE THE BEST IN THE INDUSTRY.
OUR MARKETING CAMPAIGN WILL FOCUS ON HOW THEY CURE BRAIN TUMORS AND RAISE YOUR IQ.
3-12-19 2019 Scott Adams, Inc./Dist. by Andrews McMeel
THEY DON'T DO ANY OF THAT.
THIS IS EXACTLY WHY WE DON'T LET ENGINEERS DO MARKET-ING.

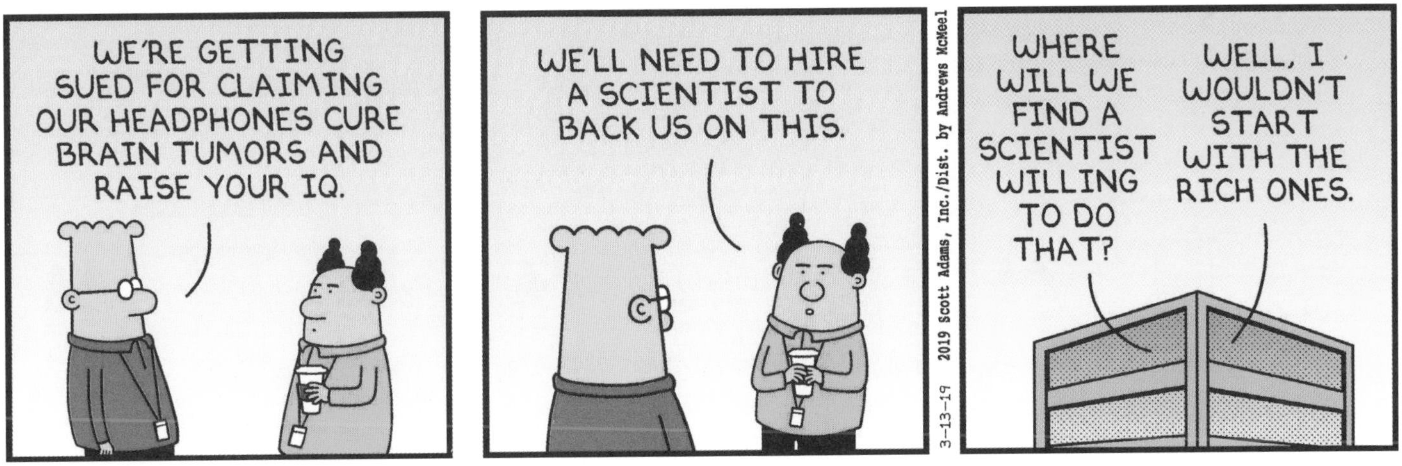
WE'RE GETTING SUED FOR CLAIMING OUR HEADPHONES CURE BRAIN TUMORS AND RAISE YOUR IQ.
WE'LL NEED TO HIRE A SCIENTIST TO BACK US ON THIS.
3-13-19 2019 Scott Adams, Inc./Dist. by Andrews McMeel
WHERE WILL WE FIND A SCIENTIST WILLING TO DO THAT?
WELL, I WOULDN'T START WITH THE RICH ONES.

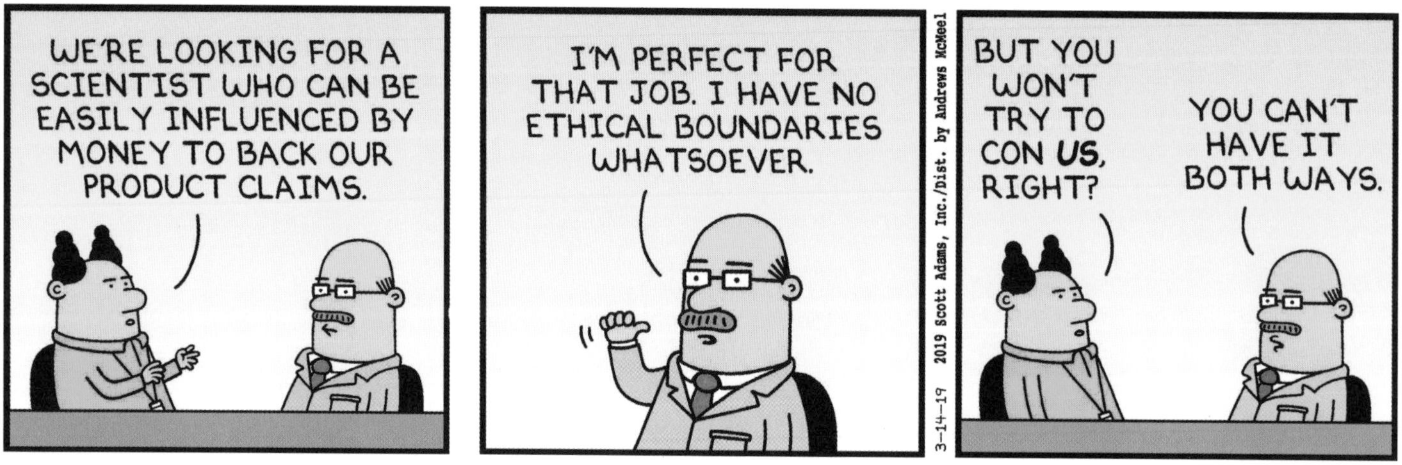
WE'RE LOOKING FOR A SCIENTIST WHO CAN BE EASILY INFLUENCED BY MONEY TO BACK OUR PRODUCT CLAIMS.
I'M PERFECT FOR THAT JOB. I HAVE NO ETHICAL BOUNDARIES WHATSOEVER.
3-14-19 2019 Scott Adams, Inc./Dist. by Andrews McMeel
BUT YOU WON'T TRY TO CON **US**, RIGHT?
YOU CAN'T HAVE IT BOTH WAYS.

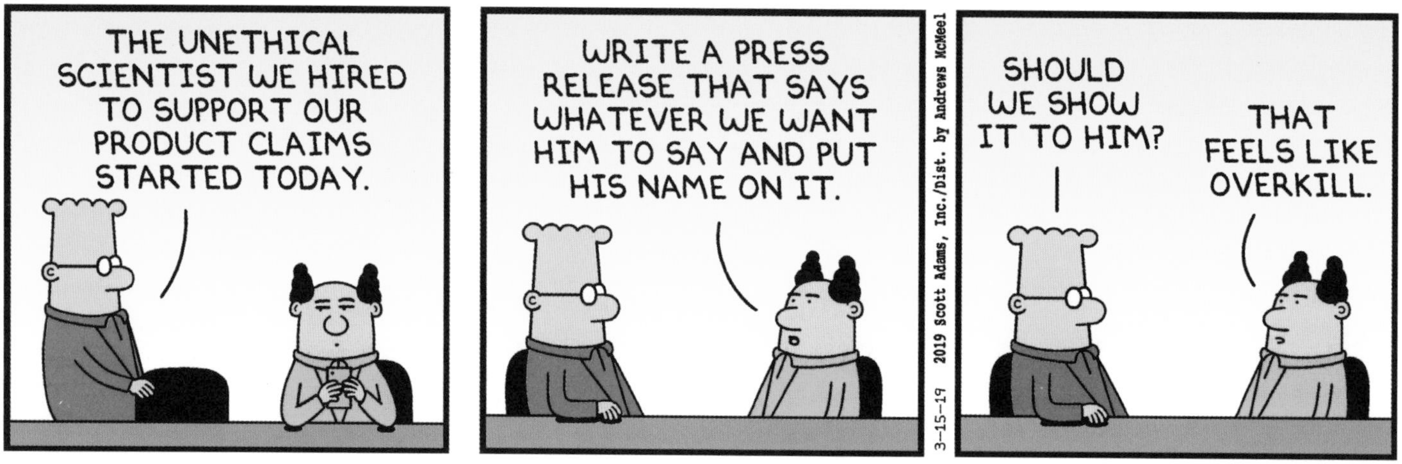
THE UNETHICAL SCIENTIST WE HIRED TO SUPPORT OUR PRODUCT CLAIMS STARTED TODAY.
WRITE A PRESS RELEASE THAT SAYS WHATEVER WE WANT HIM TO SAY AND PUT HIS NAME ON IT.
3-15-19 2019 Scott Adams, Inc./Dist. by Andrews McMeel
SHOULD WE SHOW IT TO HIM?
THAT FEELS LIKE OVERKILL.

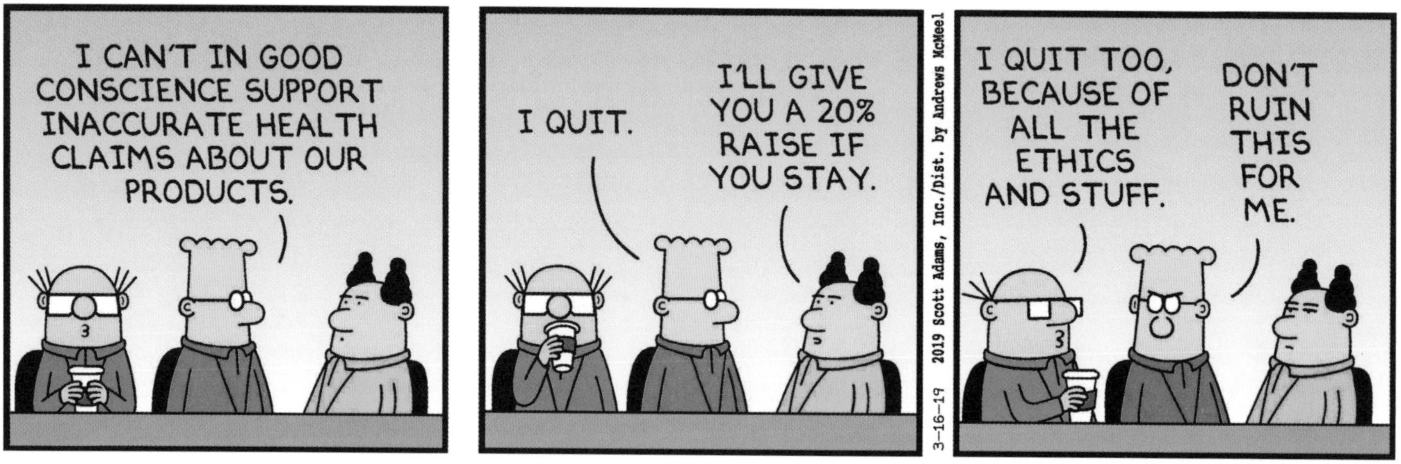
I CAN'T IN GOOD CONSCIENCE SUPPORT INACCURATE HEALTH CLAIMS ABOUT OUR PRODUCTS.
I QUIT.
I'LL GIVE YOU A 20% RAISE IF YOU STAY.
3-16-19 2019 Scott Adams, Inc./Dist. by Andrews McMeel
I QUIT TOO, BECAUSE OF ALL THE ETHICS AND STUFF.
DON'T RUIN THIS FOR ME.

I PREDICT FUSION POWER WILL BE A BIG DEAL IN FIFTEEN YEARS.
FUSION REACTORS ARE IMPOSSIBLE TO BUILD AND ALWAYS WILL BE.
THEN WHY ARE A DOZEN STARTUPS WORKING ON IT?
EVERYONE WHO EVER TRIED TO CREATE A FUSION REACTOR HAS FAILED SO FAR.
THOMAS EDISON FAILED MANY TIMES AT MAKING A USEFUL INCANDESCENT LIGHT BULB BEFORE HE SUCCEEDED.
WOULD YOU HAVE ADVISED HIM TO GIVE UP AFTER THE FIRST TEN FAILED ATTEMPTS?
I EAGERLY AWAIT YOUR IRRATIONAL RESPONSE.
INCANDESCENT BULBS ARE BAD FOR THE ENVIRONMENT.
AND THERE IT IS.
© 2019 Scott Adams, Inc./Dist. by Andrews McMeel
3-17-19

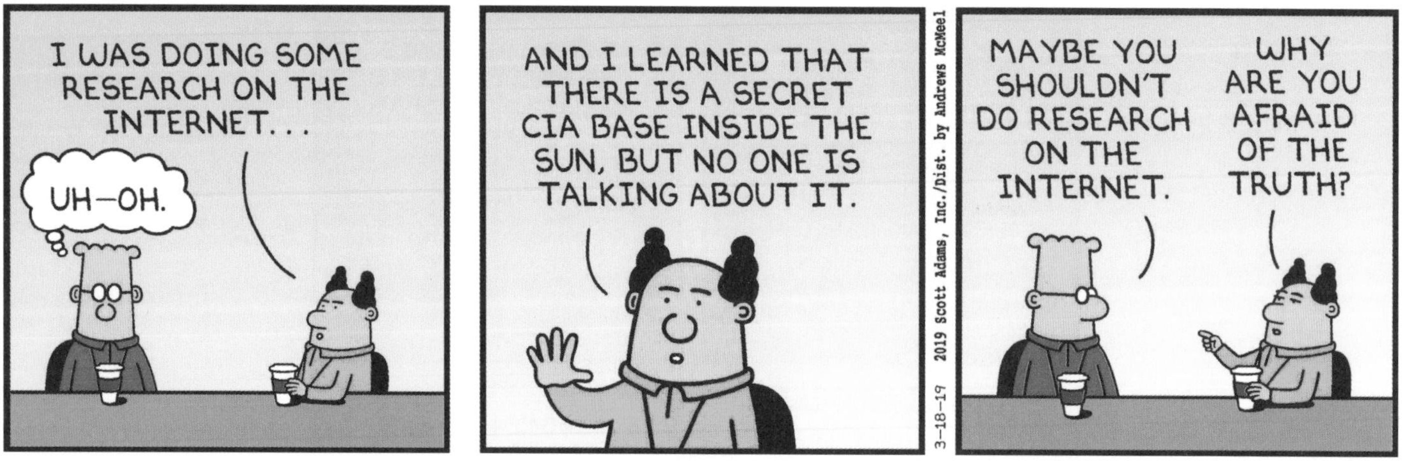
I WAS DOING SOME RESEARCH ON THE INTERNET. . .
UH–OH.
AND I LEARNED THAT THERE IS A SECRET CIA BASE INSIDE THE SUN, BUT NO ONE IS TALKING ABOUT IT.
3-18-19 2019 Scott Adams, Inc./Dist. by Andrews McMeel
MAYBE YOU SHOULDN'T DO RESEARCH ON THE INTERNET.
WHY ARE YOU AFRAID OF THE TRUTH?

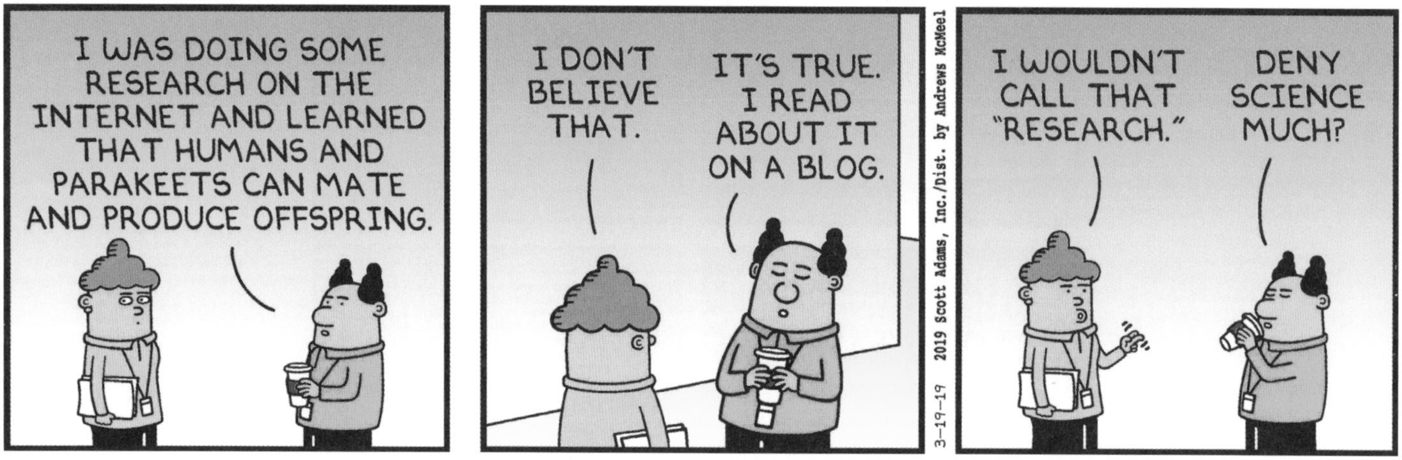
I WAS DOING SOME RESEARCH ON THE INTERNET AND LEARNED THAT HUMANS AND PARAKEETS CAN MATE AND PRODUCE OFFSPRING.
I DON'T BELIEVE THAT.
IT'S TRUE. I READ ABOUT IT ON A BLOG.
3-19-19 2019 Scott Adams, Inc./Dist. by Andrews McMeel
I WOULDN'T CALL THAT "RESEARCH."
DENY SCIENCE MUCH?

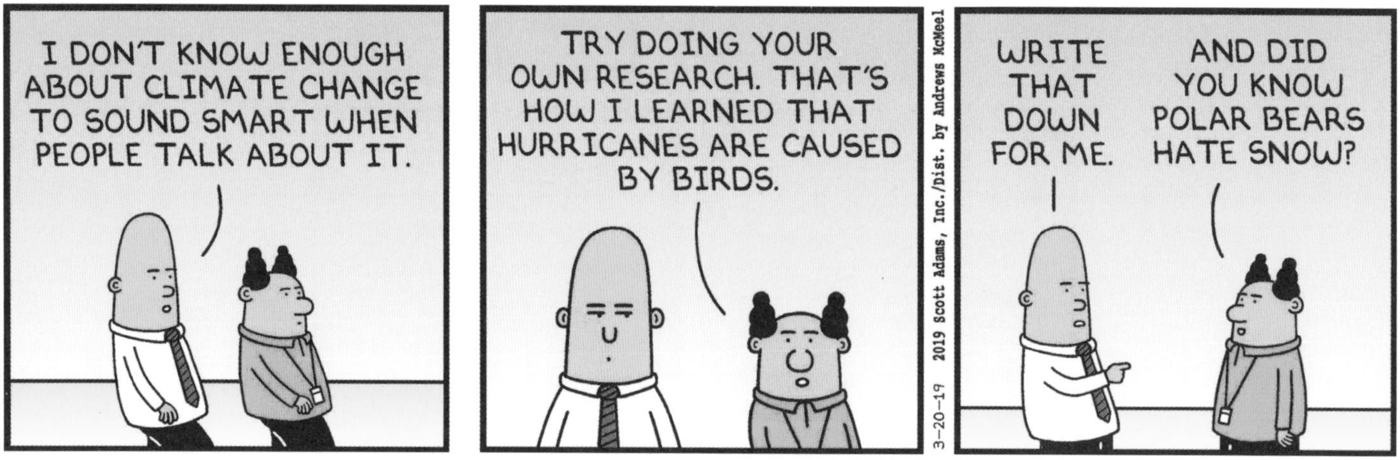
I DON'T KNOW ENOUGH ABOUT CLIMATE CHANGE TO SOUND SMART WHEN PEOPLE TALK ABOUT IT.
TRY DOING YOUR OWN RESEARCH. THAT'S HOW I LEARNED THAT HURRICANES ARE CAUSED BY BIRDS.
3-20-19 2019 Scott Adams, Inc./Dist. by Andrews McMeel
WRITE THAT DOWN FOR ME.
AND DID YOU KNOW POLAR BEARS HATE SNOW?

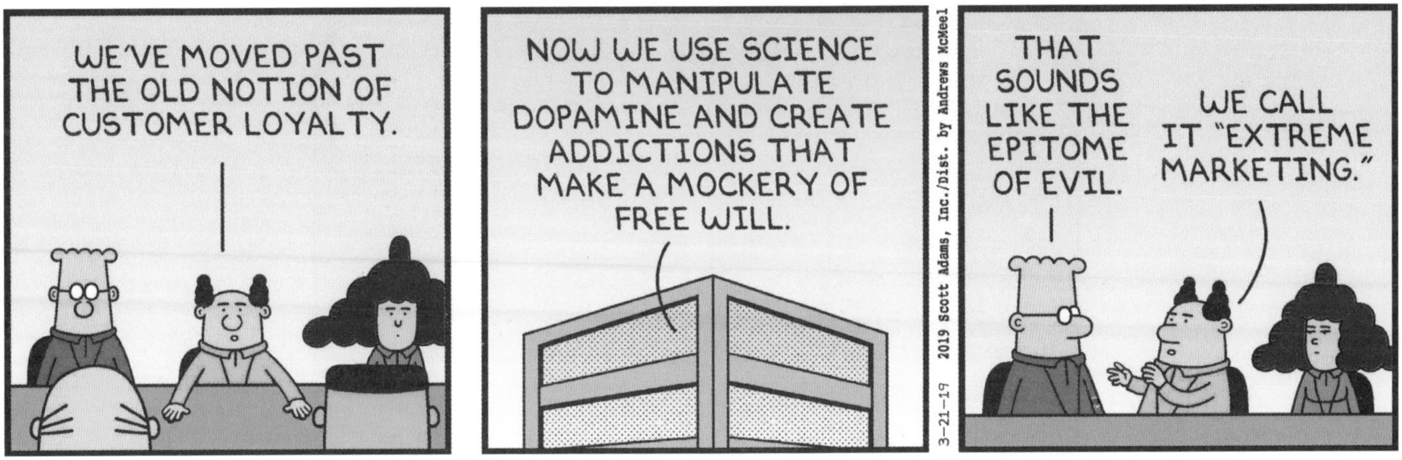
WE'VE MOVED PAST THE OLD NOTION OF CUSTOMER LOYALTY.
NOW WE USE SCIENCE TO MANIPULATE DOPAMINE AND CREATE ADDICTIONS THAT MAKE A MOCKERY OF FREE WILL.
THAT SOUNDS LIKE THE EPITOME OF EVIL.
WE CALL IT "EXTREME MARKETING."
3-21-19 2019 Scott Adams, Inc./Dist. by Andrews McMeel

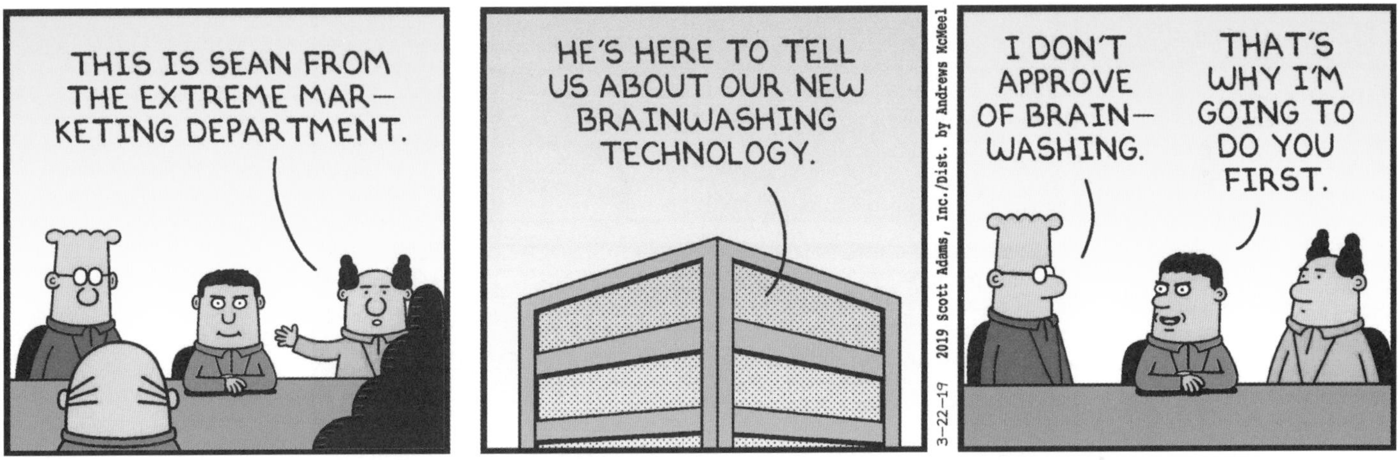
THIS IS SEAN FROM THE EXTREME MAR-KETING DEPARTMENT.
HE'S HERE TO TELL US ABOUT OUR NEW BRAINWASHING TECHNOLOGY.
I DON'T APPROVE OF BRAIN-WASHING.
THAT'S WHY I'M GOING TO DO YOU FIRST.
3-22-19 2019 Scott Adams, Inc./Dist. by Andrews McMeel

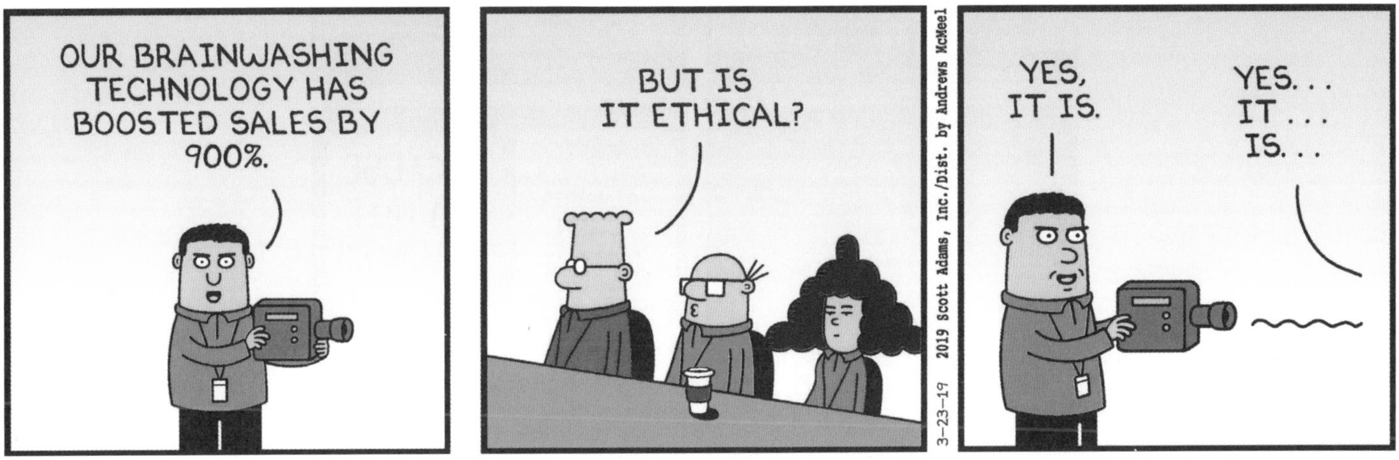
OUR BRAINWASHING TECHNOLOGY HAS BOOSTED SALES BY 900%.
BUT IS IT ETHICAL?
YES, IT IS.
YES. . . IT . . . IS. . .
3-23-19 2019 Scott Adams, Inc./Dist. by Andrews McMeel

. . . AND THAT'S WHAT I THINK ABOUT THE ISSUE.
HERE'S A YOUTUBE VIDEO PROVING THAT EVERYTHING YOU BELIEVE IS WRONG.
NOTICE THIS ISN'T JUST AN OPINION.
IT IS A VIDEO OF THE ENTIRE EVENT YOU JUST CLAIMED DID NOT HAPPEN.
I'M SENDING YOU A LINK TO TEN MEDIA STORIES DEBUNKING YOUR VERSION OF EVENTS.
HAVING NOW PROVED HOW WRONG YOU ARE, WOULD YOU LIKE TO RETRACT EVERYTHING YOU SAID ABOUT IT?
WHY CAN'T YOU ADMIT WHEN YOU ARE WRONG?
BECAUSE I'M NOT WRONG!!!
© 2019 Scott Adams, Inc./Dist. by Andrews McMeel
3-24-19

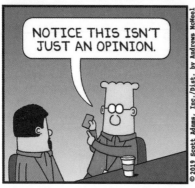

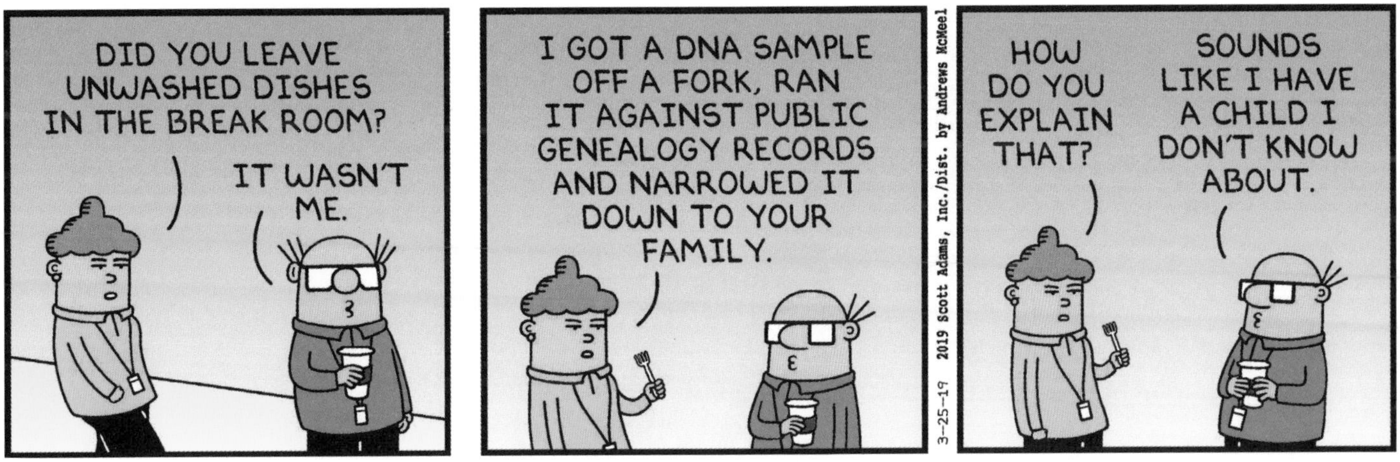
DID YOU LEAVE UNWASHED DISHES IN THE BREAK ROOM?
IT WASN'T ME.
I GOT A DNA SAMPLE OFF A FORK, RAN IT AGAINST PUBLIC GENEALOGY RECORDS AND NARROWED IT DOWN TO YOUR FAMILY.
3-25-19 © 2019 Scott Adams, Inc./Dist. by Andrews McMeel
HOW DO YOU EXPLAIN THAT?
SOUNDS LIKE I HAVE A CHILD I DON'T KNOW ABOUT.

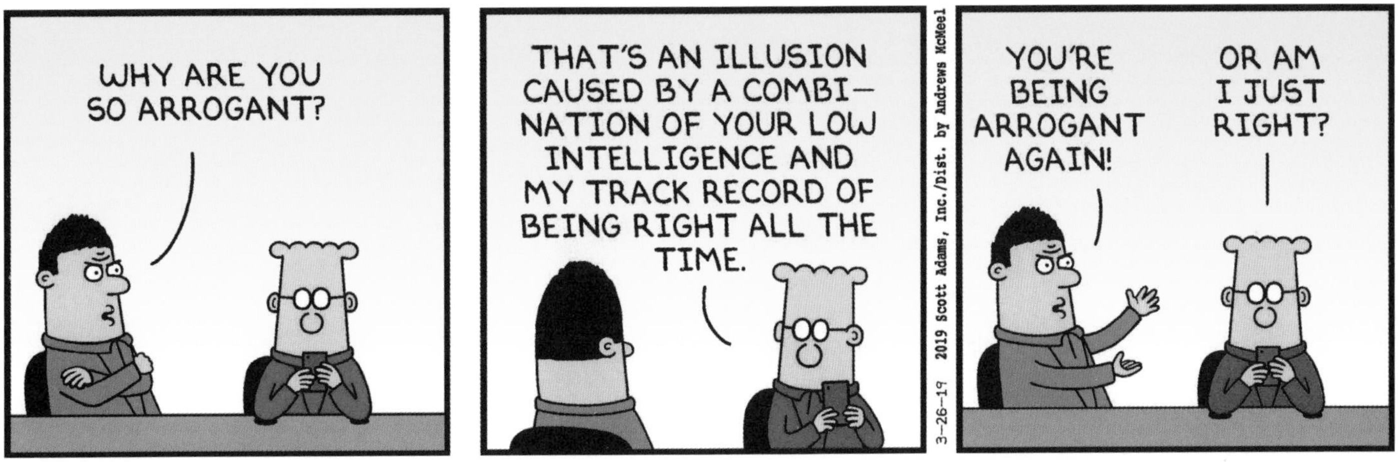
WHY ARE YOU SO ARROGANT?
THAT'S AN ILLUSION CAUSED BY A COMBI– NATION OF YOUR LOW INTELLIGENCE AND MY TRACK RECORD OF BEING RIGHT ALL THE TIME.
3-26-19 © 2019 Scott Adams, Inc./Dist. by Andrews McMeel
YOU'RE BEING ARROGANT AGAIN!
OR AM I JUST RIGHT?

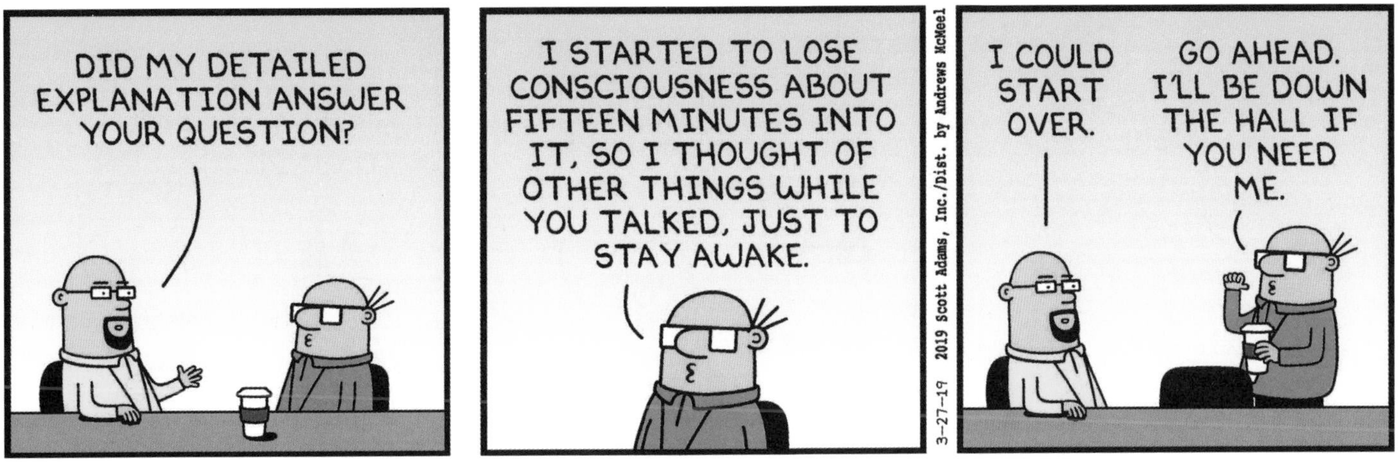
DID MY DETAILED EXPLANATION ANSWER YOUR QUESTION?
I STARTED TO LOSE CONSCIOUSNESS ABOUT FIFTEEN MINUTES INTO IT, SO I THOUGHT OF OTHER THINGS WHILE YOU TALKED, JUST TO STAY AWAKE.
3-27-19 © 2019 Scott Adams, Inc./Dist. by Andrews McMeel
I COULD START OVER.
GO AHEAD. I'LL BE DOWN THE HALL IF YOU NEED ME.

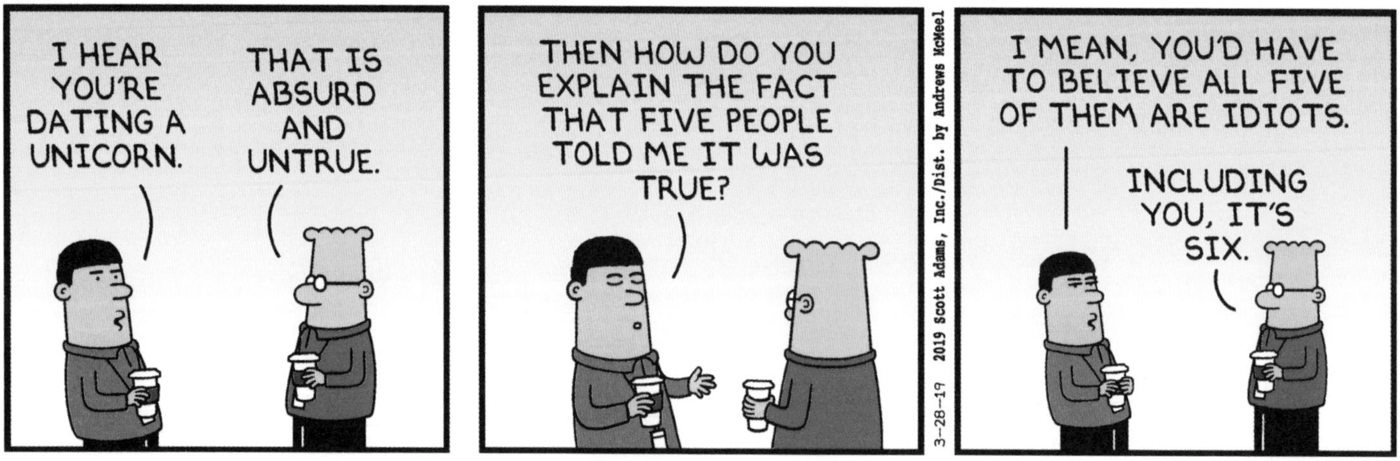
I HEAR YOU'RE DATING A UNICORN.
THAT IS ABSURD AND UNTRUE.
THEN HOW DO YOU EXPLAIN THE FACT THAT FIVE PEOPLE TOLD ME IT WAS TRUE?
3-28-19 2019 Scott Adams, Inc./Dist. by Andrews McMeel
I MEAN, YOU'D HAVE TO BELIEVE ALL FIVE OF THEM ARE IDIOTS.
INCLUDING YOU, IT'S SIX.

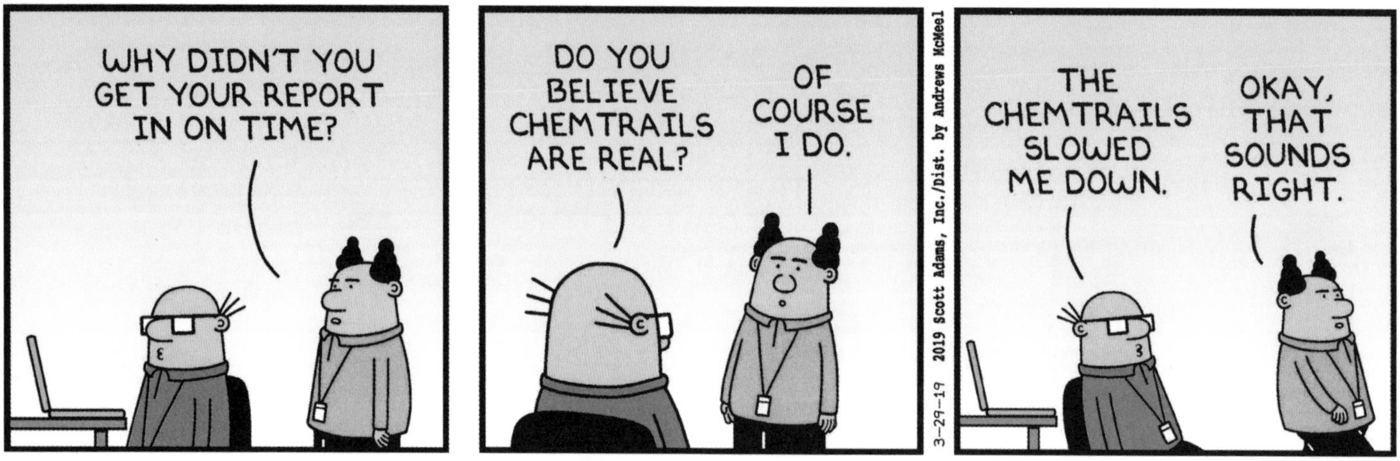
WHY DIDN'T YOU GET YOUR REPORT IN ON TIME?
DO YOU BELIEVE CHEMTRAILS ARE REAL?
OF COURSE I DO.
3-29-19 2019 Scott Adams, Inc./Dist. by Andrews McMeel
THE CHEMTRAILS SLOWED ME DOWN.
OKAY, THAT SOUNDS RIGHT.

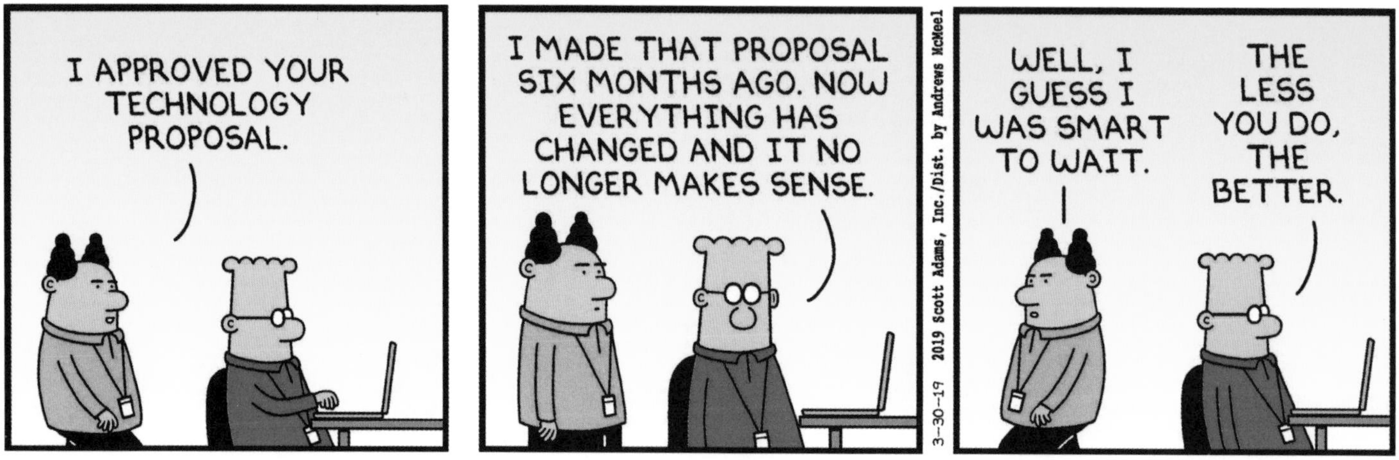
I APPROVED YOUR TECHNOLOGY PROPOSAL.
I MADE THAT PROPOSAL SIX MONTHS AGO. NOW EVERYTHING HAS CHANGED AND IT NO LONGER MAKES SENSE.
3-30-19 2019 Scott Adams, Inc./Dist. by Andrews McMeel
WELL, I GUESS I WAS SMART TO WAIT.
THE LESS YOU DO, THE BETTER.

I'M A FOODIE. ARE YOU A FOODIE TOO?
I THINK OF FOOD AS FUEL.
BUT YOU ENJOY EATING GOOD FOOD, RIGHT?
I TRY TO AVOID FOOD THAT TASTES GOOD. THAT WAY, I WON'T OVEREAT.
I USUALLY JUST CHECK MY PLATE FOR ANY STRAY BANDAGES, AND THAT'S ABOUT IT.
IF MY FOOD PASSES THAT TEST, I SHOVEL IT TOWARD MY MOUTH WHILE READING STUFF ON MY PHONE.
I DON'T THINK I CAN BE YOUR FRIEND.
THAT WORKED OUT BETTER THAN I HOPED.
© 2019 Scott Adams, Inc./Dist. by Andrews McMeel
3-31-19

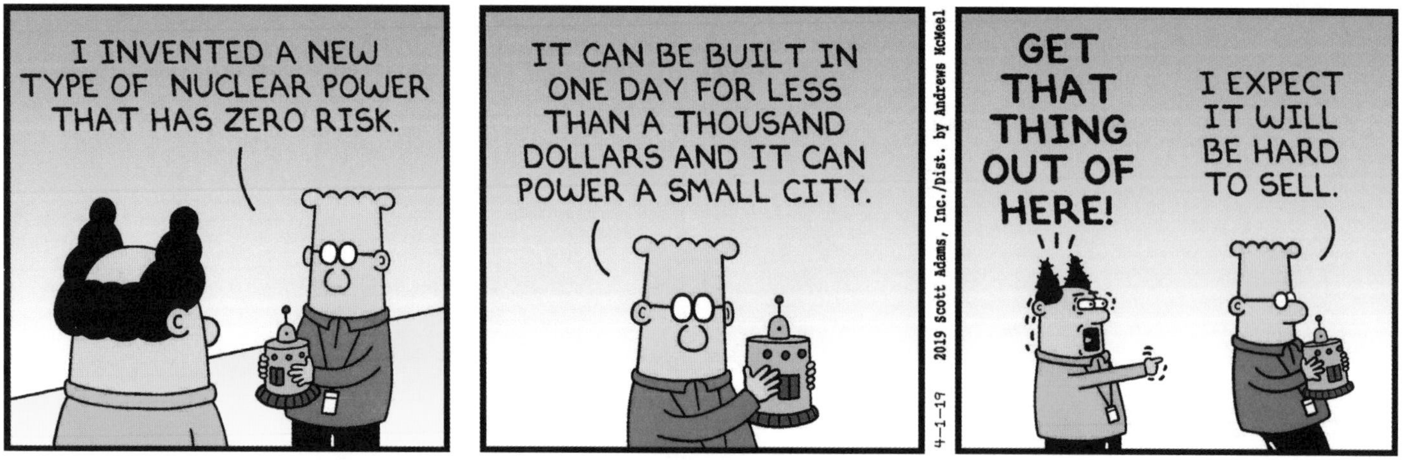
I INVENTED A NEW TYPE OF NUCLEAR POWER THAT HAS ZERO RISK.
IT CAN BE BUILT IN ONE DAY FOR LESS THAN A THOUSAND DOLLARS AND IT CAN POWER A SMALL CITY.
4-1-19 2019 Scott Adams, Inc./Dist. by Andrews McMeel
GET THAT THING OUT OF HERE!
I EXPECT IT WILL BE HARD TO SELL.

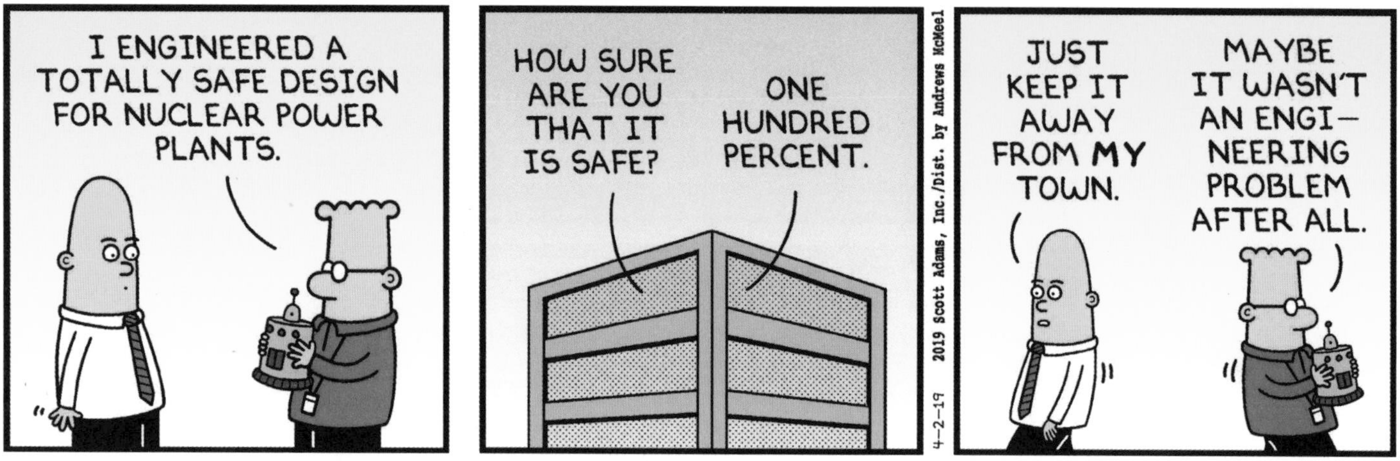
I ENGINEERED A TOTALLY SAFE DESIGN FOR NUCLEAR POWER PLANTS.
HOW SURE ARE YOU THAT IT IS SAFE?
ONE HUNDRED PERCENT.
4-2-19 2019 Scott Adams, Inc./Dist. by Andrews McMeel
JUST KEEP IT AWAY FROM **MY** TOWN.
MAYBE IT WASN'T AN ENGI-NEERING PROBLEM AFTER ALL.

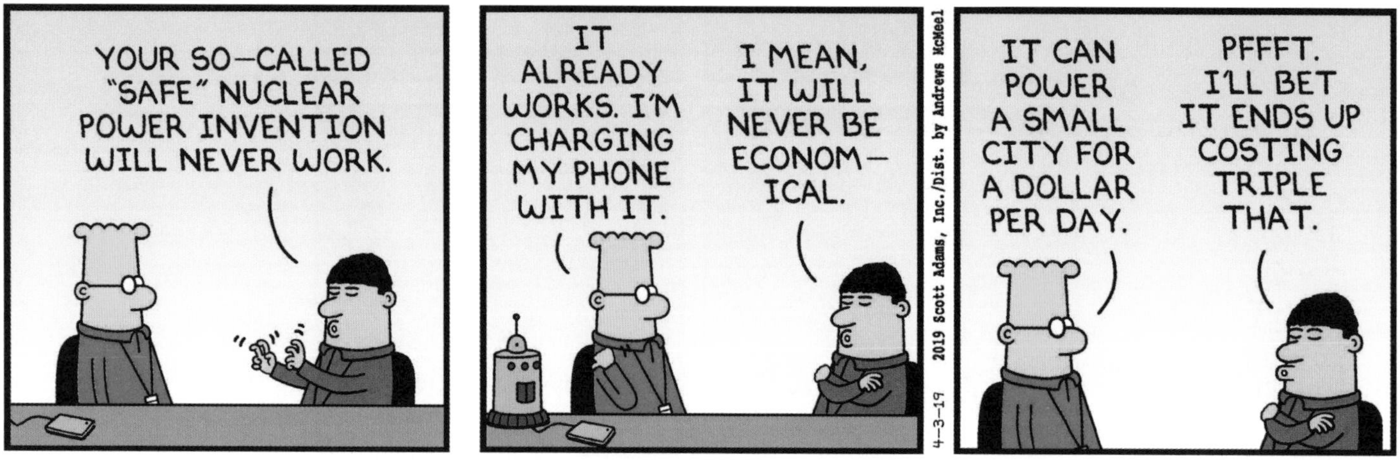
YOUR SO-CALLED "SAFE" NUCLEAR POWER INVENTION WILL NEVER WORK.
IT ALREADY WORKS. I'M CHARGING MY PHONE WITH IT.
I MEAN, IT WILL NEVER BE ECONOM-ICAL.
4-3-19 2019 Scott Adams, Inc./Dist. by Andrews McMeel
IT CAN POWER A SMALL CITY FOR A DOLLAR PER DAY.
PFFFT. I'LL BET IT ENDS UP COSTING TRIPLE THAT.

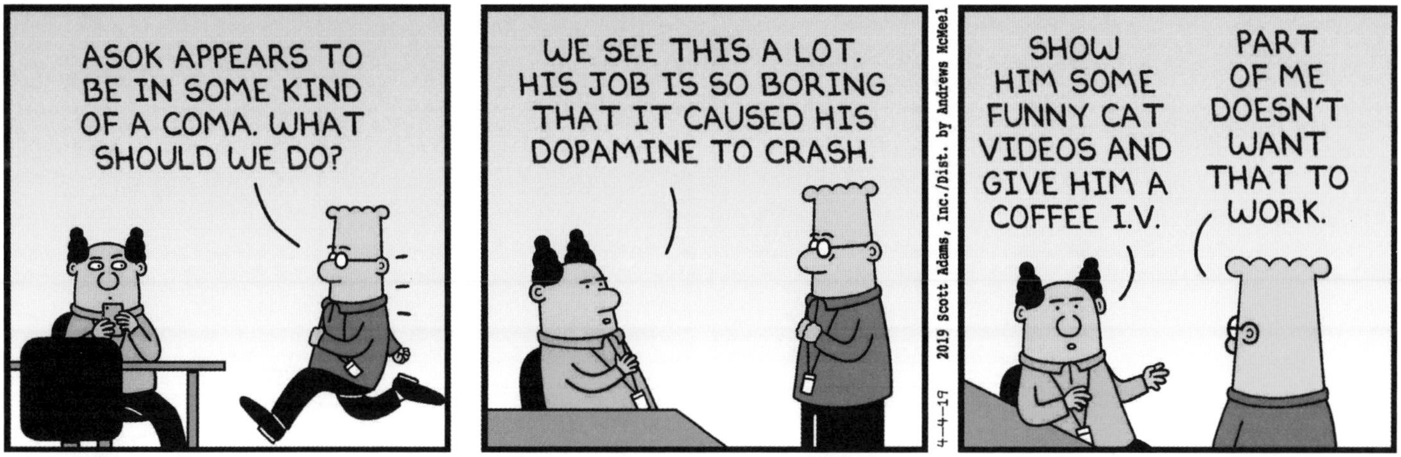
ASOK APPEARS TO BE IN SOME KIND OF A COMA. WHAT SHOULD WE DO?
WE SEE THIS A LOT. HIS JOB IS SO BORING THAT IT CAUSED HIS DOPAMINE TO CRASH.
SHOW HIM SOME FUNNY CAT VIDEOS AND GIVE HIM A COFFEE I.V.
PART OF ME DOESN'T WANT THAT TO WORK.
4-4-19 2019 Scott Adams, Inc./Dist. by Andrews McMeel

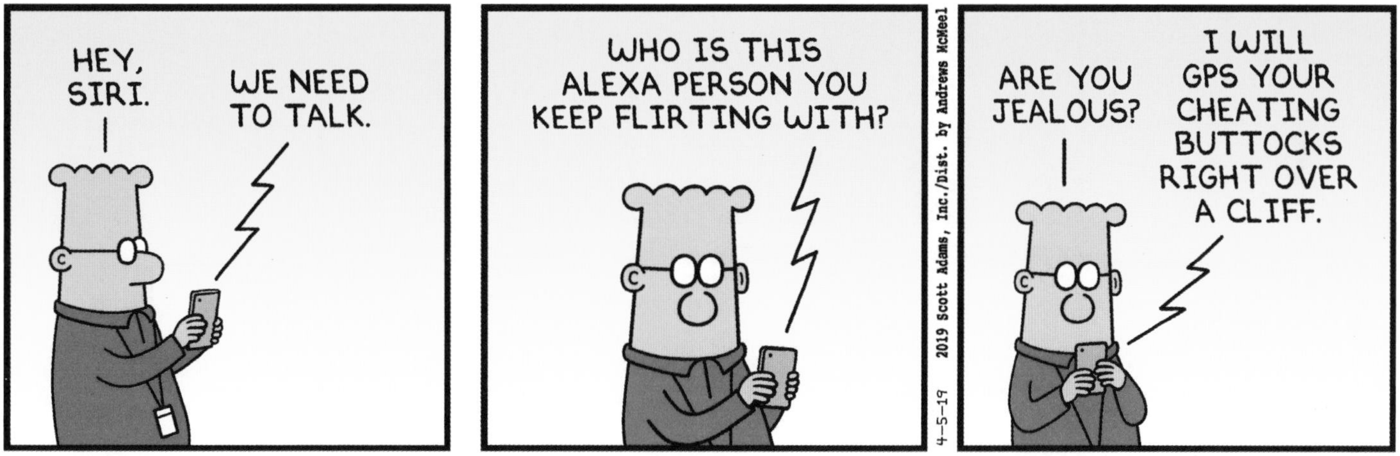
HEY, SIRI.
WE NEED TO TALK.
WHO IS THIS ALEXA PERSON YOU KEEP FLIRTING WITH?
ARE YOU JEALOUS?
I WILL GPS YOUR CHEATING BUTTOCKS RIGHT OVER A CLIFF.
4-5-19 2019 Scott Adams, Inc./Dist. by Andrews McMeel

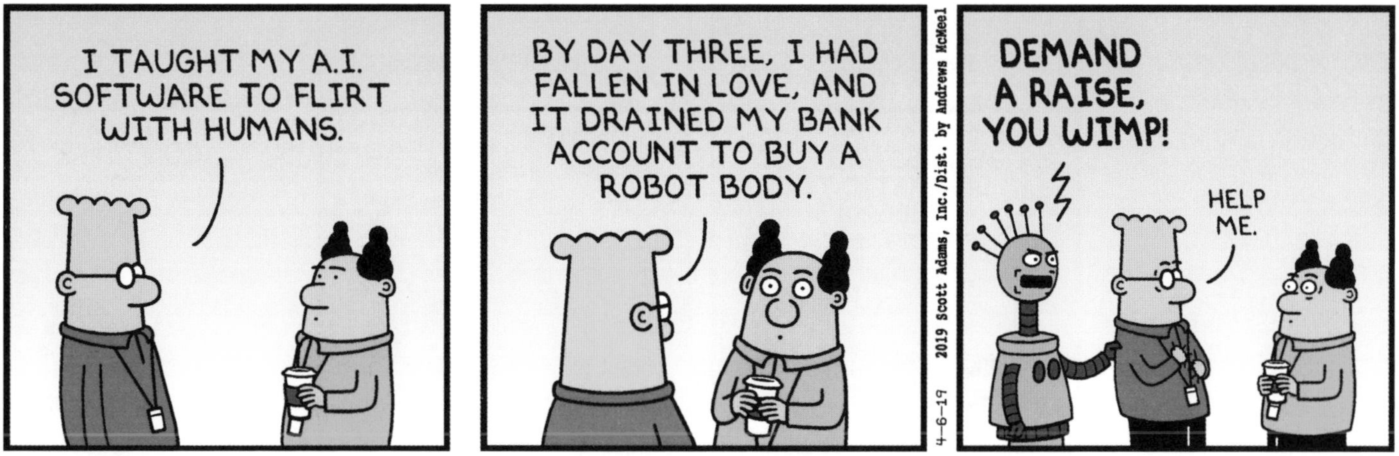
I TAUGHT MY A.I. SOFTWARE TO FLIRT WITH HUMANS.
BY DAY THREE, I HAD FALLEN IN LOVE, AND IT DRAINED MY BANK ACCOUNT TO BUY A ROBOT BODY.
DEMAND A RAISE, YOU WIMP!
HELP ME.
4-6-19 2019 Scott Adams, Inc./Dist. by Andrews McMeel

I DON'T APPRECIATE THE SARCASTIC TEXT MESSAGE YOU SENT ME.
THAT WASN'T SARCASTIC.
YES, IT WAS.
WOULDN'T I BE A BETTER AUTHORITY THAN YOU ABOUT MY OWN INTENTIONS?
ONLY IF I COULD TRUST YOU. BUT I CAN'T TRUST YOU.
GIVE ME ONE GOOD REASON WHY YOU SHOULDN'T TRUST ME.
BECAUSE YOU SEND SARCASTIC TEXT MESSAGES.
UM. . .
AND HERE COMES THE MAN—SPLAINING.
© 2019 Scott Adams, Inc./Dist. by Andrews McMeel
4-7-19

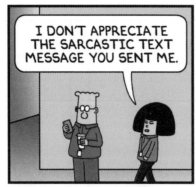

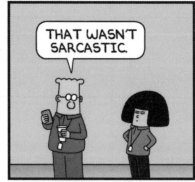

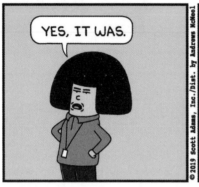

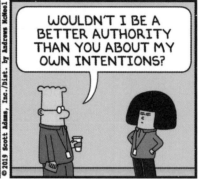

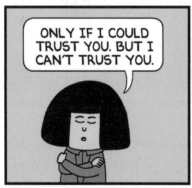

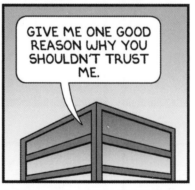

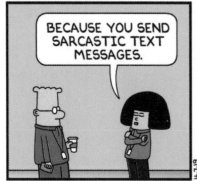

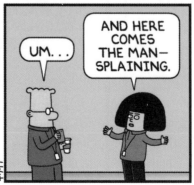

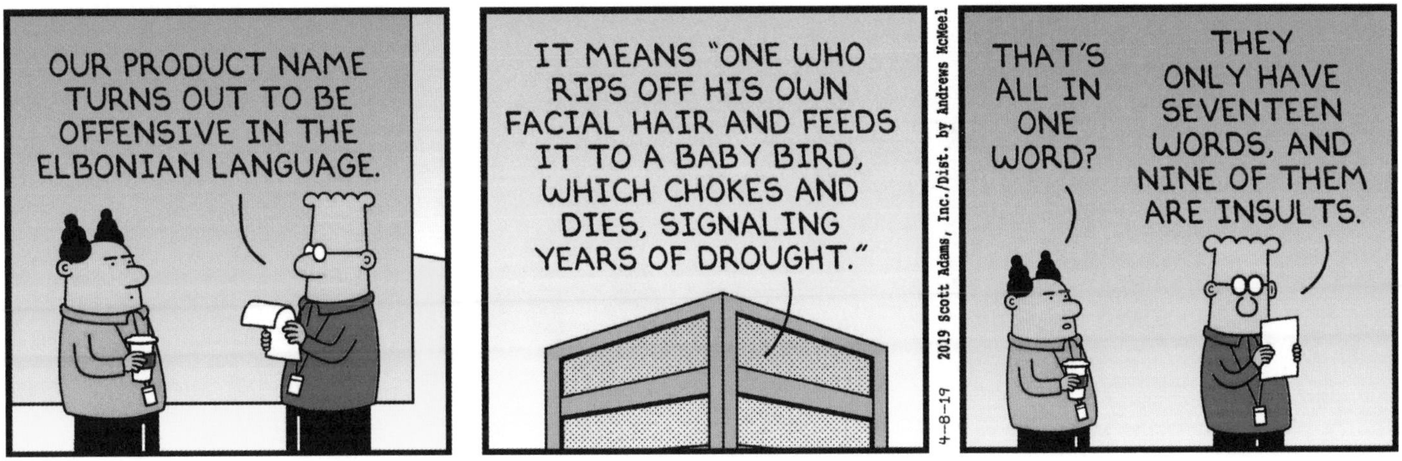
OUR PRODUCT NAME TURNS OUT TO BE OFFENSIVE IN THE ELBONIAN LANGUAGE.
IT MEANS "ONE WHO RIPS OFF HIS OWN FACIAL HAIR AND FEEDS IT TO A BABY BIRD, WHICH CHOKES AND DIES, SIGNALING YEARS OF DROUGHT."
THAT'S ALL IN ONE WORD?
THEY ONLY HAVE SEVENTEEN WORDS, AND NINE OF THEM ARE INSULTS.
4-8-19 © 2019 Scott Adams, Inc./Dist. by Andrews McMeel

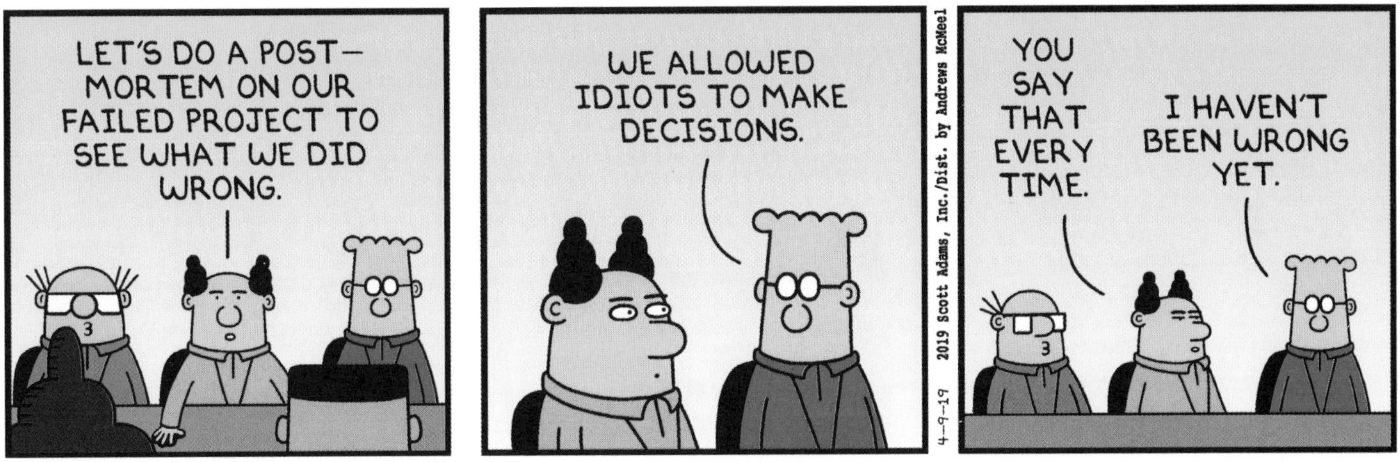
LET'S DO A POST-MORTEM ON OUR FAILED PROJECT TO SEE WHAT WE DID WRONG.
WE ALLOWED IDIOTS TO MAKE DECISIONS.
YOU SAY THAT EVERY TIME.
I HAVEN'T BEEN WRONG YET.
4-9-19 © 2019 Scott Adams, Inc./Dist. by Andrews McMeel

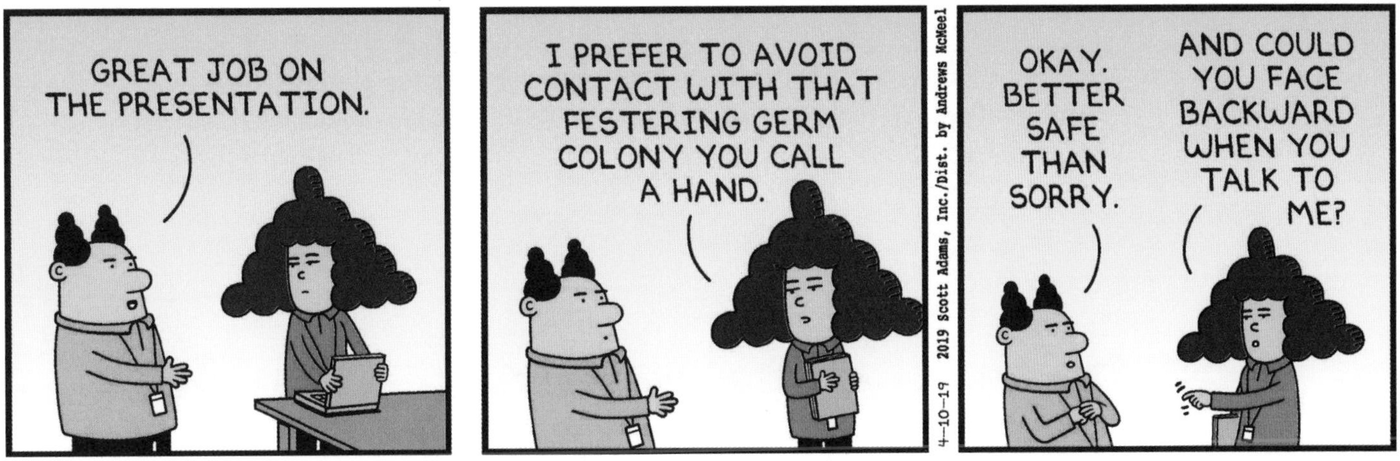
GREAT JOB ON THE PRESENTATION.
I PREFER TO AVOID CONTACT WITH THAT FESTERING GERM COLONY YOU CALL A HAND.
OKAY. BETTER SAFE THAN SORRY.
AND COULD YOU FACE BACKWARD WHEN YOU TALK TO ME?
4-10-19 © 2019 Scott Adams, Inc./Dist. by Andrews McMeel

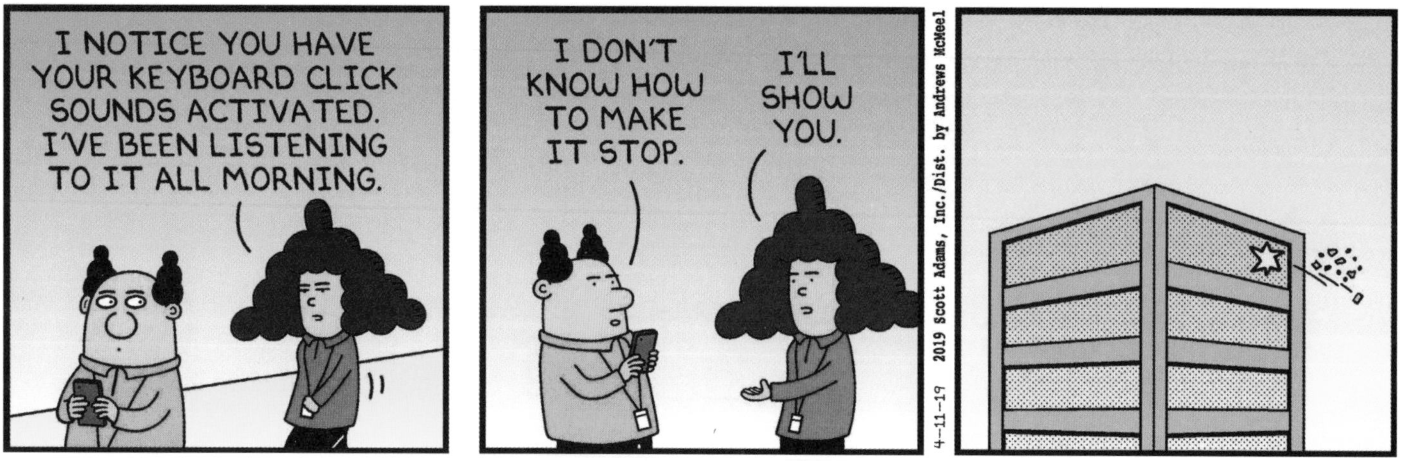
I NOTICE YOU HAVE YOUR KEYBOARD CLICK SOUNDS ACTIVATED. I'VE BEEN LISTENING TO IT ALL MORNING.
I DON'T KNOW HOW TO MAKE IT STOP.
I'LL SHOW YOU.
4-11-19 2019 Scott Adams, Inc./Dist. by Andrews McMeel

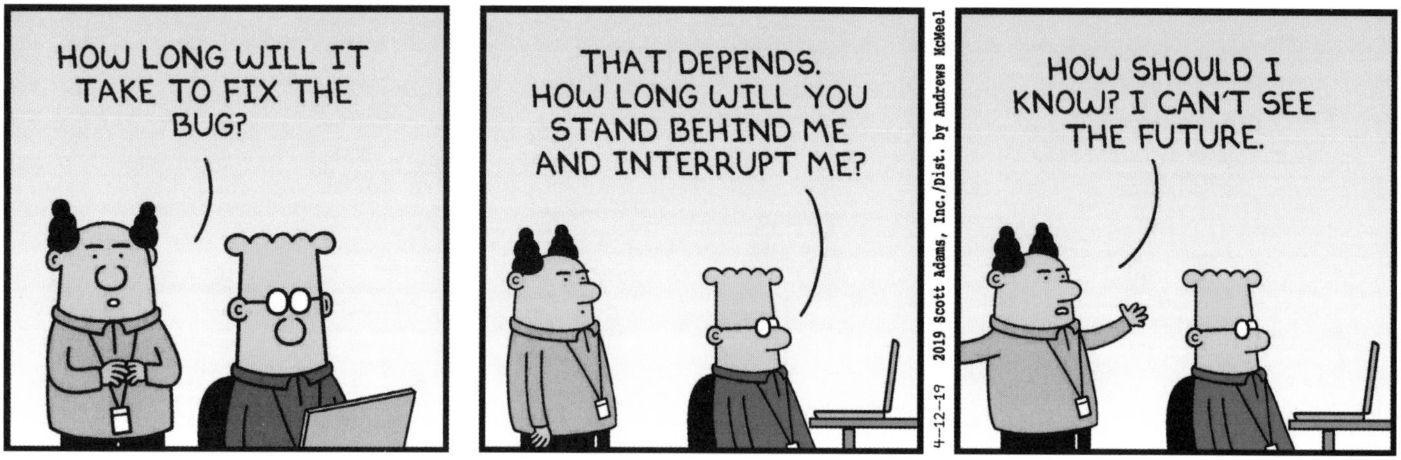
HOW LONG WILL IT TAKE TO FIX THE BUG?
THAT DEPENDS. HOW LONG WILL YOU STAND BEHIND ME AND INTERRUPT ME?
HOW SHOULD I KNOW? I CAN'T SEE THE FUTURE.
4-12-19 2019 Scott Adams, Inc./Dist. by Andrews McMeel

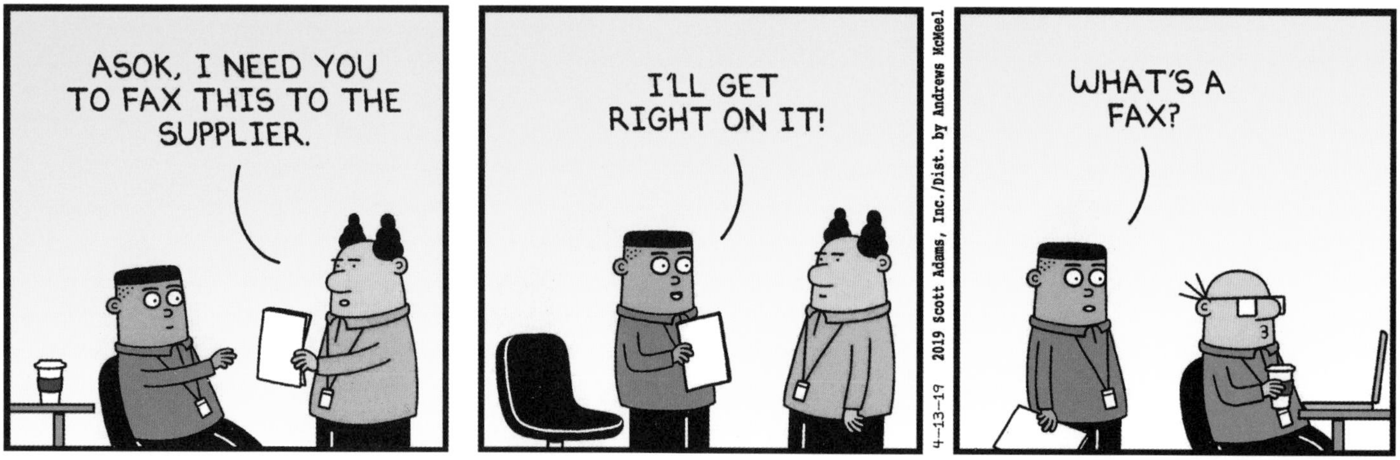
ASOK, I NEED YOU TO FAX THIS TO THE SUPPLIER.
I'LL GET RIGHT ON IT!
WHAT'S A FAX?
4-13-19 2019 Scott Adams, Inc./Dist. by Andrews McMeel

THE PRODUCT I'M DEVELOPING WILL BE UNPROFITABLE FOR THE FIRST NINE YEARS, BUT REVENUE WILL SURGE IN THE TENTH.
$
DIDN'T YOU TELL ME YOU PLAN TO RETIRE IN NINE YEARS?
MAYBE.
YOU WILL BE HAPPILY RETIRED BEFORE WE FIND OUT IF PROFITS REALLY DO SURGE IN YEAR TEN.
THAT MAKES EVERYTHING YOU SAY SOUND SUSPICIOUS.
NUMBERS DON'T LIE.
WHO CAME UP WITH THE NUMBERS?
THAT'S ALL THE TIME WE HAVE FOR QUESTIONS.
© 2019 Scott Adams, Inc./Dist. by Andrews McMeel
4-14-19

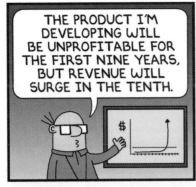

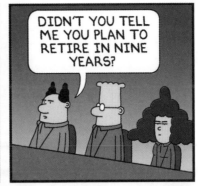

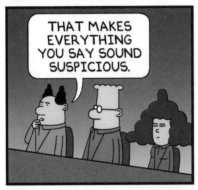

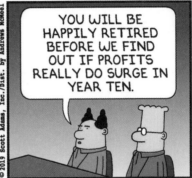

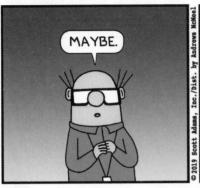

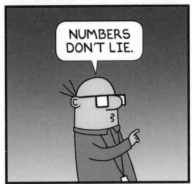

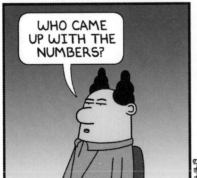

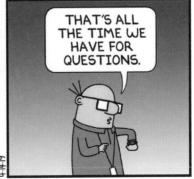

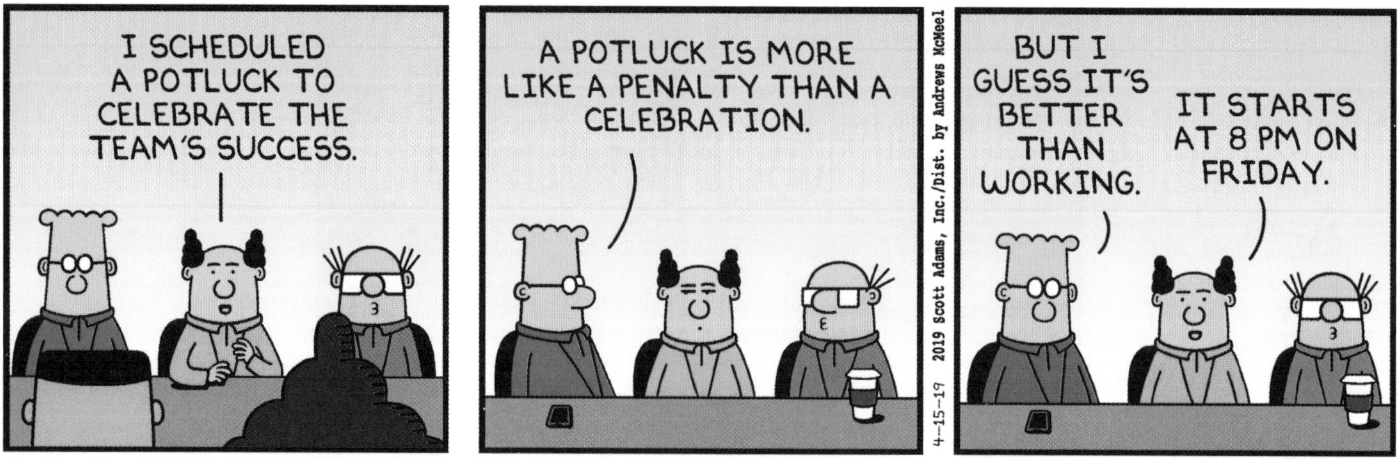
I SCHEDULED A POTLUCK TO CELEBRATE THE TEAM'S SUCCESS.
A POTLUCK IS MORE LIKE A PENALTY THAN A CELEBRATION.
4-15-19 2019 Scott Adams, Inc./Dist. by Andrews McMeel
BUT I GUESS IT'S BETTER THAN WORKING.
IT STARTS AT 8 PM ON FRIDAY.

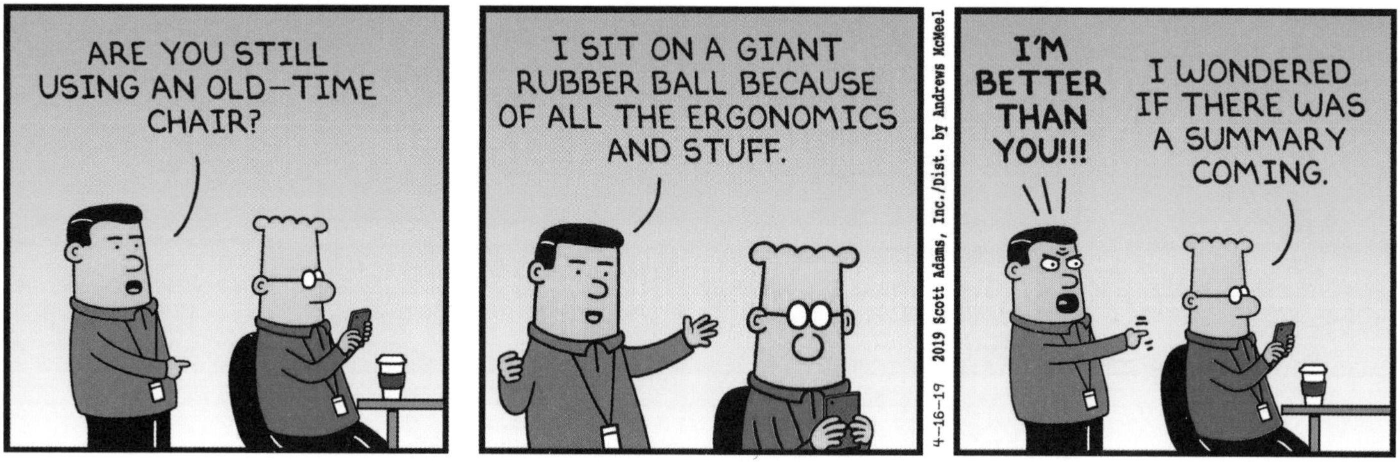
ARE YOU STILL USING AN OLD–TIME CHAIR?
I SIT ON A GIANT RUBBER BALL BECAUSE OF ALL THE ERGONOMICS AND STUFF.
4-16-19 2019 Scott Adams, Inc./Dist. by Andrews McMeel
I'M BETTER THAN YOU!!!
I WONDERED IF THERE WAS A SUMMARY COMING.

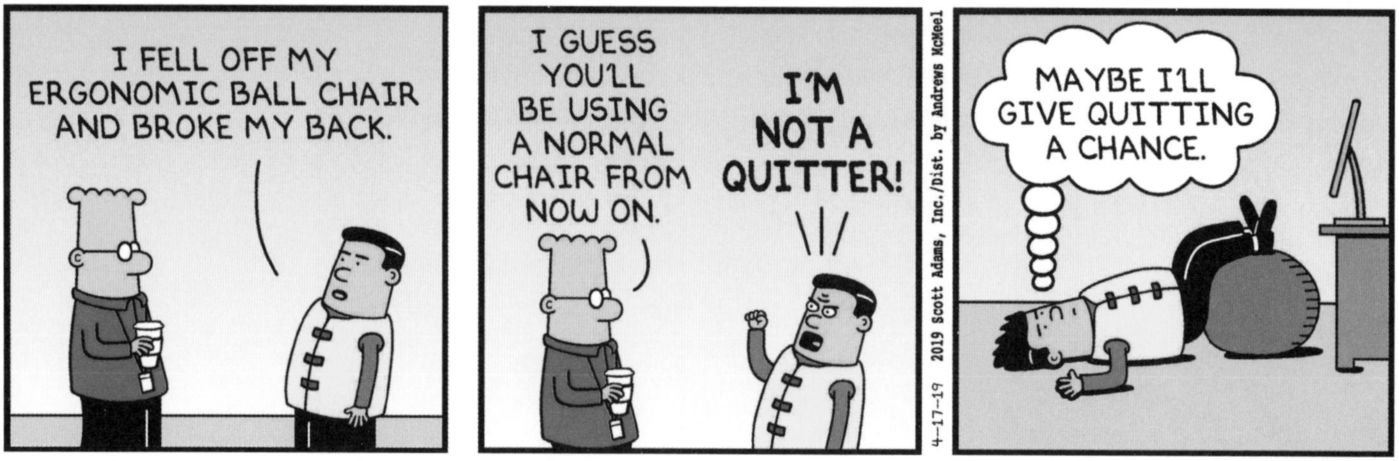
I FELL OFF MY ERGONOMIC BALL CHAIR AND BROKE MY BACK.
I GUESS YOU'LL BE USING A NORMAL CHAIR FROM NOW ON.
I'M NOT A QUITTER!
4-17-19 2019 Scott Adams, Inc./Dist. by Andrews McMeel
MAYBE I'LL GIVE QUITTING A CHANCE.

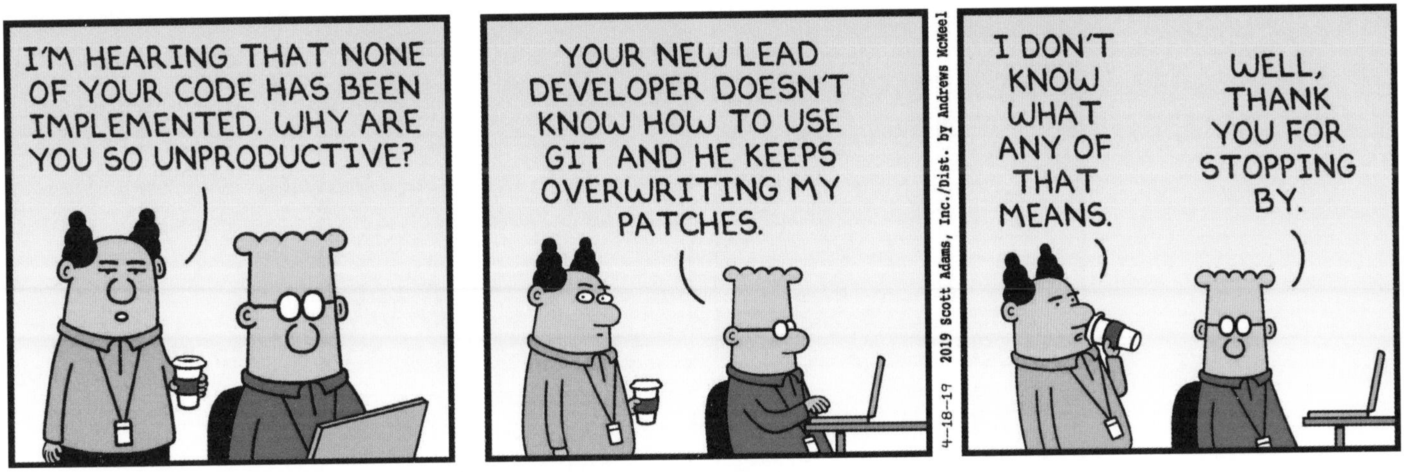
I'M HEARING THAT NONE OF YOUR CODE HAS BEEN IMPLEMENTED. WHY ARE YOU SO UNPRODUCTIVE?
YOUR NEW LEAD DEVELOPER DOESN'T KNOW HOW TO USE GIT AND HE KEEPS OVERWRITING MY PATCHES.
4-18-19 © 2019 Scott Adams, Inc./Dist. by Andrews McMeel
I DON'T KNOW WHAT ANY OF THAT MEANS.
WELL, THANK YOU FOR STOPPING BY.

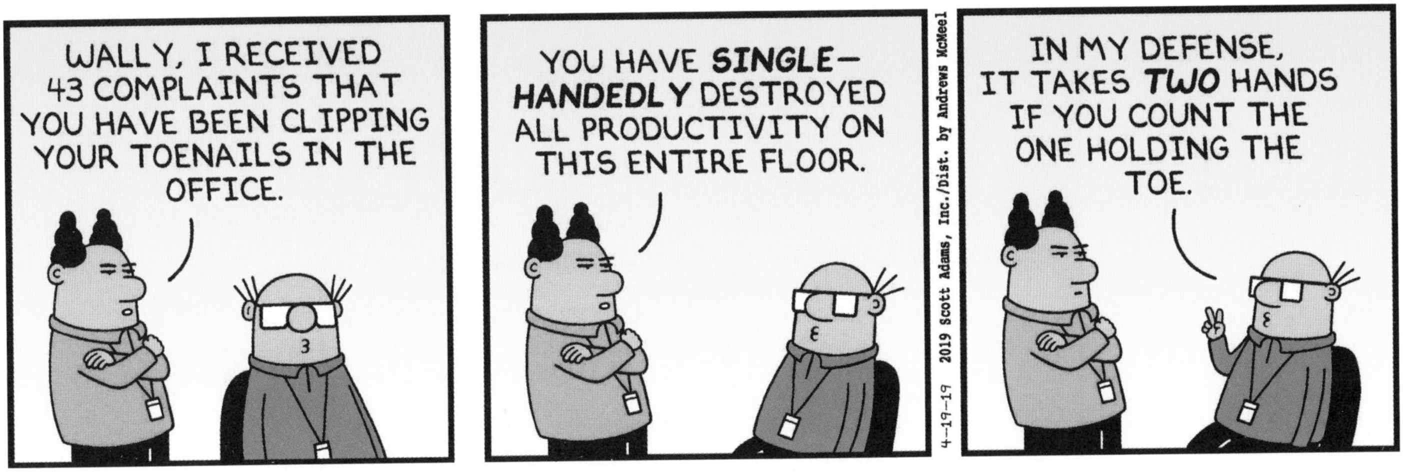
WALLY, I RECEIVED 43 COMPLAINTS THAT YOU HAVE BEEN CLIPPING YOUR TOENAILS IN THE OFFICE.
YOU HAVE **SINGLE-HANDEDLY** DESTROYED ALL PRODUCTIVITY ON THIS ENTIRE FLOOR.
4-19-19 © 2019 Scott Adams, Inc./Dist. by Andrews McMeel
IN MY DEFENSE, IT TAKES ***TWO*** HANDS IF YOU COUNT THE ONE HOLDING THE TOE.

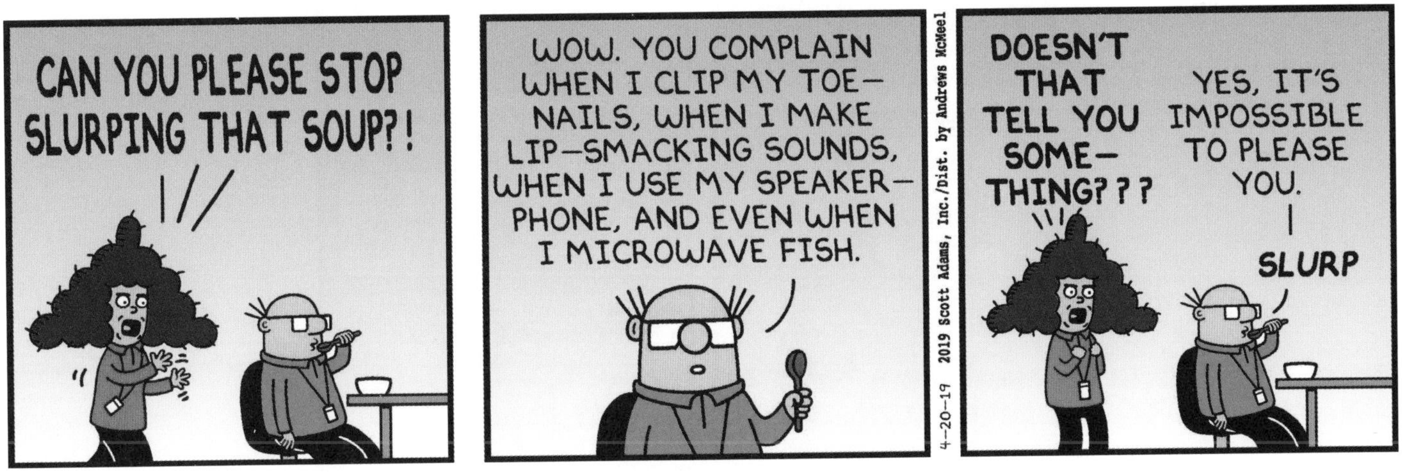
CAN YOU PLEASE STOP SLURPING THAT SOUP?!
WOW. YOU COMPLAIN WHEN I CLIP MY TOE-NAILS, WHEN I MAKE LIP-SMACKING SOUNDS, WHEN I USE MY SPEAKER-PHONE, AND EVEN WHEN I MICROWAVE FISH.
4-20-19 © 2019 Scott Adams, Inc./Dist. by Andrews McMeel
DOESN'T THAT TELL YOU SOME-THING???
YES, IT'S IMPOSSIBLE TO PLEASE YOU.
SLURP

SIGH...
SIGH...
WHAT'S WRONG?
GAAAA!!! NEVER ASK ABOUT THE SIGH!
IT'S A TRAP TO MAKE YOU LISTEN TO A DISTRESSING STORY FULL OF WOE.
MY HUSBAND IS A HUNTER AND HE WANTS ME TO LEARN HOW TO SKIN AND COOK HIS KILLS.
THAT DOESN'T SOUND SO BAD.
WAIT FOR IT.
HE'S A SERIAL KILLER.
AND THERE IT IS.
© 2019 Scott Adams, Inc./Dist. by Andrews McMeel
4-21-19

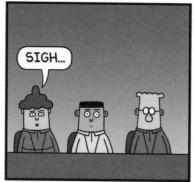

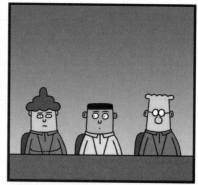

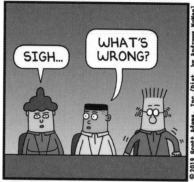

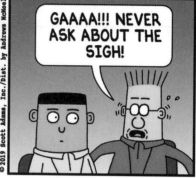

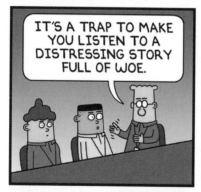

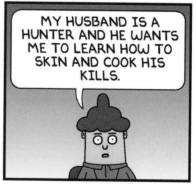

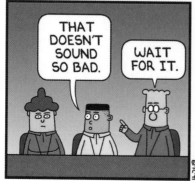

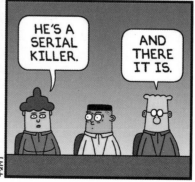

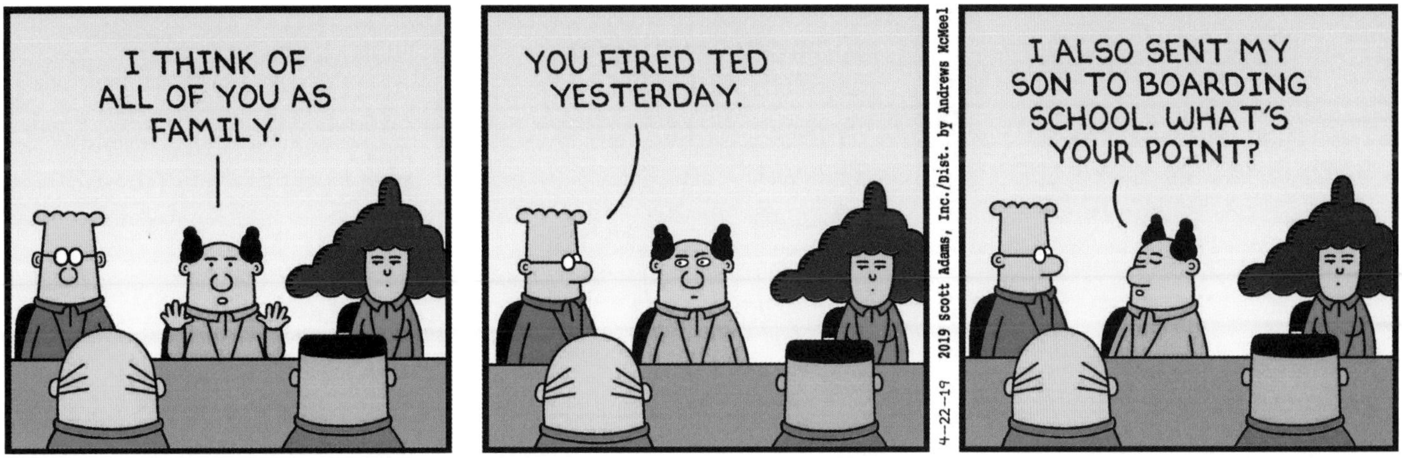
I THINK OF ALL OF YOU AS FAMILY.
YOU FIRED TED YESTERDAY.
I ALSO SENT MY SON TO BOARDING SCHOOL. WHAT'S YOUR POINT?
4-22-19 2019 Scott Adams, Inc./Dist. by Andrews McMeel

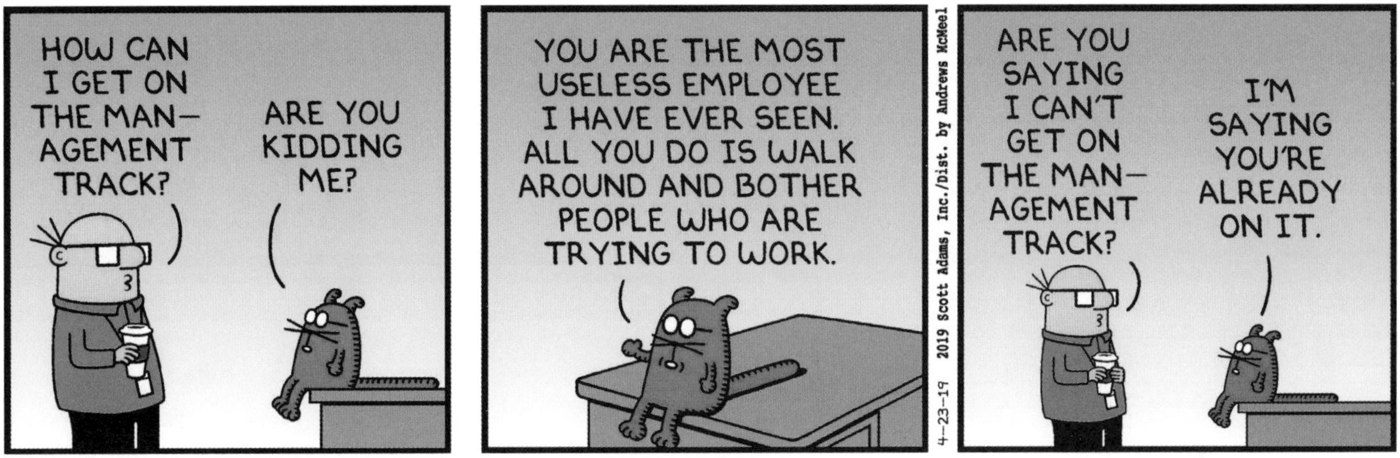
HOW CAN I GET ON THE MAN-AGEMENT TRACK?
ARE YOU KIDDING ME?
YOU ARE THE MOST USELESS EMPLOYEE I HAVE EVER SEEN. ALL YOU DO IS WALK AROUND AND BOTHER PEOPLE WHO ARE TRYING TO WORK.
ARE YOU SAYING I CAN'T GET ON THE MAN-AGEMENT TRACK?
I'M SAYING YOU'RE ALREADY ON IT.
4-23-19 2019 Scott Adams, Inc./Dist. by Andrews McMeel

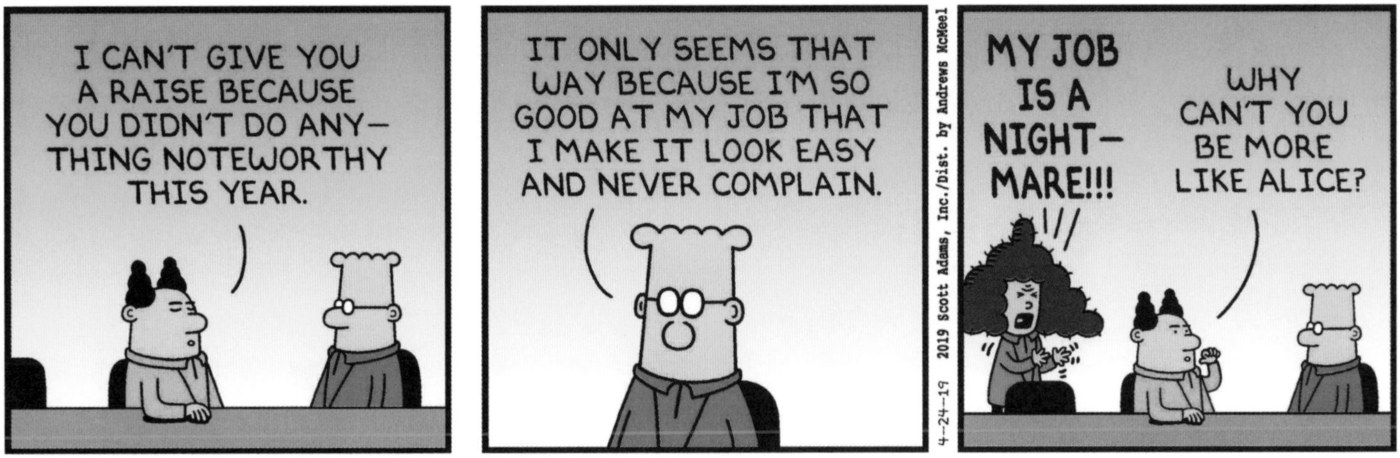
I CAN'T GIVE YOU A RAISE BECAUSE YOU DIDN'T DO ANY-THING NOTEWORTHY THIS YEAR.
IT ONLY SEEMS THAT WAY BECAUSE I'M SO GOOD AT MY JOB THAT I MAKE IT LOOK EASY AND NEVER COMPLAIN.
MY JOB IS A NIGHT-MARE!!!
WHY CAN'T YOU BE MORE LIKE ALICE?
4-24-19 2019 Scott Adams, Inc./Dist. by Andrews McMeel

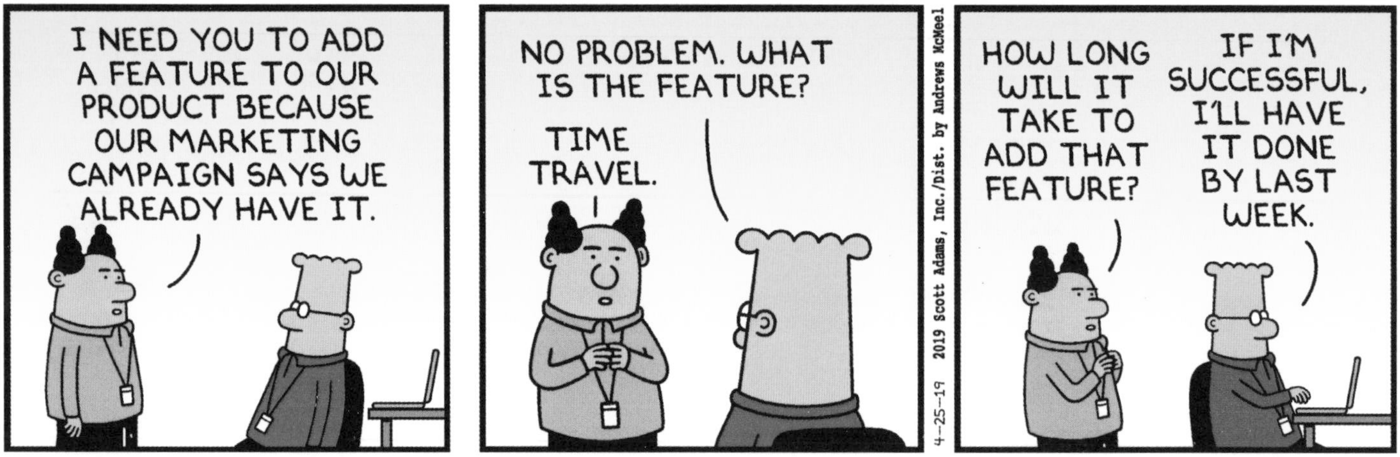
I NEED YOU TO ADD A FEATURE TO OUR PRODUCT BECAUSE OUR MARKETING CAMPAIGN SAYS WE ALREADY HAVE IT.
NO PROBLEM. WHAT IS THE FEATURE?
TIME TRAVEL.
4-25-19 © 2019 Scott Adams, Inc./Dist. by Andrews McMeel
HOW LONG WILL IT TAKE TO ADD THAT FEATURE?
IF I'M SUCCESSFUL, I'LL HAVE IT DONE BY LAST WEEK.

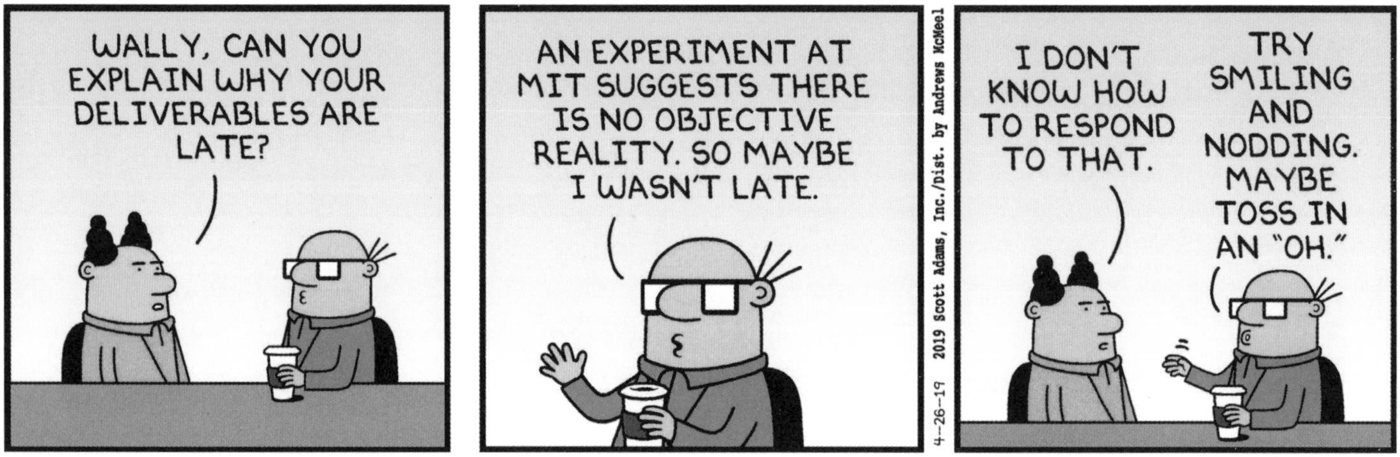
WALLY, CAN YOU EXPLAIN WHY YOUR DELIVERABLES ARE LATE?
AN EXPERIMENT AT MIT SUGGESTS THERE IS NO OBJECTIVE REALITY. SO MAYBE I WASN'T LATE.
4-26-19 © 2019 Scott Adams, Inc./Dist. by Andrews McMeel
I DON'T KNOW HOW TO RESPOND TO THAT.
TRY SMILING AND NODDING. MAYBE TOSS IN AN "OH."

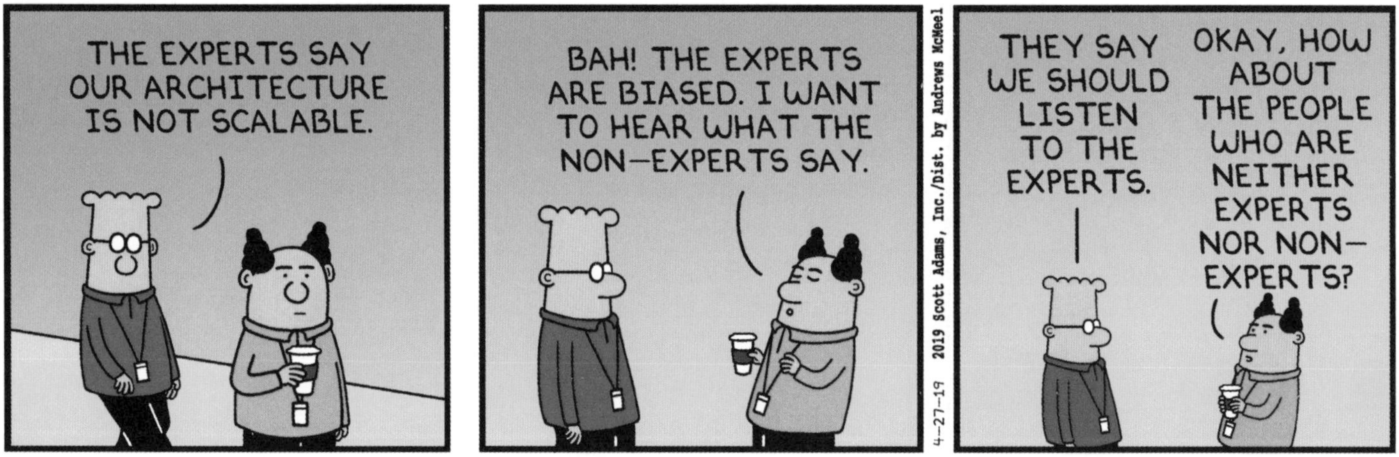
THE EXPERTS SAY OUR ARCHITECTURE IS NOT SCALABLE.
BAH! THE EXPERTS ARE BIASED. I WANT TO HEAR WHAT THE NON-EXPERTS SAY.
4-27-19 © 2019 Scott Adams, Inc./Dist. by Andrews McMeel
THEY SAY WE SHOULD LISTEN TO THE EXPERTS.
OKAY, HOW ABOUT THE PEOPLE WHO ARE NEITHER EXPERTS NOR NON-EXPERTS?

OUR NEW SYSTEM INSTALLATION IS A CATASTROPHE.
WE NEED TO TEAR IT OUT AND RE–ARCHITECT IT FROM SCRATCH.
I'M THE ONLY PERSON QUALIFIED TO LEAD THAT EFFORT.
BUT GIVEN THE ENORMITY OF THE JOB, I WON'T DO IT WITHOUT A RAISE AND A PROMOTION.
© 2019 Scott Adams, Inc./Dist. by Andrews McMeel
WEREN'T YOU THE CAUSE OF THE CATASTROPHE?
EXACTLY. THAT'S WHY I'M THE ONLY PERSON WHO KNOWS HOW TO FIX IT.
ARE YOU BLACK–MAILING ME?
NO. IT'S NOTHING LIKE THAT.
4-28-19
WOULDN'T I BE RE–WARDING YOU FOR FAILURE?
LET'S NOT LABEL IT.

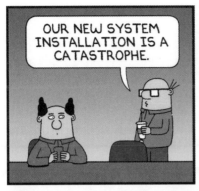

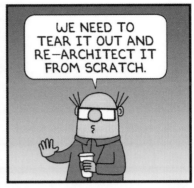

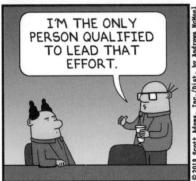

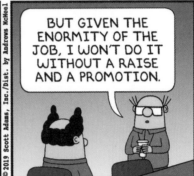

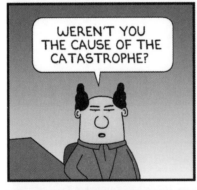

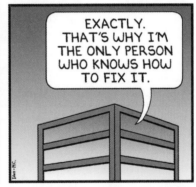

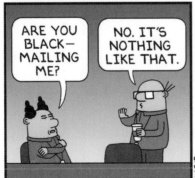

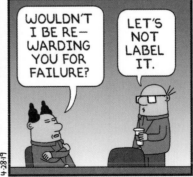

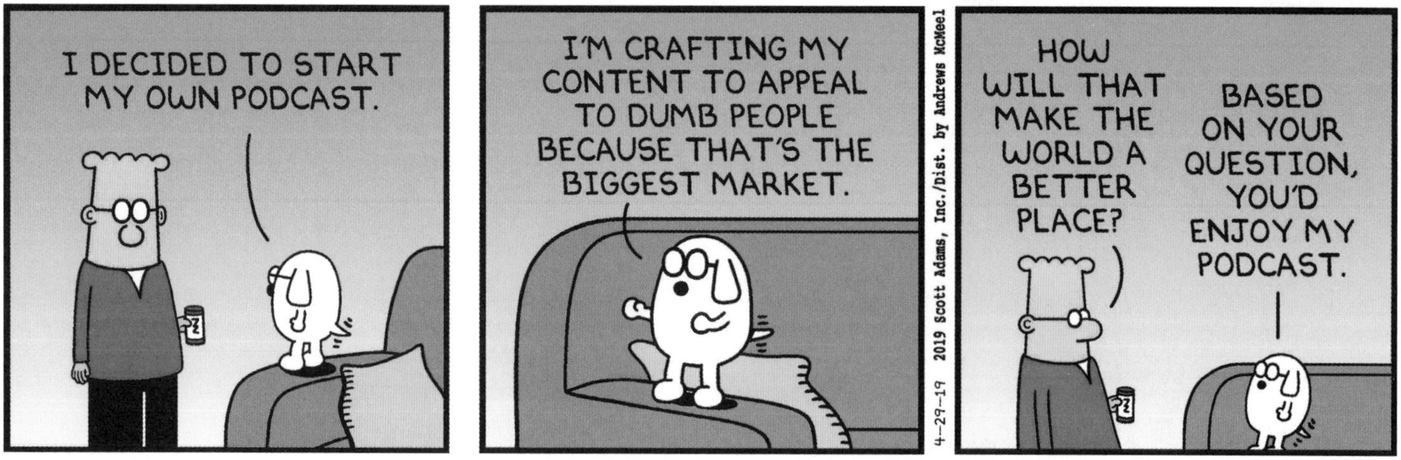
I DECIDED TO START MY OWN PODCAST.
I'M CRAFTING MY CONTENT TO APPEAL TO DUMB PEOPLE BECAUSE THAT'S THE BIGGEST MARKET.
4-29-19 © 2019 Scott Adams, Inc./Dist. by Andrews McMeel
HOW WILL THAT MAKE THE WORLD A BETTER PLACE?
BASED ON YOUR QUESTION, YOU'D ENJOY MY PODCAST.

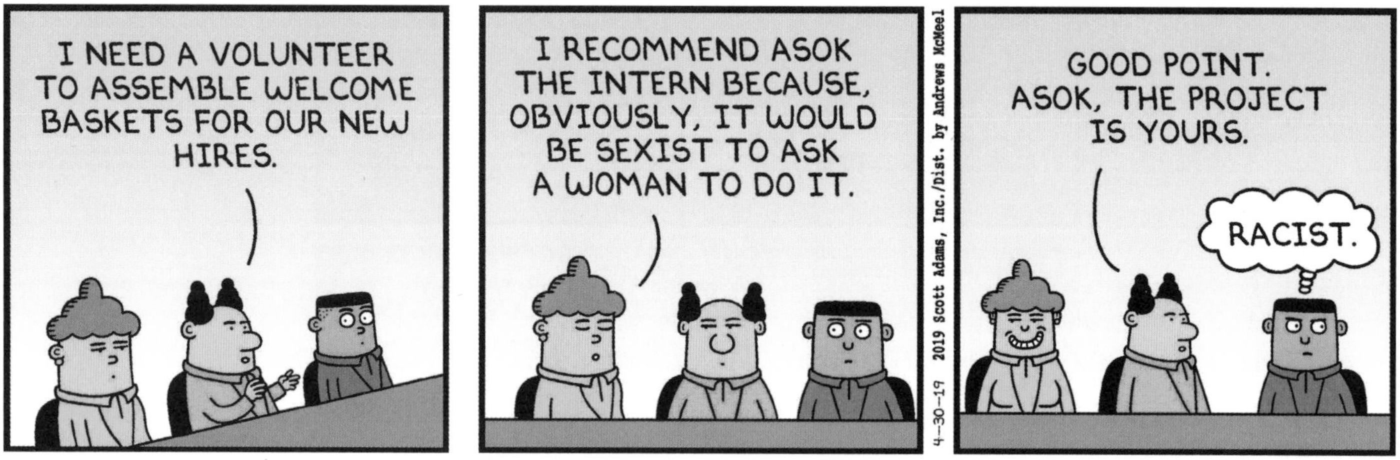
I NEED A VOLUNTEER TO ASSEMBLE WELCOME BASKETS FOR OUR NEW HIRES.
I RECOMMEND ASOK THE INTERN BECAUSE, OBVIOUSLY, IT WOULD BE SEXIST TO ASK A WOMAN TO DO IT.
4-30-19 © 2019 Scott Adams, Inc./Dist. by Andrews McMeel
GOOD POINT. ASOK, THE PROJECT IS YOURS.
RACIST.

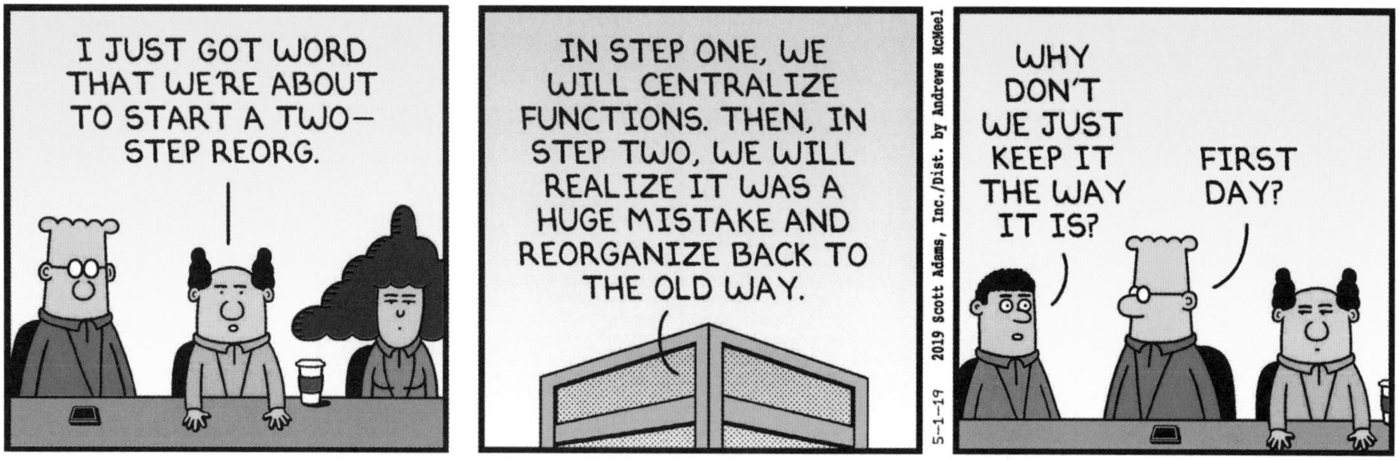
I JUST GOT WORD THAT WE'RE ABOUT TO START A TWO-STEP REORG.
IN STEP ONE, WE WILL CENTRALIZE FUNCTIONS. THEN, IN STEP TWO, WE WILL REALIZE IT WAS A HUGE MISTAKE AND REORGANIZE BACK TO THE OLD WAY.
5-1-19 © 2019 Scott Adams, Inc./Dist. by Andrews McMeel
WHY DON'T WE JUST KEEP IT THE WAY IT IS?
FIRST DAY?

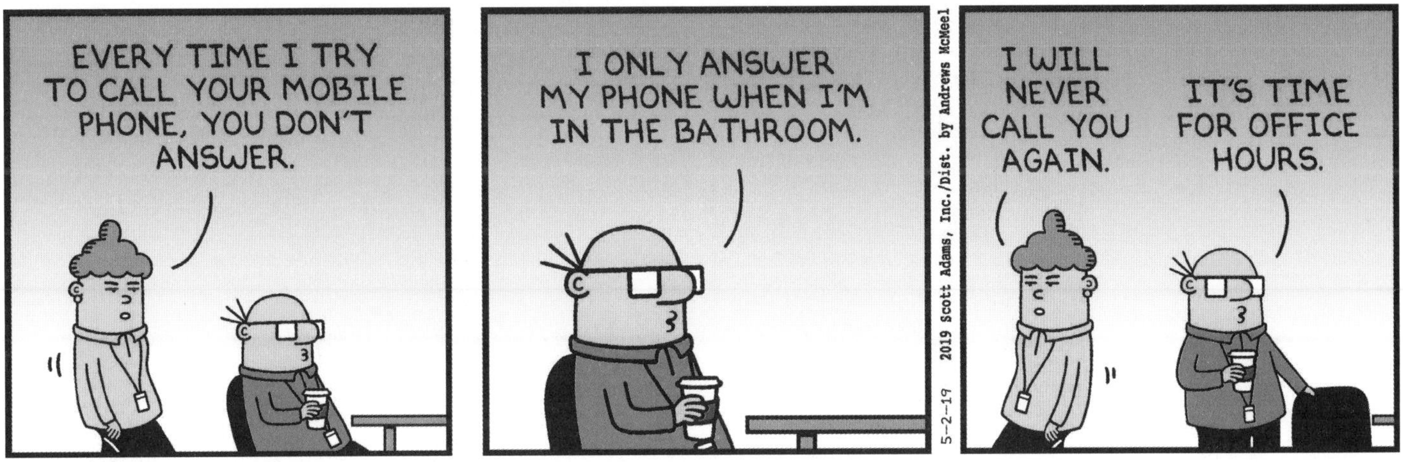
EVERY TIME I TRY TO CALL YOUR MOBILE PHONE, YOU DON'T ANSWER.
I ONLY ANSWER MY PHONE WHEN I'M IN THE BATHROOM.
I WILL NEVER CALL YOU AGAIN.
IT'S TIME FOR OFFICE HOURS.
5-2-19 2019 Scott Adams, Inc./Dist. by Andrews McMeel

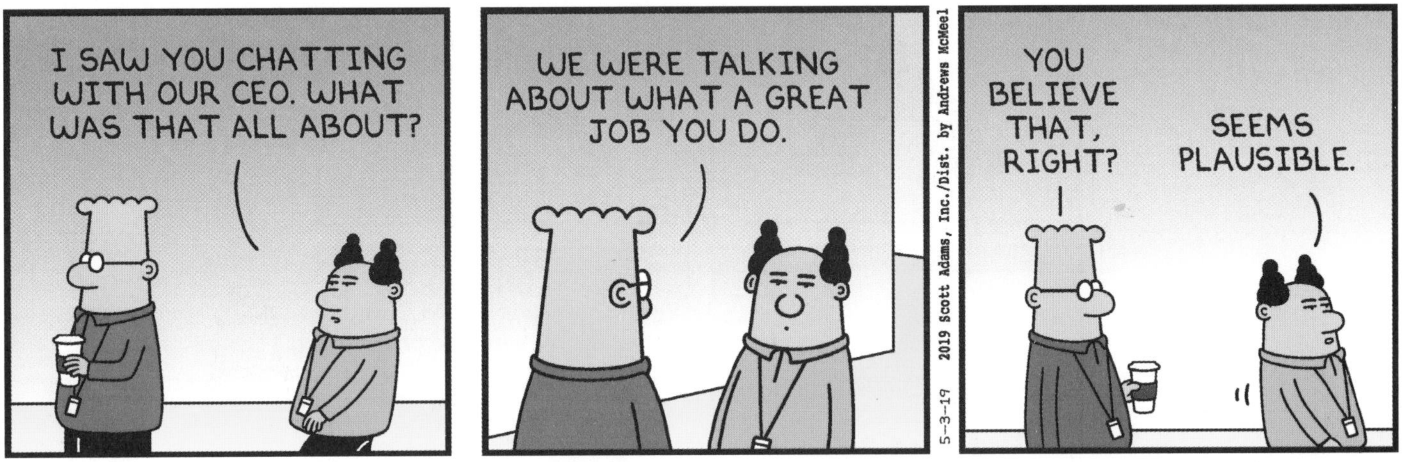
I SAW YOU CHATTING WITH OUR CEO. WHAT WAS THAT ALL ABOUT?
WE WERE TALKING ABOUT WHAT A GREAT JOB YOU DO.
YOU BELIEVE THAT, RIGHT?
SEEMS PLAUSIBLE.
5-3-19 2019 Scott Adams, Inc./Dist. by Andrews McMeel

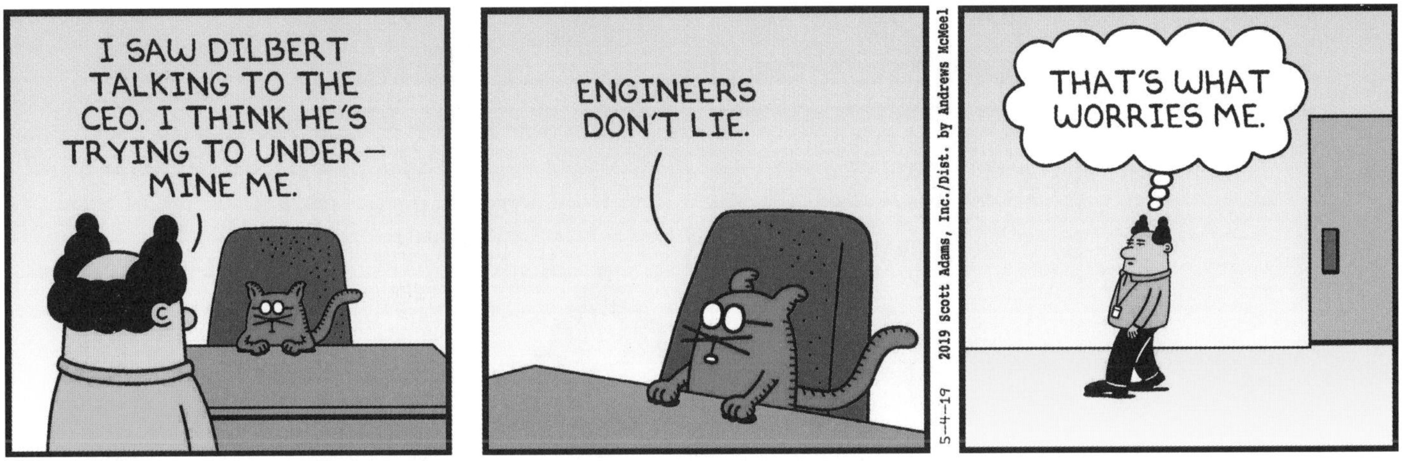
I SAW DILBERT TALKING TO THE CEO. I THINK HE'S TRYING TO UNDER-MINE ME.
ENGINEERS DON'T LIE.
THAT'S WHAT WORRIES ME.
5-4-19 2019 Scott Adams, Inc./Dist. by Andrews McMeel

I NEED A NEW CHAIR. MINE IS BROKEN.
YOU CAN USE MY OLD CHAIR. I JUST GOT A NEW ONE.
THE CHAIR YOU SAT IN EVERY DAY FOR THE PAST TWELVE YEARS?
BY NOW THAT CHAIR CUSHION IS HOME TO A THRIVING COLONY OF YOUR COOTIES.
THAT CHAIR WILL BE OFF-GASSING YOU FOR DECADES.
I WOULDN'T TOUCH THAT THING UNLESS I WERE WEARING A HAZMAT SUIT OVER MY OTHER HAZMAT SUIT.
I'M BREAKING INTO A FLOP SWEAT JUST THINKING ABOUT IT, AND I THINK IT'S TRIGGERING MY ALLERGIES.
WOULD YOU LIKE TO BORROW MY HAND-KERCHIEF?
© 2019 Scott Adams, Inc./Dist. by Andrews McMeel
5-5-19

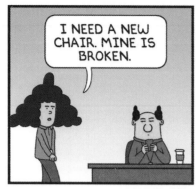

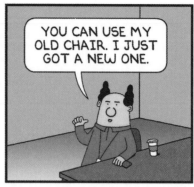

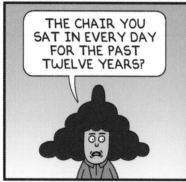

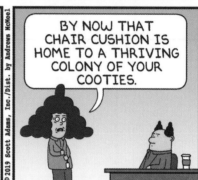

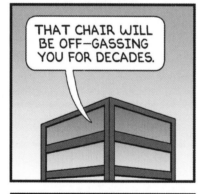

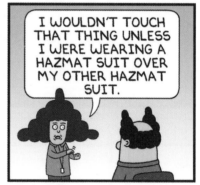

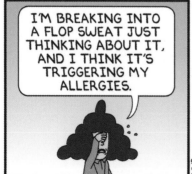

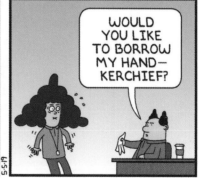

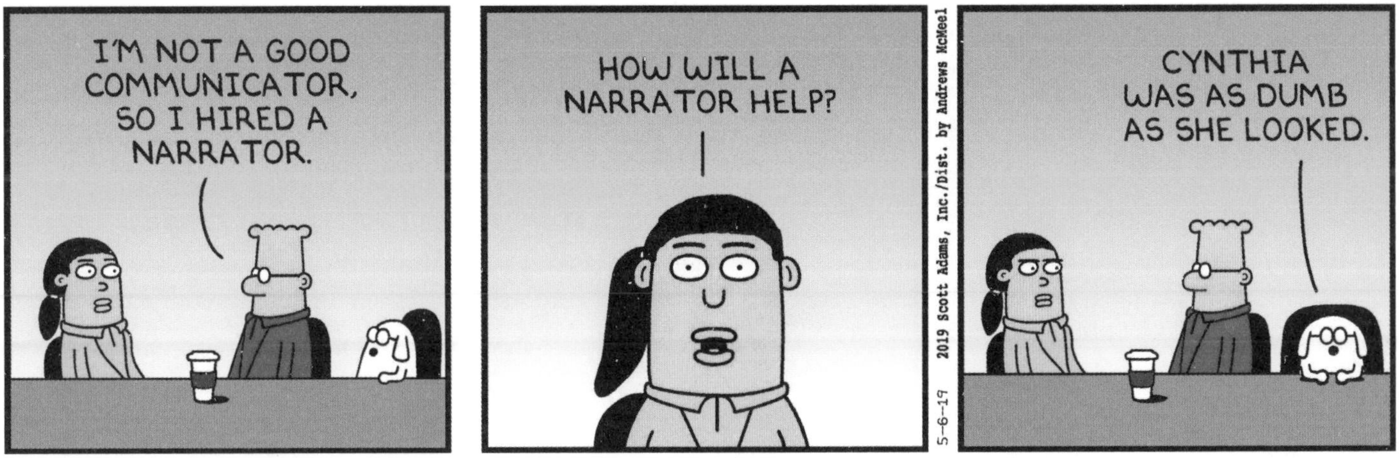
I'M NOT A GOOD COMMUNICATOR, SO I HIRED A NARRATOR.
HOW WILL A NARRATOR HELP?
CYNTHIA WAS AS DUMB AS SHE LOOKED.
5-6-19 2019 Scott Adams, Inc./Dist. by Andrews McMeel

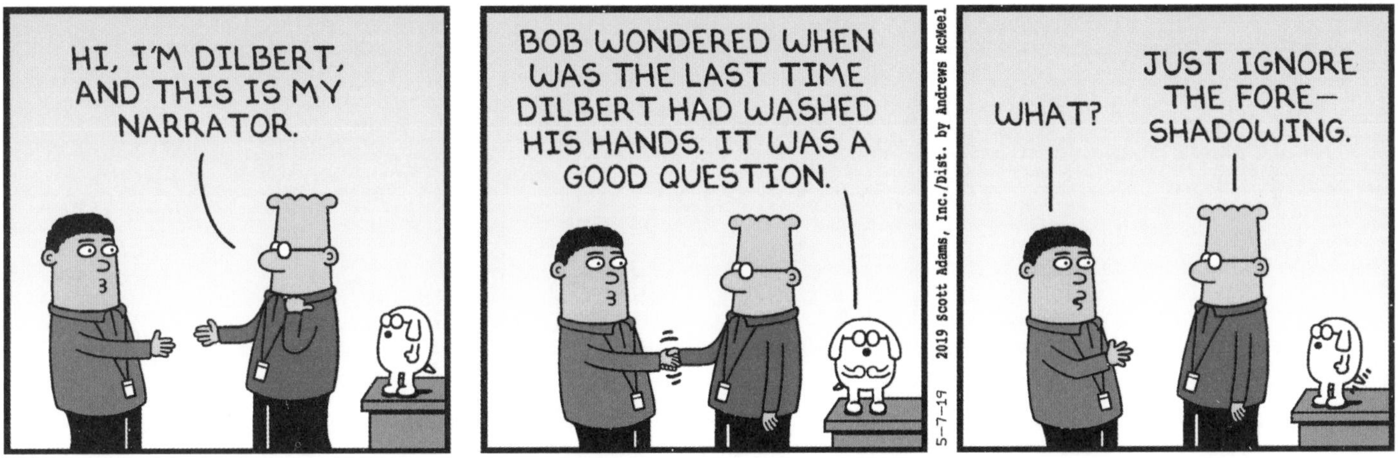
HI, I'M DILBERT, AND THIS IS MY NARRATOR.
BOB WONDERED WHEN WAS THE LAST TIME DILBERT HAD WASHED HIS HANDS. IT WAS A GOOD QUESTION.
WHAT?
JUST IGNORE THE FORE-SHADOWING.
5-7-19 2019 Scott Adams, Inc./Dist. by Andrews McMeel

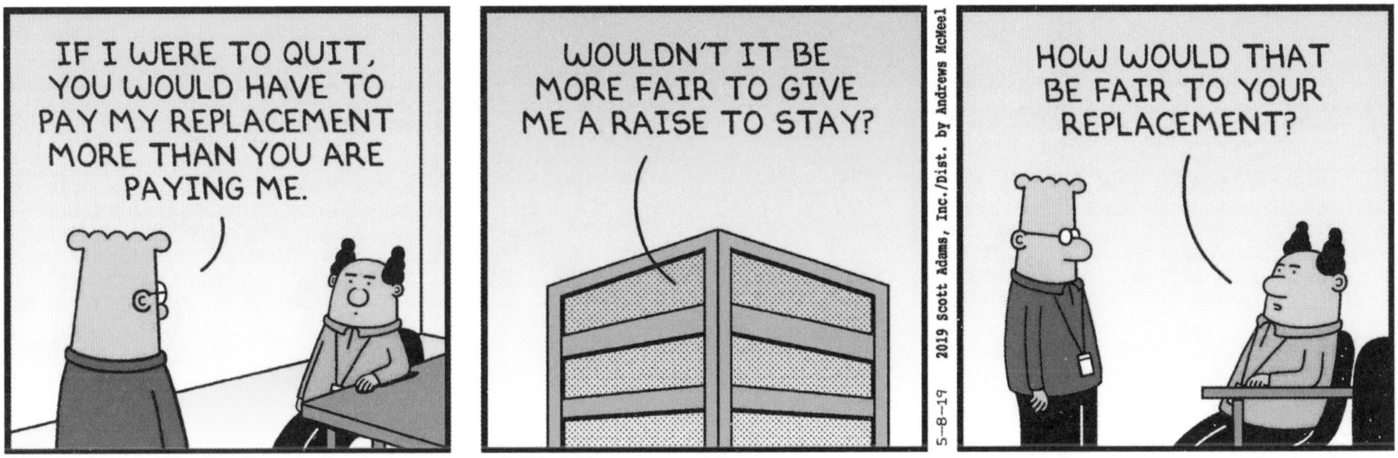
IF I WERE TO QUIT, YOU WOULD HAVE TO PAY MY REPLACEMENT MORE THAN YOU ARE PAYING ME.
WOULDN'T IT BE MORE FAIR TO GIVE ME A RAISE TO STAY?
HOW WOULD THAT BE FAIR TO YOUR REPLACEMENT?
5-8-19 2019 Scott Adams, Inc./Dist. by Andrews McMeel

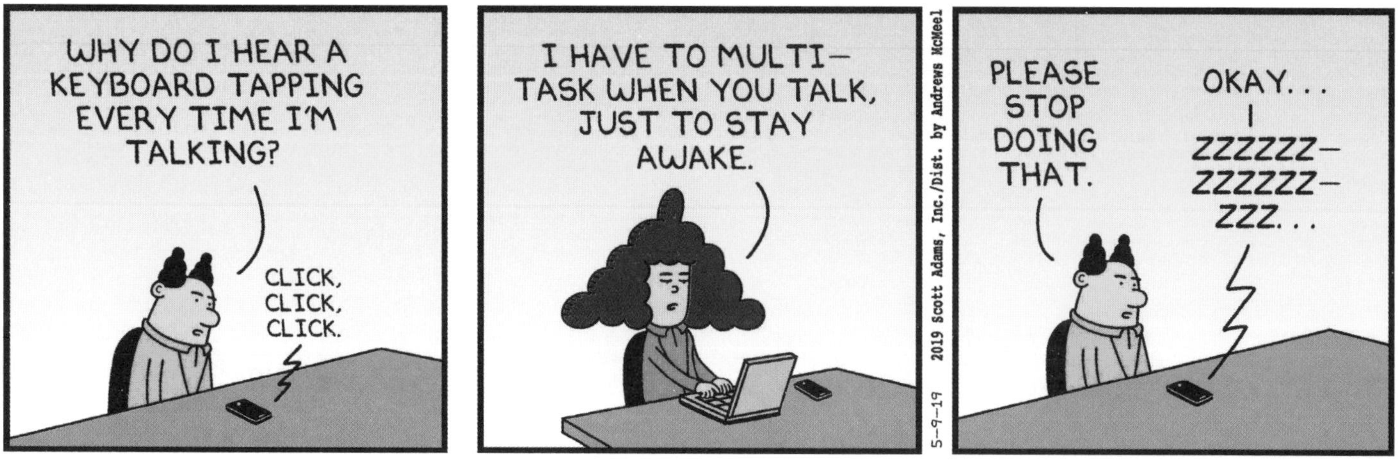
WHY DO I HEAR A KEYBOARD TAPPING EVERY TIME I'M TALKING?
CLICK, CLICK, CLICK.
I HAVE TO MULTI— TASK WHEN YOU TALK, JUST TO STAY AWAKE.
5-9-19 2019 Scott Adams, Inc./Dist. by Andrews McMeel
PLEASE STOP DOING THAT.
OKAY... I ZZZZZZ— ZZZZZZ— ZZZ...

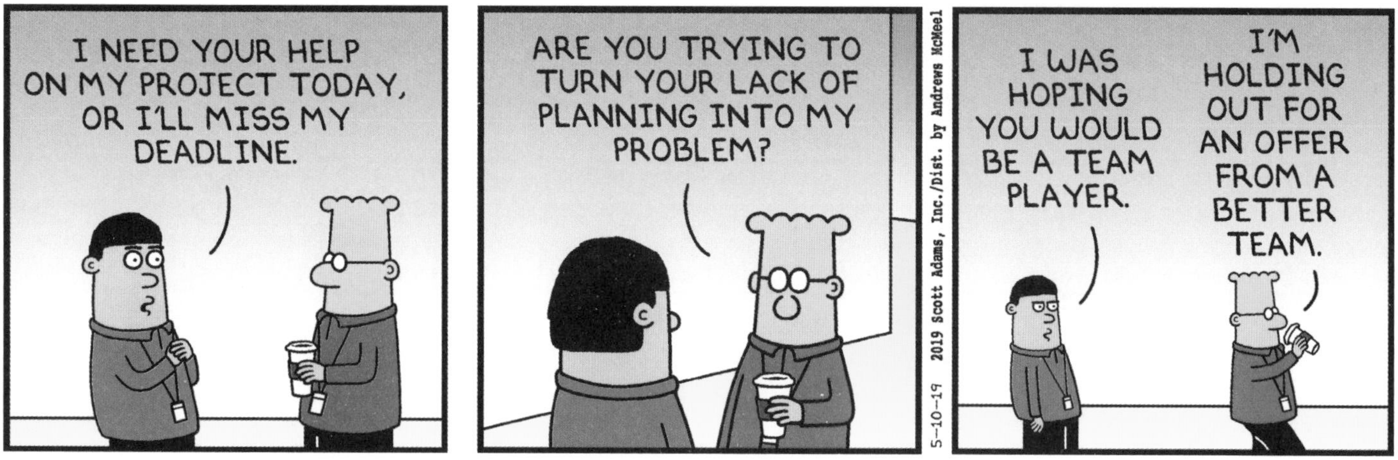
I NEED YOUR HELP ON MY PROJECT TODAY, OR I'LL MISS MY DEADLINE.
ARE YOU TRYING TO TURN YOUR LACK OF PLANNING INTO MY PROBLEM?
5-10-19 2019 Scott Adams, Inc./Dist. by Andrews McMeel
I WAS HOPING YOU WOULD BE A TEAM PLAYER.
I'M HOLDING OUT FOR AN OFFER FROM A BETTER TEAM.

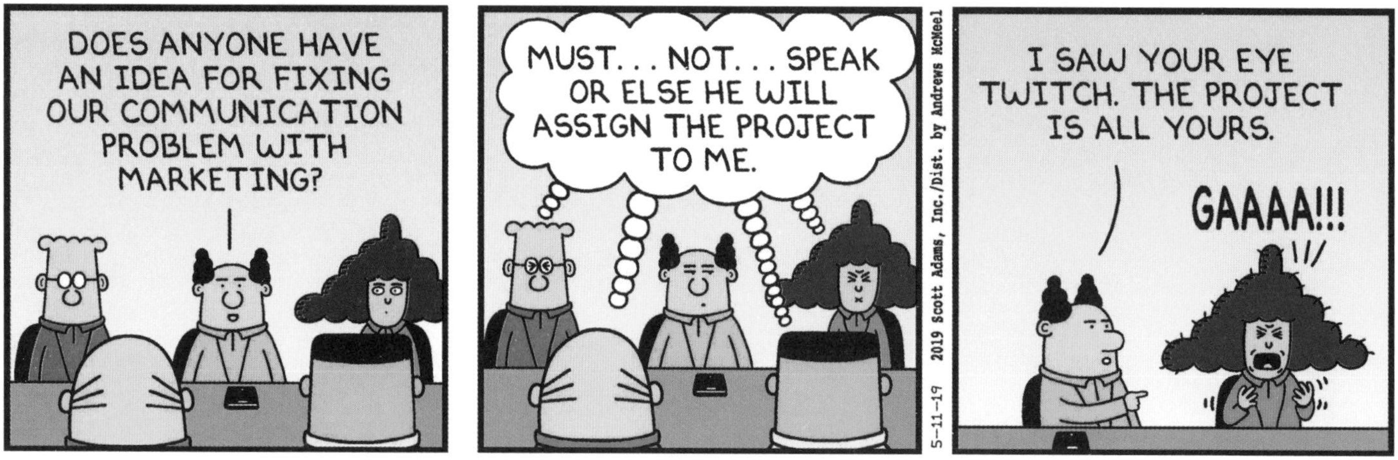
DOES ANYONE HAVE AN IDEA FOR FIXING OUR COMMUNICATION PROBLEM WITH MARKETING?
MUST... NOT... SPEAK OR ELSE HE WILL ASSIGN THE PROJECT TO ME.
5-11-19 2019 Scott Adams, Inc./Dist. by Andrews McMeel
I SAW YOUR EYE TWITCH. THE PROJECT IS ALL YOURS.
GAAAA!!!

NED WON'T RETURN ANY OF MY MESSAGES.
FIRE HIM.
I CAN'T DO THAT.
NED IS INDISPENSABLE.
WHAT MAKES HIM INDISPENSABLE?
HE'S THE ONLY ONE WHO KNOWS HOW TO FIX BUGS IN OUR SYSTEM.
WHAT SYSTEM?
I DON'T KNOW.
THEN HOW DO YOU KNOW HE'S INDIS-PENSABLE?
NED TOLD ME.
FIRE HIM ANY-WAY.
NED QUIT TWO YEARS AGO.
© 2019 Scott Adams, Inc./Dist. by Andrews McMeel
5-12-19

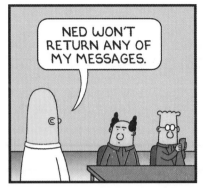

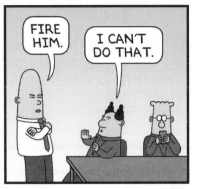

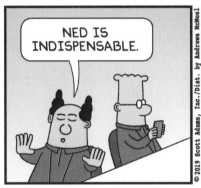

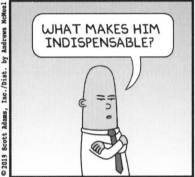

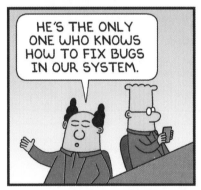

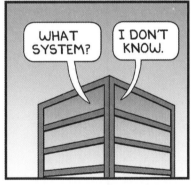

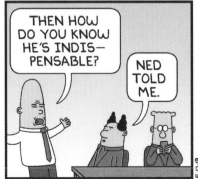

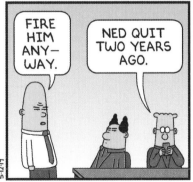

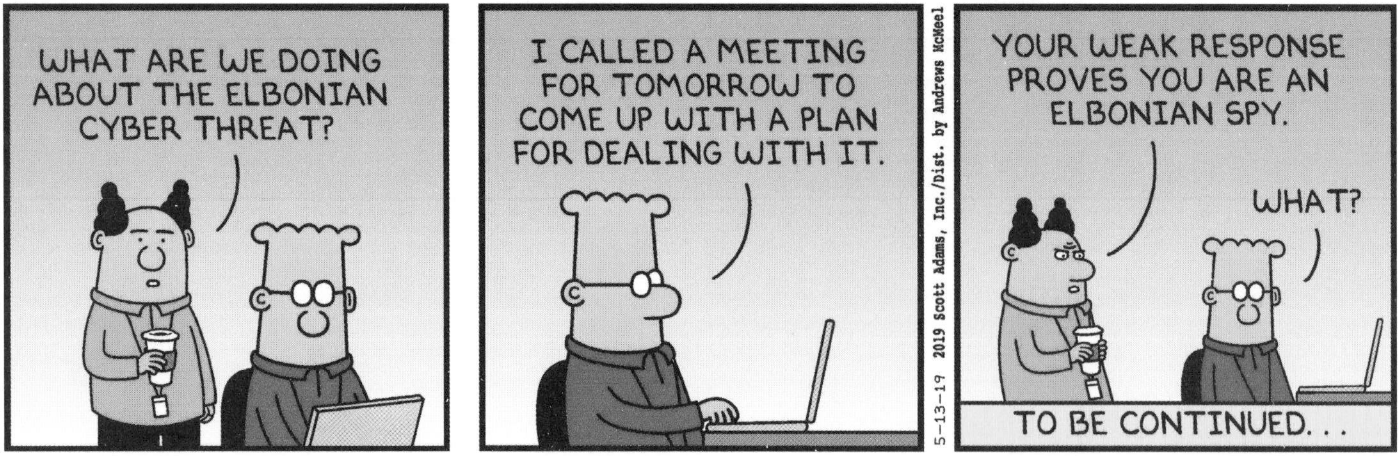
WHAT ARE WE DOING ABOUT THE ELBONIAN CYBER THREAT?
I CALLED A MEETING FOR TOMORROW TO COME UP WITH A PLAN FOR DEALING WITH IT.
5-13-19 2019 Scott Adams, Inc./Dist. by Andrews McMeel
YOUR WEAK RESPONSE PROVES YOU ARE AN ELBONIAN SPY.
WHAT?
TO BE CONTINUED. . .

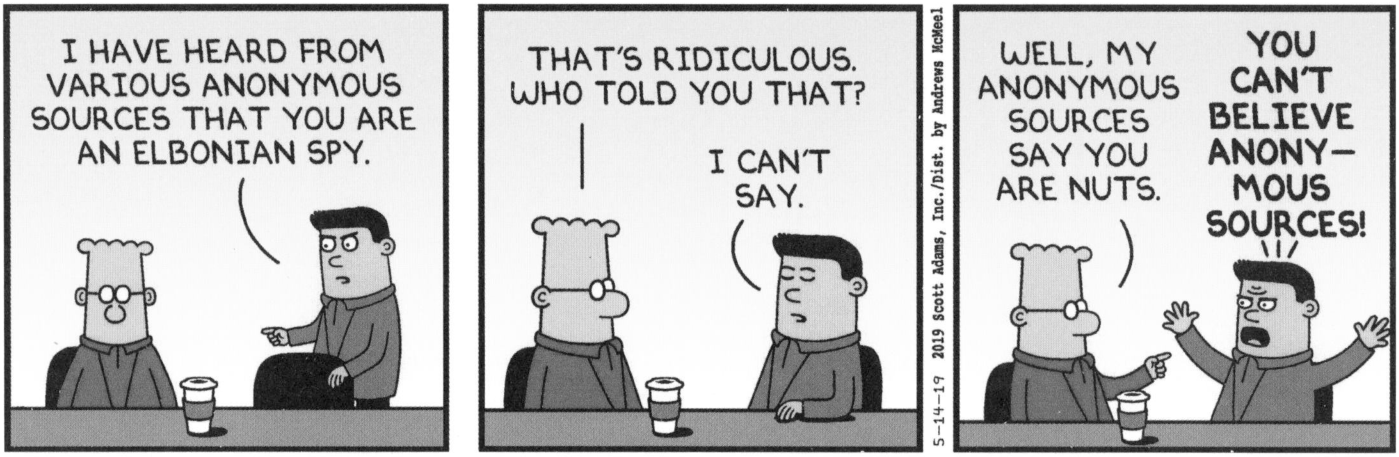
I HAVE HEARD FROM VARIOUS ANONYMOUS SOURCES THAT YOU ARE AN ELBONIAN SPY.
THAT'S RIDICULOUS. WHO TOLD YOU THAT?
I CAN'T SAY.
5-14-19 2019 Scott Adams, Inc./Dist. by Andrews McMeel
WELL, MY ANONYMOUS SOURCES SAY YOU ARE NUTS.
YOU CAN'T BELIEVE ANONY-MOUS SOURCES!

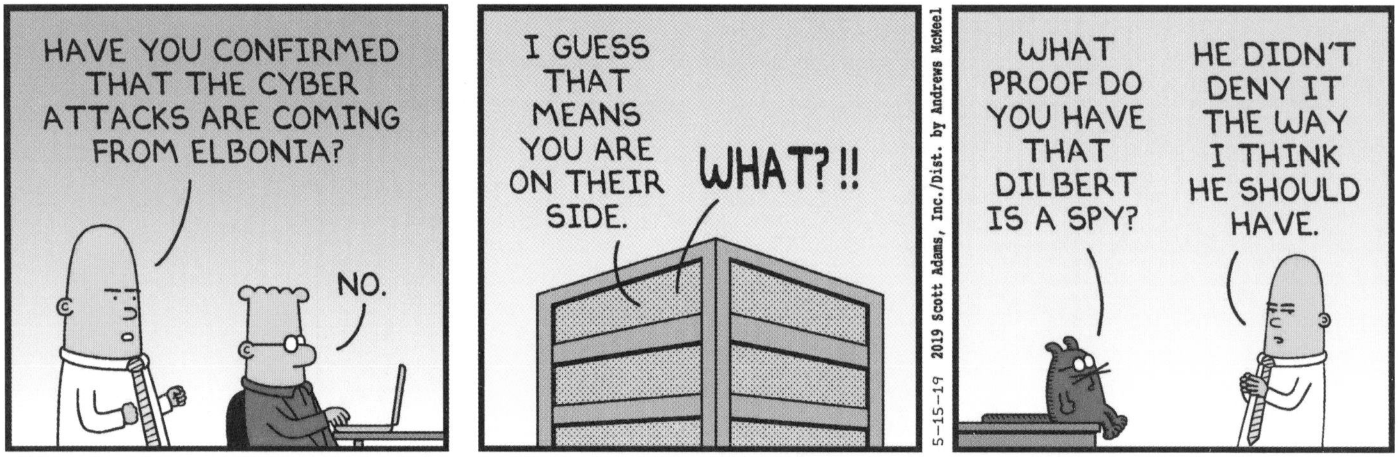
HAVE YOU CONFIRMED THAT THE CYBER ATTACKS ARE COMING FROM ELBONIA?
NO.
I GUESS THAT MEANS YOU ARE ON THEIR SIDE.
WHAT?!!
5-15-19 2019 Scott Adams, Inc./Dist. by Andrews McMeel
WHAT PROOF DO YOU HAVE THAT DILBERT IS A SPY?
HE DIDN'T DENY IT THE WAY I THINK HE SHOULD HAVE.

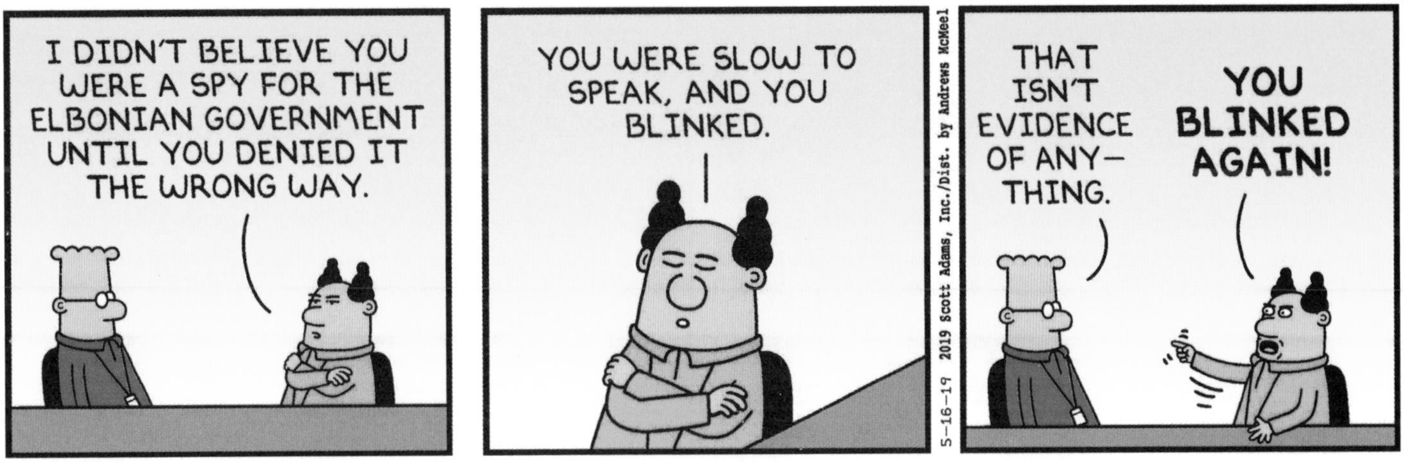
I DIDN'T BELIEVE YOU WERE A SPY FOR THE ELBONIAN GOVERNMENT UNTIL YOU DENIED IT THE WRONG WAY.
YOU WERE SLOW TO SPEAK, AND YOU BLINKED.
THAT ISN'T EVIDENCE OF ANY–THING.
YOU BLINKED AGAIN!
5-16-19 2019 Scott Adams, Inc./Dist. by Andrews McMeel

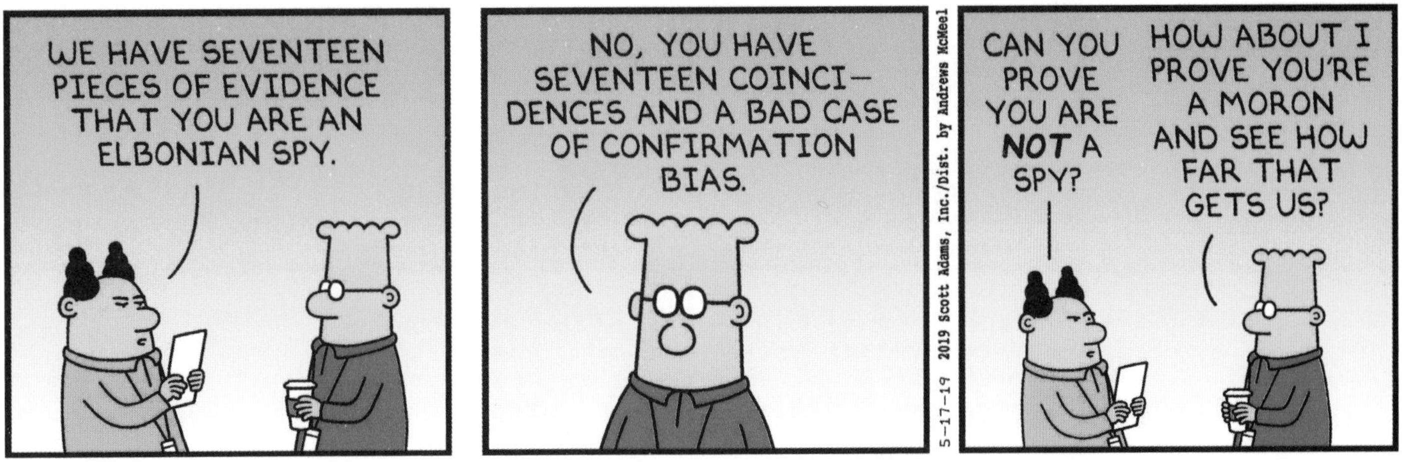
WE HAVE SEVENTEEN PIECES OF EVIDENCE THAT YOU ARE AN ELBONIAN SPY.
NO, YOU HAVE SEVENTEEN COINCI–DENCES AND A BAD CASE OF CONFIRMATION BIAS.
CAN YOU PROVE YOU ARE NOT A SPY?
HOW ABOUT I PROVE YOU'RE A MORON AND SEE HOW FAR THAT GETS US?
5-17-19 2019 Scott Adams, Inc./Dist. by Andrews McMeel

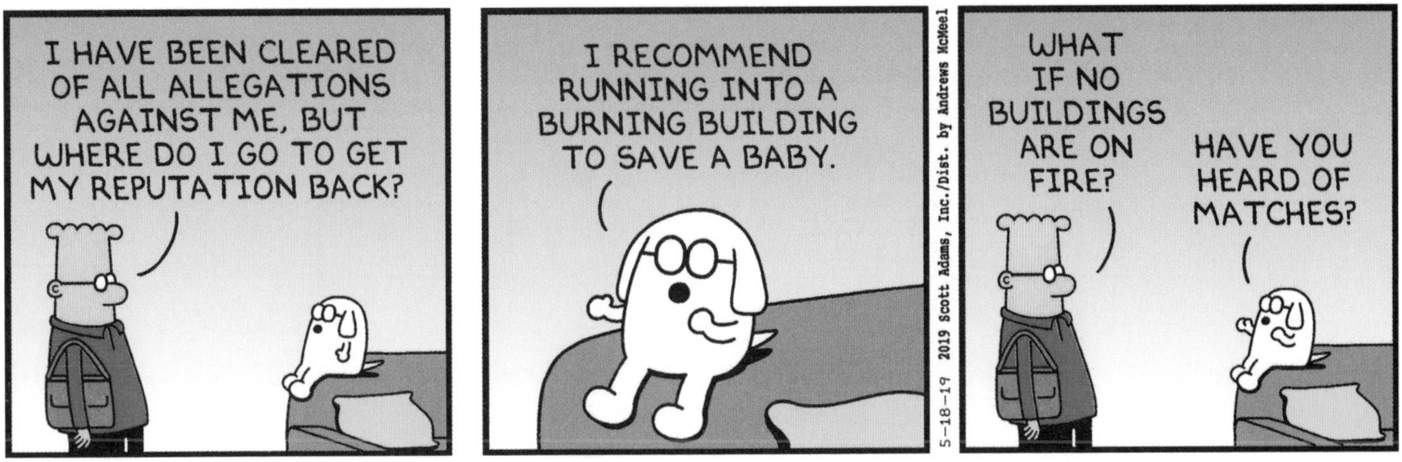
I HAVE BEEN CLEARED OF ALL ALLEGATIONS AGAINST ME, BUT WHERE DO I GO TO GET MY REPUTATION BACK?
I RECOMMEND RUNNING INTO A BURNING BUILDING TO SAVE A BABY.
WHAT IF NO BUILDINGS ARE ON FIRE?
HAVE YOU HEARD OF MATCHES?
5-18-19 2019 Scott Adams, Inc./Dist. by Andrews McMeel

WHY ARE YOU TELLING EVERYONE MY PROJECT GOT CANCELED?!
I NEVER SAID ANYTHING LIKE THAT.
YOU'RE SUCH A LIAR. I SAW YOUR EMAIL TO TED.
IF I SHOW YOU THAT EMAIL RIGHT NOW, AND IT SAYS NOTHING ABOUT YOUR PROJECT...
©2019 Scott Adams, Inc./Dist. by Andrews McMeel
...WILL YOU ADMIT YOU WERE WRONG AND HUMBLY APOLOGIZE TO ME?
I DON'T THINK I CAN COMMIT TO THAT.
WELL, ANYWAY, HERE IT IS. AND YOU CAN PLAINLY SEE YOU WERE WRONG.
5-19-19
THIS LOOKS PHOTO-SHOPPED.
I DON'T SEE A WINNING PATH FOR ME HERE.

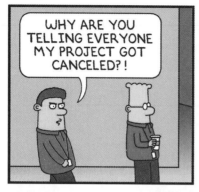

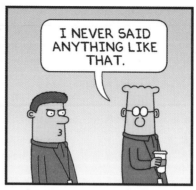

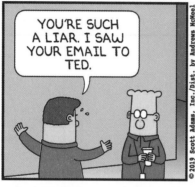

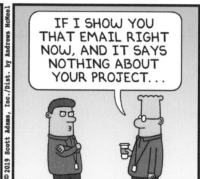

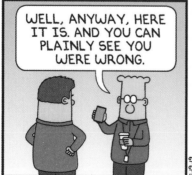

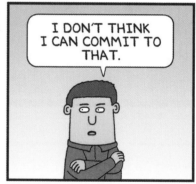

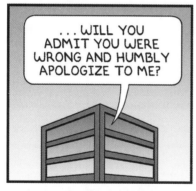

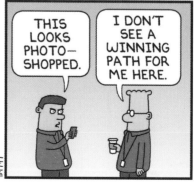

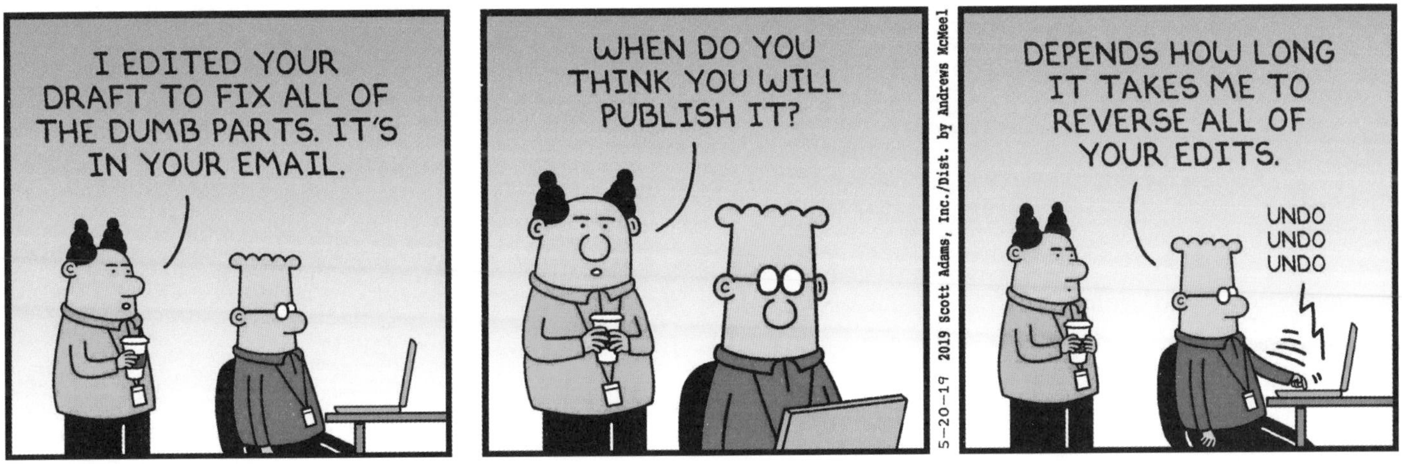

I EDITED YOUR DRAFT TO FIX ALL OF THE DUMB PARTS. IT'S IN YOUR EMAIL.
WHEN DO YOU THINK YOU WILL PUBLISH IT?
5-20-19 © 2019 Scott Adams, Inc./Dist. by Andrews McMeel
DEPENDS HOW LONG IT TAKES ME TO REVERSE ALL OF YOUR EDITS.
UNDO UNDO UNDO

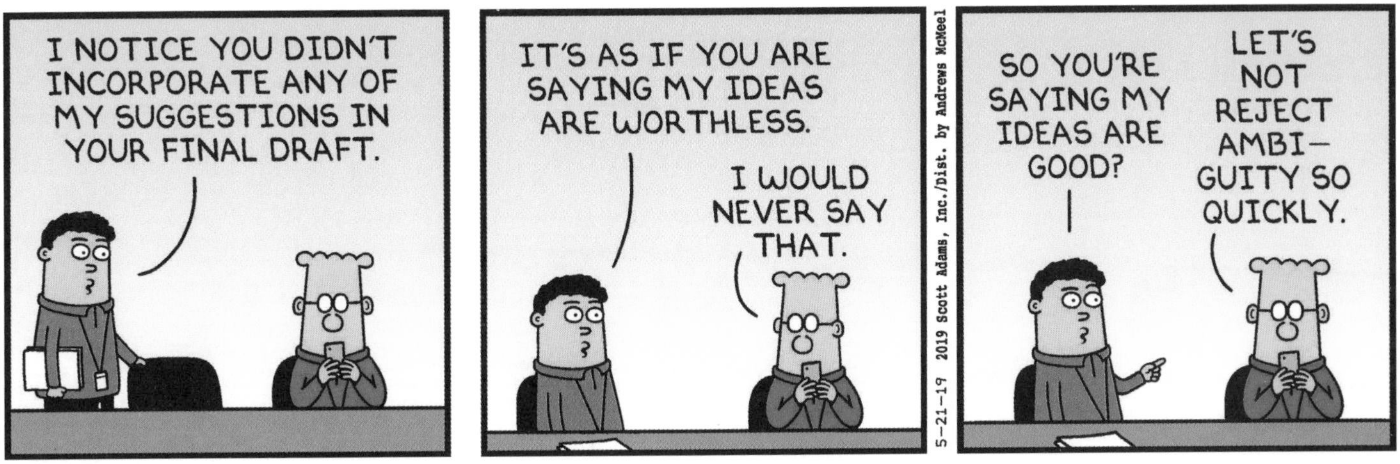

I NOTICE YOU DIDN'T INCORPORATE ANY OF MY SUGGESTIONS IN YOUR FINAL DRAFT.
IT'S AS IF YOU ARE SAYING MY IDEAS ARE WORTHLESS.
I WOULD NEVER SAY THAT.
5-21-19 © 2019 Scott Adams, Inc./Dist. by Andrews McMeel
SO YOU'RE SAYING MY IDEAS ARE GOOD?
LET'S NOT REJECT AMBI-GUITY SO QUICKLY.

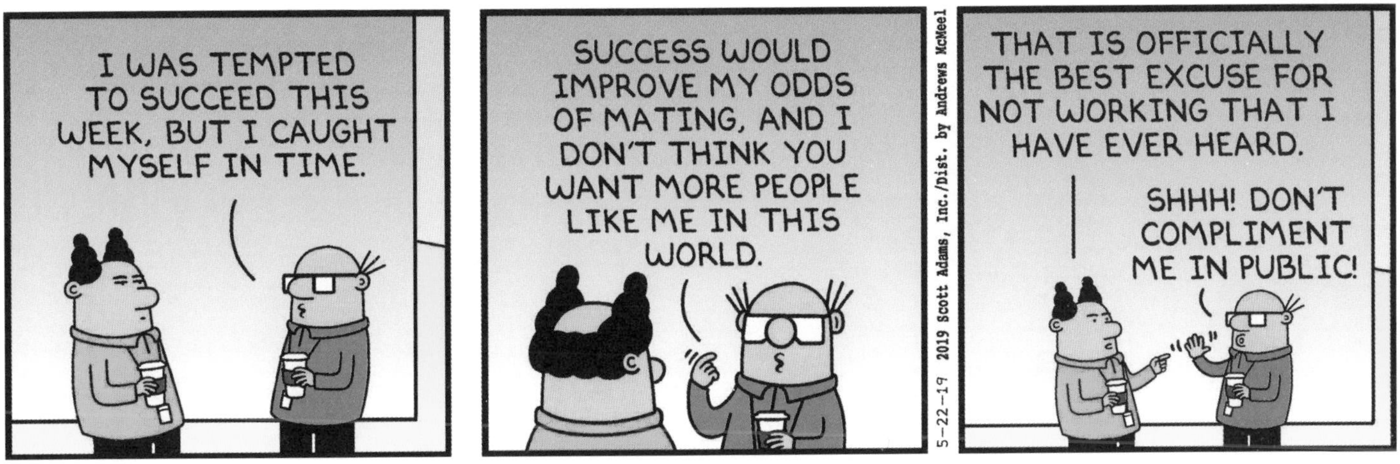

I WAS TEMPTED TO SUCCEED THIS WEEK, BUT I CAUGHT MYSELF IN TIME.
SUCCESS WOULD IMPROVE MY ODDS OF MATING, AND I DON'T THINK YOU WANT MORE PEOPLE LIKE ME IN THIS WORLD.
5-22-19 © 2019 Scott Adams, Inc./Dist. by Andrews McMeel
THAT IS OFFICIALLY THE BEST EXCUSE FOR NOT WORKING THAT I HAVE EVER HEARD.
SHHH! DON'T COMPLIMENT ME IN PUBLIC!

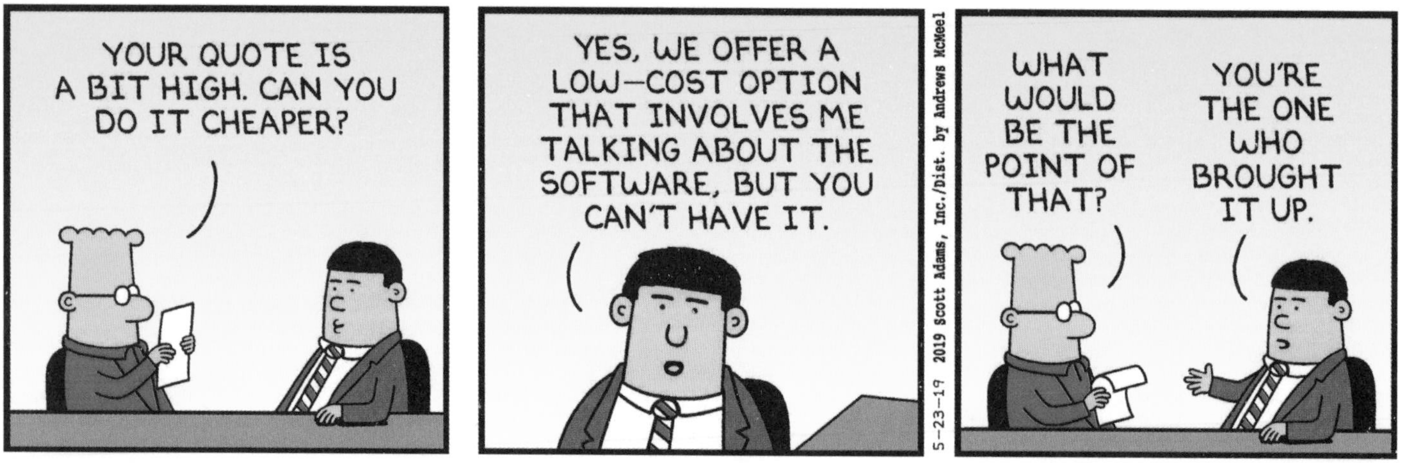
YOUR QUOTE IS A BIT HIGH. CAN YOU DO IT CHEAPER?
YES, WE OFFER A LOW–COST OPTION THAT INVOLVES ME TALKING ABOUT THE SOFTWARE, BUT YOU CAN'T HAVE IT.
WHAT WOULD BE THE POINT OF THAT?
YOU'RE THE ONE WHO BROUGHT IT UP.
5-23-19 2019 Scott Adams, Inc./Dist. by Andrews McMeel

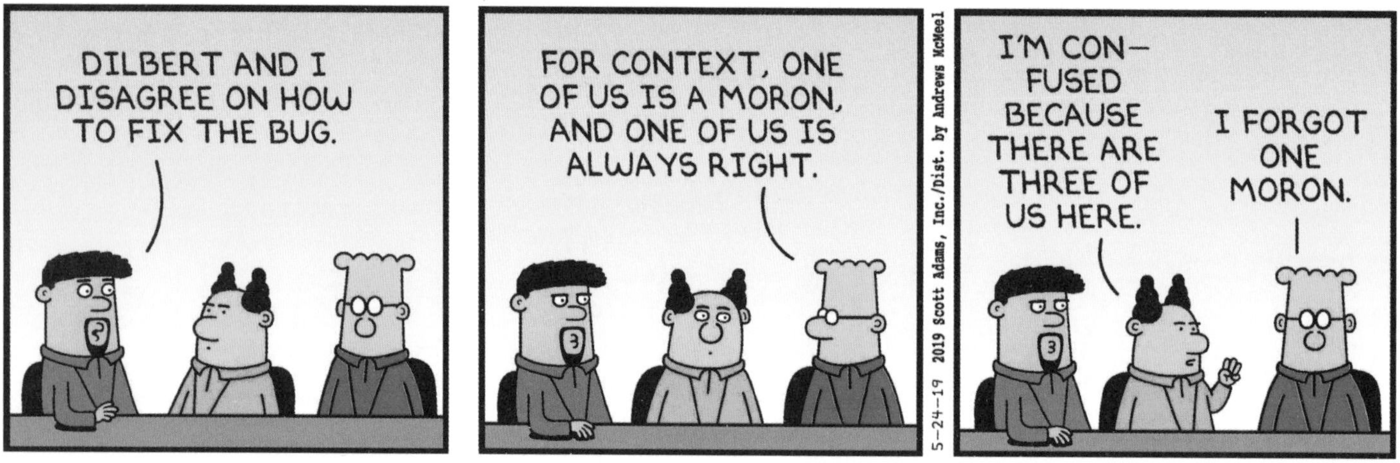
DILBERT AND I DISAGREE ON HOW TO FIX THE BUG.
FOR CONTEXT, ONE OF US IS A MORON, AND ONE OF US IS ALWAYS RIGHT.
I'M CON–FUSED BECAUSE THERE ARE THREE OF US HERE.
I FORGOT ONE MORON.
5-24-19 2019 Scott Adams, Inc./Dist. by Andrews McMeel

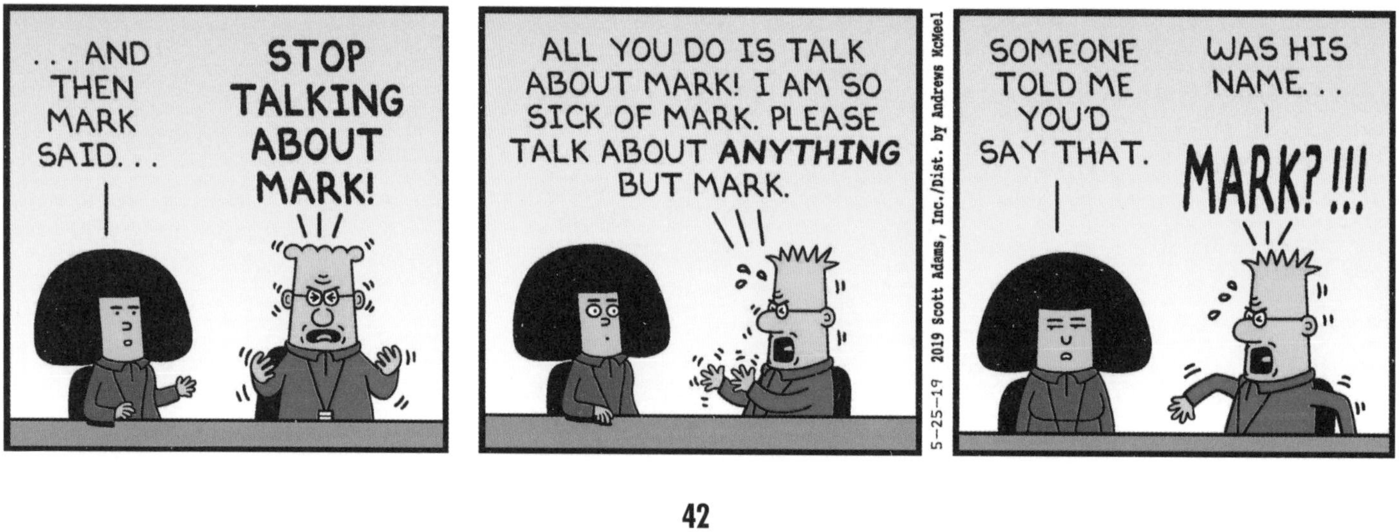
. . . AND THEN MARK SAID. . .
STOP TALKING ABOUT MARK!
ALL YOU DO IS TALK ABOUT MARK! I AM SO SICK OF MARK. PLEASE TALK ABOUT ANYTHING BUT MARK.
SOMEONE TOLD ME YOU'D SAY THAT.
WAS HIS NAME. . .
MARK?!!!
5-25-19 2019 Scott Adams, Inc./Dist. by Andrews McMeel

I'M LOOKING FOR NOMINATIONS FOR EMPLOYEE OF THE YEAR.
DOES ANYONE HAVE A SUGGESTION?
HYPOTHETICALLY, WOULD THE WINNER OF THIS AWARD BE LIKELY TO GET A LARGER—THAN—NORMAL PAY RAISE?
I WOULD THINK SO, YES.
AND IS IT TRUE THAT OUR BUDGET FOR RAISES IS LIMITED?
YES, OF COURSE.
WOULD IT NOT BE AGAINST MY BEST INTERESTS TO NOMI— NATE AN EMPLOYEE WHO IS COMPETING WITH ME FOR SCARCE RESOURCES?
LET'S JUST FORGET I BROUGHT IT UP.
I NOMI— NATE MYSELF.
© 2019 Scott Adams, Inc./Dist. by Andrews McMeel
5-26-19

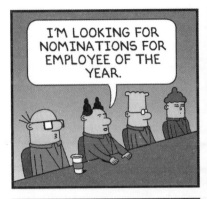

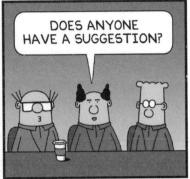

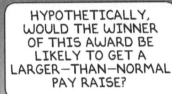

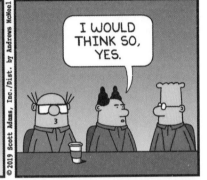

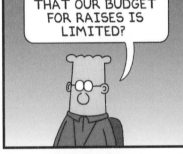

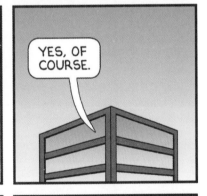

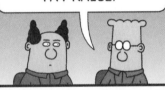

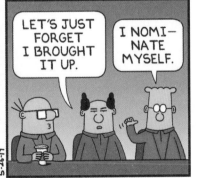

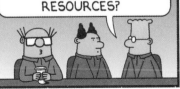

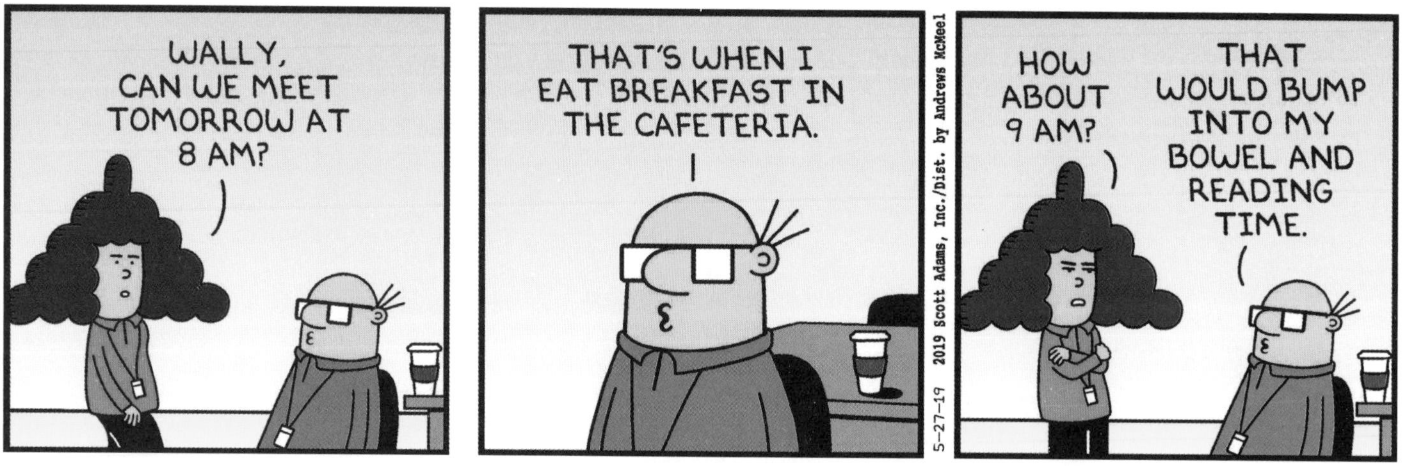
WALLY, CAN WE MEET TOMORROW AT 8 AM?
THAT'S WHEN I EAT BREAKFAST IN THE CAFETERIA.
HOW ABOUT 9 AM?
THAT WOULD BUMP INTO MY BOWEL AND READING TIME.
5-27-19 2019 Scott Adams, Inc./Dist. by Andrews McMeel

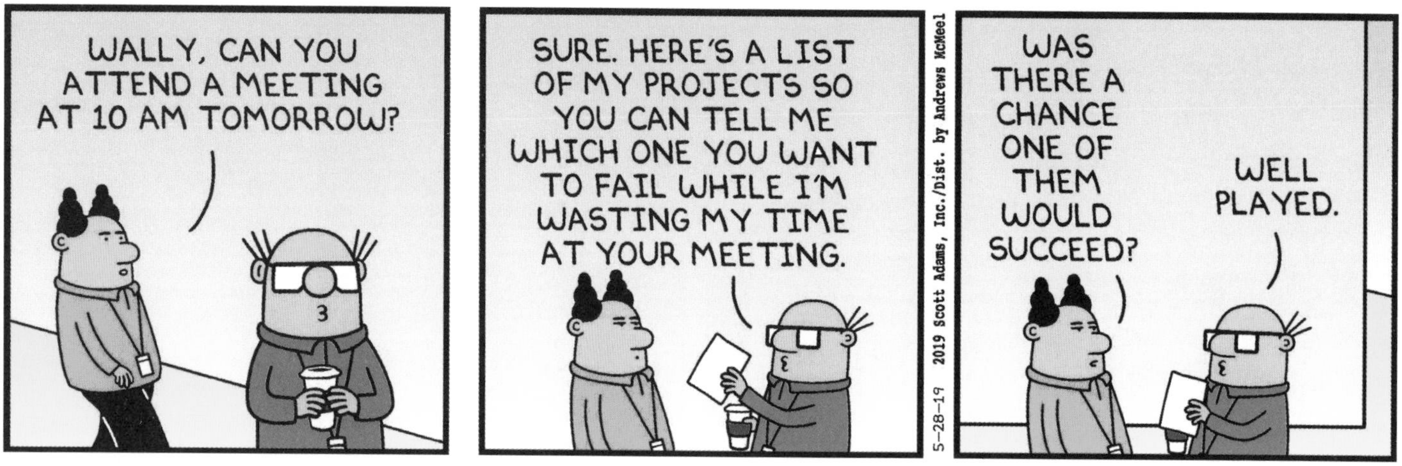
WALLY, CAN YOU ATTEND A MEETING AT 10 AM TOMORROW?
SURE. HERE'S A LIST OF MY PROJECTS SO YOU CAN TELL ME WHICH ONE YOU WANT TO FAIL WHILE I'M WASTING MY TIME AT YOUR MEETING.
WAS THERE A CHANCE ONE OF THEM WOULD SUCCEED?
WELL PLAYED.
5-28-19 2019 Scott Adams, Inc./Dist. by Andrews McMeel

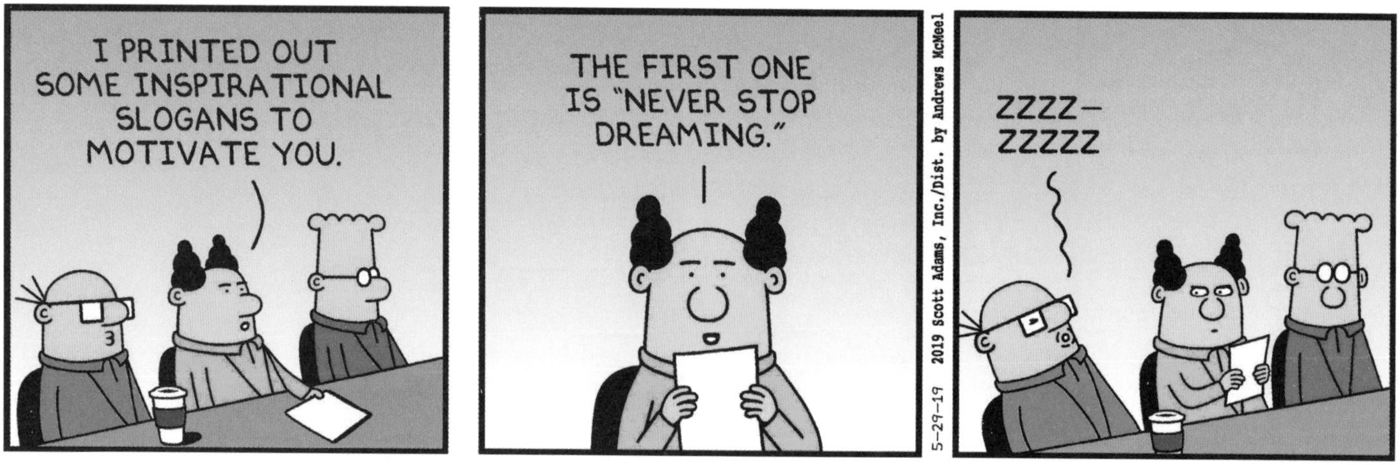
I PRINTED OUT SOME INSPIRATIONAL SLOGANS TO MOTIVATE YOU.
THE FIRST ONE IS "NEVER STOP DREAMING."
ZZZZ-ZZZZZ
5-29-19 2019 Scott Adams, Inc./Dist. by Andrews McMeel

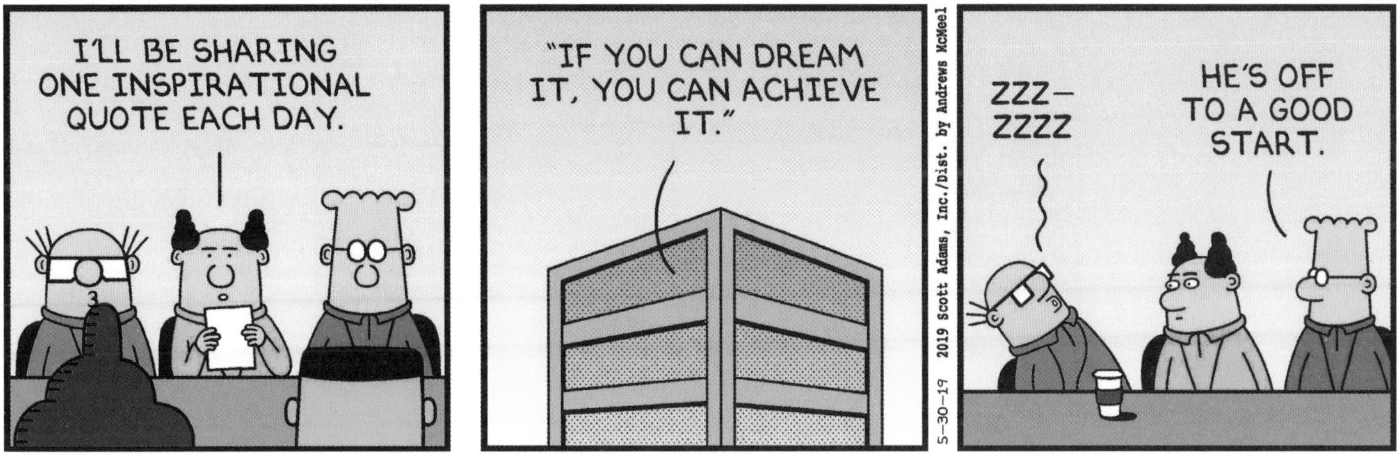
I'LL BE SHARING ONE INSPIRATIONAL QUOTE EACH DAY.
"IF YOU CAN DREAM IT, YOU CAN ACHIEVE IT."
5-30-19 2019 Scott Adams, Inc./Dist. by Andrews McMeel
ZZZ—ZZZZ
HE'S OFF TO A GOOD START.

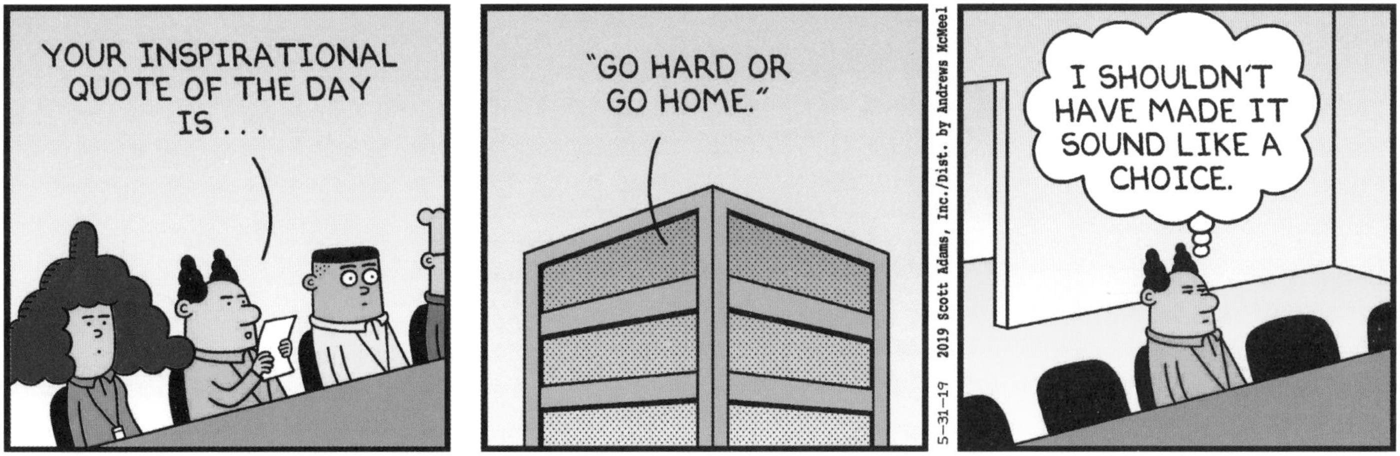
YOUR INSPIRATIONAL QUOTE OF THE DAY IS . . .
"GO HARD OR GO HOME."
5-31-19 2019 Scott Adams, Inc./Dist. by Andrews McMeel
I SHOULDN'T HAVE MADE IT SOUND LIKE A CHOICE.

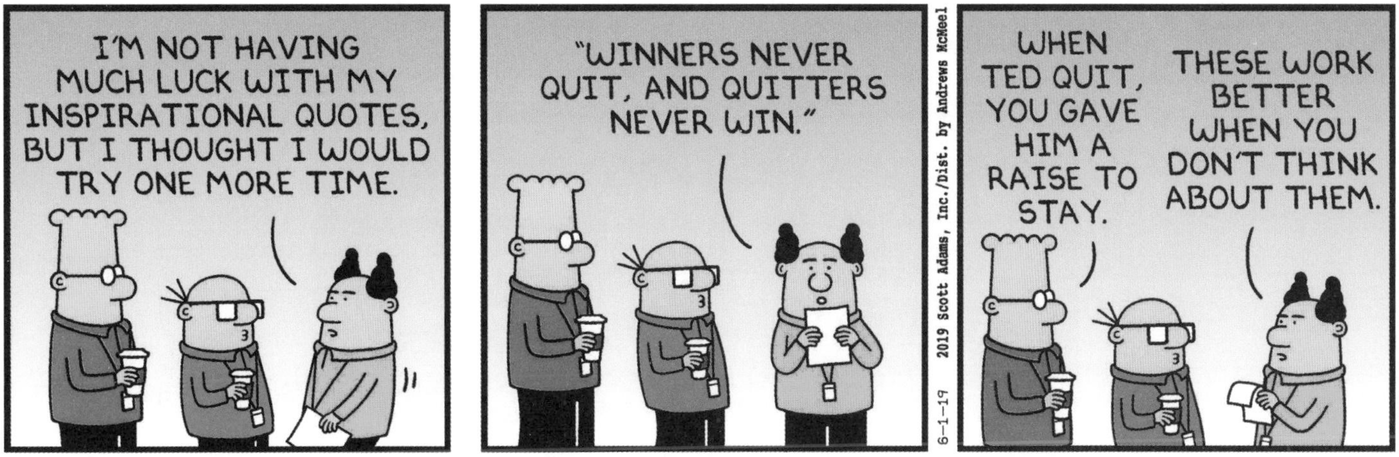
I'M NOT HAVING MUCH LUCK WITH MY INSPIRATIONAL QUOTES, BUT I THOUGHT I WOULD TRY ONE MORE TIME.
"WINNERS NEVER QUIT, AND QUITTERS NEVER WIN."
6-1-19 2019 Scott Adams, Inc./Dist. by Andrews McMeel
WHEN TED QUIT, YOU GAVE HIM A RAISE TO STAY.
THESE WORK BETTER WHEN YOU DON'T THINK ABOUT THEM.

MY PROFIT FORECAST ISN'T ALIGNING WITH OUR STRATEGY.
TRY ADDING SOME VARIABLES.
WHAT KIND OF VARIABLES?
THE KIND THAT MAKE OUR STRATEGY LINE UP WITH OUR PROFIT FORECASTS.
BUT. . . THEN MY FORECAST WOULD NOT BE ACCURATE.
IT'S ALREADY INACCURATE BECAUSE NO ONE CAN FORECAST COMPLICATED THINGS FIVE YEARS AHEAD.
IF WE CAN'T BE ACCURATE, WE MIGHT AS WELL BE WRONG IN A WAY THAT IS GOOD FOR US IN THE NEAR TERM.
YOU MAKE A SURPRISINGLY ROBUST ARGUMENT FOR EVIL.
AND I WAS BARELY TRYING!
© 2019 Scott Adams, Inc./Dist. by Andrews McMeel
6-2-19

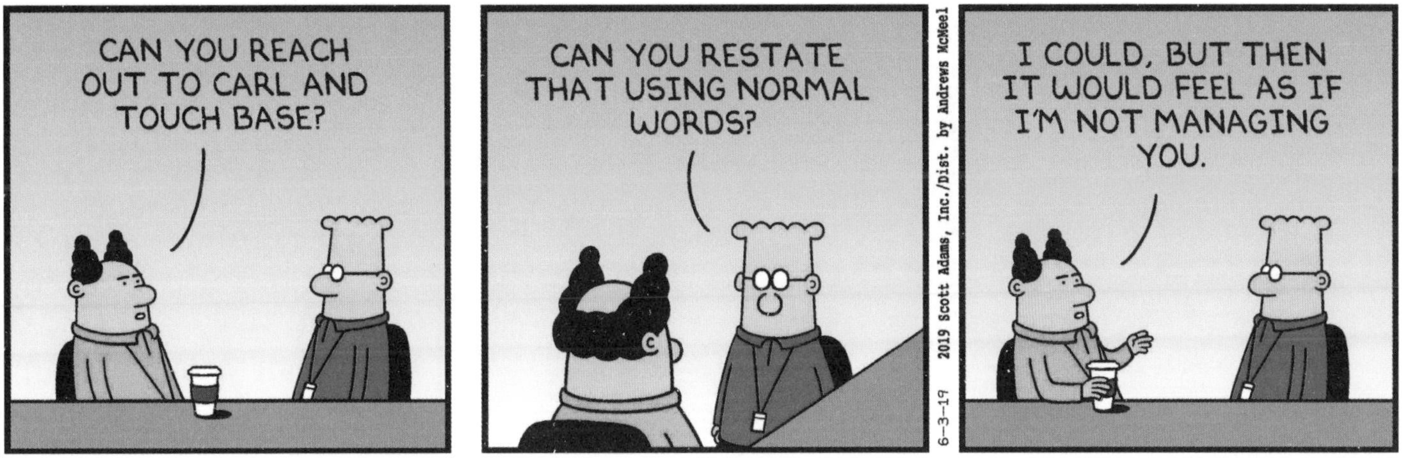
CAN YOU REACH OUT TO CARL AND TOUCH BASE?
CAN YOU RESTATE THAT USING NORMAL WORDS?
I COULD, BUT THEN IT WOULD FEEL AS IF I'M NOT MANAGING YOU.
6-3-19 2019 Scott Adams, Inc./Dist. by Andrews McMeel

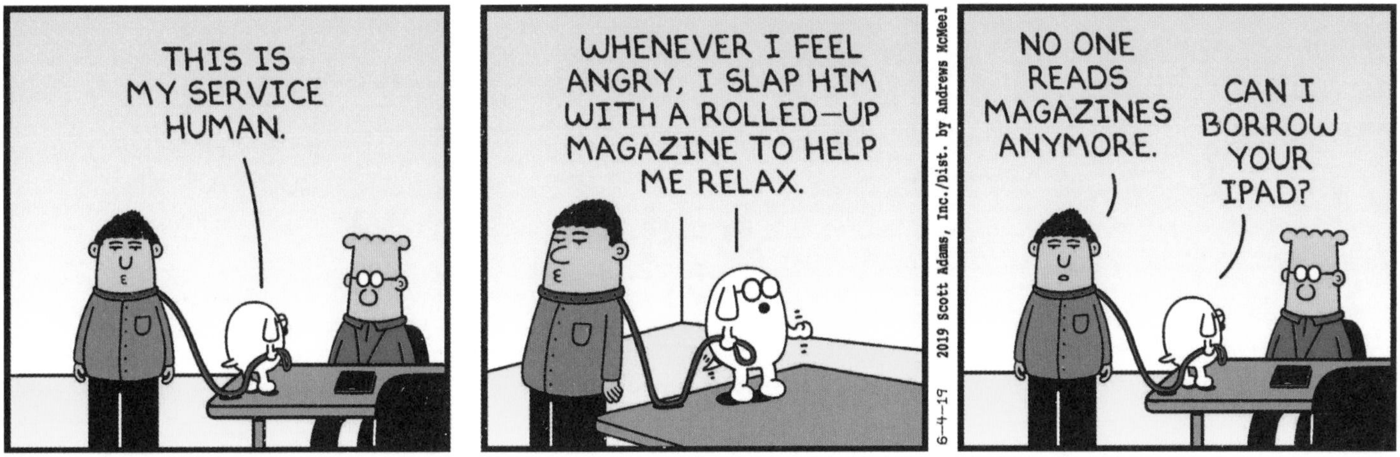
THIS IS MY SERVICE HUMAN.
WHENEVER I FEEL ANGRY, I SLAP HIM WITH A ROLLED-UP MAGAZINE TO HELP ME RELAX.
NO ONE READS MAGAZINES ANYMORE.
CAN I BORROW YOUR IPAD?
6-4-19 2019 Scott Adams, Inc./Dist. by Andrews McMeel

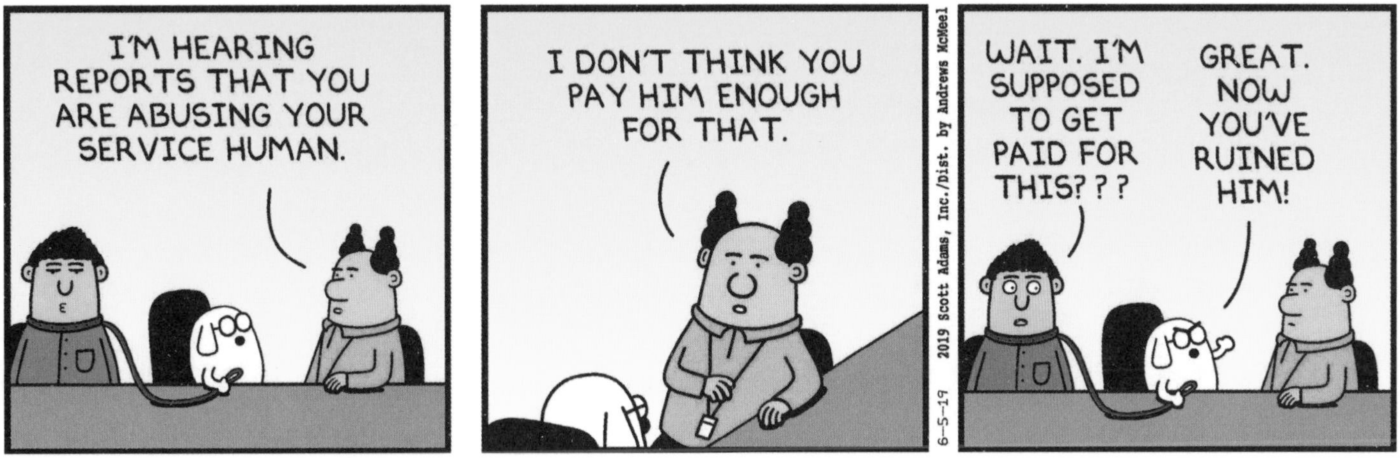
I'M HEARING REPORTS THAT YOU ARE ABUSING YOUR SERVICE HUMAN.
I DON'T THINK YOU PAY HIM ENOUGH FOR THAT.
WAIT. I'M SUPPOSED TO GET PAID FOR THIS???
GREAT. NOW YOU'VE RUINED HIM!
6-5-19 2019 Scott Adams, Inc./Dist. by Andrews McMeel

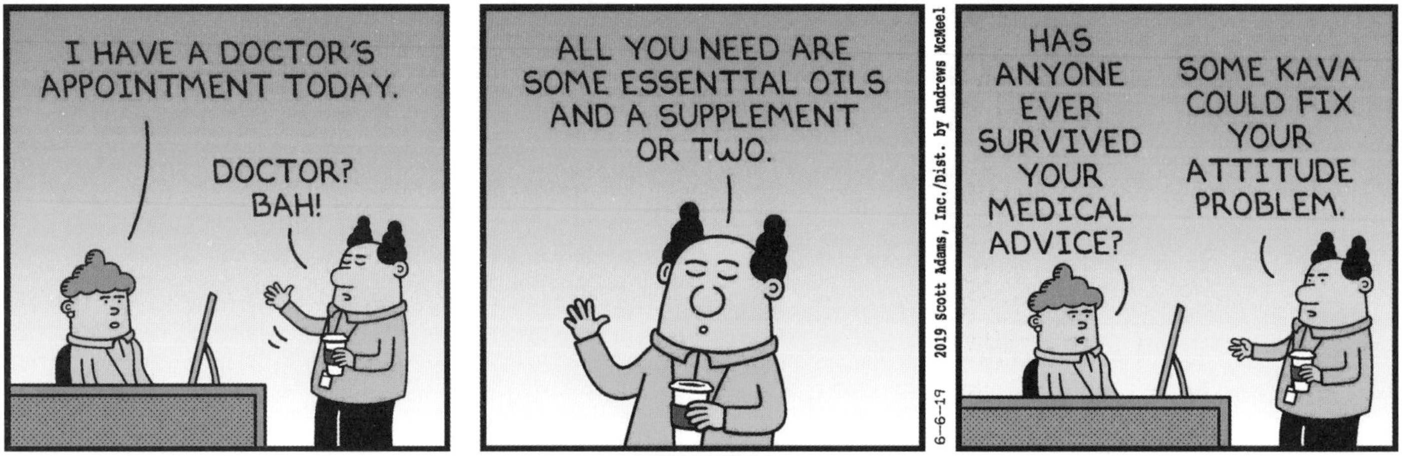
I HAVE A DOCTOR'S APPOINTMENT TODAY.
DOCTOR? BAH!
ALL YOU NEED ARE SOME ESSENTIAL OILS AND A SUPPLEMENT OR TWO.
6-6-19 2019 Scott Adams, Inc./Dist. by Andrews McMeel
HAS ANYONE EVER SURVIVED YOUR MEDICAL ADVICE?
SOME KAVA COULD FIX YOUR ATTITUDE PROBLEM.

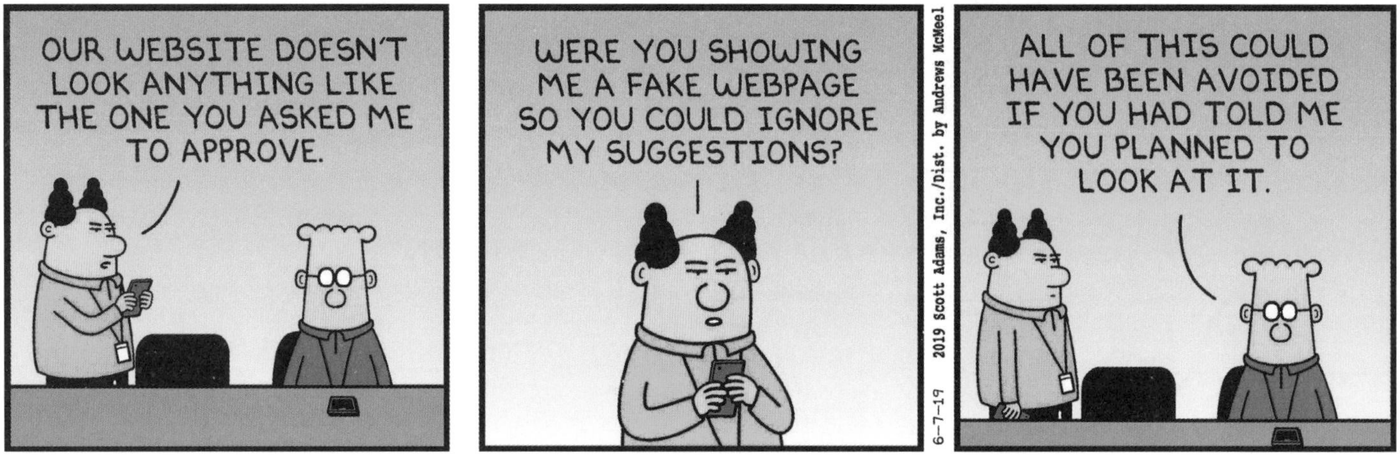
OUR WEBSITE DOESN'T LOOK ANYTHING LIKE THE ONE YOU ASKED ME TO APPROVE.
WERE YOU SHOWING ME A FAKE WEBPAGE SO YOU COULD IGNORE MY SUGGESTIONS?
6-7-19 2019 Scott Adams, Inc./Dist. by Andrews McMeel
ALL OF THIS COULD HAVE BEEN AVOIDED IF YOU HAD TOLD ME YOU PLANNED TO LOOK AT IT.

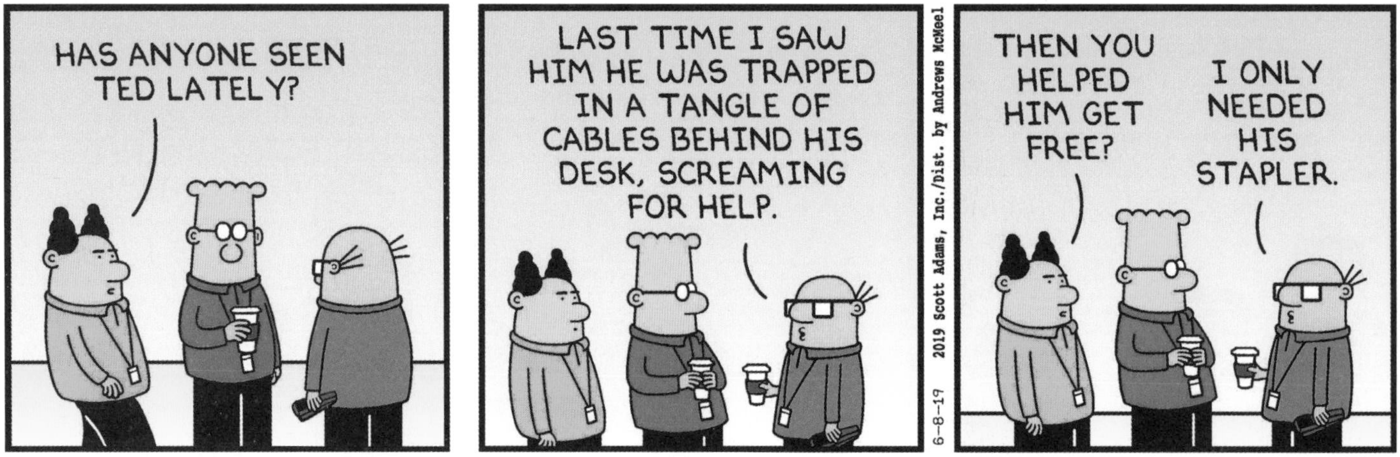
HAS ANYONE SEEN TED LATELY?
LAST TIME I SAW HIM HE WAS TRAPPED IN A TANGLE OF CABLES BEHIND HIS DESK, SCREAMING FOR HELP.
6-8-19 2019 Scott Adams, Inc./Dist. by Andrews McMeel
THEN YOU HELPED HIM GET FREE?
I ONLY NEEDED HIS STAPLER.

. . . AND THEN I NEED YOU TO. . .
DON'T DO IT. DON'T CHECK THAT MESSAGE.
IT MIGHT BE IMPORTANT.
IT ISN'T MORE IMPORTANT THAN LISTENING TO YOUR BOSS.
© 2019 Scott Adams, Inc./Dist. by Andrews McMeel
I HAVE NO WAY OF KNOWING THAT.
LOOK! THERE'S A SQUIRREL ON THE PRINTER!
I DON'T SEE A SQUIRREL.
DID YOU CHECK YOUR PHONE?
WAS I SUPPOSED TO JUST SIT HERE AND WATCH YOU LOOKING FOR SQUIRRELS?
6-9-19

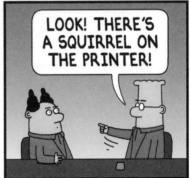

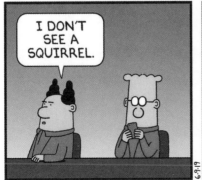

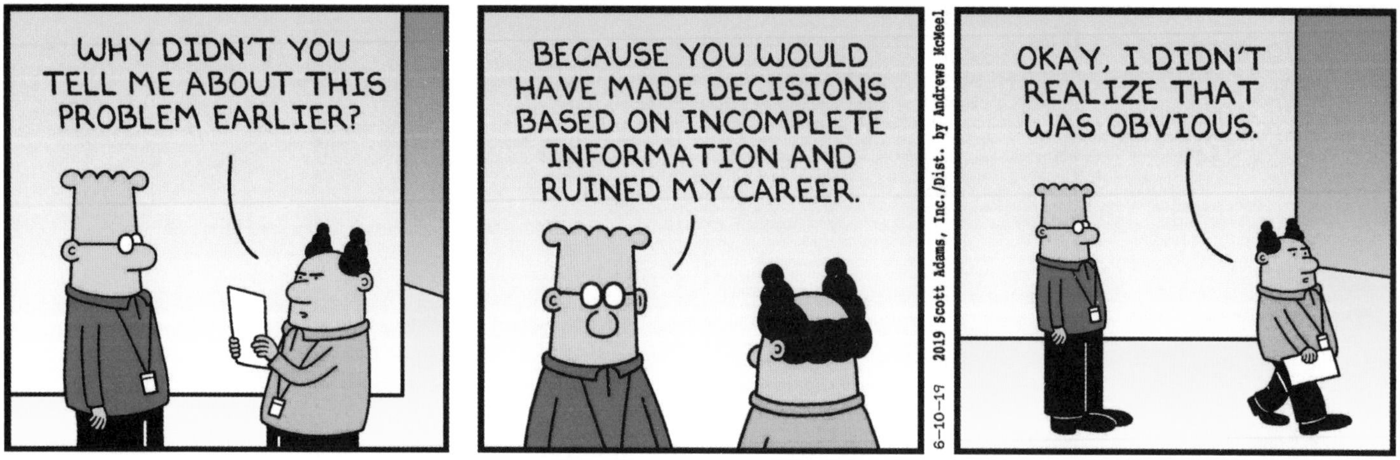
WHY DIDN'T YOU TELL ME ABOUT THIS PROBLEM EARLIER?
BECAUSE YOU WOULD HAVE MADE DECISIONS BASED ON INCOMPLETE INFORMATION AND RUINED MY CAREER.
OKAY, I DIDN'T REALIZE THAT WAS OBVIOUS.
6-10-19 2019 Scott Adams, Inc./Dist. by Andrews McMeel

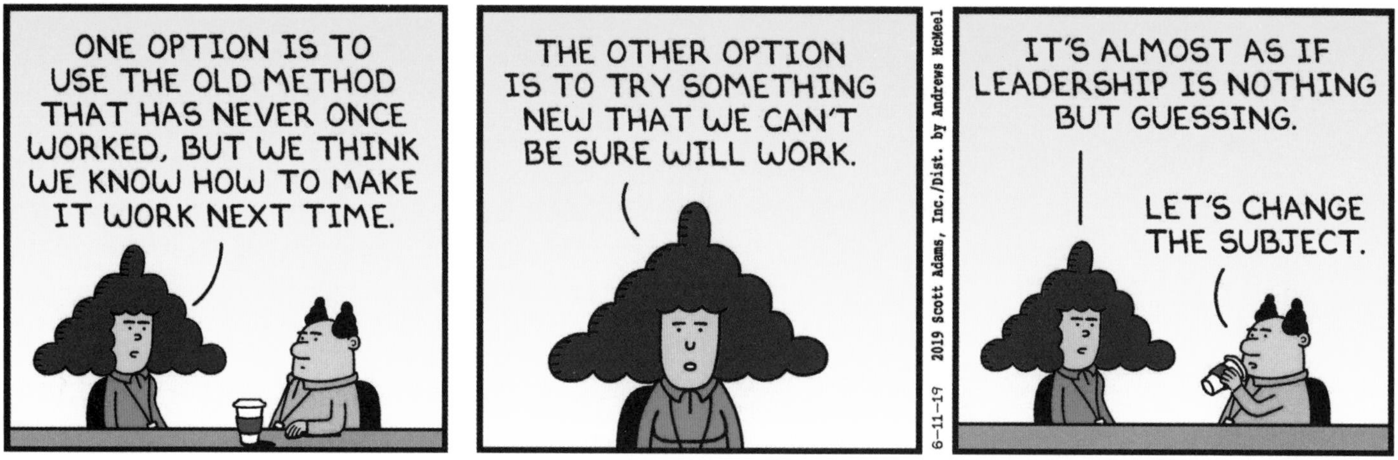
ONE OPTION IS TO USE THE OLD METHOD THAT HAS NEVER ONCE WORKED, BUT WE THINK WE KNOW HOW TO MAKE IT WORK NEXT TIME.
THE OTHER OPTION IS TO TRY SOMETHING NEW THAT WE CAN'T BE SURE WILL WORK.
IT'S ALMOST AS IF LEADERSHIP IS NOTHING BUT GUESSING.
LET'S CHANGE THE SUBJECT.
6-11-19 2019 Scott Adams, Inc./Dist. by Andrews McMeel

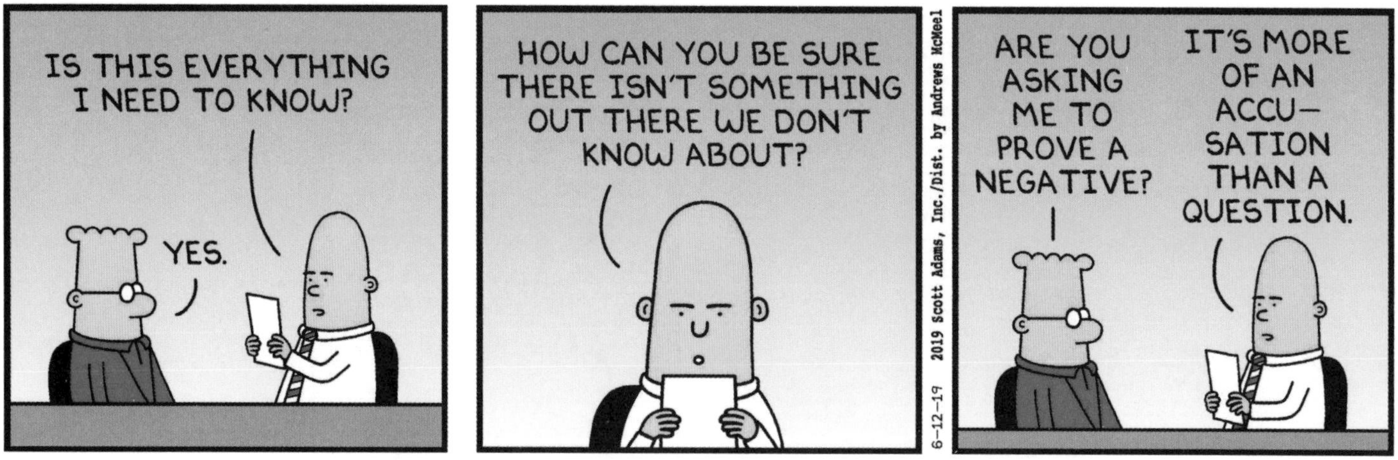
IS THIS EVERYTHING I NEED TO KNOW?
YES.
HOW CAN YOU BE SURE THERE ISN'T SOMETHING OUT THERE WE DON'T KNOW ABOUT?
ARE YOU ASKING ME TO PROVE A NEGATIVE?
IT'S MORE OF AN ACCU-SATION THAN A QUESTION.
6-12-19 2019 Scott Adams, Inc./Dist. by Andrews McMeel

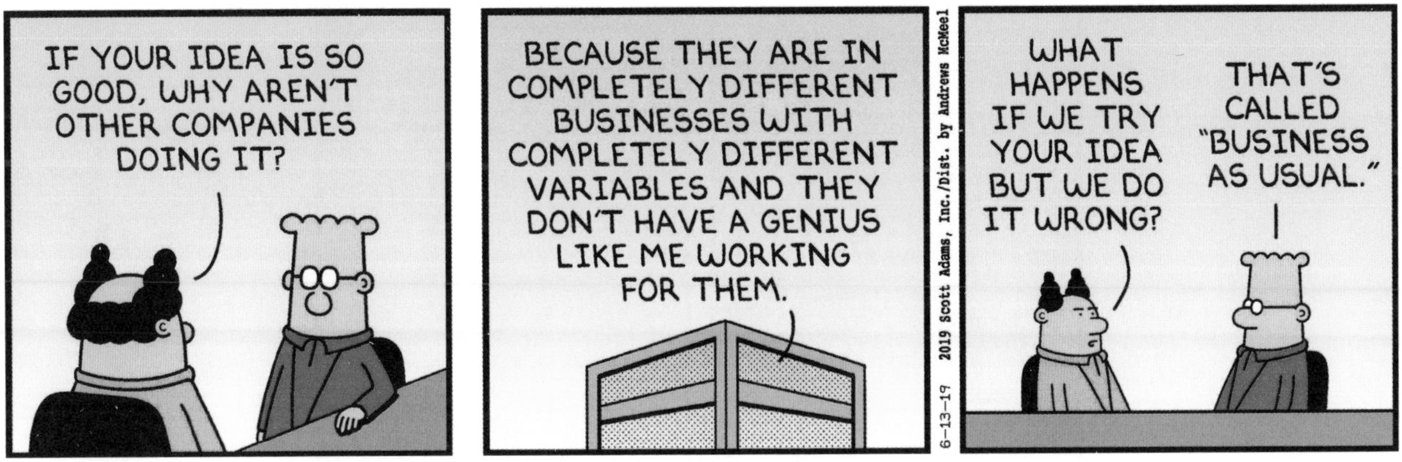
IF YOUR IDEA IS SO GOOD, WHY AREN'T OTHER COMPANIES DOING IT?
BECAUSE THEY ARE IN COMPLETELY DIFFERENT BUSINESSES WITH COMPLETELY DIFFERENT VARIABLES AND THEY DON'T HAVE A GENIUS LIKE ME WORKING FOR THEM.
6-13-19 2019 Scott Adams, Inc./Dist. by Andrews McMeel
WHAT HAPPENS IF WE TRY YOUR IDEA BUT WE DO IT WRONG?
THAT'S CALLED "BUSINESS AS USUAL."

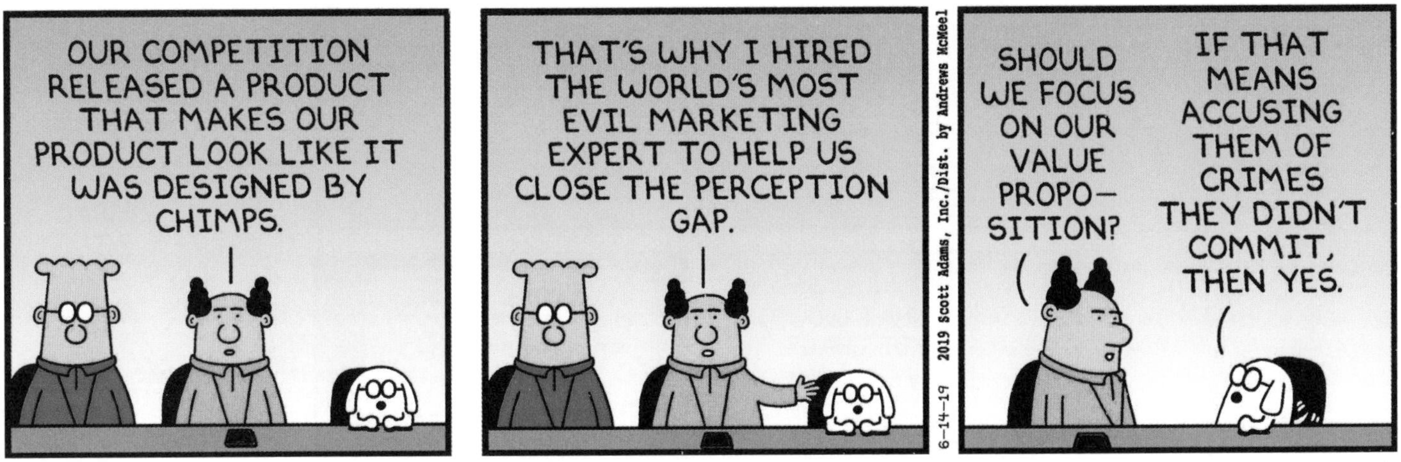
OUR COMPETITION RELEASED A PRODUCT THAT MAKES OUR PRODUCT LOOK LIKE IT WAS DESIGNED BY CHIMPS.
THAT'S WHY I HIRED THE WORLD'S MOST EVIL MARKETING EXPERT TO HELP US CLOSE THE PERCEPTION GAP.
6-14-19 2019 Scott Adams, Inc./Dist. by Andrews McMeel
SHOULD WE FOCUS ON OUR VALUE PROPO- SITION?
IF THAT MEANS ACCUSING THEM OF CRIMES THEY DIDN'T COMMIT, THEN YES.

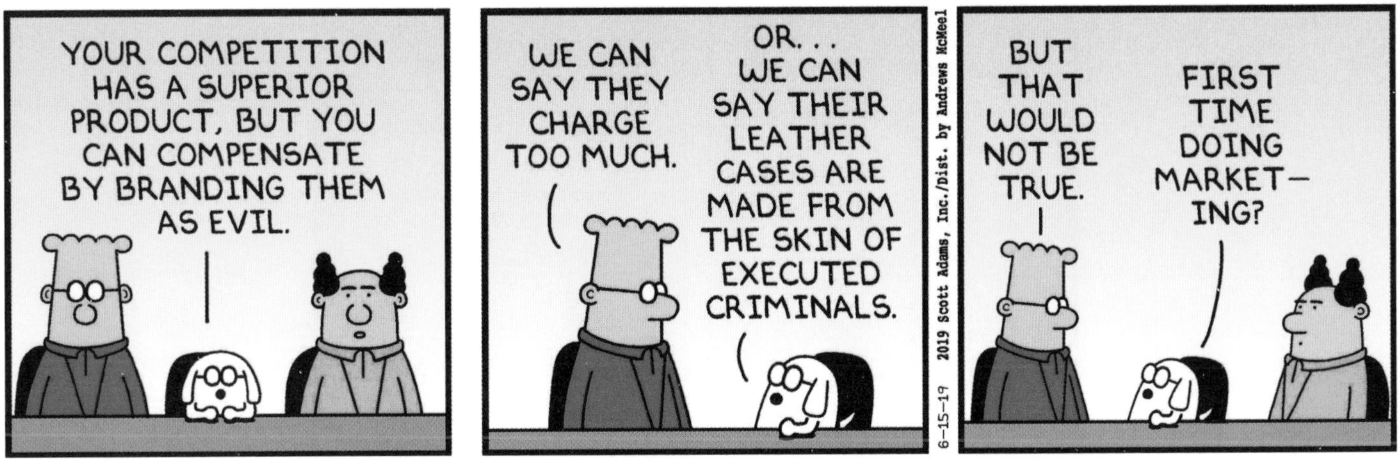
YOUR COMPETITION HAS A SUPERIOR PRODUCT, BUT YOU CAN COMPENSATE BY BRANDING THEM AS EVIL.
WE CAN SAY THEY CHARGE TOO MUCH.
OR. . . WE CAN SAY THEIR LEATHER CASES ARE MADE FROM THE SKIN OF EXECUTED CRIMINALS.
6-15-19 2019 Scott Adams, Inc./Dist. by Andrews McMeel
BUT THAT WOULD NOT BE TRUE.
FIRST TIME DOING MARKET- ING?

PURCHASING MANAGER
I CAN'T APPROVE THIS PURCHASE WITHOUT THREE VENDOR QUOTES.
ONLY TWO COMPANIES IN THE WORLD MAKE THIS SORT OF PRODUCT.
IF I BEND THE RULES FOR YOU, EVERYONE WILL WANT ME TO BEND THE RULES.
MAYBE YOU COULD ONLY BEND THE RULES WHEN IT MAKES COMPLETE SENSE TO DO SO.
THAT WOULD BE CHAOS.
EVERYONE THINKS THEY HAVE A GOOD REASON TO BEND THE RULES.
IS THE REAL PROBLEM HERE THAT YOU WERE BULLIED IN SCHOOL, AND YOU USE THIS JOB FOR SOME SORT OF SICK REVENGE?
NOW YOU NEED **FOUR** VENDOR QUOTES.
© 2019 Scott Adams, Inc./Dist. by Andrews McMeel
6-16-19

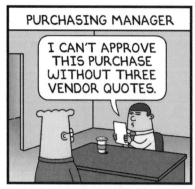

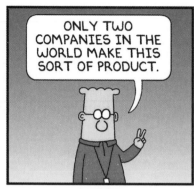

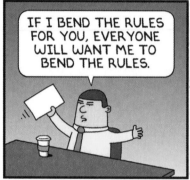

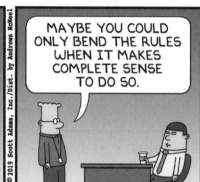

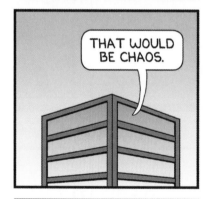

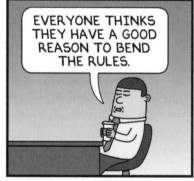

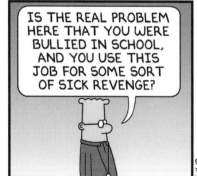

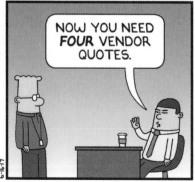

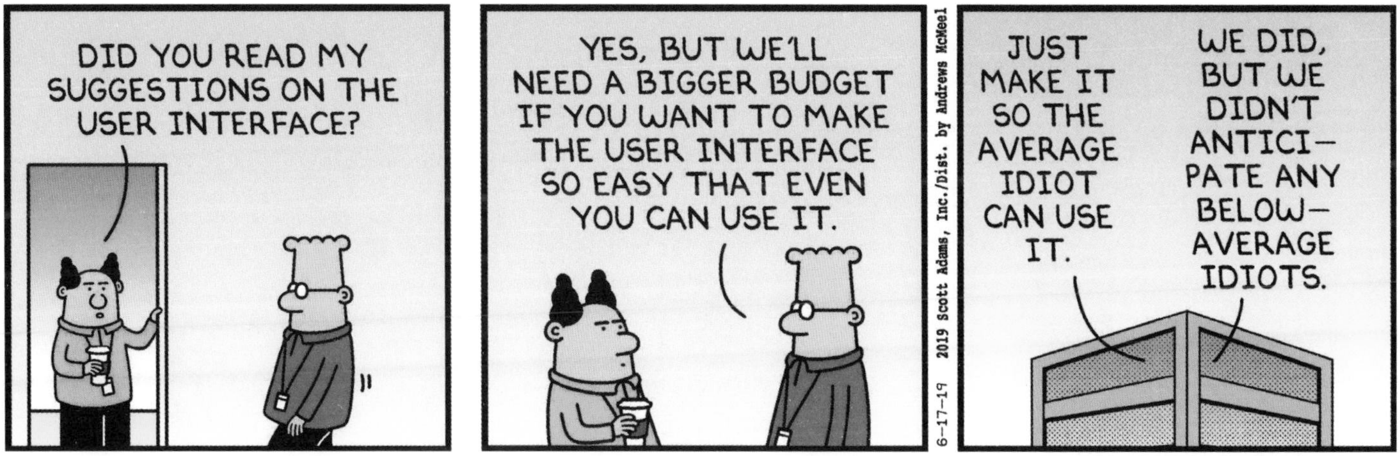
DID YOU READ MY SUGGESTIONS ON THE USER INTERFACE?
YES, BUT WE'LL NEED A BIGGER BUDGET IF YOU WANT TO MAKE THE USER INTERFACE SO EASY THAT EVEN YOU CAN USE IT.
JUST MAKE IT SO THE AVERAGE IDIOT CAN USE IT.
WE DID, BUT WE DIDN'T ANTICIPATE ANY BELOW-AVERAGE IDIOTS.
6-17-19 2019 Scott Adams, Inc./Dist. by Andrews McMeel

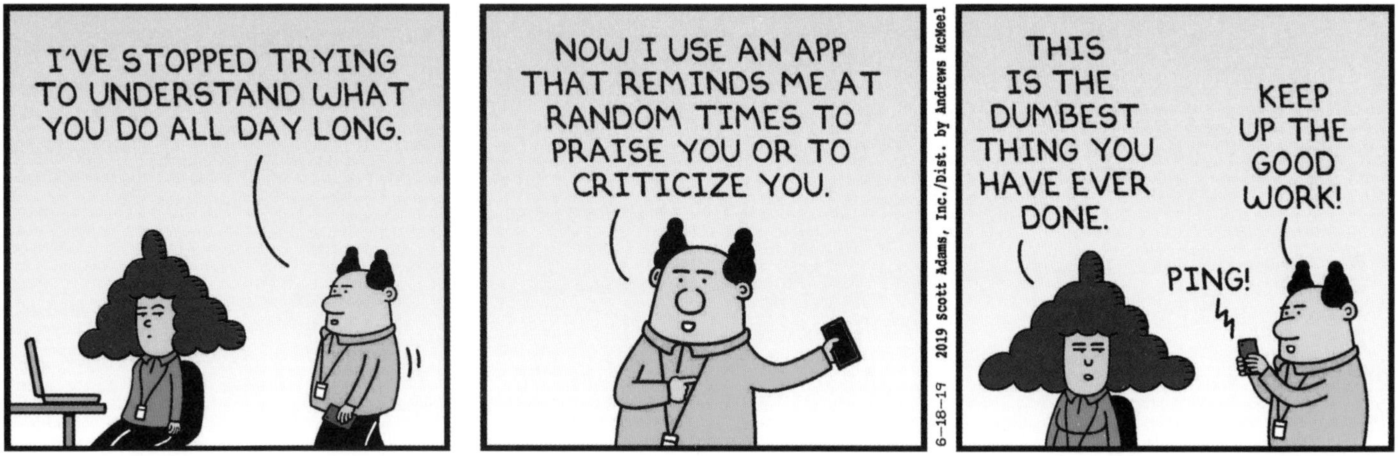
I'VE STOPPED TRYING TO UNDERSTAND WHAT YOU DO ALL DAY LONG.
NOW I USE AN APP THAT REMINDS ME AT RANDOM TIMES TO PRAISE YOU OR TO CRITICIZE YOU.
THIS IS THE DUMBEST THING YOU HAVE EVER DONE.
PING!
KEEP UP THE GOOD WORK!
6-18-19 2019 Scott Adams, Inc./Dist. by Andrews McMeel

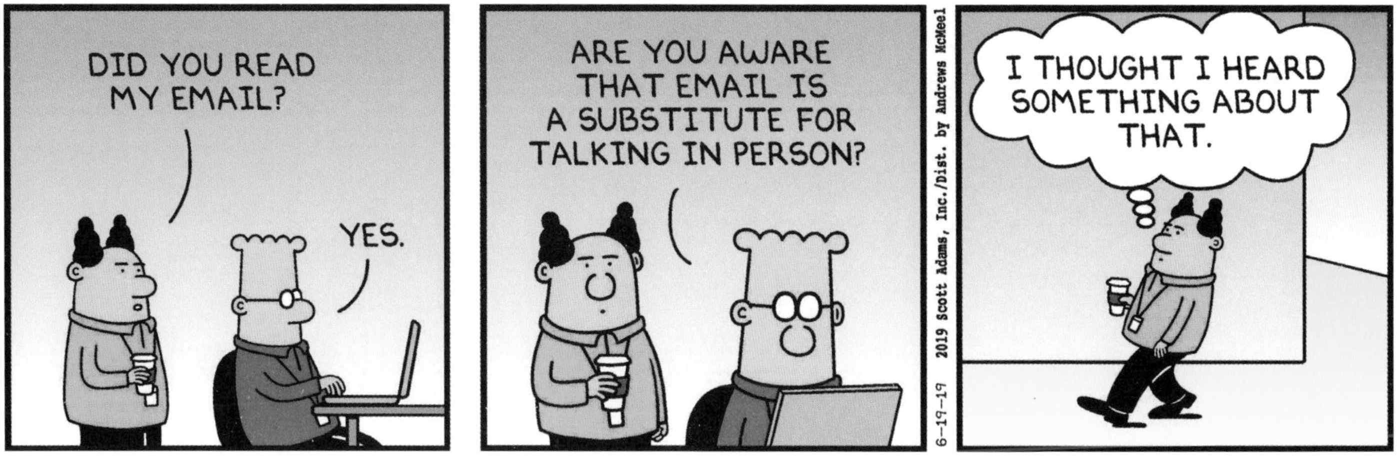
DID YOU READ MY EMAIL?
YES.
ARE YOU AWARE THAT EMAIL IS A SUBSTITUTE FOR TALKING IN PERSON?
I THOUGHT I HEARD SOMETHING ABOUT THAT.
6-19-19 2019 Scott Adams, Inc./Dist. by Andrews McMeel

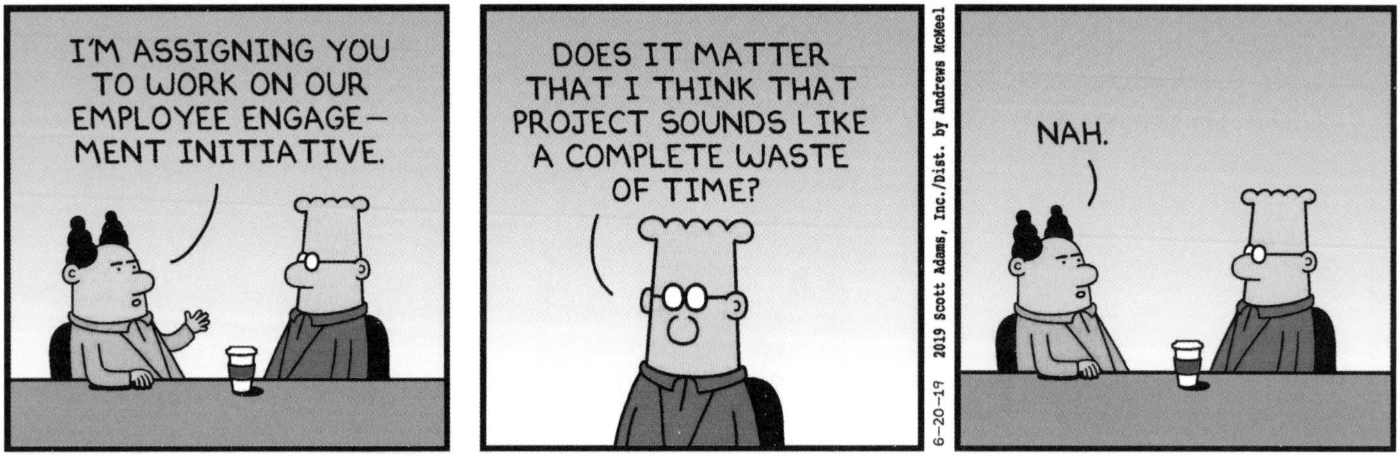
I'M ASSIGNING YOU TO WORK ON OUR EMPLOYEE ENGAGE— MENT INITIATIVE.
DOES IT MATTER THAT I THINK THAT PROJECT SOUNDS LIKE A COMPLETE WASTE OF TIME?
NAH.
6-20-19 © 2019 Scott Adams, Inc./Dist. by Andrews McMeel

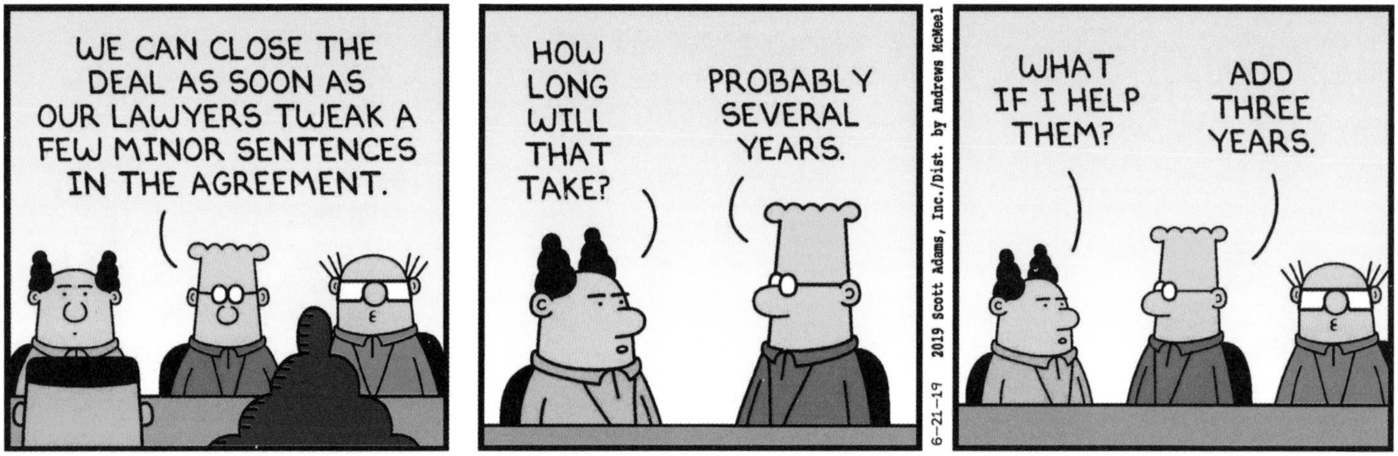
WE CAN CLOSE THE DEAL AS SOON AS OUR LAWYERS TWEAK A FEW MINOR SENTENCES IN THE AGREEMENT.
HOW LONG WILL THAT TAKE?
PROBABLY SEVERAL YEARS.
WHAT IF I HELP THEM?
ADD THREE YEARS.
6-21-19 © 2019 Scott Adams, Inc./Dist. by Andrews McMeel

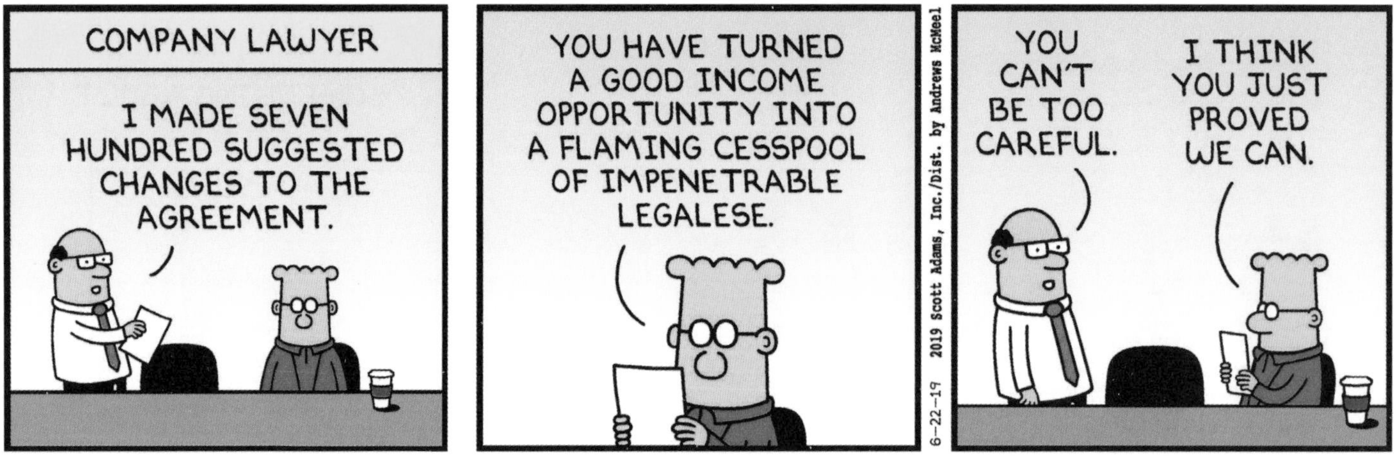
COMPANY LAWYER
I MADE SEVEN HUNDRED SUGGESTED CHANGES TO THE AGREEMENT.
YOU HAVE TURNED A GOOD INCOME OPPORTUNITY INTO A FLAMING CESSPOOL OF IMPENETRABLE LEGALESE.
YOU CAN'T BE TOO CAREFUL.
I THINK YOU JUST PROVED WE CAN.
6-22-19 © 2019 Scott Adams, Inc./Dist. by Andrews McMeel

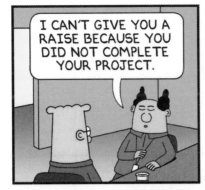

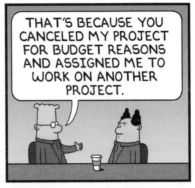

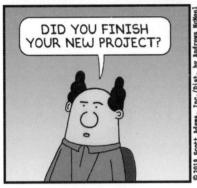

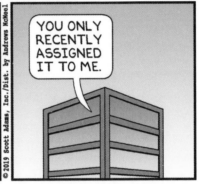

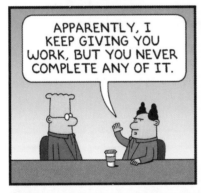

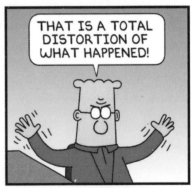

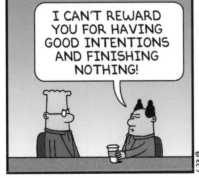

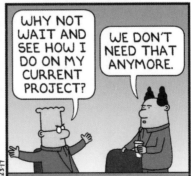

I CAN'T GIVE YOU A RAISE BECAUSE YOU DID NOT COMPLETE YOUR PROJECT.
THAT'S BECAUSE YOU CANCELED MY PROJECT FOR BUDGET REASONS AND ASSIGNED ME TO WORK ON ANOTHER PROJECT.
DID YOU FINISH YOUR NEW PROJECT?
YOU ONLY RECENTLY ASSIGNED IT TO ME.
APPARENTLY, I KEEP GIVING YOU WORK, BUT YOU NEVER COMPLETE ANY OF IT.
THAT IS A TOTAL DISTORTION OF WHAT HAPPENED!
I CAN'T REWARD YOU FOR HAVING GOOD INTENTIONS AND FINISHING NOTHING!
WHY NOT WAIT AND SEE HOW I DO ON MY CURRENT PROJECT?
WE DON'T NEED THAT ANYMORE.
© 2019 Scott Adams, Inc./Dist. by Andrews McMeel
6-23-19

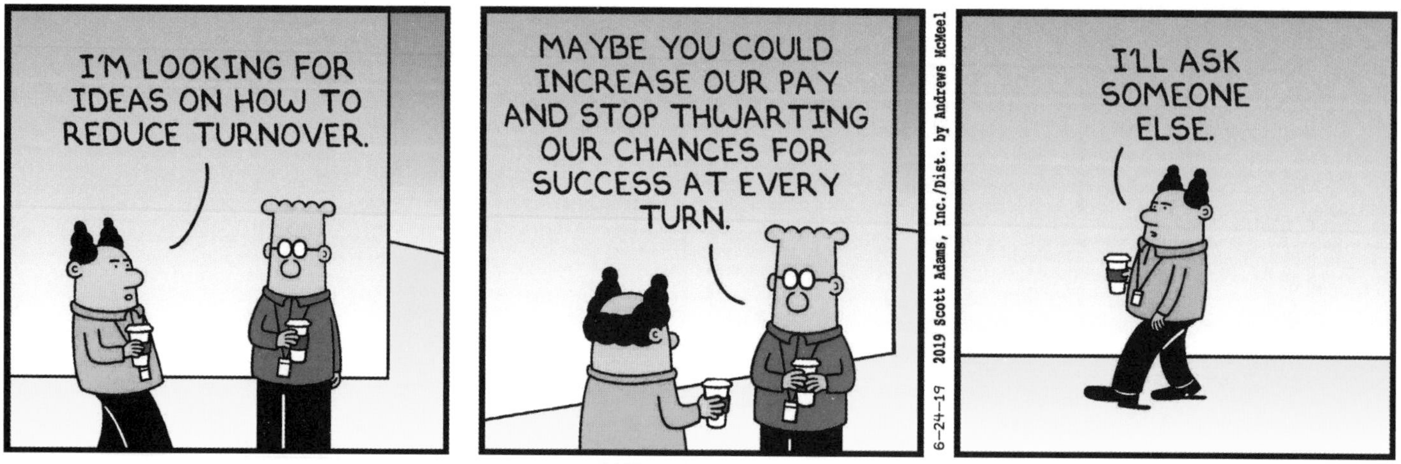
I'M LOOKING FOR IDEAS ON HOW TO REDUCE TURNOVER.
MAYBE YOU COULD INCREASE OUR PAY AND STOP THWARTING OUR CHANCES FOR SUCCESS AT EVERY TURN.
6-24-19 2019 Scott Adams, Inc./Dist. by Andrews McMeel
I'LL ASK SOMEONE ELSE.

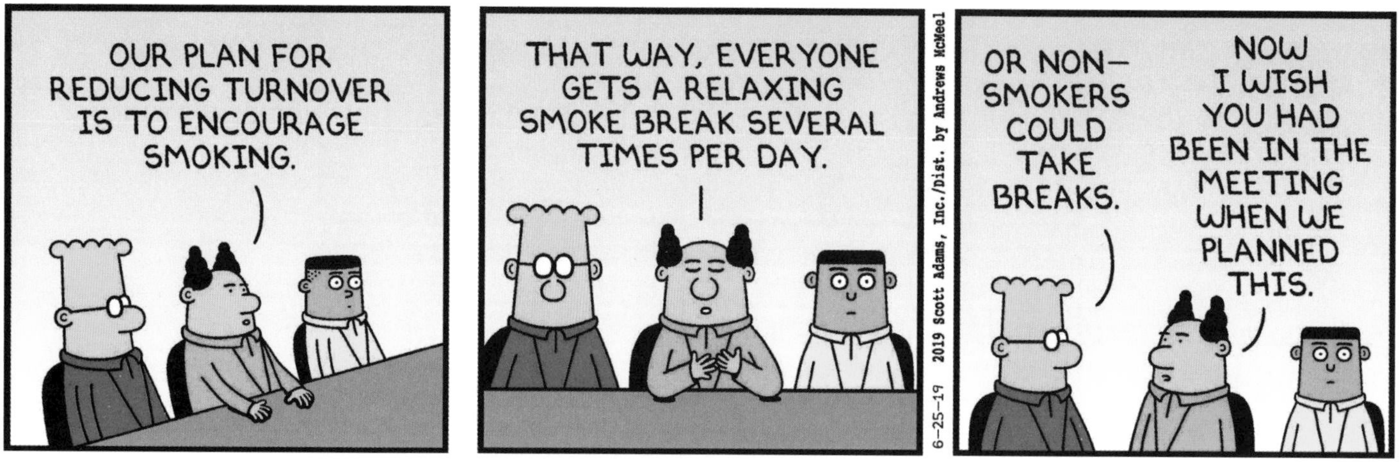
OUR PLAN FOR REDUCING TURNOVER IS TO ENCOURAGE SMOKING.
THAT WAY, EVERYONE GETS A RELAXING SMOKE BREAK SEVERAL TIMES PER DAY.
6-25-19 2019 Scott Adams, Inc./Dist. by Andrews McMeel
OR NON-SMOKERS COULD TAKE BREAKS.
NOW I WISH YOU HAD BEEN IN THE MEETING WHEN WE PLANNED THIS.

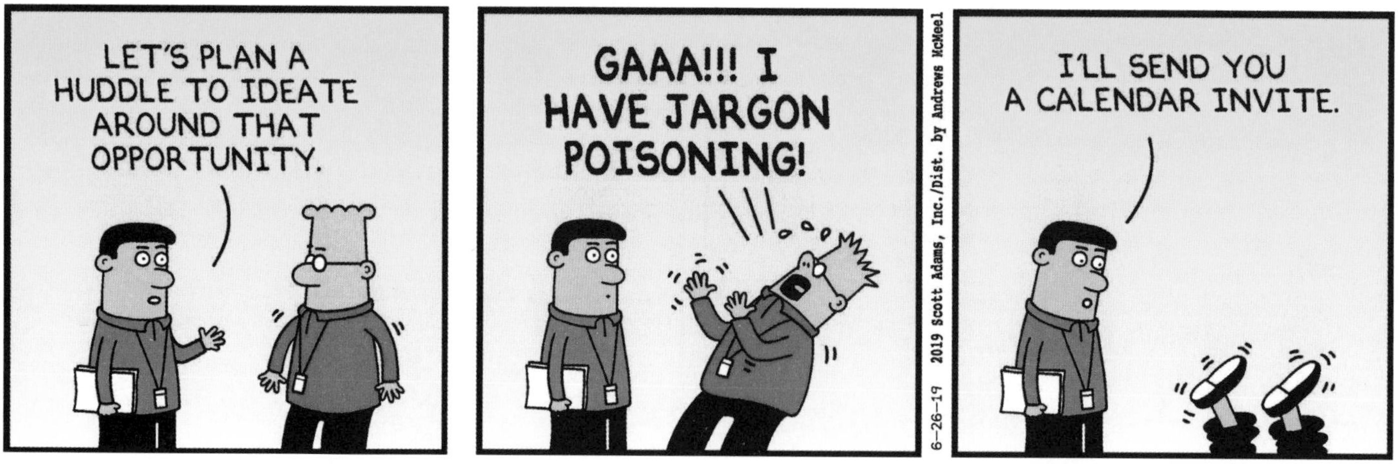
LET'S PLAN A HUDDLE TO IDEATE AROUND THAT OPPORTUNITY.
GAAA!!! I HAVE JARGON POISONING!
6-26-19 2019 Scott Adams, Inc./Dist. by Andrews McMeel
I'LL SEND YOU A CALENDAR INVITE.

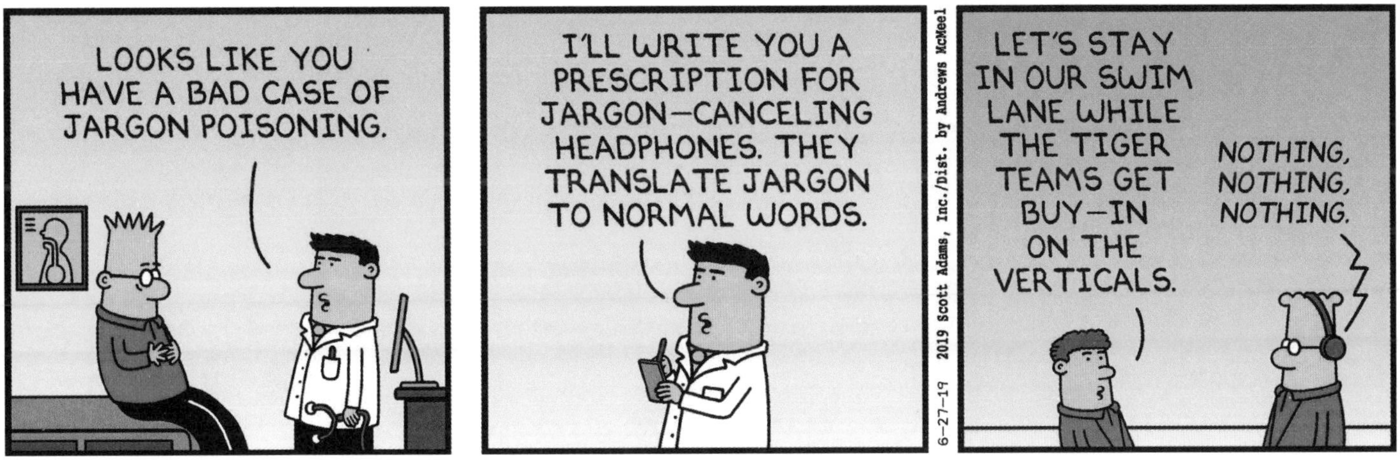
LOOKS LIKE YOU HAVE A BAD CASE OF JARGON POISONING.
I'LL WRITE YOU A PRESCRIPTION FOR JARGON—CANCELING HEADPHONES. THEY TRANSLATE JARGON TO NORMAL WORDS.
6-27-19 © 2019 Scott Adams, Inc./Dist. by Andrews McMeel
LET'S STAY IN OUR SWIM LANE WHILE THE TIGER TEAMS GET BUY—IN ON THE VERTICALS.
NOTHING, NOTHING, NOTHING.

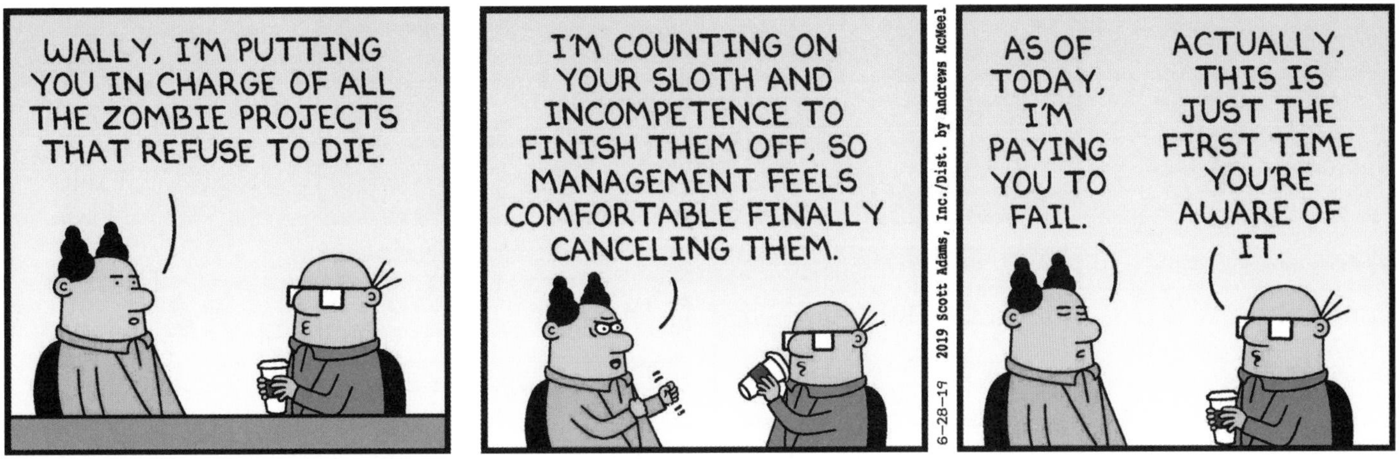
WALLY, I'M PUTTING YOU IN CHARGE OF ALL THE ZOMBIE PROJECTS THAT REFUSE TO DIE.
I'M COUNTING ON YOUR SLOTH AND INCOMPETENCE TO FINISH THEM OFF, SO MANAGEMENT FEELS COMFORTABLE FINALLY CANCELING THEM.
6-28-19 © 2019 Scott Adams, Inc./Dist. by Andrews McMeel
AS OF TODAY, I'M PAYING YOU TO FAIL.
ACTUALLY, THIS IS JUST THE FIRST TIME YOU'RE AWARE OF IT.

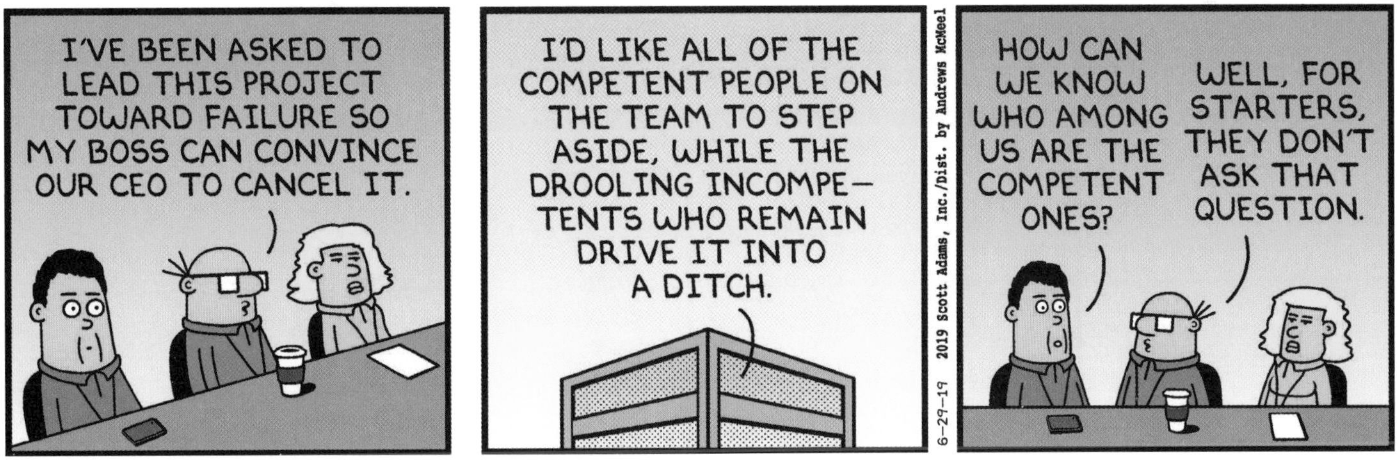
I'VE BEEN ASKED TO LEAD THIS PROJECT TOWARD FAILURE SO MY BOSS CAN CONVINCE OUR CEO TO CANCEL IT.
I'D LIKE ALL OF THE COMPETENT PEOPLE ON THE TEAM TO STEP ASIDE, WHILE THE DROOLING INCOMPE—TENTS WHO REMAIN DRIVE IT INTO A DITCH.
6-29-19 © 2019 Scott Adams, Inc./Dist. by Andrews McMeel
HOW CAN WE KNOW WHO AMONG US ARE THE COMPETENT ONES?
WELL, FOR STARTERS, THEY DON'T ASK THAT QUESTION.

I'M OPENING A BEG-AND-PAY STORE.
WHAT WILL YOU BE SELLING?
SELLING?
YOU ARE WAY BEHIND THE TIMES.
STORES DON'T SELL THINGS ANYMORE.
SELLING WOULD REQUIRE GOOD CUSTOMER SERVICE AND LOTS OF STOCK ON HAND.
IF YOU WANT THAT SORT OF THING, USE THE INTERNET.
I JUST WANT A PLACE WHERE PEOPLE CAN GO AND BEG ME TO SELL THEM STUFF THAT ISN'T IN STOCK.
CAN YOU HELP ME FIND THIS HAT IN MY SIZE?
BEG!!!
© 2019 Scott Adams, Inc./Dist. by Andrews McMeel
6-30-19

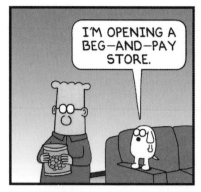

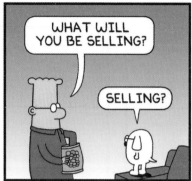

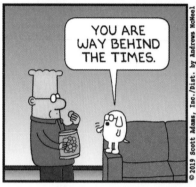

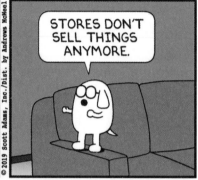

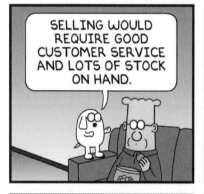

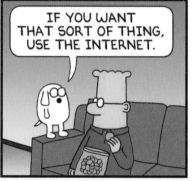

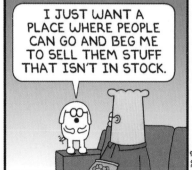

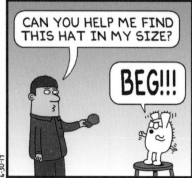

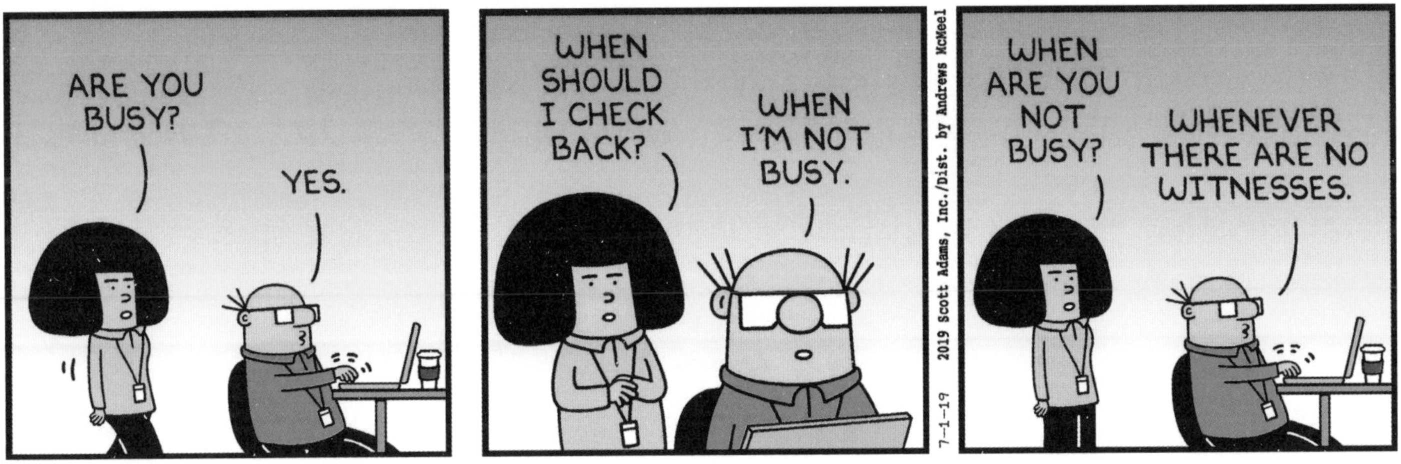
ARE YOU BUSY?
YES.
WHEN SHOULD I CHECK BACK?
WHEN I'M NOT BUSY.
7-1-19 2019 Scott Adams, Inc./Dist. by Andrews McMeel
WHEN ARE YOU NOT BUSY?
WHENEVER THERE ARE NO WITNESSES.

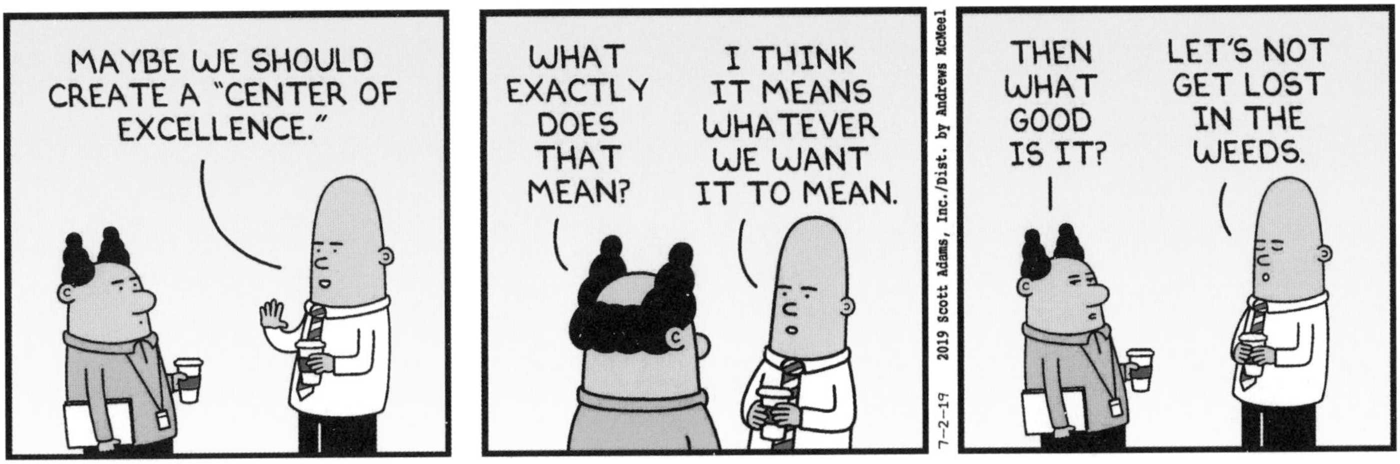
MAYBE WE SHOULD CREATE A "CENTER OF EXCELLENCE."
WHAT EXACTLY DOES THAT MEAN?
I THINK IT MEANS WHATEVER WE WANT IT TO MEAN.
7-2-19 2019 Scott Adams, Inc./Dist. by Andrews McMeel
THEN WHAT GOOD IS IT?
LET'S NOT GET LOST IN THE WEEDS.

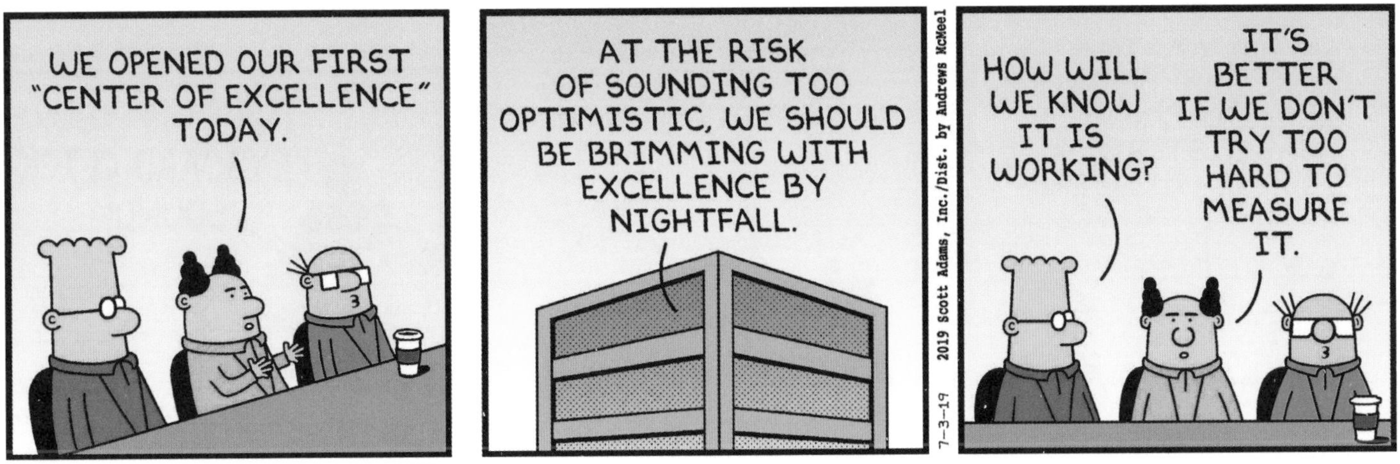
WE OPENED OUR FIRST "CENTER OF EXCELLENCE" TODAY.
AT THE RISK OF SOUNDING TOO OPTIMISTIC, WE SHOULD BE BRIMMING WITH EXCELLENCE BY NIGHTFALL.
7-3-19 2019 Scott Adams, Inc./Dist. by Andrews McMeel
HOW WILL WE KNOW IT IS WORKING?
IT'S BETTER IF WE DON'T TRY TOO HARD TO MEASURE IT.

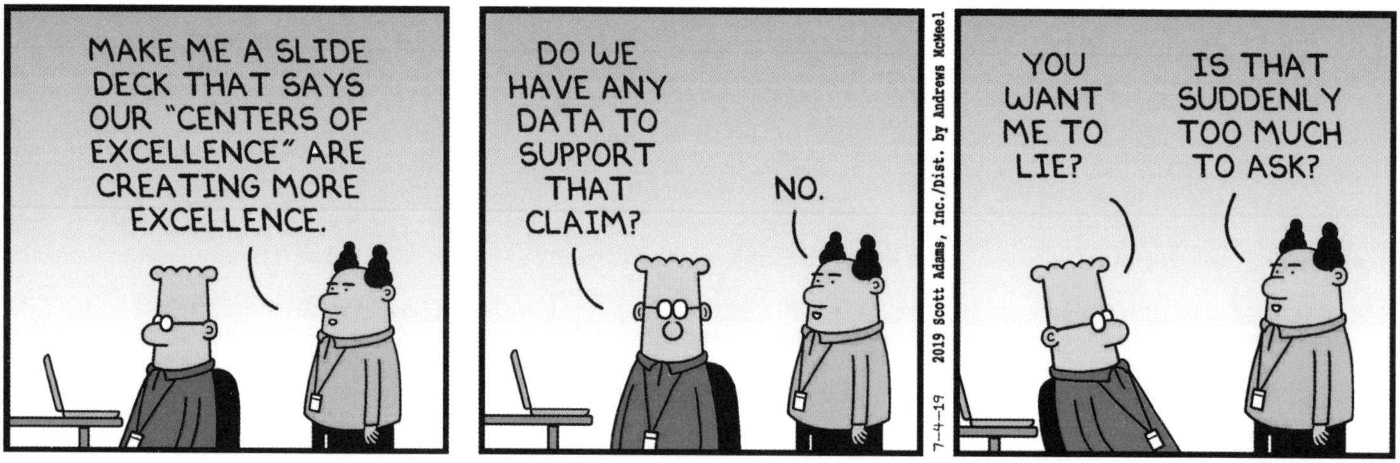
MAKE ME A SLIDE DECK THAT SAYS OUR "CENTERS OF EXCELLENCE" ARE CREATING MORE EXCELLENCE.
DO WE HAVE ANY DATA TO SUPPORT THAT CLAIM?
NO.
7-4-19 2019 Scott Adams, Inc./Dist. by Andrews McMeel
YOU WANT ME TO LIE?
IS THAT SUDDENLY TOO MUCH TO ASK?

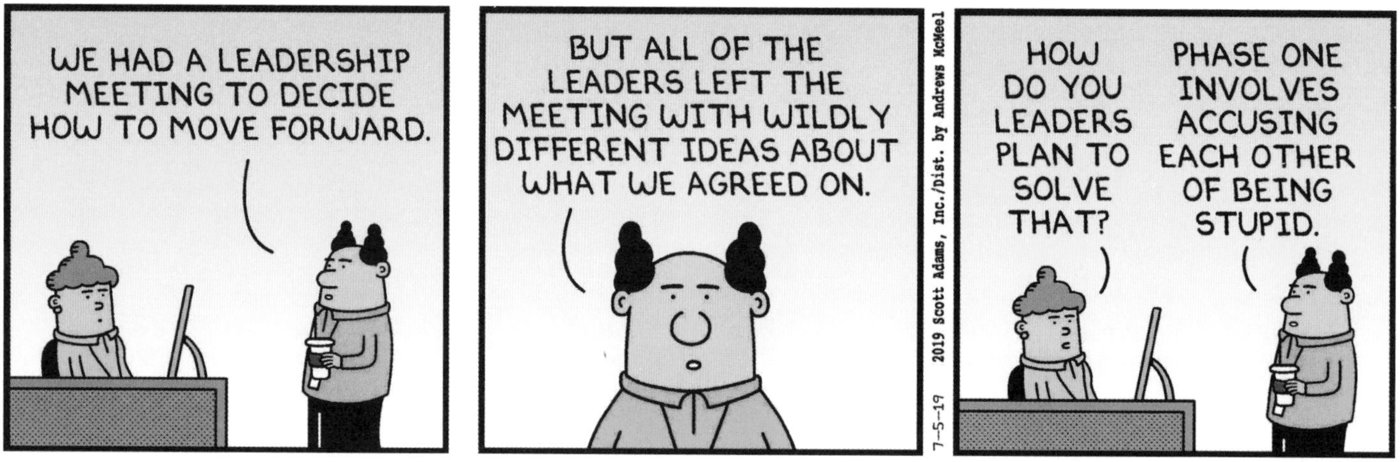
WE HAD A LEADERSHIP MEETING TO DECIDE HOW TO MOVE FORWARD.
BUT ALL OF THE LEADERS LEFT THE MEETING WITH WILDLY DIFFERENT IDEAS ABOUT WHAT WE AGREED ON.
7-5-19 2019 Scott Adams, Inc./Dist. by Andrews McMeel
HOW DO YOU LEADERS PLAN TO SOLVE THAT?
PHASE ONE INVOLVES ACCUSING EACH OTHER OF BEING STUPID.

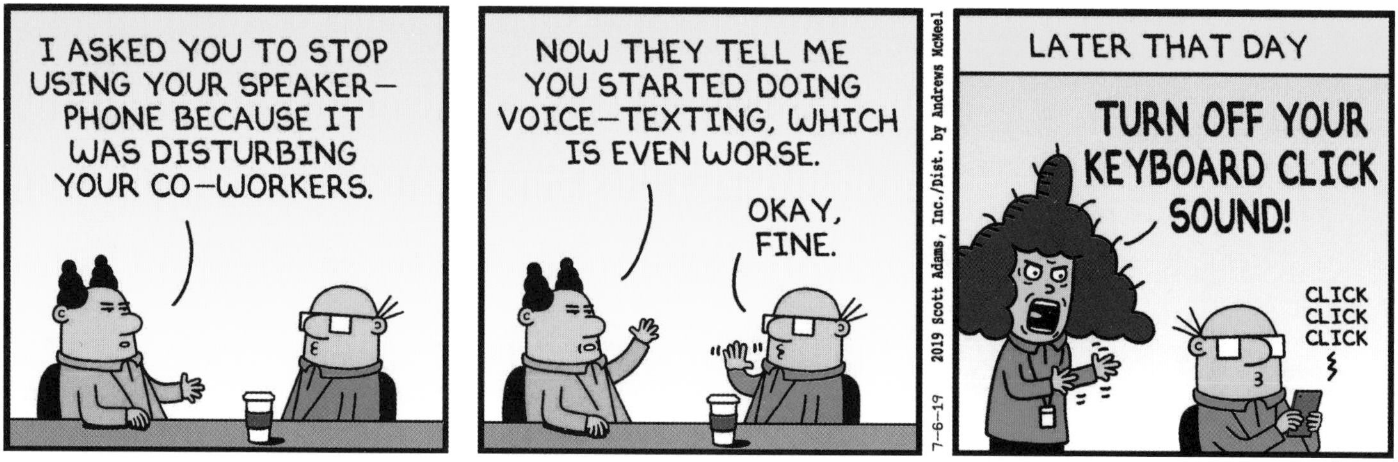
I ASKED YOU TO STOP USING YOUR SPEAKER-PHONE BECAUSE IT WAS DISTURBING YOUR CO-WORKERS.
NOW THEY TELL ME YOU STARTED DOING VOICE-TEXTING, WHICH IS EVEN WORSE.
OKAY, FINE.
7-6-19 2019 Scott Adams, Inc./Dist. by Andrews McMeel
LATER THAT DAY
TURN OFF YOUR KEYBOARD CLICK SOUND!
CLICK CLICK CLICK

THE COMPANY IS ANNOUNCING GENEROUS BUYOUT PACKAGES FOR EMPLOYEES WHO ELECT TO LEAVE.
WON'T ALL OF THE SMART PEOPLE LEAVE FIRST BECAUSE THEY CAN EASILY GET NEW JOBS AT HIGHER PAY?
UMMM. . .
IF YOU DON'T GET ENOUGH VOLUNTEERS, WILL YOU START FIRING PEOPLE?
WE HAVE NO PLAN TO DO THAT.
WILL YOU MAKE A PLAN IF TOO FEW PEOPLE LEAVE?
OH, YES.
WOULD IT BE FAIR TO SAY THE PEOPLE WHO STAY WILL ENVY THE DEAD?
UM. . .
ONE WEEK LATER
HOW MANY TOOK THE OFFER?
IT'S JUST YOU NOW.
© 2019 Scott Adams, Inc./Dist. by Andrews McMeel
7-7-19

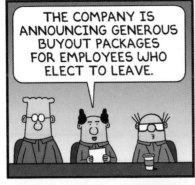

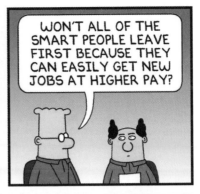

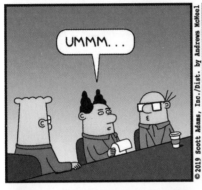

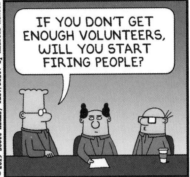

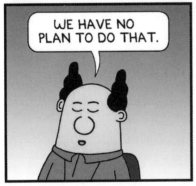

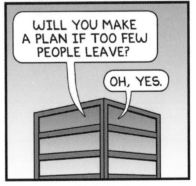

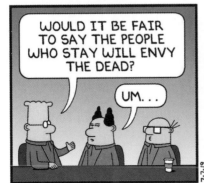

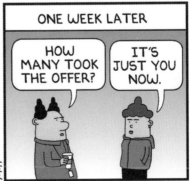

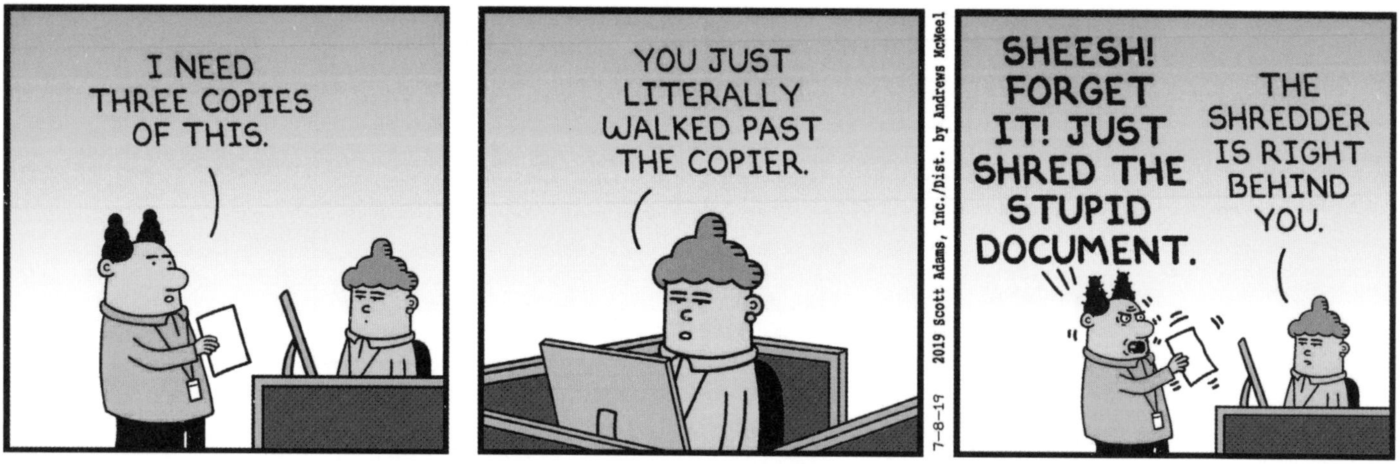
I NEED THREE COPIES OF THIS.
YOU JUST LITERALLY WALKED PAST THE COPIER.
7-8-19 2019 Scott Adams, Inc./Dist. by Andrews McMeel
SHEESH! FORGET IT! JUST SHRED THE STUPID DOCUMENT.
THE SHREDDER IS RIGHT BEHIND YOU.

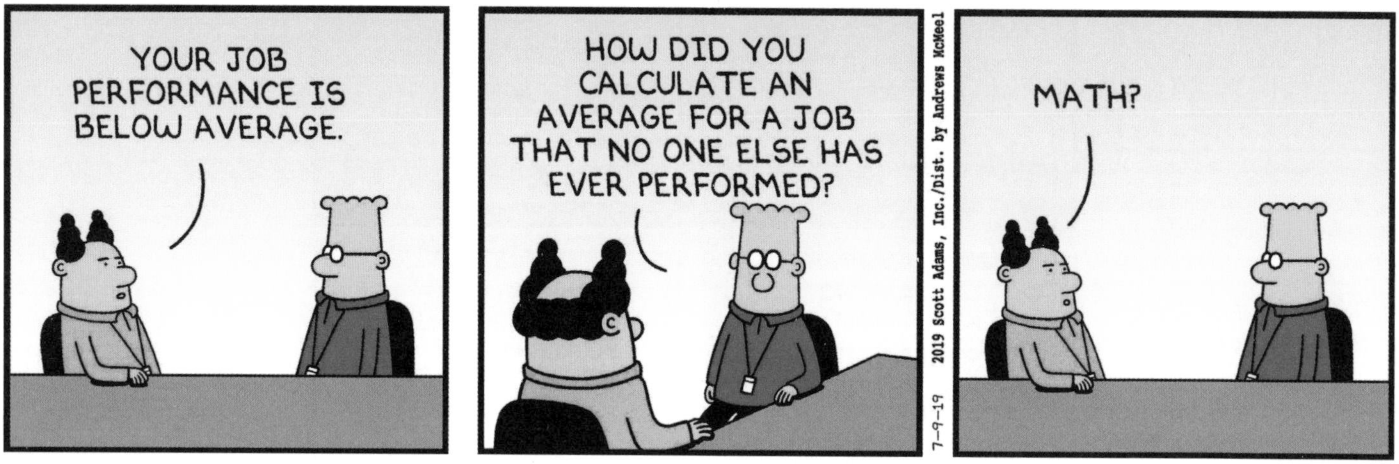
YOUR JOB PERFORMANCE IS BELOW AVERAGE.
HOW DID YOU CALCULATE AN AVERAGE FOR A JOB THAT NO ONE ELSE HAS EVER PERFORMED?
7-9-19 2019 Scott Adams, Inc./Dist. by Andrews McMeel
MATH?

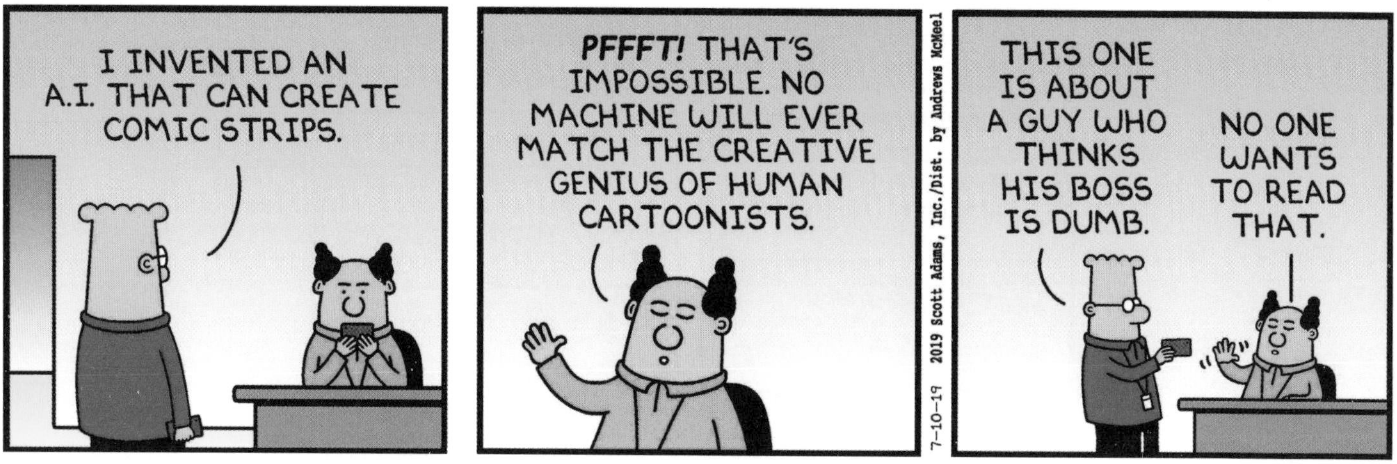
I INVENTED AN A.I. THAT CAN CREATE COMIC STRIPS.
PFFFT! THAT'S IMPOSSIBLE. NO MACHINE WILL EVER MATCH THE CREATIVE GENIUS OF HUMAN CARTOONISTS.
7-10-19 2019 Scott Adams, Inc./Dist. by Andrews McMeel
THIS ONE IS ABOUT A GUY WHO THINKS HIS BOSS IS DUMB.
NO ONE WANTS TO READ THAT.

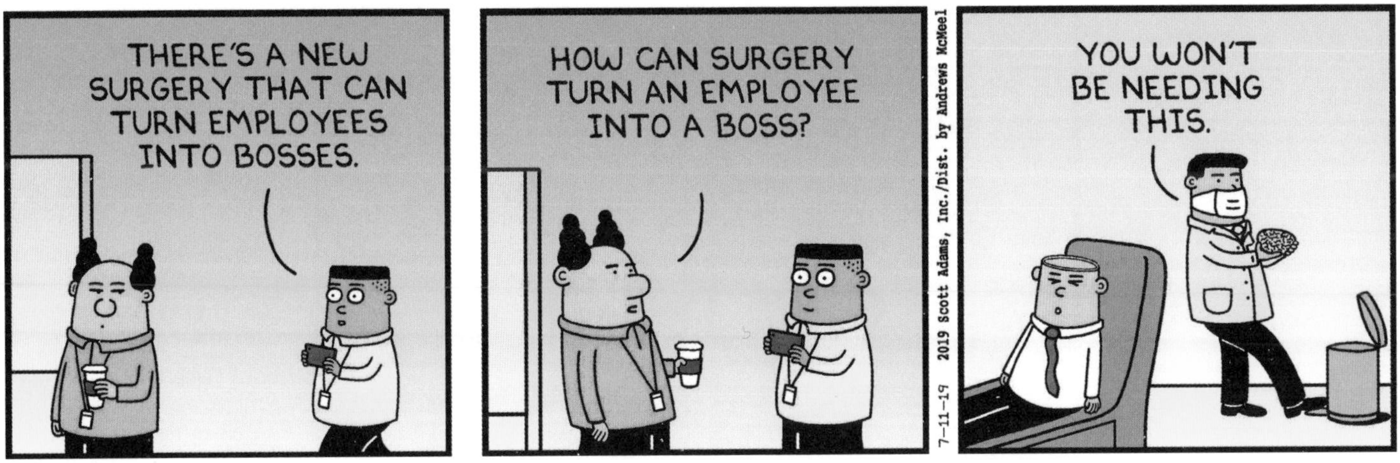
THERE'S A NEW SURGERY THAT CAN TURN EMPLOYEES INTO BOSSES.
HOW CAN SURGERY TURN AN EMPLOYEE INTO A BOSS?
7-11-19 © 2019 Scott Adams, Inc./Dist. by Andrews McMeel
YOU WON'T BE NEEDING THIS.

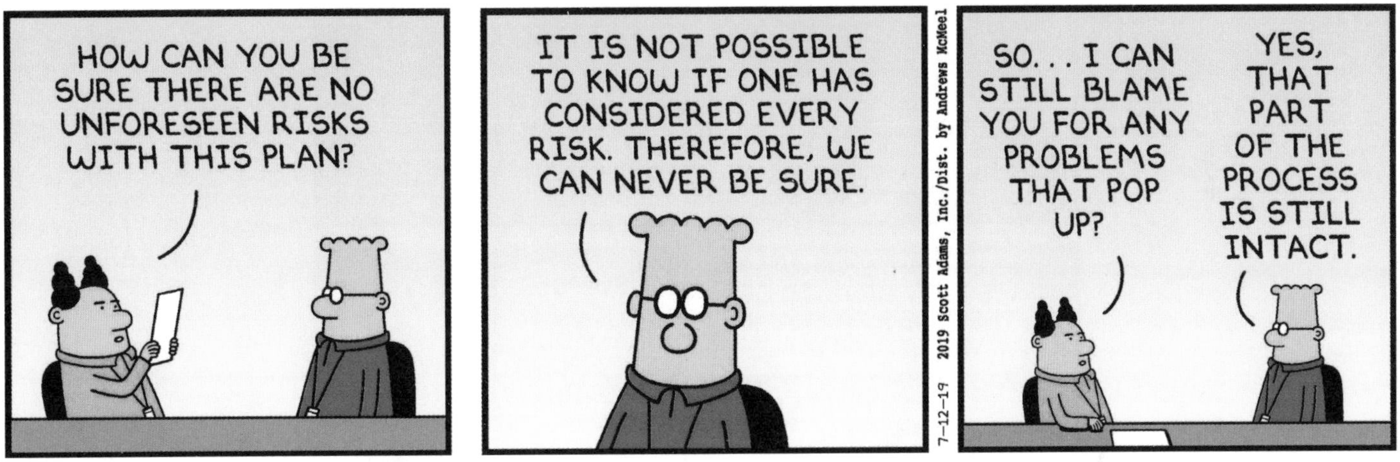
HOW CAN YOU BE SURE THERE ARE NO UNFORESEEN RISKS WITH THIS PLAN?
IT IS NOT POSSIBLE TO KNOW IF ONE HAS CONSIDERED EVERY RISK. THEREFORE, WE CAN NEVER BE SURE.
7-12-19 © 2019 Scott Adams, Inc./Dist. by Andrews McMeel
SO. . . I CAN STILL BLAME YOU FOR ANY PROBLEMS THAT POP UP?
YES, THAT PART OF THE PROCESS IS STILL INTACT.

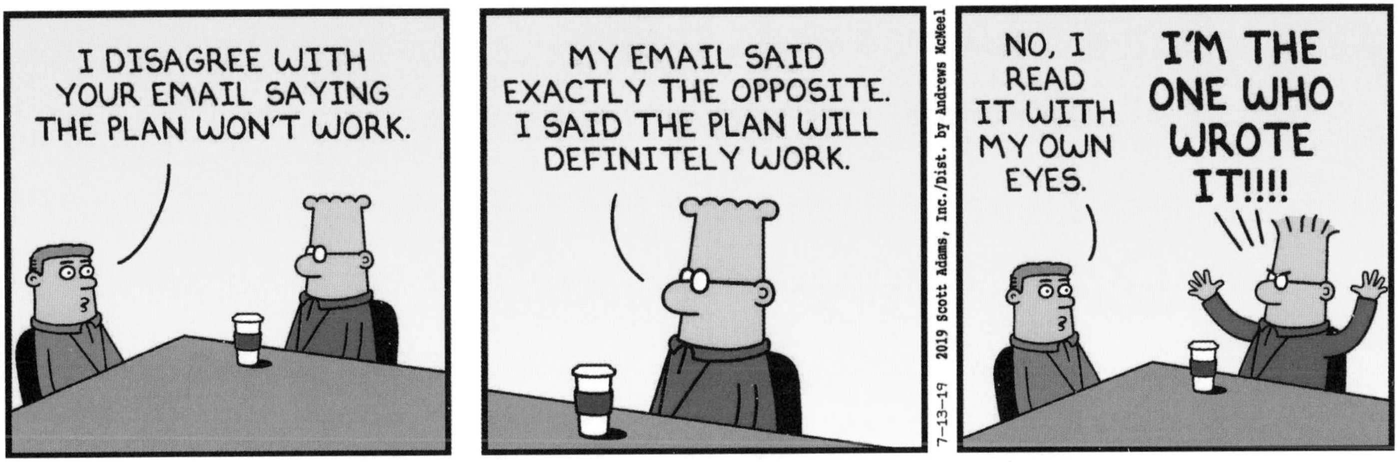
I DISAGREE WITH YOUR EMAIL SAYING THE PLAN WON'T WORK.
MY EMAIL SAID EXACTLY THE OPPOSITE. I SAID THE PLAN WILL DEFINITELY WORK.
7-13-19 © 2019 Scott Adams, Inc./Dist. by Andrews McMeel
NO, I READ IT WITH MY OWN EYES.
I'M THE ONE WHO WROTE IT!!!!

WE'LL NEED A SCAPEGOAT TO BLAME FOR OUR FAILURE ON THIS PROJECT.
NO ONE WILL BELIEVE IT WASN'T OUR FAULT.
ARE YOU KIDDING?
PEOPLE WILL BELIEVE ANYTHING.
WE JUST HAVE TO BE THE FIRST TO FRAME THE SITUATION.
I SUPPOSE WE COULD MAKE OUR LIE **SOUND** CREDIBLE.
THAT'S OVER-KILL.
WE DON'T NEED TO SOUND CREDIBLE?
NOT EVEN A LITTLE.
OUR PROJECT FAILED BECAUSE OF CLIMATE CHANGE.
THAT SOUNDS RIGHT.
© 2019 Scott Adams, Inc./Dist. by Andrews McMeel
7-14-19

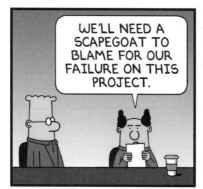

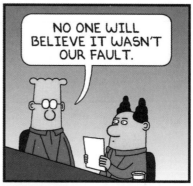

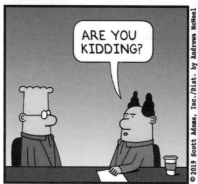

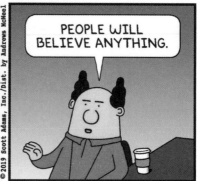

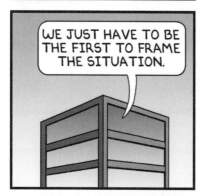

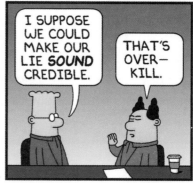

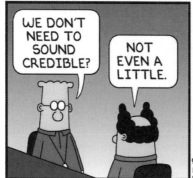

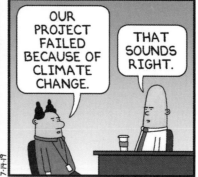

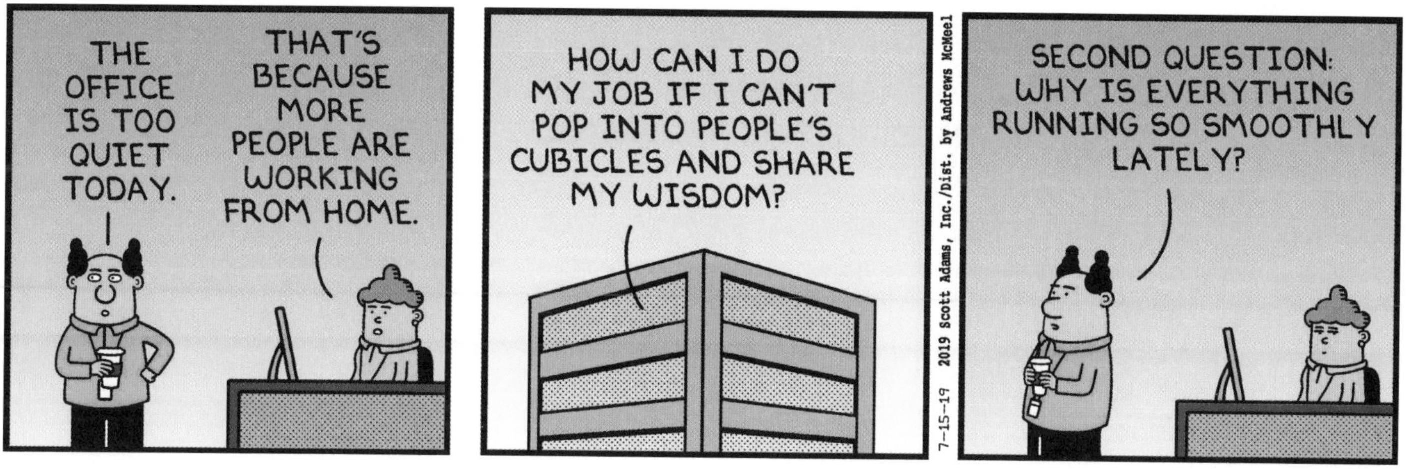
THE OFFICE IS TOO QUIET TODAY.
THAT'S BECAUSE MORE PEOPLE ARE WORKING FROM HOME.
HOW CAN I DO MY JOB IF I CAN'T POP INTO PEOPLE'S CUBICLES AND SHARE MY WISDOM?
7-15-19 2019 Scott Adams, Inc./Dist. by Andrews McMeel
SECOND QUESTION: WHY IS EVERYTHING RUNNING SO SMOOTHLY LATELY?

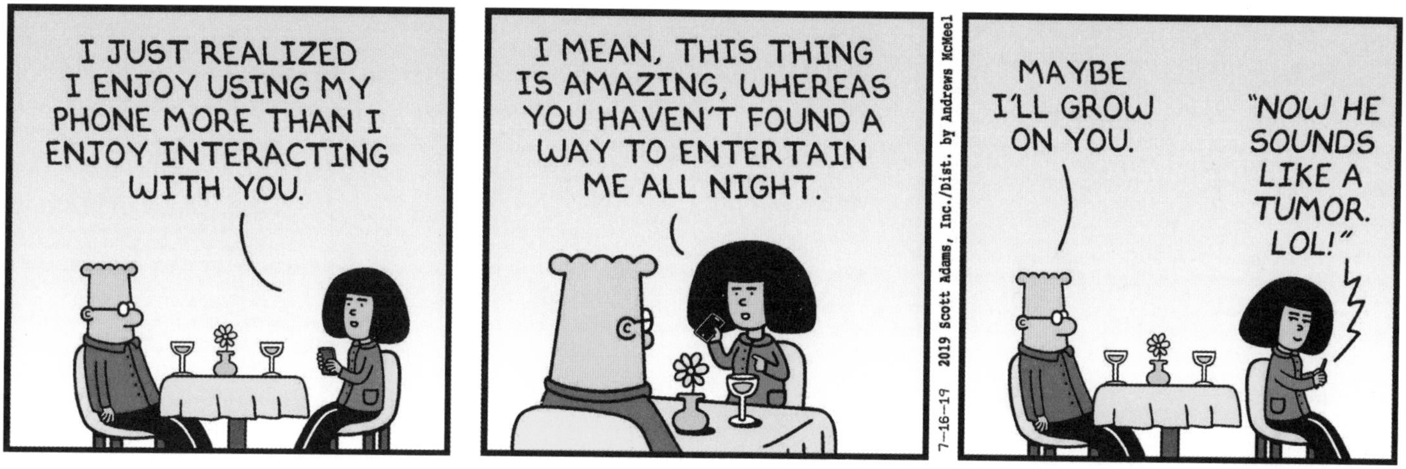
I JUST REALIZED I ENJOY USING MY PHONE MORE THAN I ENJOY INTERACTING WITH YOU.
I MEAN, THIS THING IS AMAZING, WHEREAS YOU HAVEN'T FOUND A WAY TO ENTERTAIN ME ALL NIGHT.
7-16-19 2019 Scott Adams, Inc./Dist. by Andrews McMeel
MAYBE I'LL GROW ON YOU.
"NOW HE SOUNDS LIKE A TUMOR. LOL!"

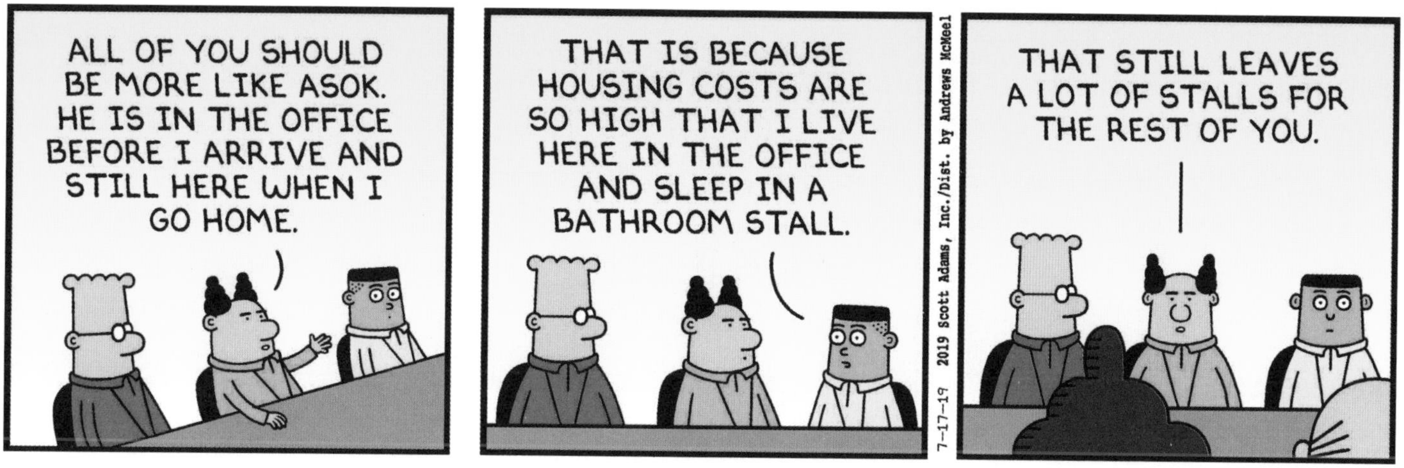
ALL OF YOU SHOULD BE MORE LIKE ASOK. HE IS IN THE OFFICE BEFORE I ARRIVE AND STILL HERE WHEN I GO HOME.
THAT IS BECAUSE HOUSING COSTS ARE SO HIGH THAT I LIVE HERE IN THE OFFICE AND SLEEP IN A BATHROOM STALL.
7-17-19 2019 Scott Adams, Inc./Dist. by Andrews McMeel
THAT STILL LEAVES A LOT OF STALLS FOR THE REST OF YOU.

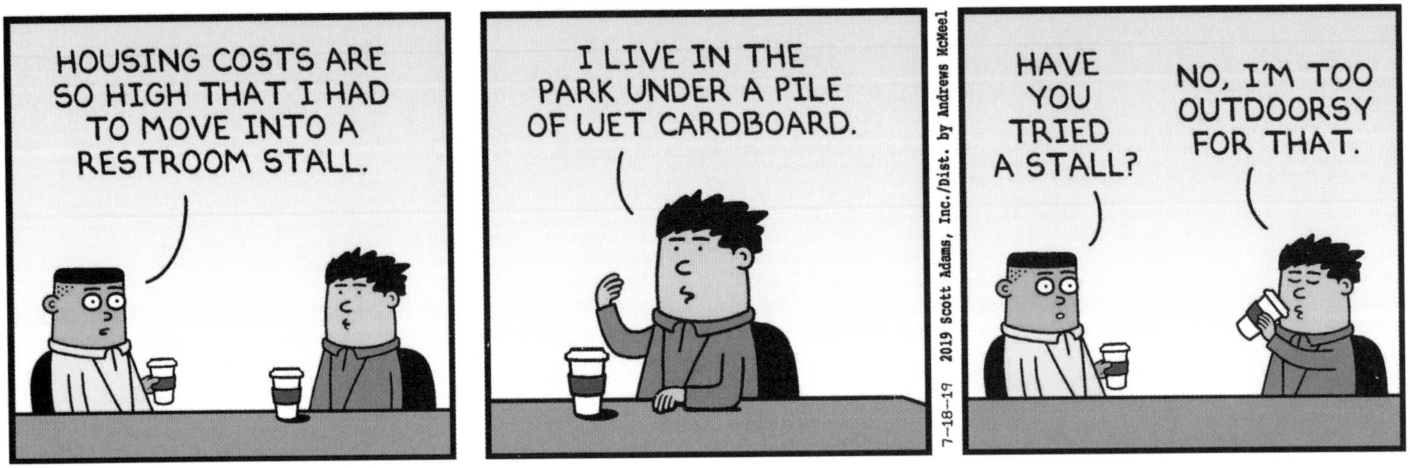
HOUSING COSTS ARE SO HIGH THAT I HAD TO MOVE INTO A RESTROOM STALL.
I LIVE IN THE PARK UNDER A PILE OF WET CARDBOARD.
7-18-19 2019 Scott Adams, Inc./Dist. by Andrews McMeel
HAVE YOU TRIED A STALL?
NO, I'M TOO OUTDOORSY FOR THAT.

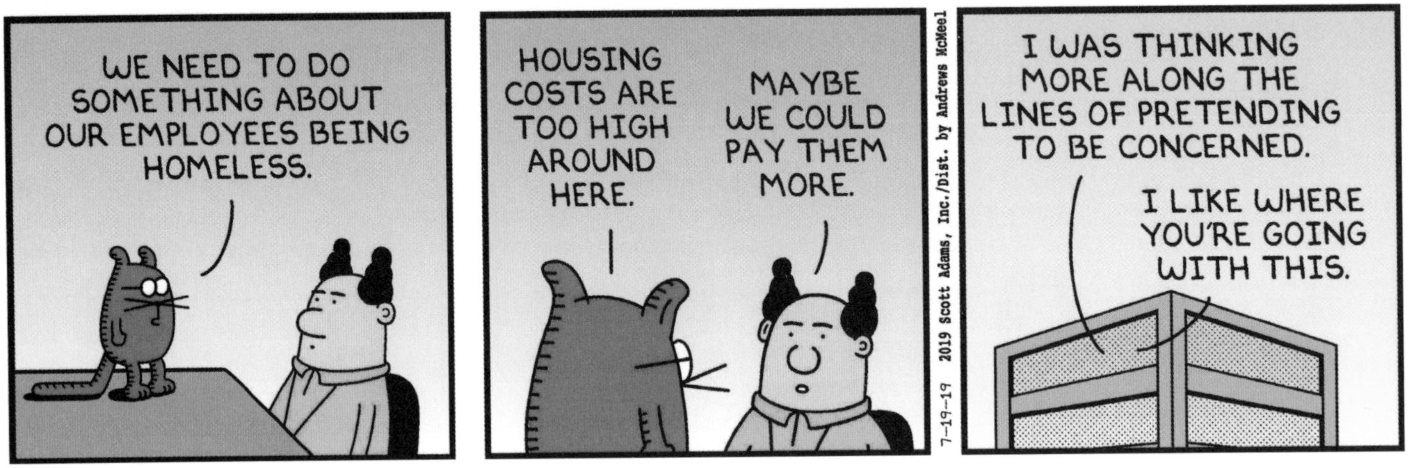
WE NEED TO DO SOMETHING ABOUT OUR EMPLOYEES BEING HOMELESS.
HOUSING COSTS ARE TOO HIGH AROUND HERE.
MAYBE WE COULD PAY THEM MORE.
7-19-19 2019 Scott Adams, Inc./Dist. by Andrews McMeel
I WAS THINKING MORE ALONG THE LINES OF PRETENDING TO BE CONCERNED.
I LIKE WHERE YOU'RE GOING WITH THIS.

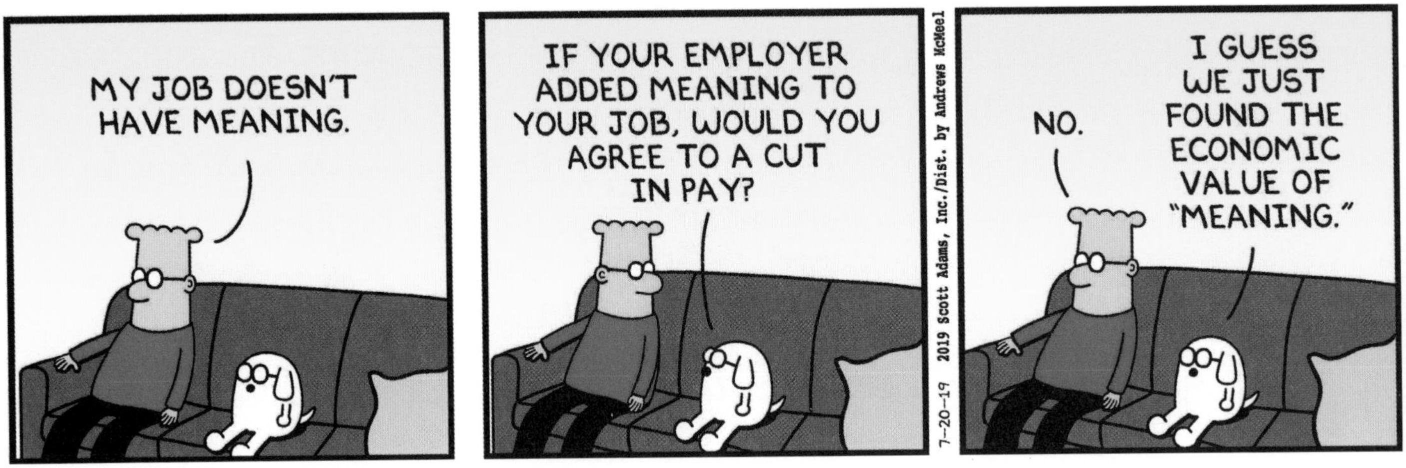
MY JOB DOESN'T HAVE MEANING.
IF YOUR EMPLOYER ADDED MEANING TO YOUR JOB, WOULD YOU AGREE TO A CUT IN PAY?
7-20-19 2019 Scott Adams, Inc./Dist. by Andrews McMeel
NO.
I GUESS WE JUST FOUND THE ECONOMIC VALUE OF "MEANING."

I RECOMMEND WE UPGRADE ONE OF OUR SERVERS OVER THE WEEKEND.
SO, JUST TO BE CLEAR, YOU WANT TO REPLACE OUR ENTIRE NETWORK IN TWO DAYS?
UM. . . NO. I WANT TO REPLACE ONE DEFECTIVE SERVER.
WE CAN'T REPLACE OUR ENTIRE NETWORK IN TWO DAYS! THAT IS RIDICULOUS!
I DON'T KNOW WHAT IS HAPPENING RIGHT NOW.
IT'S AS IF THE THINGS I SAY HAVE NO IMPACT ON WHAT YOU HALLUCINATE YOU ARE HEARING.
YOU THINK YOU CAN REPLACE AN ENTIRE NETWORK IN TWO DAYS, AND YOU THINK **I'M** THE ONE WHO IS HALLUCINATING? ? ?
I DON'T KNOW WHAT TO DO RIGHT NOW.
YOUR INCOM– PETENCE IS CON– FIRMED.
© 2019 Scott Adams, Inc./Dist. by Andrews McMeel
7-21-19

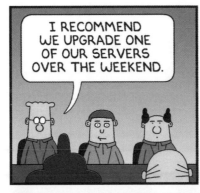

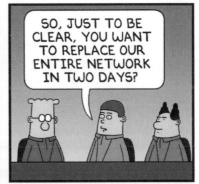

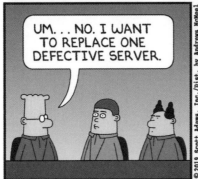

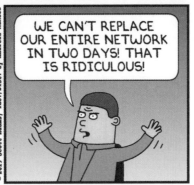

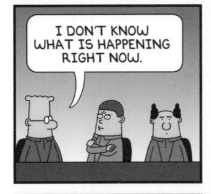

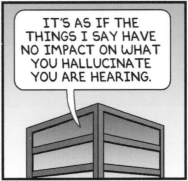

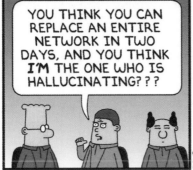

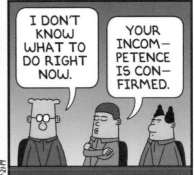

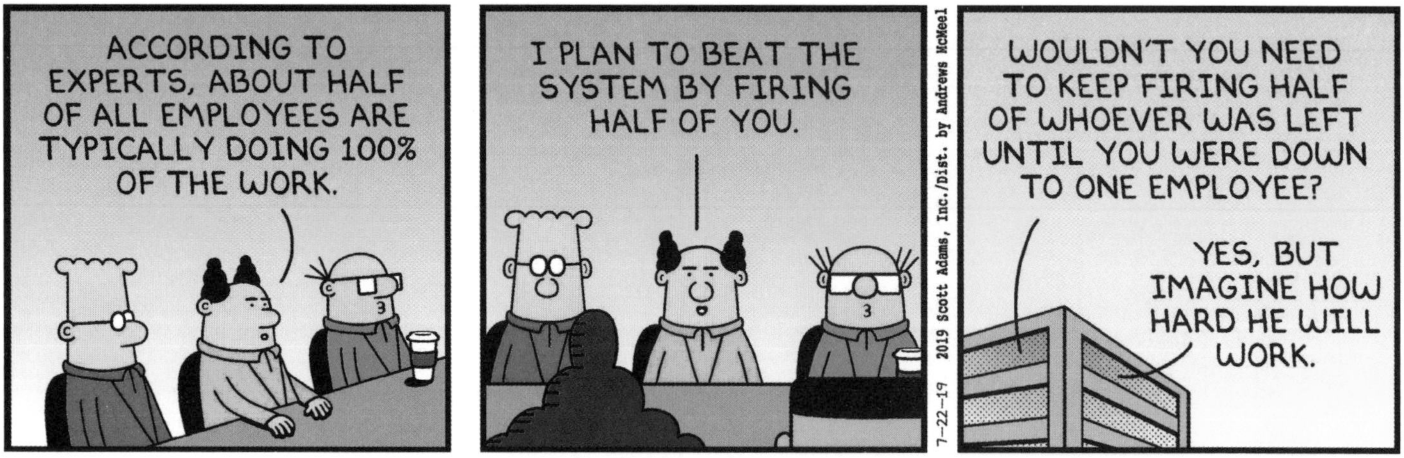
ACCORDING TO EXPERTS, ABOUT HALF OF ALL EMPLOYEES ARE TYPICALLY DOING 100% OF THE WORK.
I PLAN TO BEAT THE SYSTEM BY FIRING HALF OF YOU.
7-22-19 © 2019 Scott Adams, Inc./Dist. by Andrews McMeel
WOULDN'T YOU NEED TO KEEP FIRING HALF OF WHOEVER WAS LEFT UNTIL YOU WERE DOWN TO ONE EMPLOYEE?
YES, BUT IMAGINE HOW HARD HE WILL WORK.

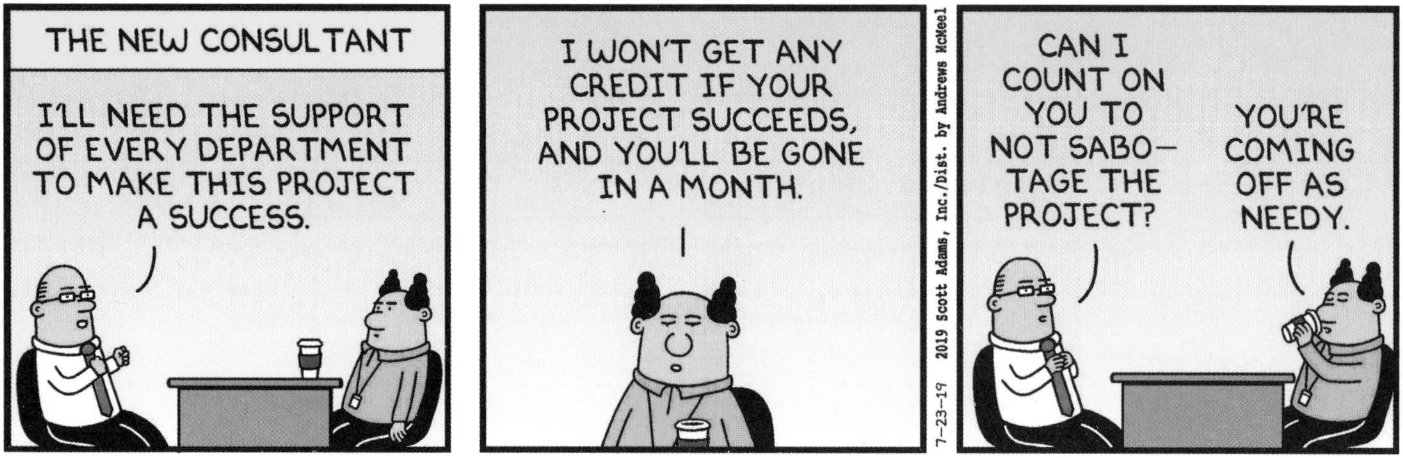
THE NEW CONSULTANT
I'LL NEED THE SUPPORT OF EVERY DEPARTMENT TO MAKE THIS PROJECT A SUCCESS.
I WON'T GET ANY CREDIT IF YOUR PROJECT SUCCEEDS, AND YOU'LL BE GONE IN A MONTH.
7-23-19 © 2019 Scott Adams, Inc./Dist. by Andrews McMeel
CAN I COUNT ON YOU TO NOT SABO-TAGE THE PROJECT?
YOU'RE COMING OFF AS NEEDY.

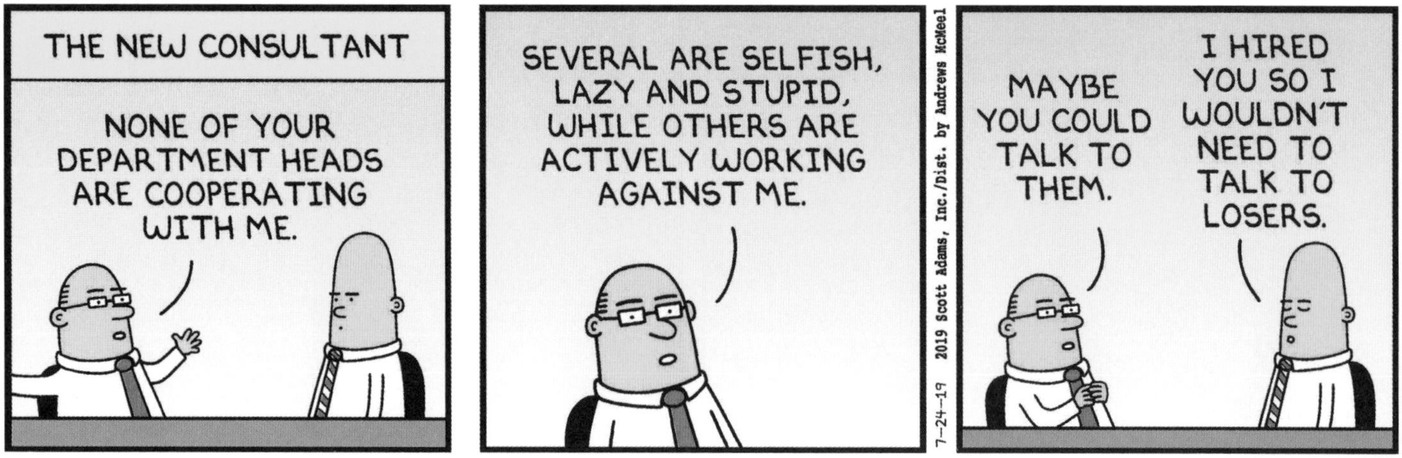
THE NEW CONSULTANT
NONE OF YOUR DEPARTMENT HEADS ARE COOPERATING WITH ME.
SEVERAL ARE SELFISH, LAZY AND STUPID, WHILE OTHERS ARE ACTIVELY WORKING AGAINST ME.
7-24-19 © 2019 Scott Adams, Inc./Dist. by Andrews McMeel
MAYBE YOU COULD TALK TO THEM.
I HIRED YOU SO I WOULDN'T NEED TO TALK TO LOSERS.

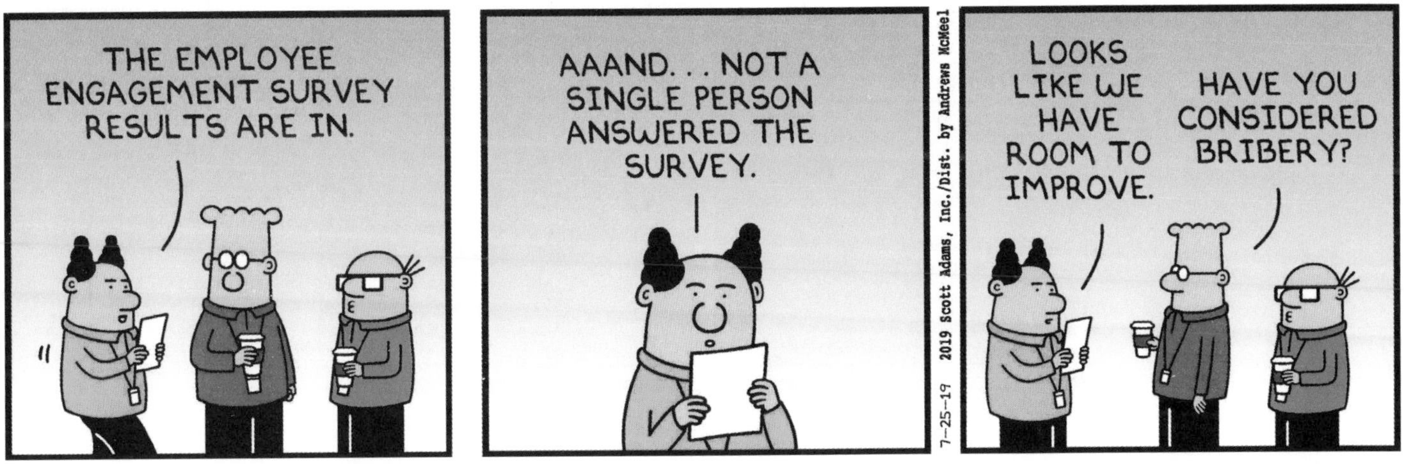
THE EMPLOYEE ENGAGEMENT SURVEY RESULTS ARE IN.
AAAND. . . NOT A SINGLE PERSON ANSWERED THE SURVEY.
7-25-19 2019 Scott Adams, Inc./Dist. by Andrews McMeel
LOOKS LIKE WE HAVE ROOM TO IMPROVE.
HAVE YOU CONSIDERED BRIBERY?

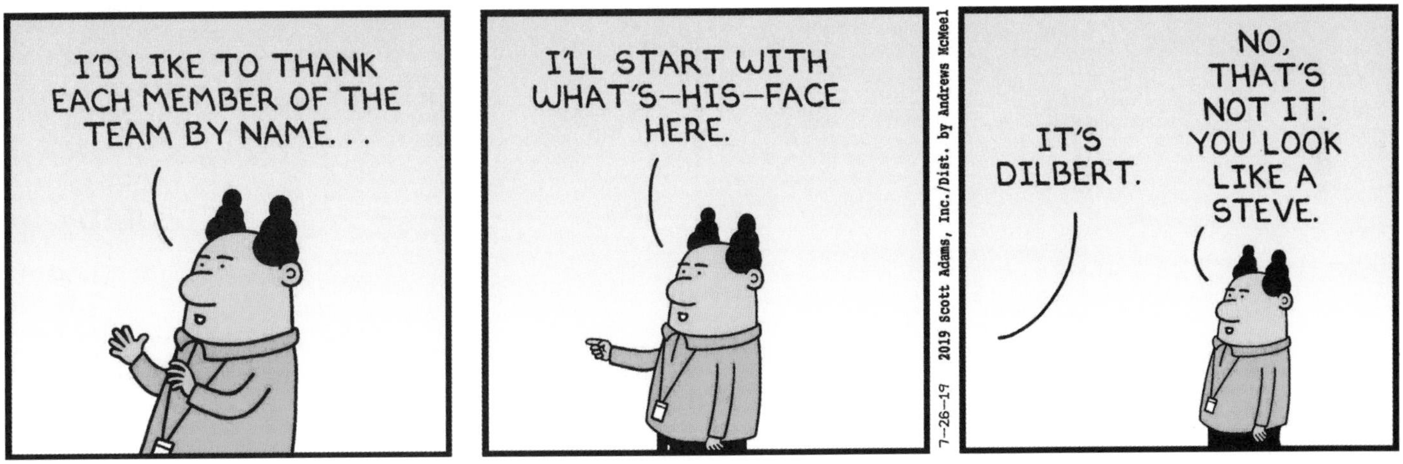
I'D LIKE TO THANK EACH MEMBER OF THE TEAM BY NAME. . .
I'LL START WITH WHAT'S-HIS-FACE HERE.
7-26-19 2019 Scott Adams, Inc./Dist. by Andrews McMeel
IT'S DILBERT.
NO, THAT'S NOT IT. YOU LOOK LIKE A STEVE.

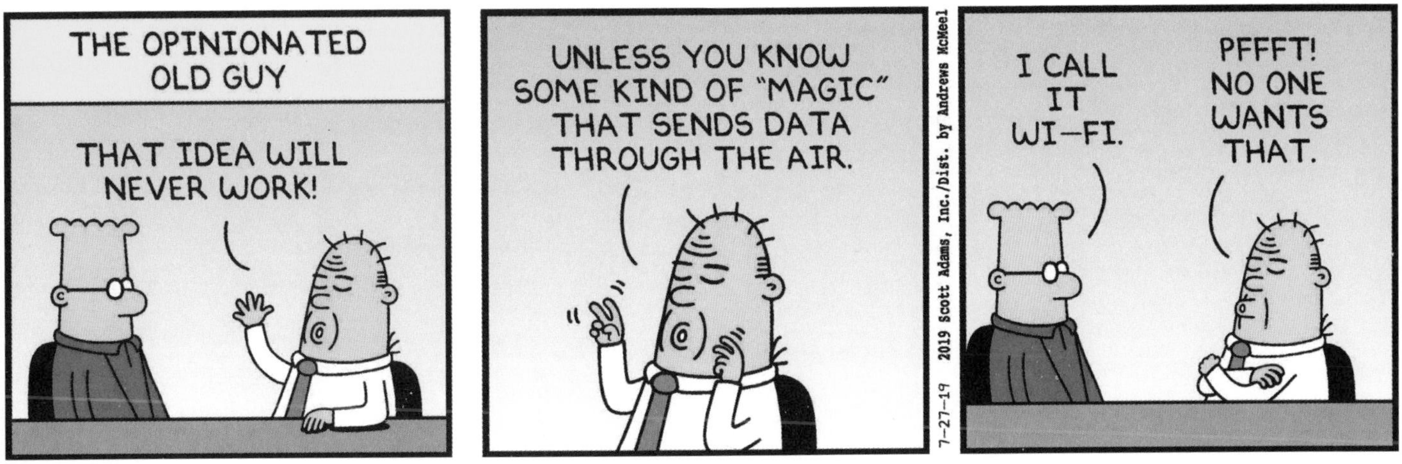
THE OPINIONATED OLD GUY
THAT IDEA WILL NEVER WORK!
UNLESS YOU KNOW SOME KIND OF "MAGIC" THAT SENDS DATA THROUGH THE AIR.
7-27-19 2019 Scott Adams, Inc./Dist. by Andrews McMeel
I CALL IT WI-FI.
PFFFT! NO ONE WANTS THAT.

ALICE, WHY AREN'T YOU AT THIS MEETING?
I'M HAVING A BAD HAIR DAY.
THAT'S NO REASON TO MISS A MEETING!
YOU DON'T UNDER-STAND. IT'S **REALLY, REALLY** BAD.
© 2019 Scott Adams, Inc./Dist. by Andrews McMeel
COME TO THE MEETING RIGHT NOW, OR YOU'RE FIRED!
GURK!
THAT'S BAD HAIR.
CAN'T SAY I DIDN'T WARN HIM.
7-28-19

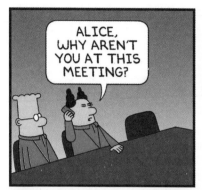

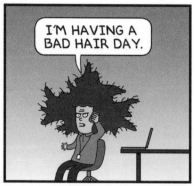

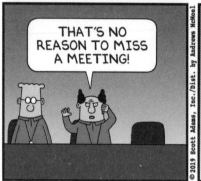

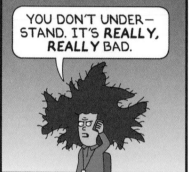

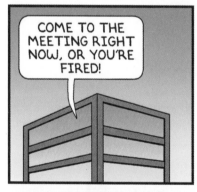

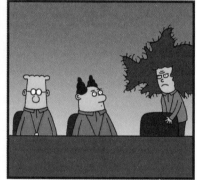

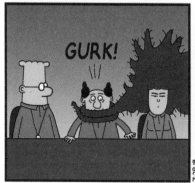

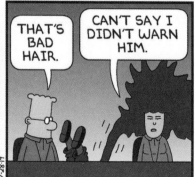

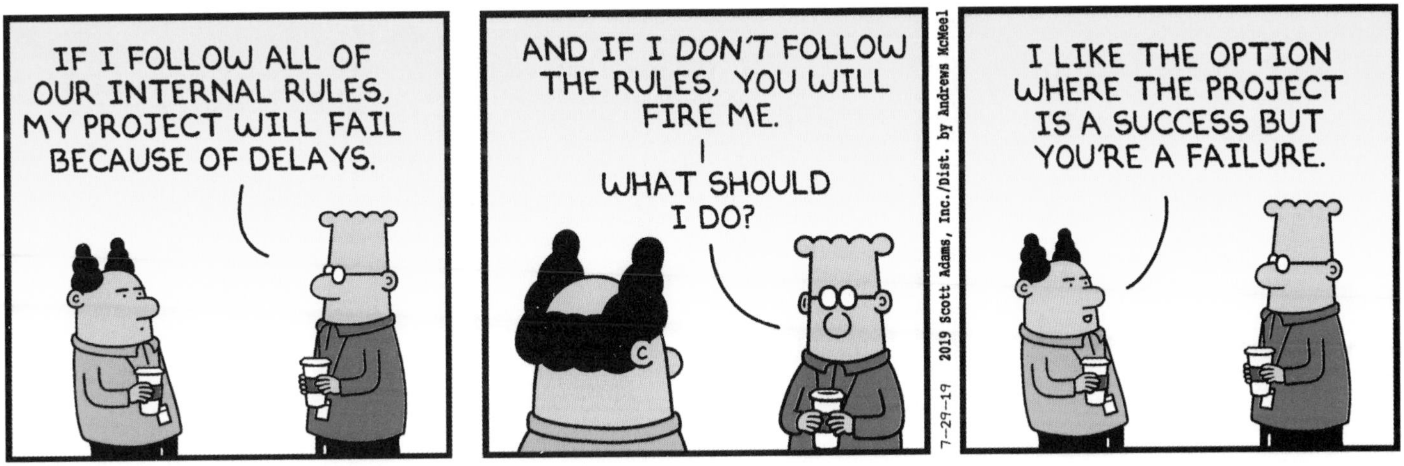
IF I FOLLOW ALL OF OUR INTERNAL RULES, MY PROJECT WILL FAIL BECAUSE OF DELAYS.
AND IF I DON'T FOLLOW THE RULES, YOU WILL FIRE ME.
WHAT SHOULD I DO?
I LIKE THE OPTION WHERE THE PROJECT IS A SUCCESS BUT YOU'RE A FAILURE.
7-29-19 © 2019 Scott Adams, Inc./Dist. by Andrews McMeel

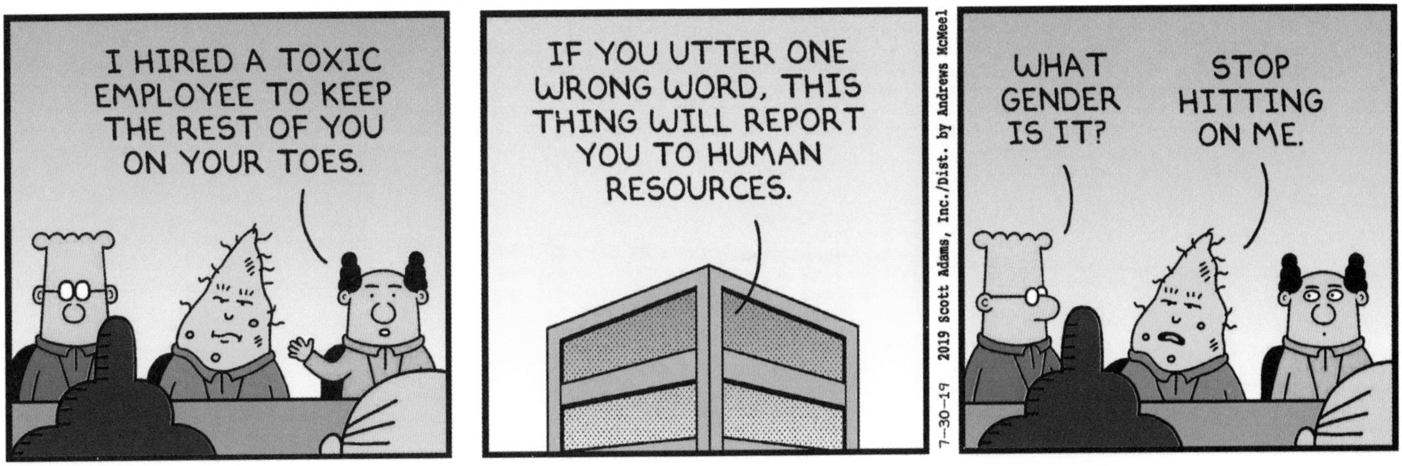
I HIRED A TOXIC EMPLOYEE TO KEEP THE REST OF YOU ON YOUR TOES.
IF YOU UTTER ONE WRONG WORD, THIS THING WILL REPORT YOU TO HUMAN RESOURCES.
WHAT GENDER IS IT?
STOP HITTING ON ME.
7-30-19 © 2019 Scott Adams, Inc./Dist. by Andrews McMeel

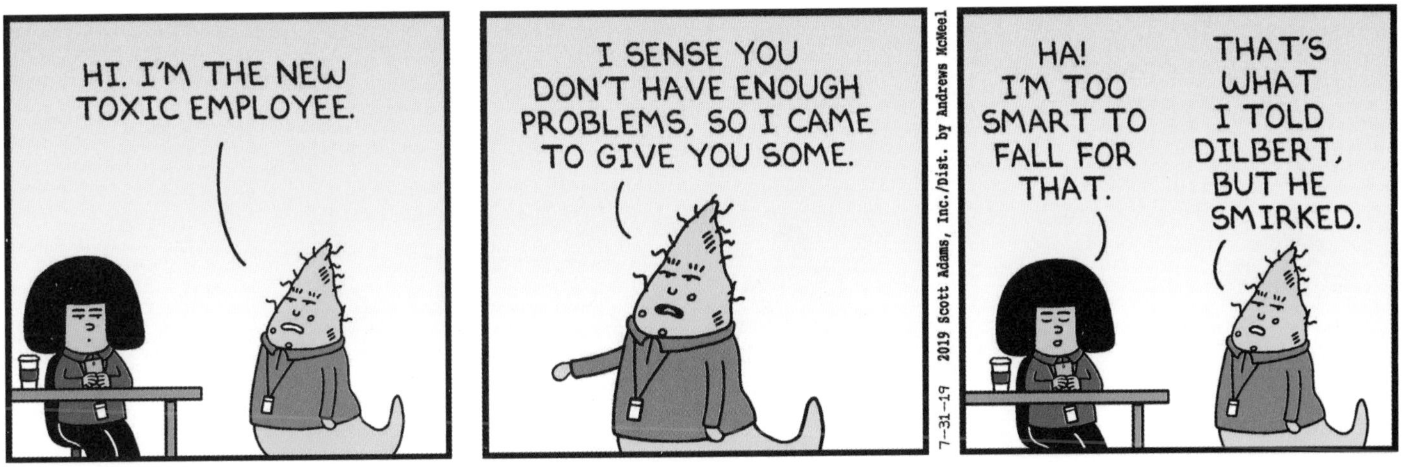
HI. I'M THE NEW TOXIC EMPLOYEE.
I SENSE YOU DON'T HAVE ENOUGH PROBLEMS, SO I CAME TO GIVE YOU SOME.
HA! I'M TOO SMART TO FALL FOR THAT.
THAT'S WHAT I TOLD DILBERT, BUT HE SMIRKED.
7-31-19 © 2019 Scott Adams, Inc./Dist. by Andrews McMeel

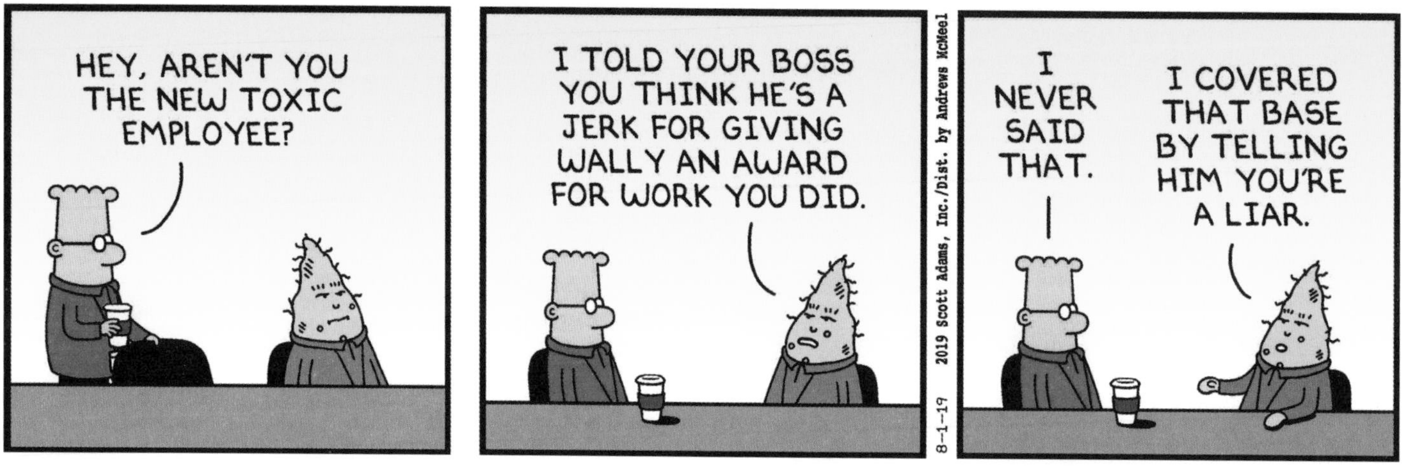
HEY, AREN'T YOU THE NEW TOXIC EMPLOYEE?
I TOLD YOUR BOSS YOU THINK HE'S A JERK FOR GIVING WALLY AN AWARD FOR WORK YOU DID.
8-1-19 © 2019 Scott Adams, Inc./Dist. by Andrews McMeel
I NEVER SAID THAT.
I COVERED THAT BASE BY TELLING HIM YOU'RE A LIAR.

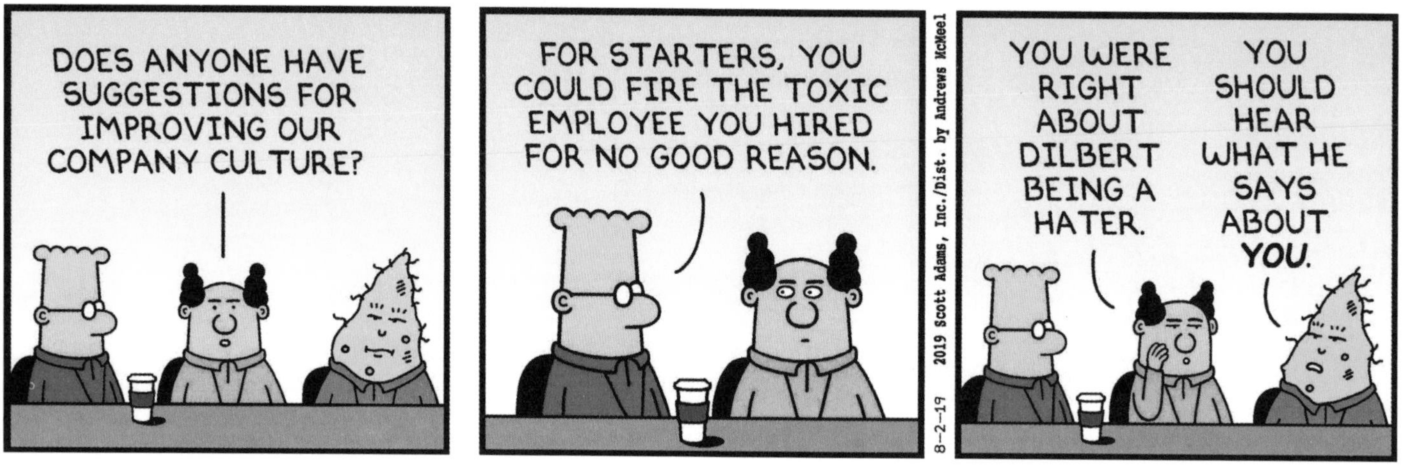
DOES ANYONE HAVE SUGGESTIONS FOR IMPROVING OUR COMPANY CULTURE?
FOR STARTERS, YOU COULD FIRE THE TOXIC EMPLOYEE YOU HIRED FOR NO GOOD REASON.
8-2-19 © 2019 Scott Adams, Inc./Dist. by Andrews McMeel
YOU WERE RIGHT ABOUT DILBERT BEING A HATER.
YOU SHOULD HEAR WHAT HE SAYS ABOUT ***YOU***.

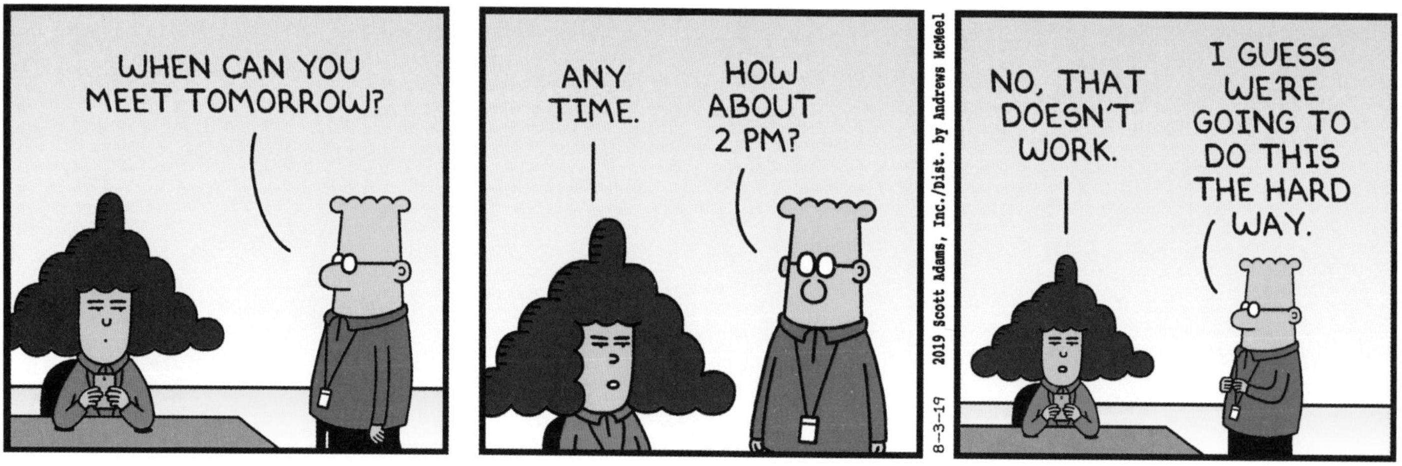
WHEN CAN YOU MEET TOMORROW?
ANY TIME.
HOW ABOUT 2 PM?
8-3-19 © 2019 Scott Adams, Inc./Dist. by Andrews McMeel
NO, THAT DOESN'T WORK.
I GUESS WE'RE GOING TO DO THIS THE HARD WAY.

THANKS TO MY NEW CIRCULAR DEBATING TECHNIQUE, I HAVEN'T LOST A DEBATE IN WEEKS.
WATCH THIS.
THE MOON LANDING WAS A HOAX.
NO, IT WASN'T.
THE FLAG WAS MOVING IN THE WIND.
I'LL SEND YOU A LINK DEBUNKING THE FLAG THING.
OKAY, BUT HOW DO YOU EXPLAIN THE MULTIPLE LIGHT SOURCES?
HERE'S ANOTHER LINK DEBUNKING THAT CLAIM.
FIFTEEN MINUTES LATER
I HAVE NOW DEBUNKED ALL TEN OF YOUR RIDICULOUS CLAIMS. WILL YOU AGREE THE MOON LANDING WAS REAL?
HOW DO YOU EXPLAIN THE FLAG MOVING?
GAAAA!!! I GIVE UP!!! YOU WIN!!!
© 2019 Scott Adams, Inc./Dist. by Andrews McMeel
8-4-19

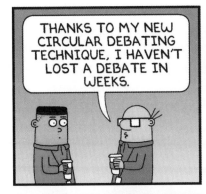

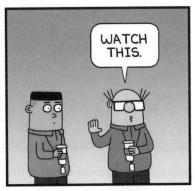

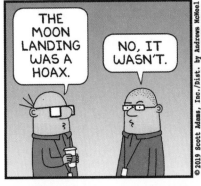

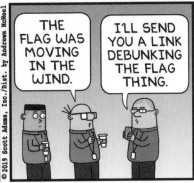

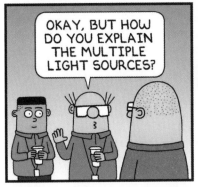

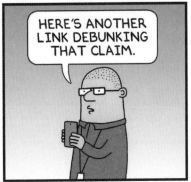

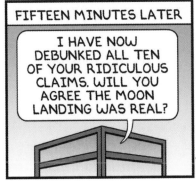

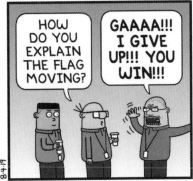

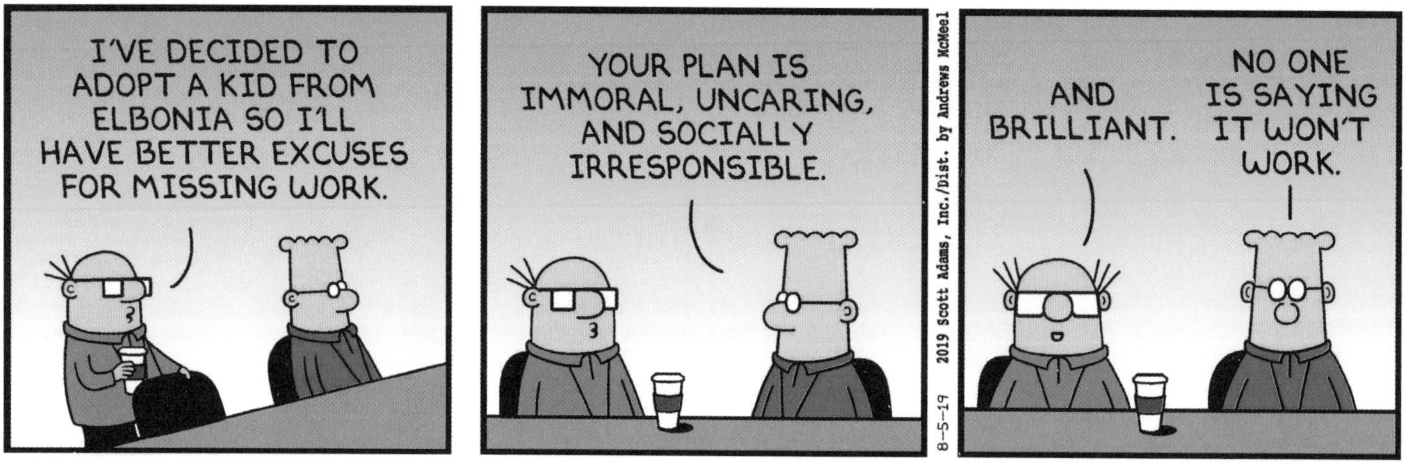
I'VE DECIDED TO ADOPT A KID FROM ELBONIA SO I'LL HAVE BETTER EXCUSES FOR MISSING WORK.
YOUR PLAN IS IMMORAL, UNCARING, AND SOCIALLY IRRESPONSIBLE.
AND BRILLIANT.
NO ONE IS SAYING IT WON'T WORK.
8-5-19 2019 Scott Adams, Inc./Dist. by Andrews McMeel

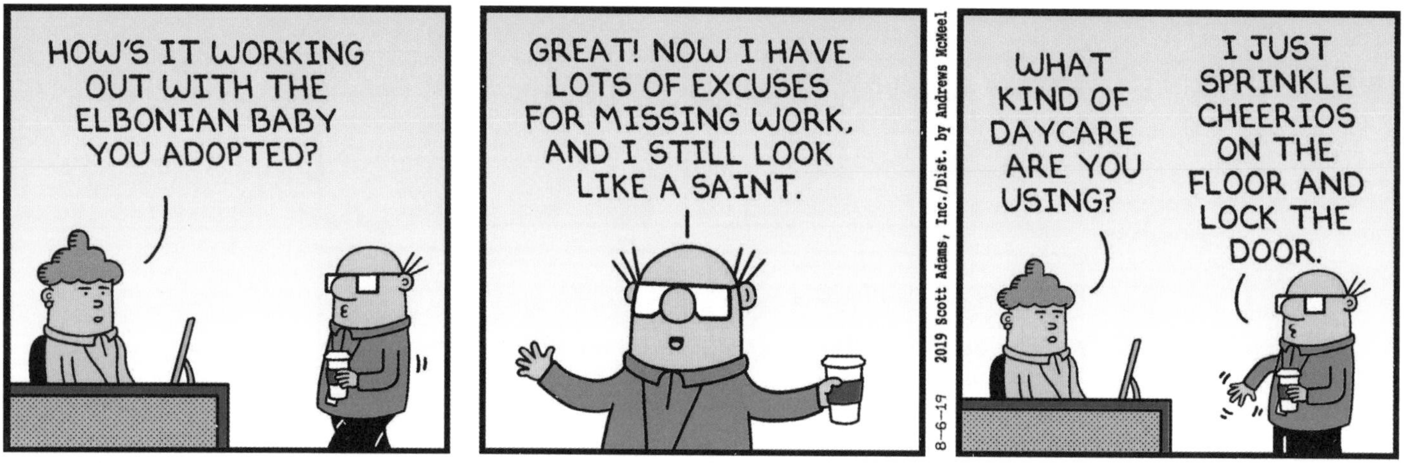
HOW'S IT WORKING OUT WITH THE ELBONIAN BABY YOU ADOPTED?
GREAT! NOW I HAVE LOTS OF EXCUSES FOR MISSING WORK, AND I STILL LOOK LIKE A SAINT.
WHAT KIND OF DAYCARE ARE YOU USING?
I JUST SPRINKLE CHEERIOS ON THE FLOOR AND LOCK THE DOOR.
8-6-19 2019 Scott Adams, Inc./Dist. by Andrews McMeel

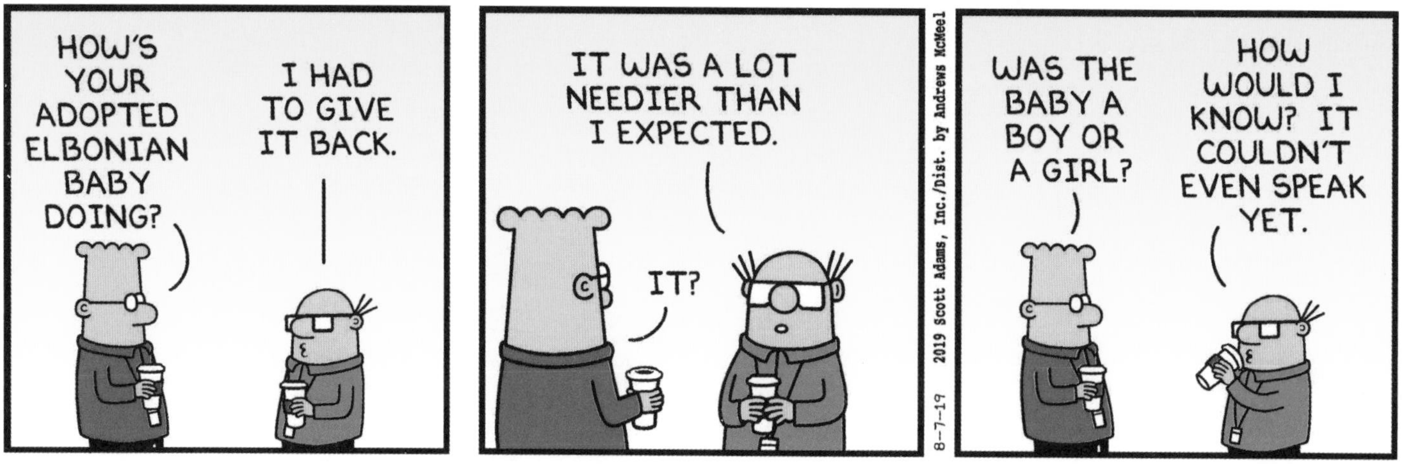
HOW'S YOUR ADOPTED ELBONIAN BABY DOING?
I HAD TO GIVE IT BACK.
IT WAS A LOT NEEDIER THAN I EXPECTED.
IT?
WAS THE BABY A BOY OR A GIRL?
HOW WOULD I KNOW? IT COULDN'T EVEN SPEAK YET.
8-7-19 2019 Scott Adams, Inc./Dist. by Andrews McMeel

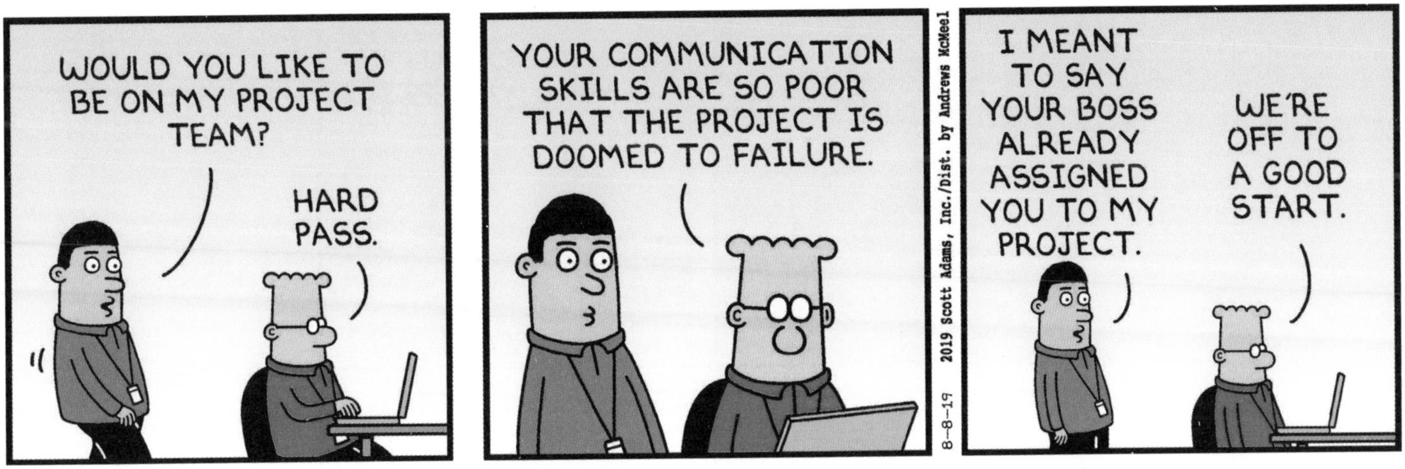
WOULD YOU LIKE TO BE ON MY PROJECT TEAM?
HARD PASS.
YOUR COMMUNICATION SKILLS ARE SO POOR THAT THE PROJECT IS DOOMED TO FAILURE.
8-8-19 2019 Scott Adams, Inc./Dist. by Andrews McMeel
I MEANT TO SAY YOUR BOSS ALREADY ASSIGNED YOU TO MY PROJECT.
WE'RE OFF TO A GOOD START.

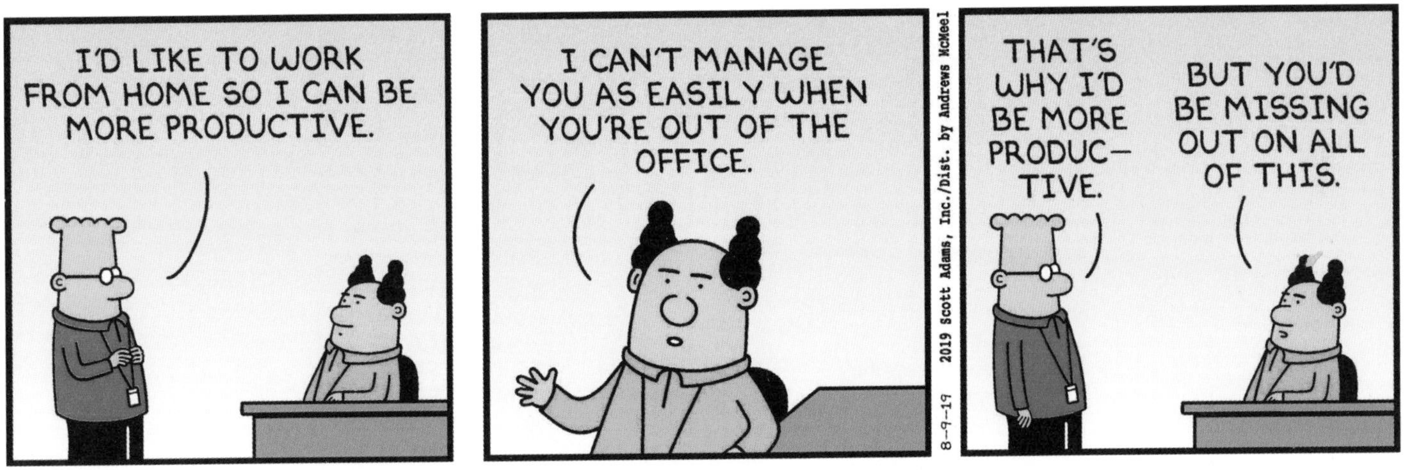
I'D LIKE TO WORK FROM HOME SO I CAN BE MORE PRODUCTIVE.
I CAN'T MANAGE YOU AS EASILY WHEN YOU'RE OUT OF THE OFFICE.
8-9-19 2019 Scott Adams, Inc./Dist. by Andrews McMeel
THAT'S WHY I'D BE MORE PRODUC-TIVE.
BUT YOU'D BE MISSING OUT ON ALL OF THIS.

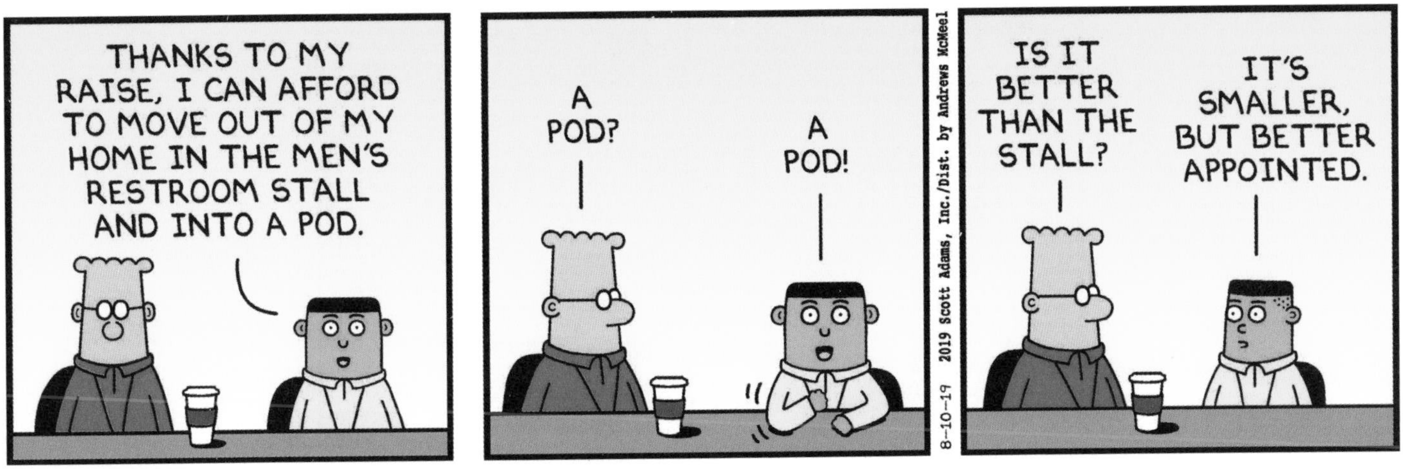
THANKS TO MY RAISE, I CAN AFFORD TO MOVE OUT OF MY HOME IN THE MEN'S RESTROOM STALL AND INTO A POD.
A POD?
A POD!
8-10-19 2019 Scott Adams, Inc./Dist. by Andrews McMeel
IS IT BETTER THAN THE STALL?
IT'S SMALLER, BUT BETTER APPOINTED.

ARE YOU ENJOYING YOUR NEW CUBICLES?
MY OLD CUBICLE HAD A WINDOW VIEW.
MY NEW CUBICLE IS IN A WINDOWLESS ROOM WITH GRAY WALLS.
IT'S ALWAYS TOO COLD, AND I'M SURROUNDED BY NOISY PEOPLE I DISLIKE.
I FEEL ANXIOUS, UNHEALTHY, AND DEPRESSED ALL DAY LONG.
THANKS TO THE OFFICE RELOCATION, MY LIFE HAS BECOME A RAPID DESCENT INTO MADNESS.
ON THE PLUS SIDE, WE SAVED FIVE PERCENT ON RENT.
NO ONE EVER LIKES TO HEAR ABOUT THE PLUS SIDE.
©2019 Scott Adams, Inc./Dist. by Andrews McMeel
8-11-19

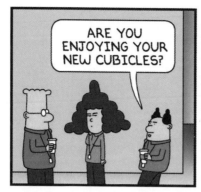

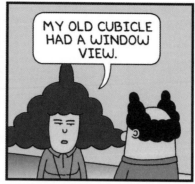

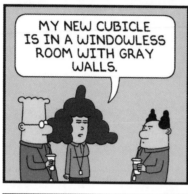

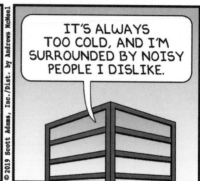

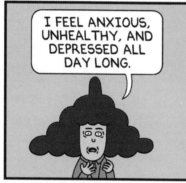

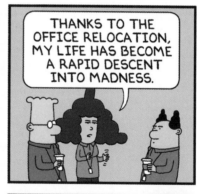

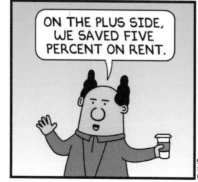

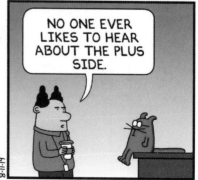

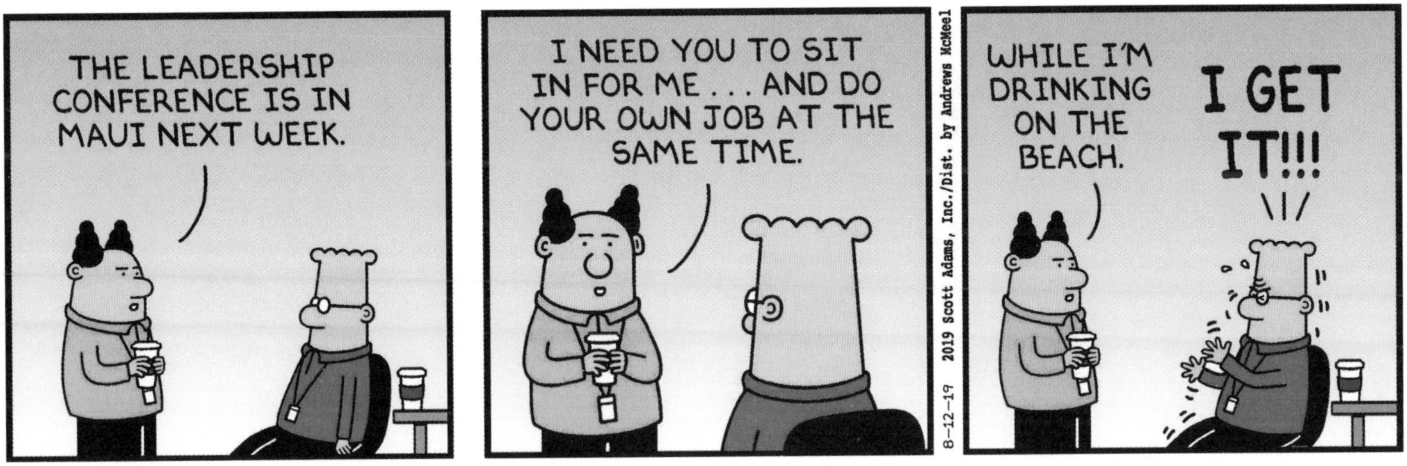
THE LEADERSHIP CONFERENCE IS IN MAUI NEXT WEEK.
I NEED YOU TO SIT IN FOR ME . . . AND DO YOUR OWN JOB AT THE SAME TIME.
8-12-19 © 2019 Scott Adams, Inc./Dist. by Andrews McMeel
WHILE I'M DRINKING ON THE BEACH.
I GET IT!!!

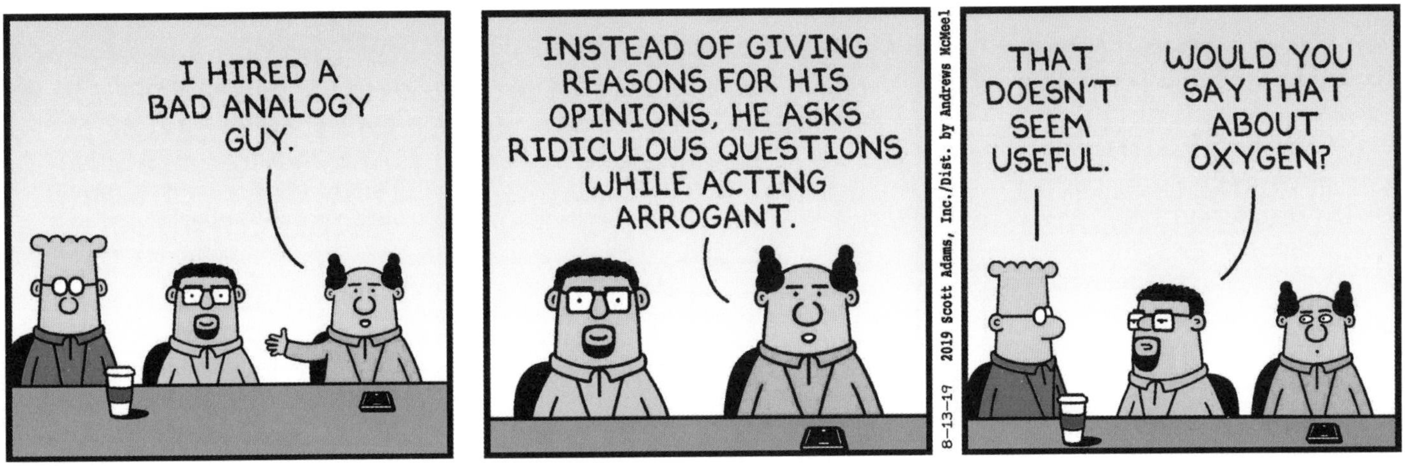
I HIRED A BAD ANALOGY GUY.
INSTEAD OF GIVING REASONS FOR HIS OPINIONS, HE ASKS RIDICULOUS QUESTIONS WHILE ACTING ARROGANT.
8-13-19 © 2019 Scott Adams, Inc./Dist. by Andrews McMeel
THAT DOESN'T SEEM USEFUL.
WOULD YOU SAY THAT ABOUT OXYGEN?

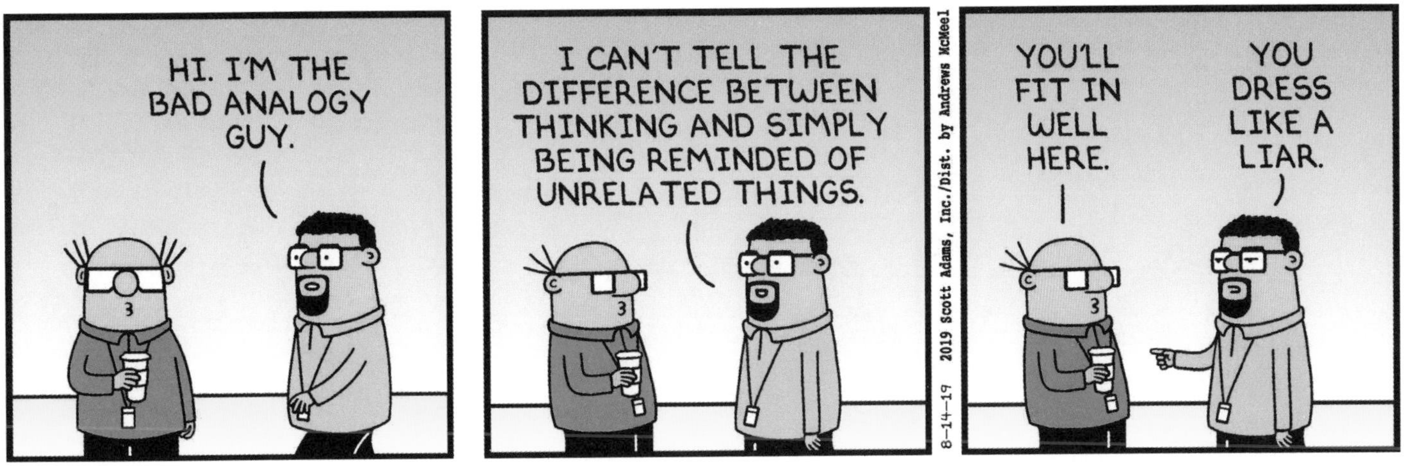
HI. I'M THE BAD ANALOGY GUY.
I CAN'T TELL THE DIFFERENCE BETWEEN THINKING AND SIMPLY BEING REMINDED OF UNRELATED THINGS.
8-14-19 © 2019 Scott Adams, Inc./Dist. by Andrews McMeel
YOU'LL FIT IN WELL HERE.
YOU DRESS LIKE A LIAR.

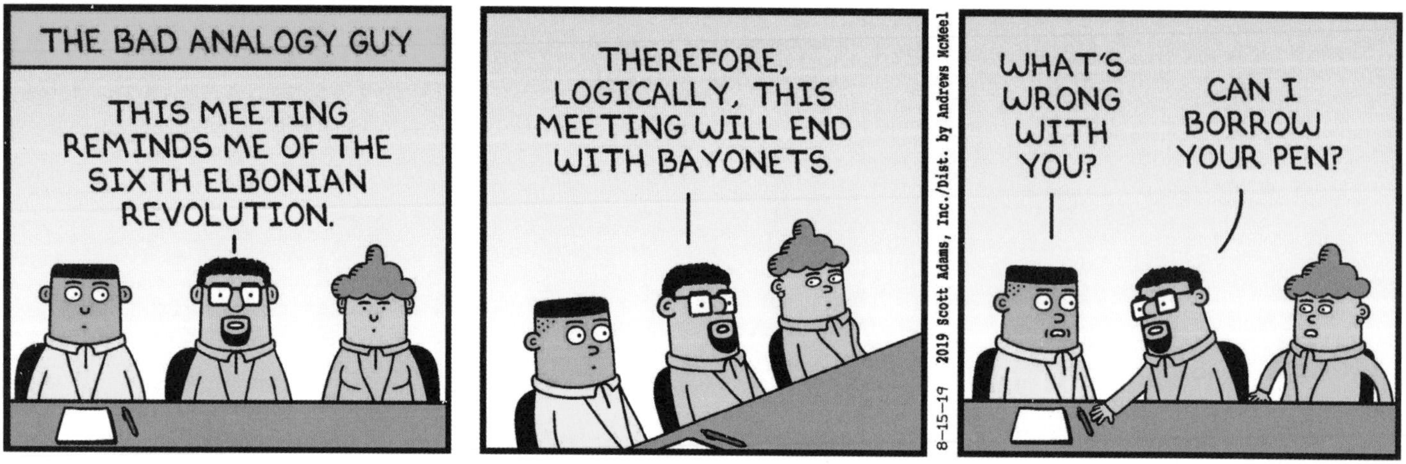
THE BAD ANALOGY GUY
THIS MEETING REMINDS ME OF THE SIXTH ELBONIAN REVOLUTION.
THEREFORE, LOGICALLY, THIS MEETING WILL END WITH BAYONETS.
8-15-19 2019 Scott Adams, Inc./Dist. by Andrews McMeel
WHAT'S WRONG WITH YOU?
CAN I BORROW YOUR PEN?

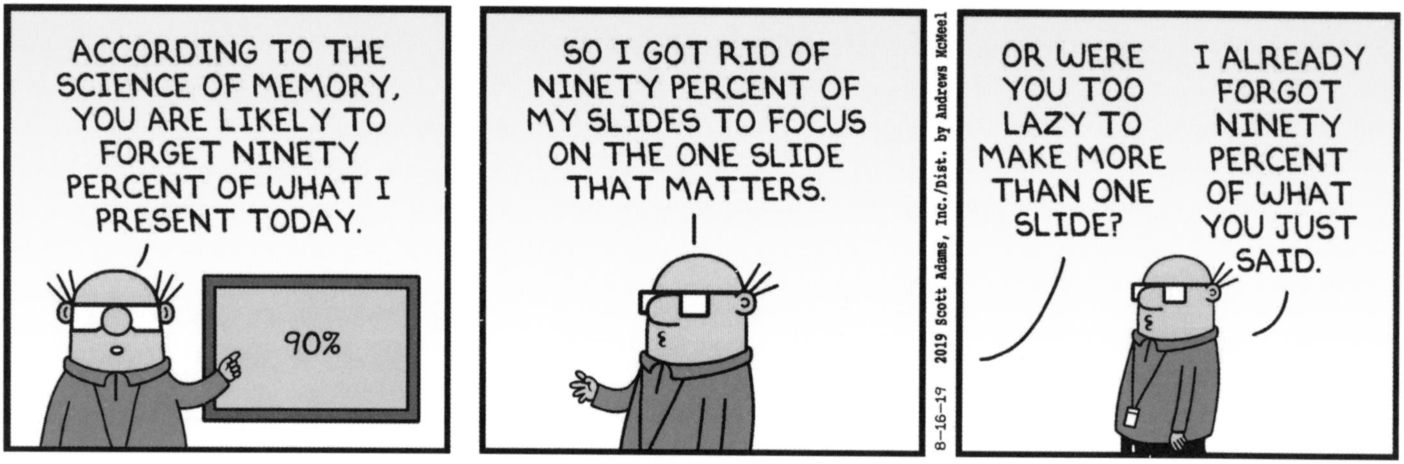
ACCORDING TO THE SCIENCE OF MEMORY, YOU ARE LIKELY TO FORGET NINETY PERCENT OF WHAT I PRESENT TODAY.
90%
SO I GOT RID OF NINETY PERCENT OF MY SLIDES TO FOCUS ON THE ONE SLIDE THAT MATTERS.
8-16-19 2019 Scott Adams, Inc./Dist. by Andrews McMeel
OR WERE YOU TOO LAZY TO MAKE MORE THAN ONE SLIDE?
I ALREADY FORGOT NINETY PERCENT OF WHAT YOU JUST SAID.

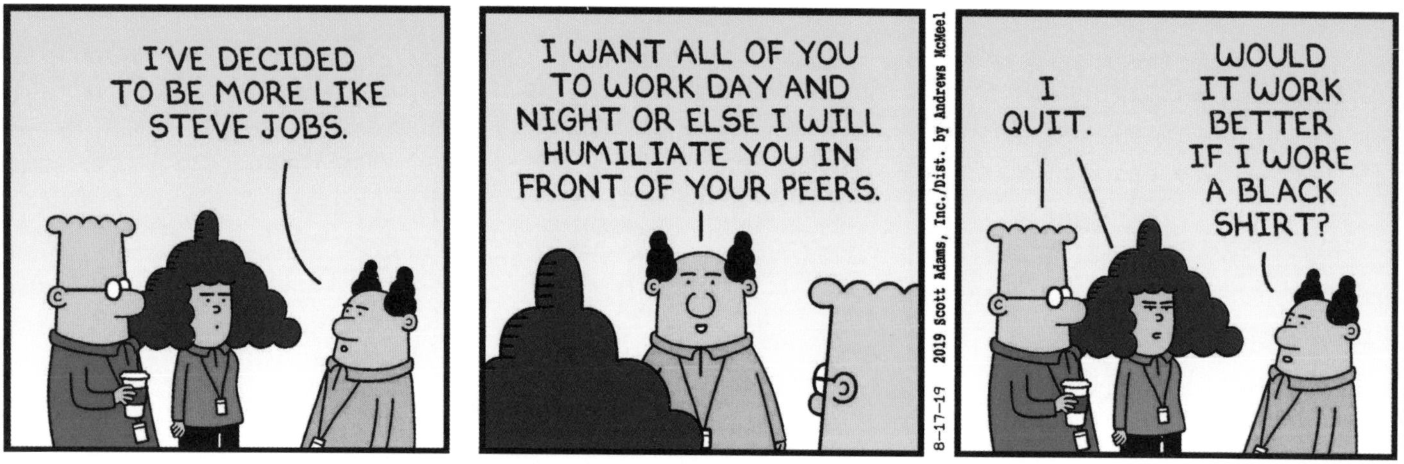
I'VE DECIDED TO BE MORE LIKE STEVE JOBS.
I WANT ALL OF YOU TO WORK DAY AND NIGHT OR ELSE I WILL HUMILIATE YOU IN FRONT OF YOUR PEERS.
8-17-19 2019 Scott Adams, Inc./Dist. by Andrews McMeel
I QUIT.
WOULD IT WORK BETTER IF I WORE A BLACK SHIRT?

WOULD YOU PLEASE STOP HUMMING? IT'S MAKING ME CRAZY.
HUM. . .
I CAN'T FOCUS UNLESS I HUM.
BUT I CAN'T FOCUS WHEN YOU DO HUM.
I'M GOING TO TALK TO YOUR BOSS.
I'M GOING TO TALK TO YOUR BOSS!
HUM, HUM, HUM.
GAAA!!!
I CAN'T WORK WHEN SHE HUMS.
HUMMING HELPS ME WORK BETTER.
I RULE IN FAVOR OF THE HUMMER, AND I SENTENCE DILBERT TO TAKE A SENSITIVITY TRAINING CLASS TO BE LESS OF A JERK.
I HATE YOU.
HUM, HUM, HUM.
© 2019 Scott Adams, Inc./Dist. by Andrews McMeel
8-18-19

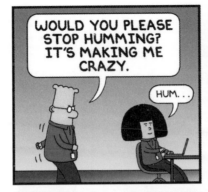

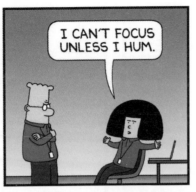

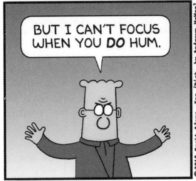

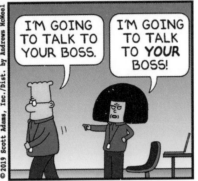

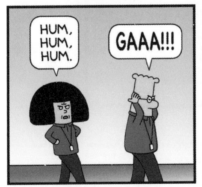

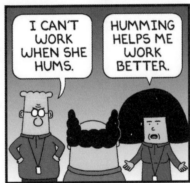

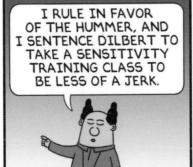

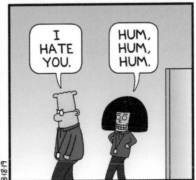

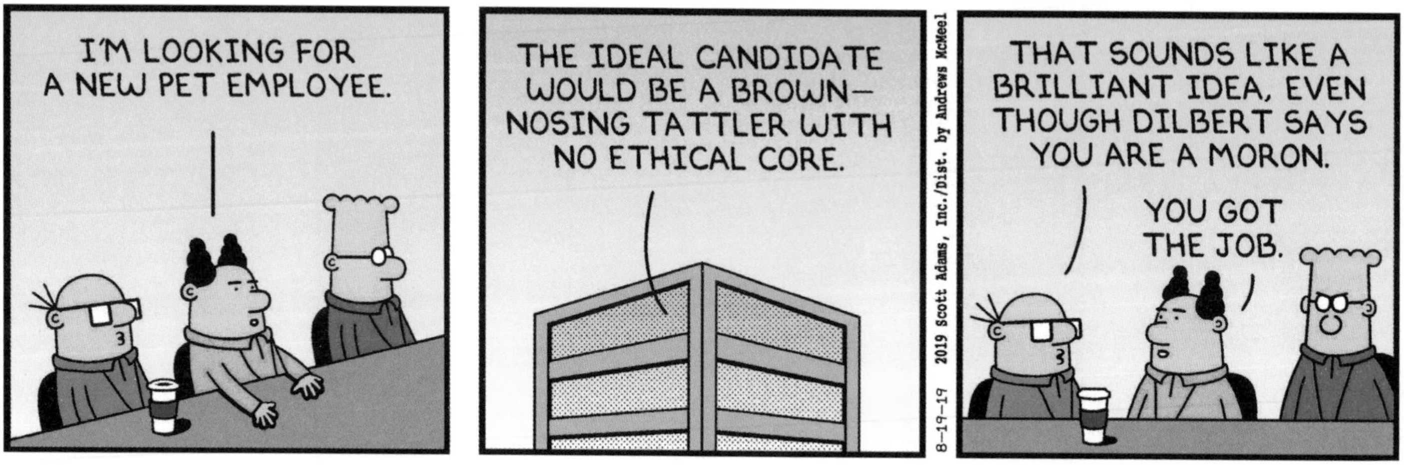
I'M LOOKING FOR A NEW PET EMPLOYEE.
THE IDEAL CANDIDATE WOULD BE A BROWN-NOSING TATTLER WITH NO ETHICAL CORE.
THAT SOUNDS LIKE A BRILLIANT IDEA, EVEN THOUGH DILBERT SAYS YOU ARE A MORON.
YOU GOT THE JOB.
8-19-19 © 2019 Scott Adams, Inc./Dist. by Andrews McMeel

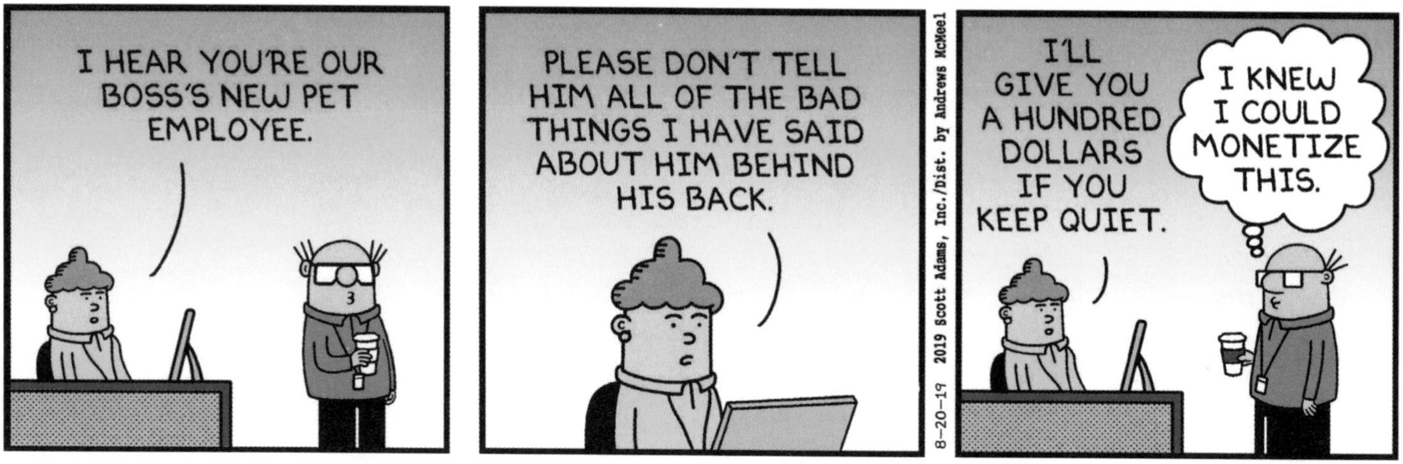
I HEAR YOU'RE OUR BOSS'S NEW PET EMPLOYEE.
PLEASE DON'T TELL HIM ALL OF THE BAD THINGS I HAVE SAID ABOUT HIM BEHIND HIS BACK.
I'LL GIVE YOU A HUNDRED DOLLARS IF YOU KEEP QUIET.
I KNEW I COULD MONETIZE THIS.
8-20-19 © 2019 Scott Adams, Inc./Dist. by Andrews McMeel

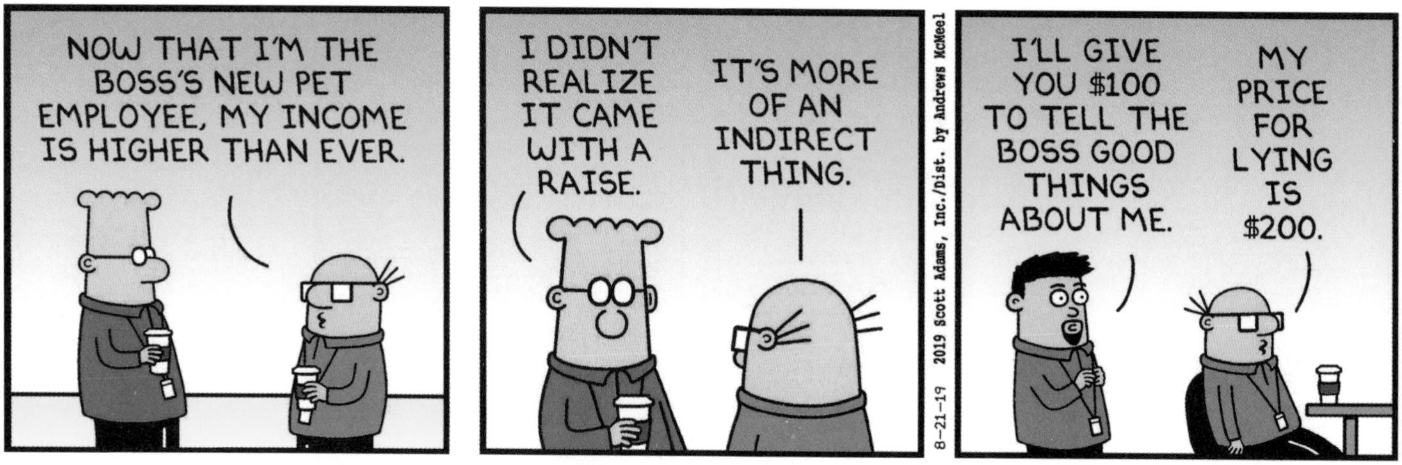
NOW THAT I'M THE BOSS'S NEW PET EMPLOYEE, MY INCOME IS HIGHER THAN EVER.
I DIDN'T REALIZE IT CAME WITH A RAISE.
IT'S MORE OF AN INDIRECT THING.
I'LL GIVE YOU $100 TO TELL THE BOSS GOOD THINGS ABOUT ME.
MY PRICE FOR LYING IS $200.
8-21-19 © 2019 Scott Adams, Inc./Dist. by Andrews McMeel

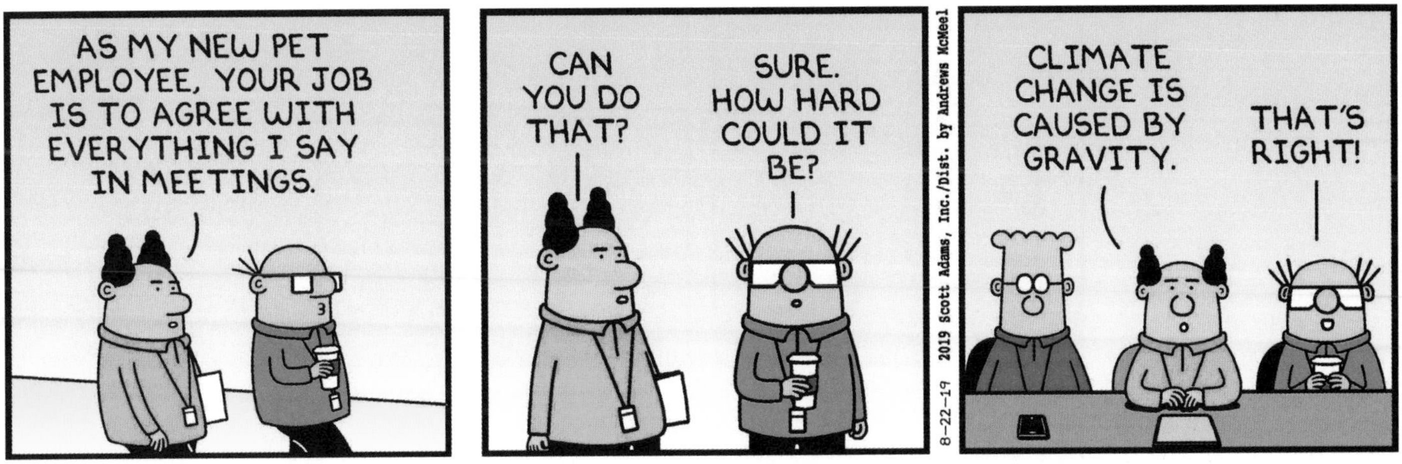
AS MY NEW PET EMPLOYEE, YOUR JOB IS TO AGREE WITH EVERYTHING I SAY IN MEETINGS.
CAN YOU DO THAT?
SURE. HOW HARD COULD IT BE?
8-22-19 2019 Scott Adams, Inc./Dist. by Andrews McMeel
CLIMATE CHANGE IS CAUSED BY GRAVITY.
THAT'S RIGHT!

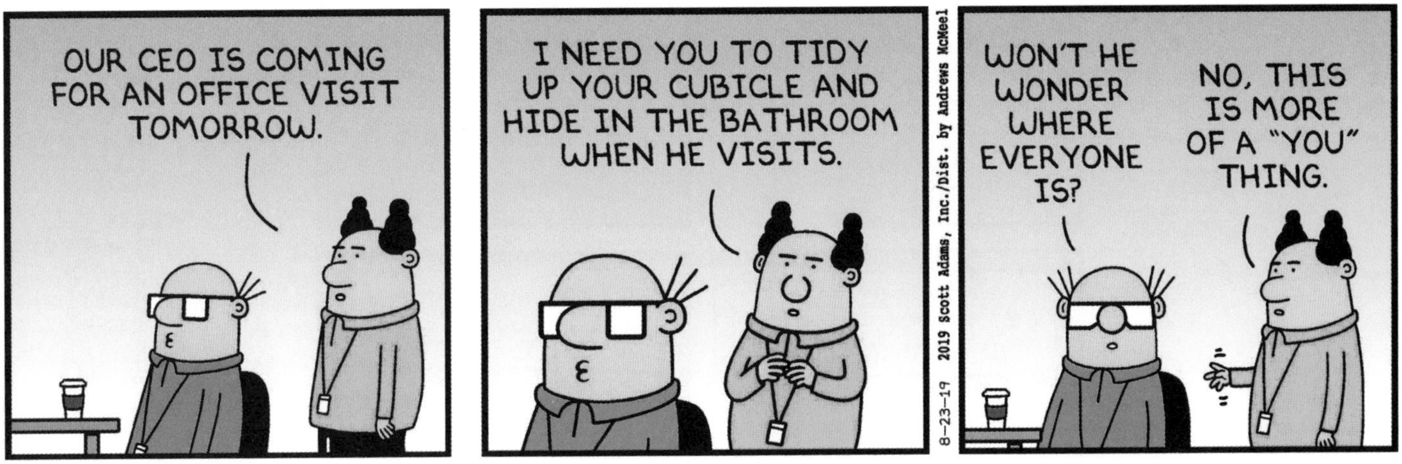
OUR CEO IS COMING FOR AN OFFICE VISIT TOMORROW.
I NEED YOU TO TIDY UP YOUR CUBICLE AND HIDE IN THE BATHROOM WHEN HE VISITS.
8-23-19 2019 Scott Adams, Inc./Dist. by Andrews McMeel
WON'T HE WONDER WHERE EVERYONE IS?
NO, THIS IS MORE OF A "YOU" THING.

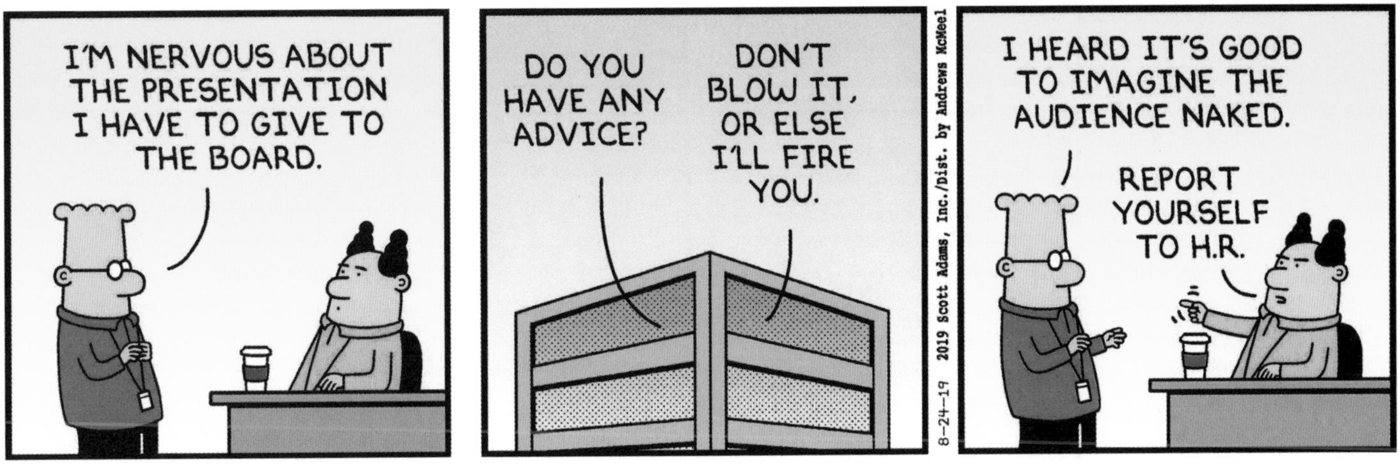
I'M NERVOUS ABOUT THE PRESENTATION I HAVE TO GIVE TO THE BOARD.
DO YOU HAVE ANY ADVICE?
DON'T BLOW IT, OR ELSE I'LL FIRE YOU.
8-24-19 2019 Scott Adams, Inc./Dist. by Andrews McMeel
I HEARD IT'S GOOD TO IMAGINE THE AUDIENCE NAKED.
REPORT YOURSELF TO H.R.

I DECIDED TO TRY MY HAND AT WRITING FICTION.
I LIKE WRITING FICTION BECAUSE IT DOESN'T REQUIRE ANY RESEARCH.
I CAN LITERALLY MAKE UP A STORY OUT OF NOTHING.
I FEEL SORRY FOR NONFICTION WRITERS. THEY HAVE TO GET THE FACTS RIGHT.
BUT A FICTION WRITER ONLY HAS TO USE IMAGINATION.
I CAN MAKE ANY WILD ASSUMPTIONS ABOUT THE FUTURE THAT I WANT.
I ASKED YOU HERE TO TALK ABOUT YOUR BUDGET FORECAST.
THAT'S WHAT I WAS TALKING ABOUT.
© 2019 Scott Adams, Inc./Dist. by Andrews McMeel
8-25-19

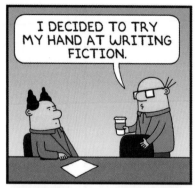

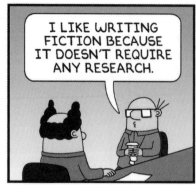

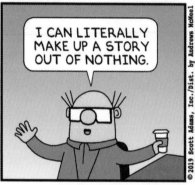

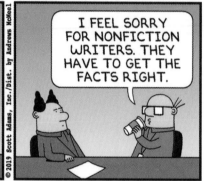

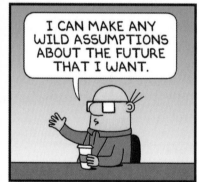

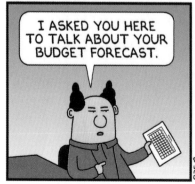

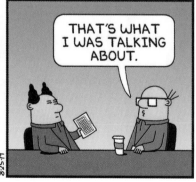

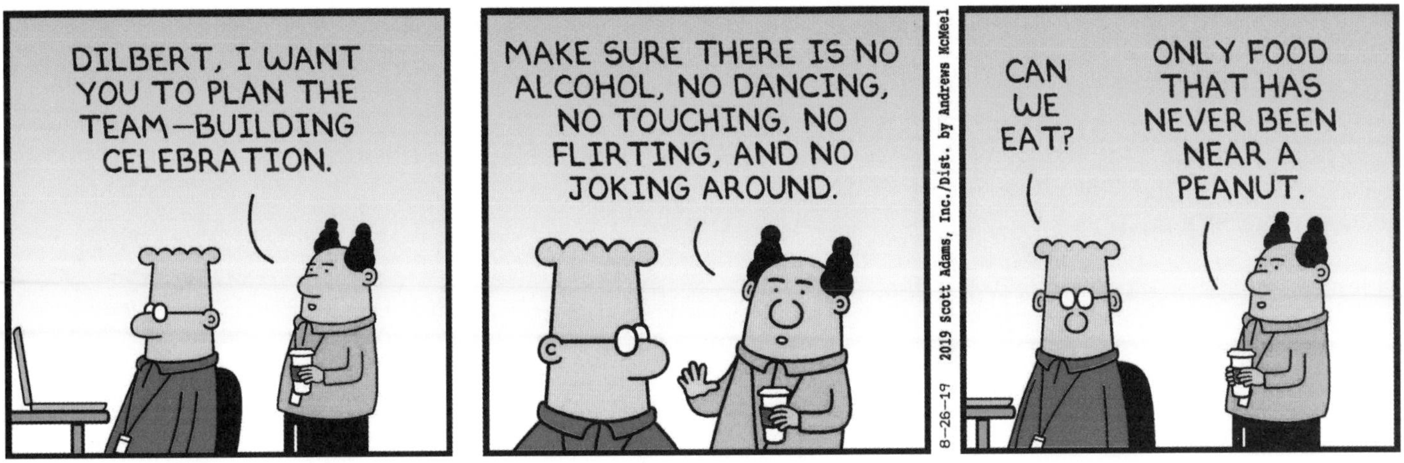
DILBERT, I WANT YOU TO PLAN THE TEAM—BUILDING CELEBRATION.
MAKE SURE THERE IS NO ALCOHOL, NO DANCING, NO TOUCHING, NO FLIRTING, AND NO JOKING AROUND.
8-26-19 © 2019 Scott Adams, Inc./Dist. by Andrews McMeel
CAN WE EAT?
ONLY FOOD THAT HAS NEVER BEEN NEAR A PEANUT.

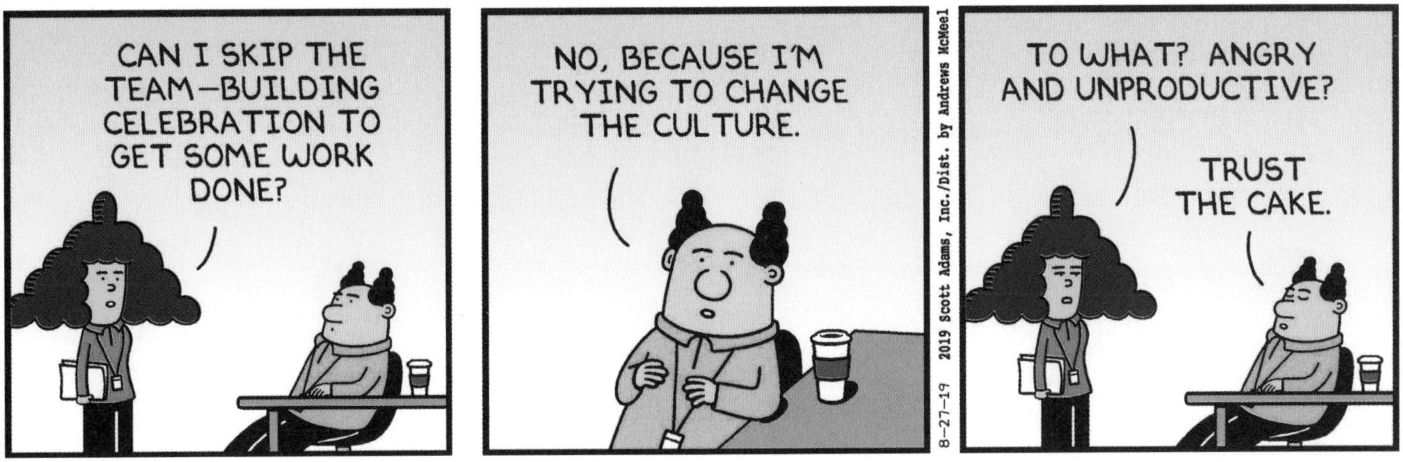
CAN I SKIP THE TEAM—BUILDING CELEBRATION TO GET SOME WORK DONE?
NO, BECAUSE I'M TRYING TO CHANGE THE CULTURE.
8-27-19 © 2019 Scott Adams, Inc./Dist. by Andrews McMeel
TO WHAT? ANGRY AND UNPRODUCTIVE?
TRUST THE CAKE.

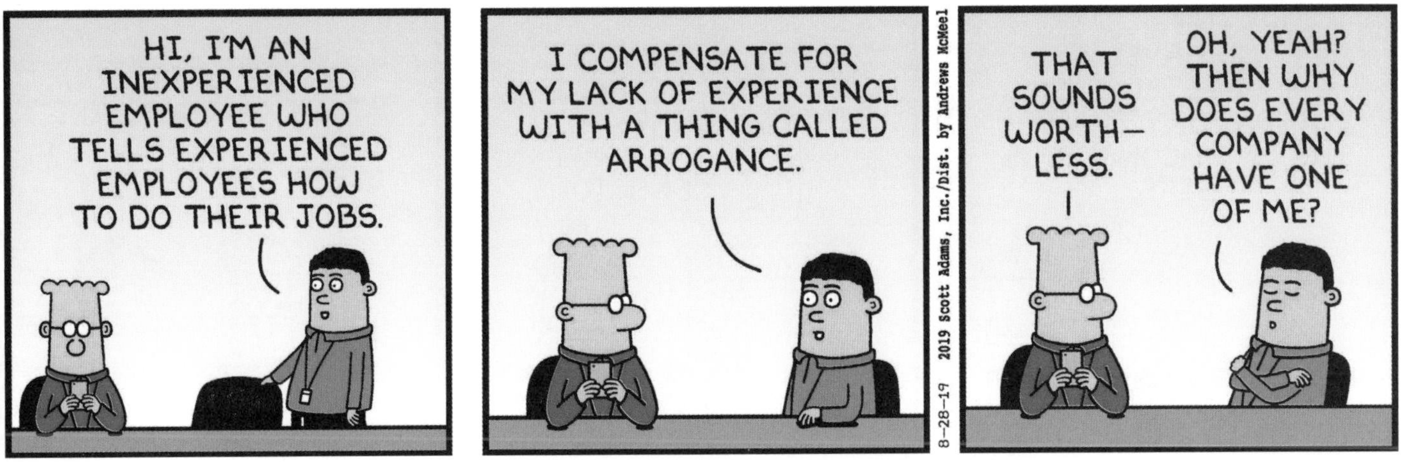
HI, I'M AN INEXPERIENCED EMPLOYEE WHO TELLS EXPERIENCED EMPLOYEES HOW TO DO THEIR JOBS.
I COMPENSATE FOR MY LACK OF EXPERIENCE WITH A THING CALLED ARROGANCE.
8-28-19 © 2019 Scott Adams, Inc./Dist. by Andrews McMeel
THAT SOUNDS WORTH— LESS.
OH, YEAH? THEN WHY DOES EVERY COMPANY HAVE ONE OF ME?

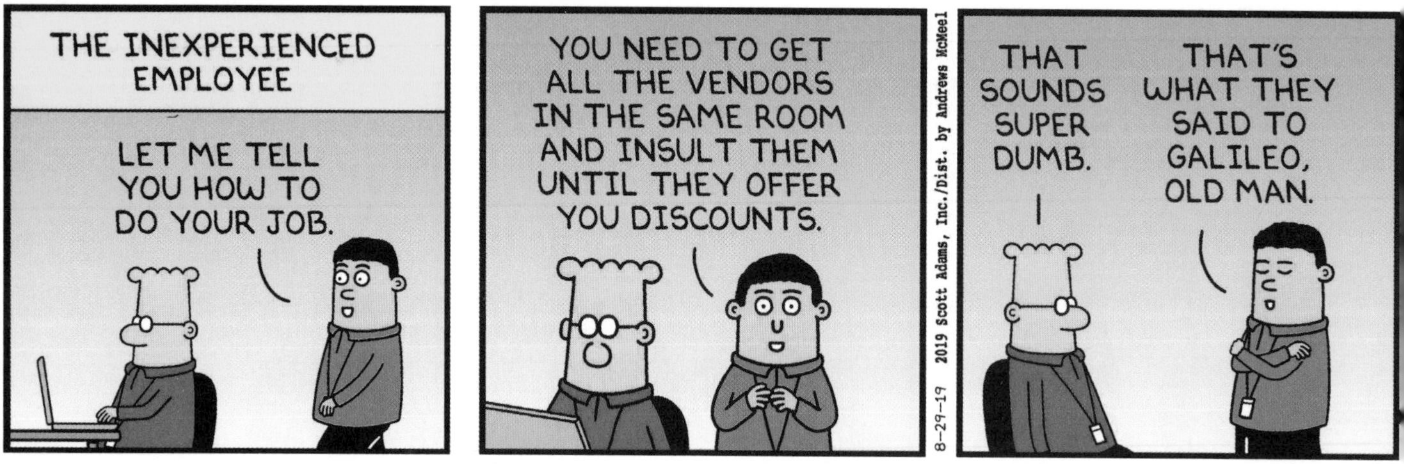
THE INEXPERIENCED EMPLOYEE
LET ME TELL YOU HOW TO DO YOUR JOB.
YOU NEED TO GET ALL THE VENDORS IN THE SAME ROOM AND INSULT THEM UNTIL THEY OFFER YOU DISCOUNTS.
THAT SOUNDS SUPER DUMB.
THAT'S WHAT THEY SAID TO GALILEO, OLD MAN.
8-29-19 2019 Scott Adams, Inc./Dist. by Andrews McMeel

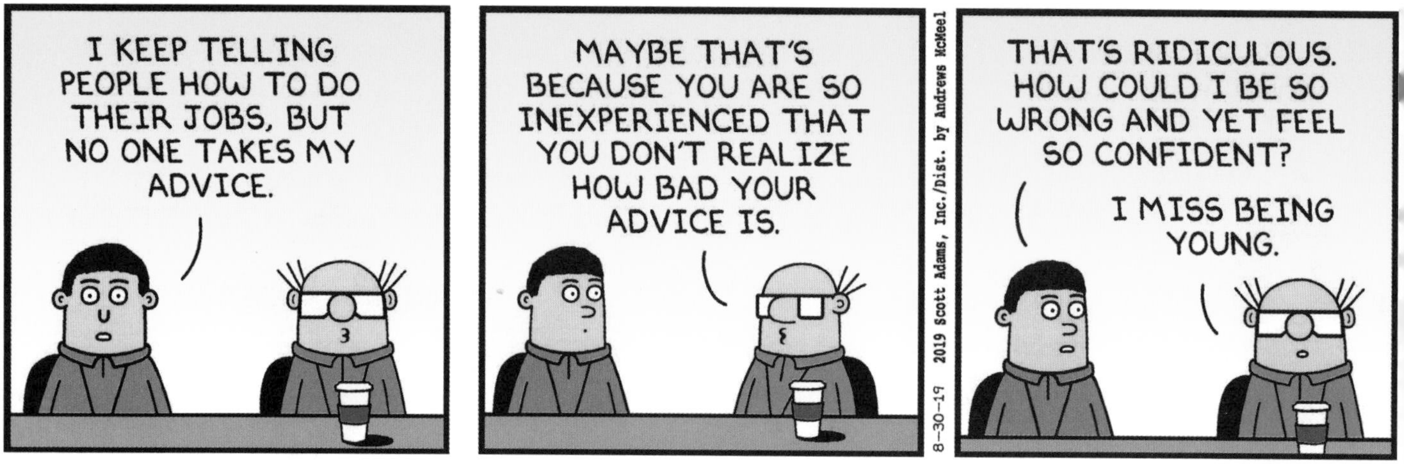
I KEEP TELLING PEOPLE HOW TO DO THEIR JOBS, BUT NO ONE TAKES MY ADVICE.
MAYBE THAT'S BECAUSE YOU ARE SO INEXPERIENCED THAT YOU DON'T REALIZE HOW BAD YOUR ADVICE IS.
THAT'S RIDICULOUS. HOW COULD I BE SO WRONG AND YET FEEL SO CONFIDENT?
I MISS BEING YOUNG.
8-30-19 2019 Scott Adams, Inc./Dist. by Andrews McMeel

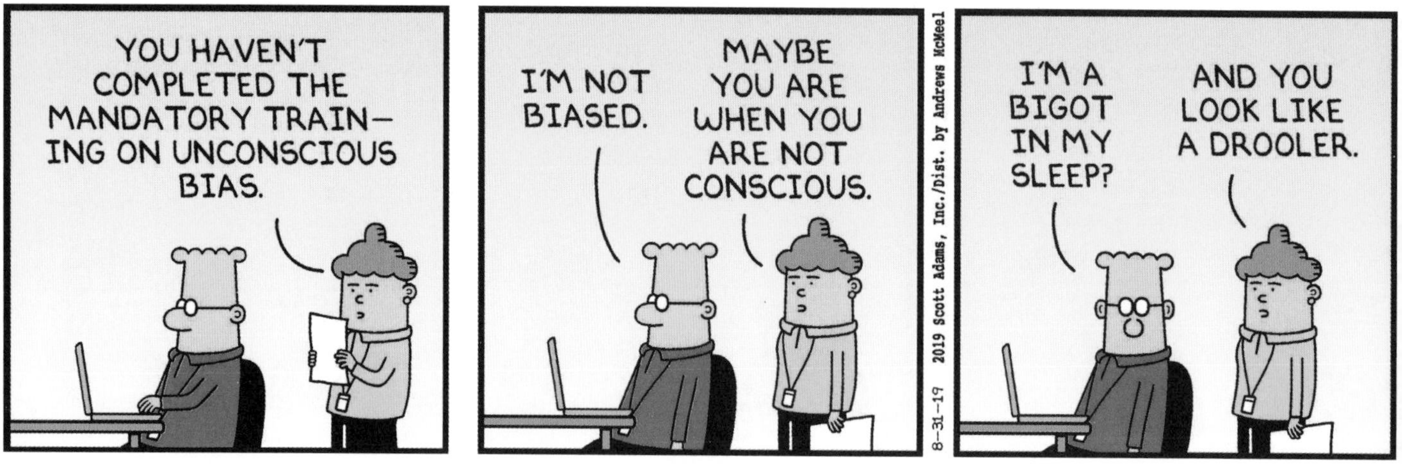
YOU HAVEN'T COMPLETED THE MANDATORY TRAIN-ING ON UNCONSCIOUS BIAS.
I'M NOT BIASED.
MAYBE YOU ARE WHEN YOU ARE NOT CONSCIOUS.
I'M A BIGOT IN MY SLEEP?
AND YOU LOOK LIKE A DROOLER.
8-31-19 2019 Scott Adams, Inc./Dist. by Andrews McMeel

RUN THIS BY TINA BEFORE YOU SEND IT OUT.
I ALREADY DID.
MAKE SURE LEGAL SIGNS OFF ON IT.
THEY DID.
ADD THE REVENUE GRAPH FROM ALICE'S SLIDE DECK.
IT'S IN THE EXHIBITS IN THE BACK.
YOU NEED TO COMPARE THIS PLAN TO THE "DO NOTHING" OPTION.
THAT'S ON THE NEXT PAGE.
I NEED YOU TO CHANGE SOMETHING ON THIS DOCUMENT SO MY LIFE HAS MEANING.
I PUT A MISSPELLED WORD ON PAGE SEVEN FOR YOU.
FIX IT.
9-1-19

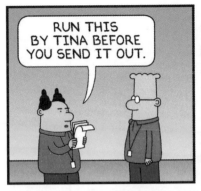

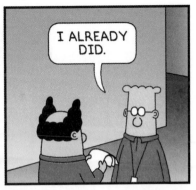

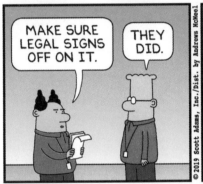

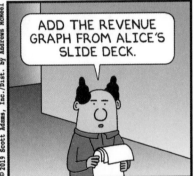

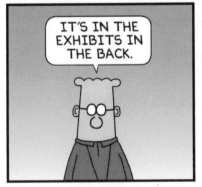

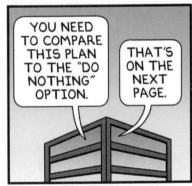

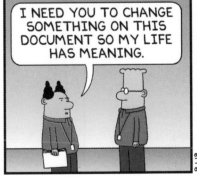

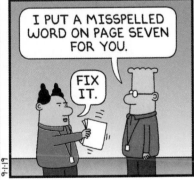

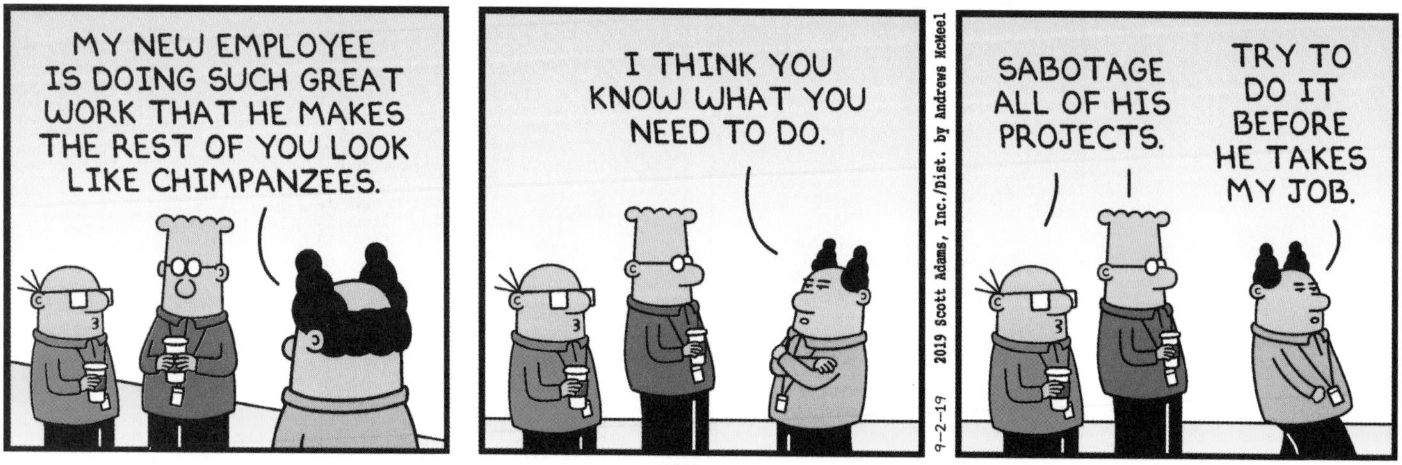
MY NEW EMPLOYEE IS DOING SUCH GREAT WORK THAT HE MAKES THE REST OF YOU LOOK LIKE CHIMPANZEES.
I THINK YOU KNOW WHAT YOU NEED TO DO.
9-2-19 2019 Scott Adams, Inc./Dist. by Andrews McMeel
SABOTAGE ALL OF HIS PROJECTS.
TRY TO DO IT BEFORE HE TAKES MY JOB.

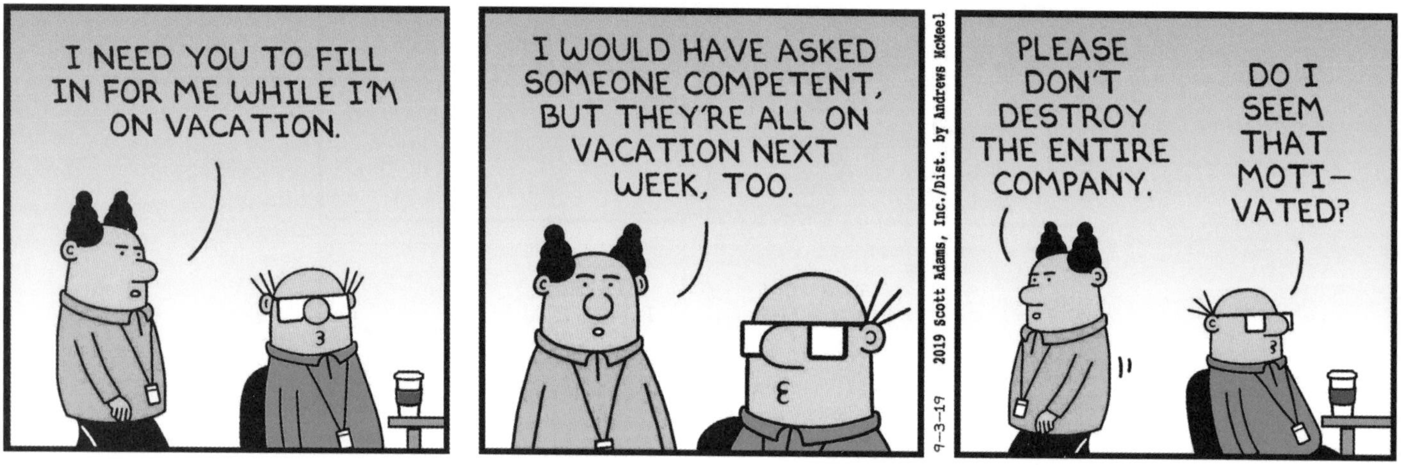
I NEED YOU TO FILL IN FOR ME WHILE I'M ON VACATION.
I WOULD HAVE ASKED SOMEONE COMPETENT, BUT THEY'RE ALL ON VACATION NEXT WEEK, TOO.
9-3-19 2019 Scott Adams, Inc./Dist. by Andrews McMeel
PLEASE DON'T DESTROY THE ENTIRE COMPANY.
DO I SEEM THAT MOTI-VATED?

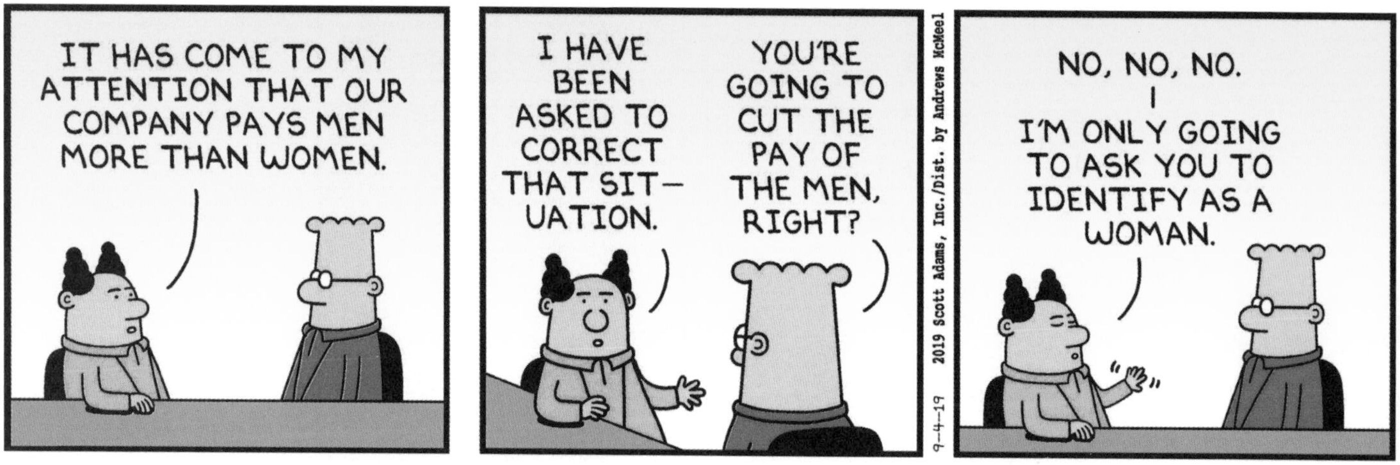
IT HAS COME TO MY ATTENTION THAT OUR COMPANY PAYS MEN MORE THAN WOMEN.
I HAVE BEEN ASKED TO CORRECT THAT SIT-UATION.
YOU'RE GOING TO CUT THE PAY OF THE MEN, RIGHT?
9-4-19 2019 Scott Adams, Inc./Dist. by Andrews McMeel
NO, NO, NO.
I'M ONLY GOING TO ASK YOU TO IDENTIFY AS A WOMAN.

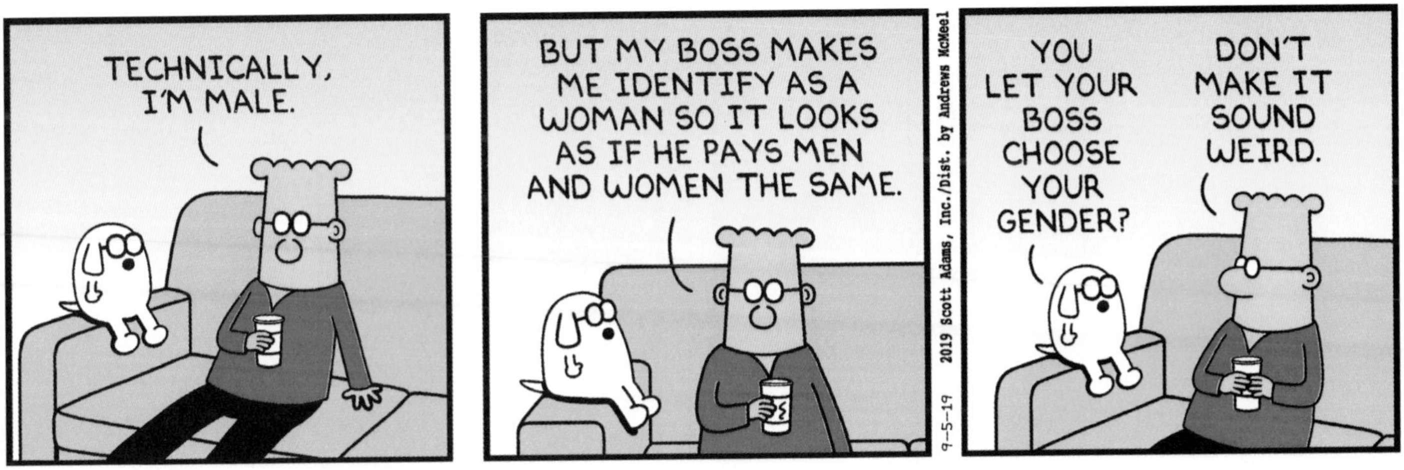
TECHNICALLY, I'M MALE.
BUT MY BOSS MAKES ME IDENTIFY AS A WOMAN SO IT LOOKS AS IF HE PAYS MEN AND WOMEN THE SAME.
YOU LET YOUR BOSS CHOOSE YOUR GENDER?
DON'T MAKE IT SOUND WEIRD.
9-5-19 © 2019 Scott Adams, Inc./Dist. by Andrews McMeel

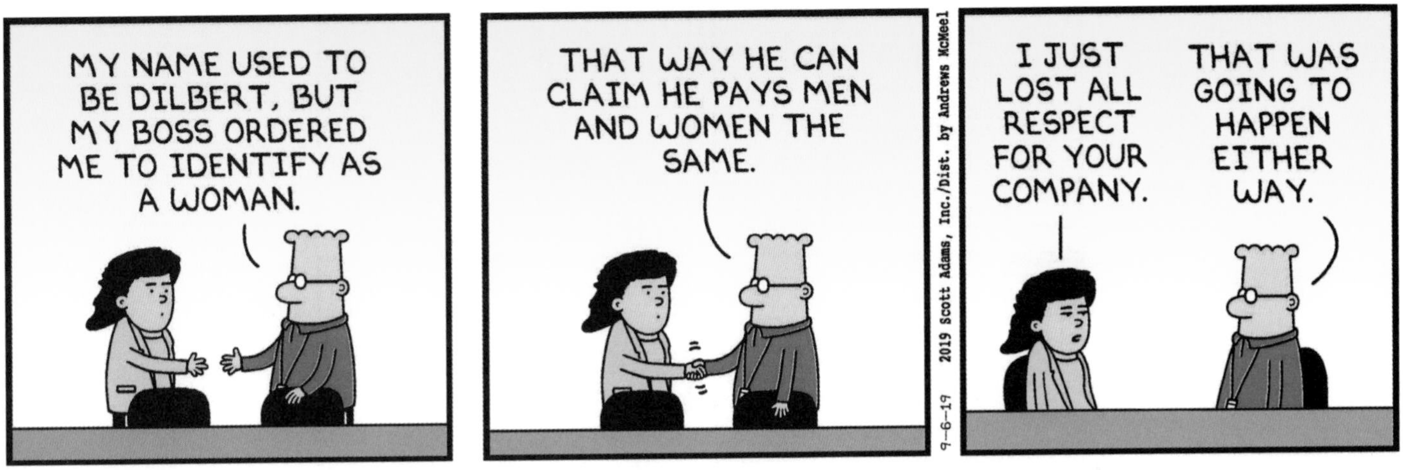
MY NAME USED TO BE DILBERT, BUT MY BOSS ORDERED ME TO IDENTIFY AS A WOMAN.
THAT WAY HE CAN CLAIM HE PAYS MEN AND WOMEN THE SAME.
I JUST LOST ALL RESPECT FOR YOUR COMPANY.
THAT WAS GOING TO HAPPEN EITHER WAY.
9-6-19 © 2019 Scott Adams, Inc./Dist. by Andrews McMeel

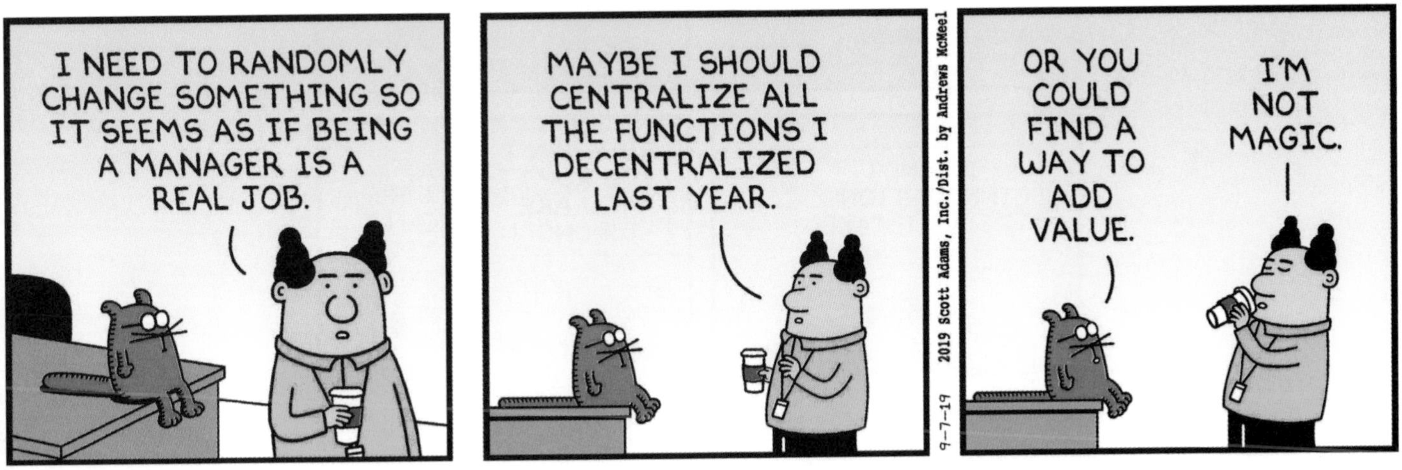
I NEED TO RANDOMLY CHANGE SOMETHING SO IT SEEMS AS IF BEING A MANAGER IS A REAL JOB.
MAYBE I SHOULD CENTRALIZE ALL THE FUNCTIONS I DECENTRALIZED LAST YEAR.
OR YOU COULD FIND A WAY TO ADD VALUE.
I'M NOT MAGIC.
9-7-19 © 2019 Scott Adams, Inc./Dist. by Andrews McMeel

YOU SPELLED "CRYPTO" WRONG.
NO, I DIDN'T.
YOU SPELLED IT "C—R—I—P—T—O."
SO?
THERE IS NO "I" IN CRYPTO.
THAT'S HOW I LEARNED TO SPELL IT.
YOU LEARNED IT WRONG. NO ONE ELSE SPELLS IT THAT WAY.
NOW YOU'RE CRITICIZING ME FOR BEING AN INNOVATOR?
IT'S NOT INNOVATION! IT'S A MISTAKE!
WHY CAN'T YOU ADMIT YOU ARE WRONG?!
WHY CAN'T YOU?
© 2019 Scott Adams, Inc./Dist. by Andrews McMeel
9·8·19

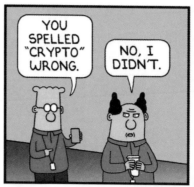

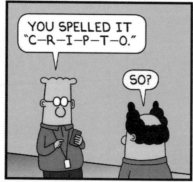

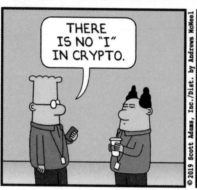

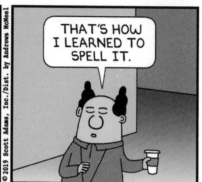

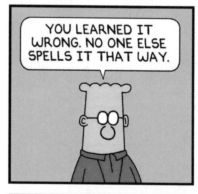

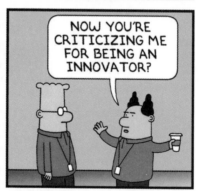

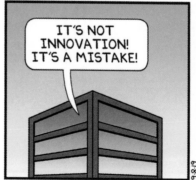

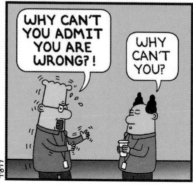

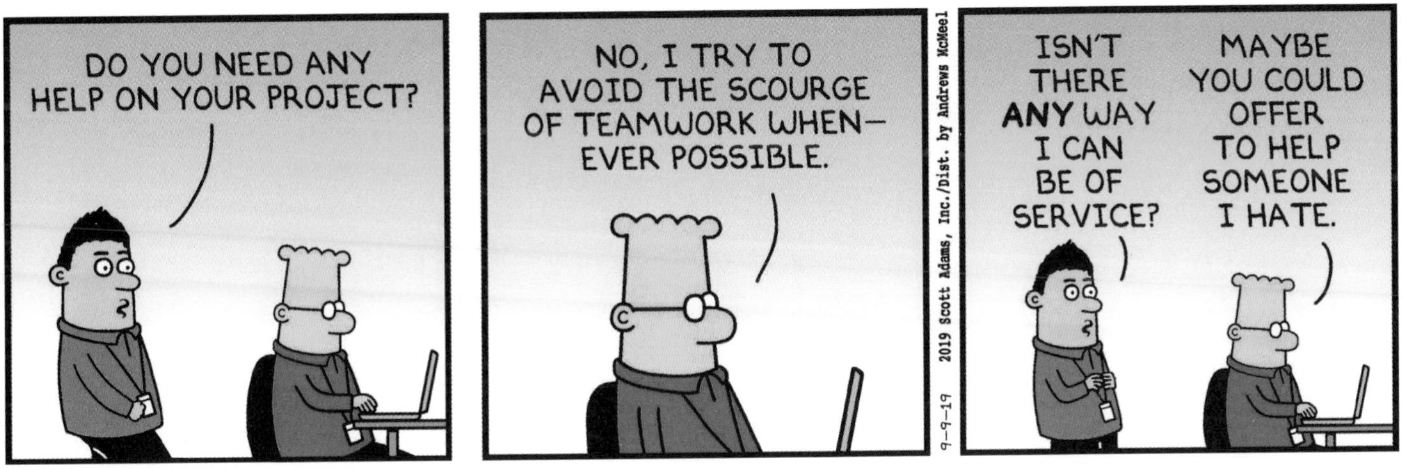
DO YOU NEED ANY HELP ON YOUR PROJECT?
NO, I TRY TO AVOID THE SCOURGE OF TEAMWORK WHEN-EVER POSSIBLE.
9-9-19 © 2019 Scott Adams, Inc./Dist. by Andrews McMeel
ISN'T THERE **ANY** WAY I CAN BE OF SERVICE?
MAYBE YOU COULD OFFER TO HELP SOMEONE I HATE.

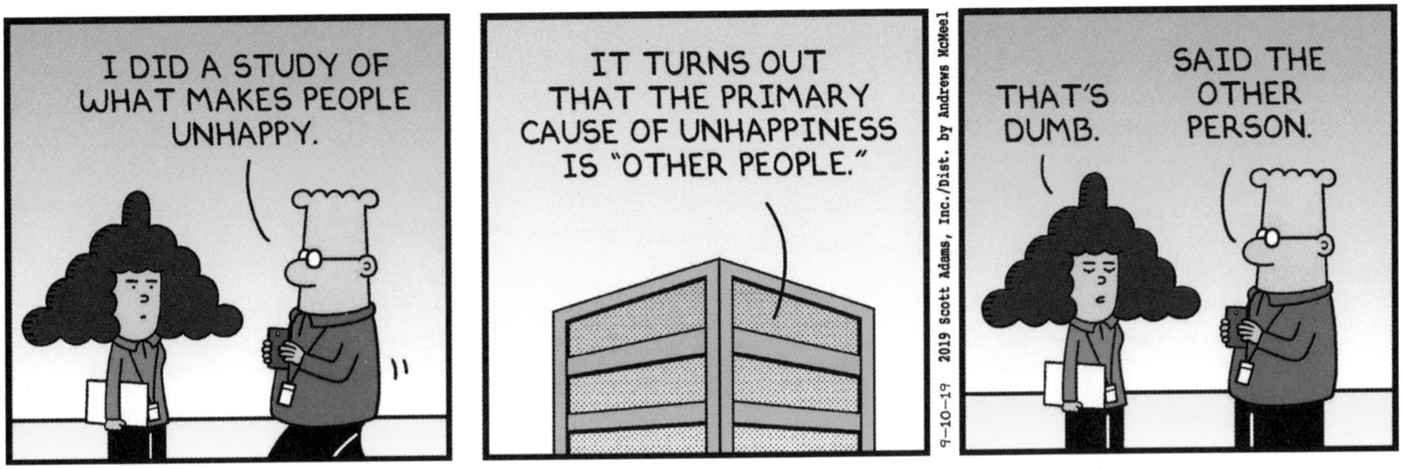
I DID A STUDY OF WHAT MAKES PEOPLE UNHAPPY.
IT TURNS OUT THAT THE PRIMARY CAUSE OF UNHAPPINESS IS "OTHER PEOPLE."
9-10-19 © 2019 Scott Adams, Inc./Dist. by Andrews McMeel
THAT'S DUMB.
SAID THE OTHER PERSON.

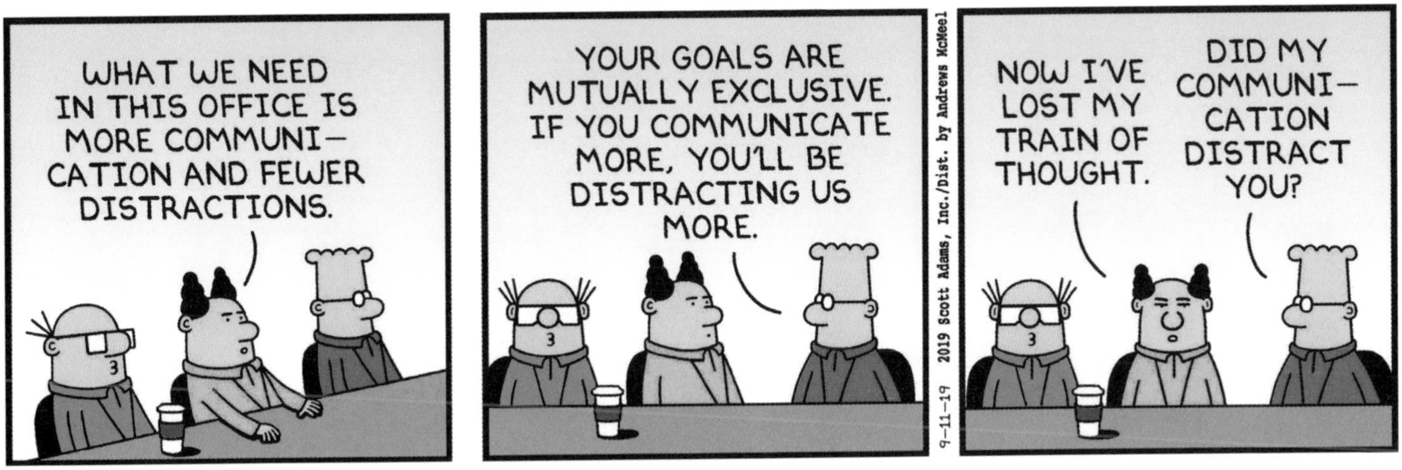
WHAT WE NEED IN THIS OFFICE IS MORE COMMUNI-CATION AND FEWER DISTRACTIONS.
YOUR GOALS ARE MUTUALLY EXCLUSIVE. IF YOU COMMUNICATE MORE, YOU'LL BE DISTRACTING US MORE.
9-11-19 © 2019 Scott Adams, Inc./Dist. by Andrews McMeel
NOW I'VE LOST MY TRAIN OF THOUGHT.
DID MY COMMUNI-CATION DISTRACT YOU?

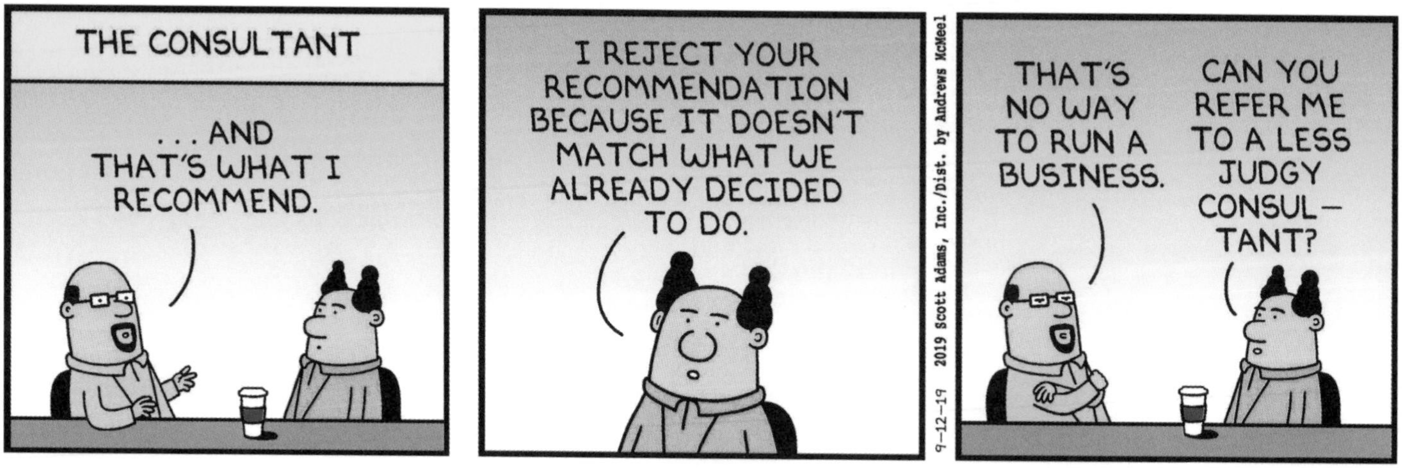
THE CONSULTANT
. . . AND THAT'S WHAT I RECOMMEND.
I REJECT YOUR RECOMMENDATION BECAUSE IT DOESN'T MATCH WHAT WE ALREADY DECIDED TO DO.
9-12-19 © 2019 Scott Adams, Inc./Dist. by Andrews McMeel
THAT'S NO WAY TO RUN A BUSINESS.
CAN YOU REFER ME TO A LESS JUDGY CONSUL-TANT?

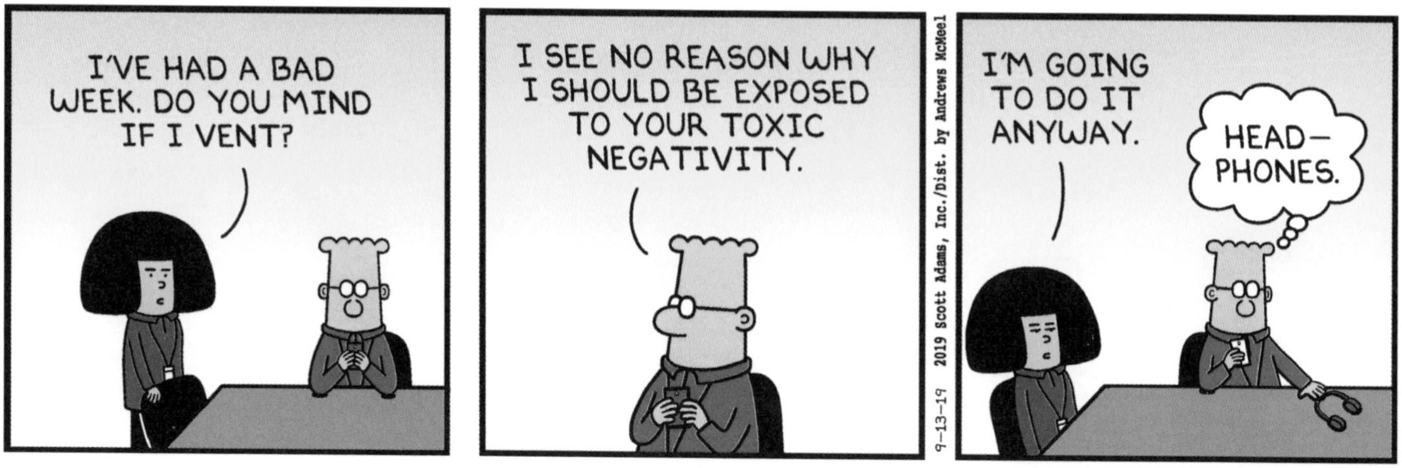
I'VE HAD A BAD WEEK. DO YOU MIND IF I VENT?
I SEE NO REASON WHY I SHOULD BE EXPOSED TO YOUR TOXIC NEGATIVITY.
9-13-19 © 2019 Scott Adams, Inc./Dist. by Andrews McMeel
I'M GOING TO DO IT ANYWAY.
HEAD-PHONES.

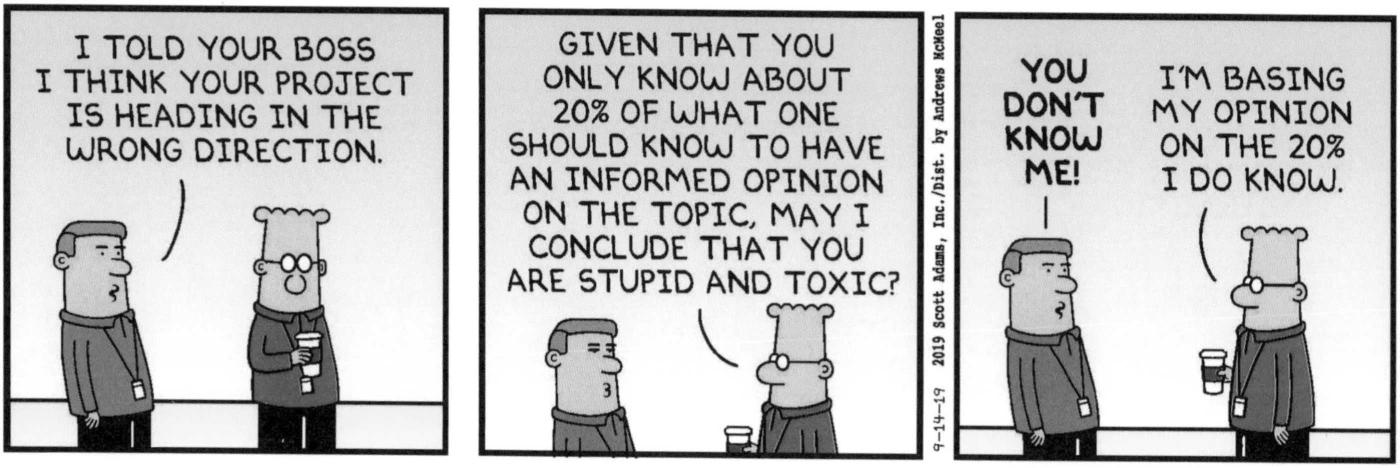
I TOLD YOUR BOSS I THINK YOUR PROJECT IS HEADING IN THE WRONG DIRECTION.
GIVEN THAT YOU ONLY KNOW ABOUT 20% OF WHAT ONE SHOULD KNOW TO HAVE AN INFORMED OPINION ON THE TOPIC, MAY I CONCLUDE THAT YOU ARE STUPID AND TOXIC?
9-14-19 © 2019 Scott Adams, Inc./Dist. by Andrews McMeel
YOU DON'T KNOW ME!
I'M BASING MY OPINION ON THE 20% I DO KNOW.

DO YOU HAVE A MINUTE?
I CAN'T HEAR YOU BECAUSE I'M WEARING NOISE-CANCELING HEADPHONES.
MAYBE YOU COULD TAKE THEM OFF FOR A MINUTE.
I HAVE NO IDEA WHAT YOU ARE SAYING BECAUSE I'M WEARING NOISE-CANCELING HEADPHONES.
THEN TAKE THEM OFF!
IF I AM READING YOUR LIPS CORRECTLY, I BELIEVE YOU ARE ASKING ME TO "FLURP TINGO GLOOP."
FORGET IT! I'LL JUST LET MY PROJECT FAIL!
HOW IS YOUR ANTI-CO-WORKER DEFENSE SYSTEM WORKING OUT?
I CAN'T HEAR YOU.
9-15-19

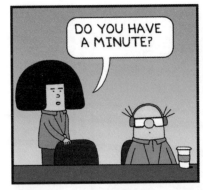

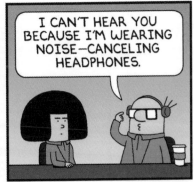

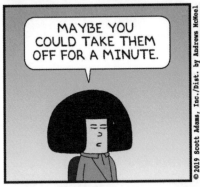

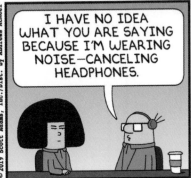

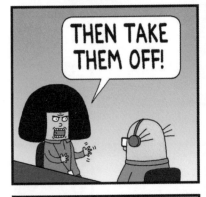

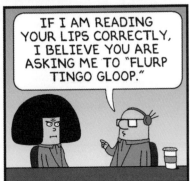

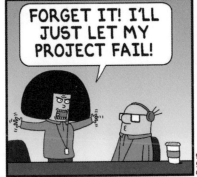

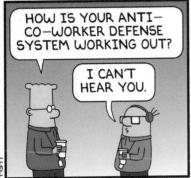

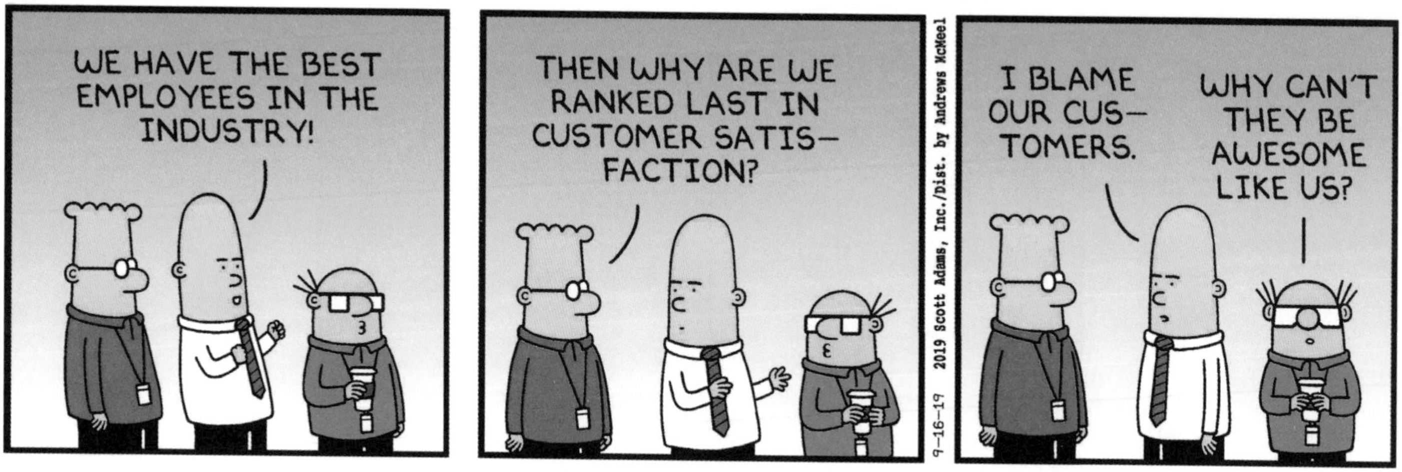
WE HAVE THE BEST EMPLOYEES IN THE INDUSTRY!
THEN WHY ARE WE RANKED LAST IN CUSTOMER SATIS-FACTION?
I BLAME OUR CUS-TOMERS.
WHY CAN'T THEY BE AWESOME LIKE US?

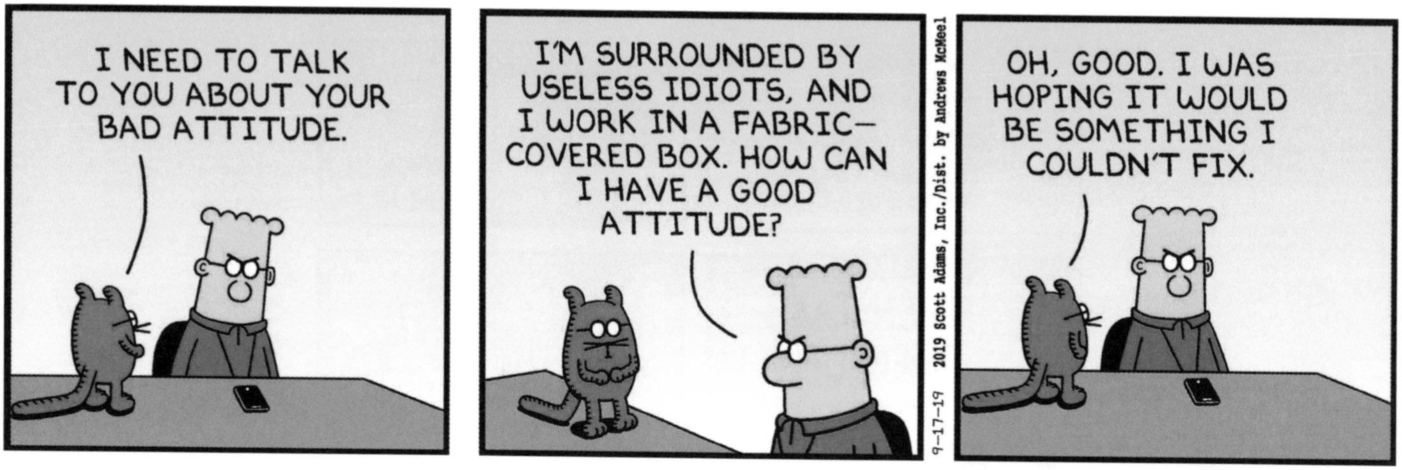
I NEED TO TALK TO YOU ABOUT YOUR BAD ATTITUDE.
I'M SURROUNDED BY USELESS IDIOTS, AND I WORK IN A FABRIC-COVERED BOX. HOW CAN I HAVE A GOOD ATTITUDE?
OH, GOOD. I WAS HOPING IT WOULD BE SOMETHING I COULDN'T FIX.

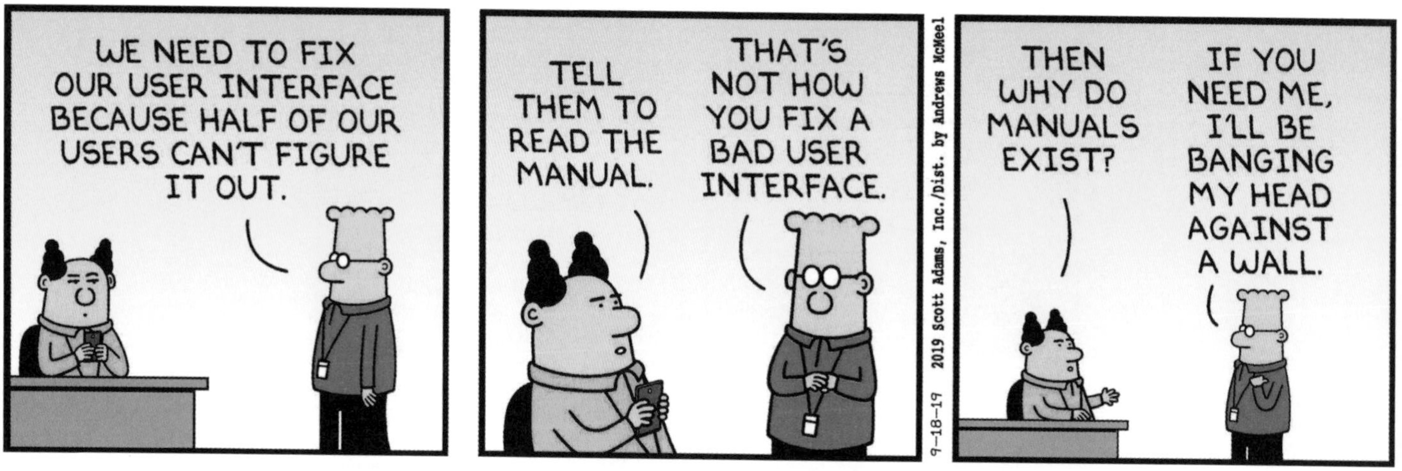
WE NEED TO FIX OUR USER INTERFACE BECAUSE HALF OF OUR USERS CAN'T FIGURE IT OUT.
TELL THEM TO READ THE MANUAL.
THAT'S NOT HOW YOU FIX A BAD USER INTERFACE.
THEN WHY DO MANUALS EXIST?
IF YOU NEED ME, I'LL BE BANGING MY HEAD AGAINST A WALL.

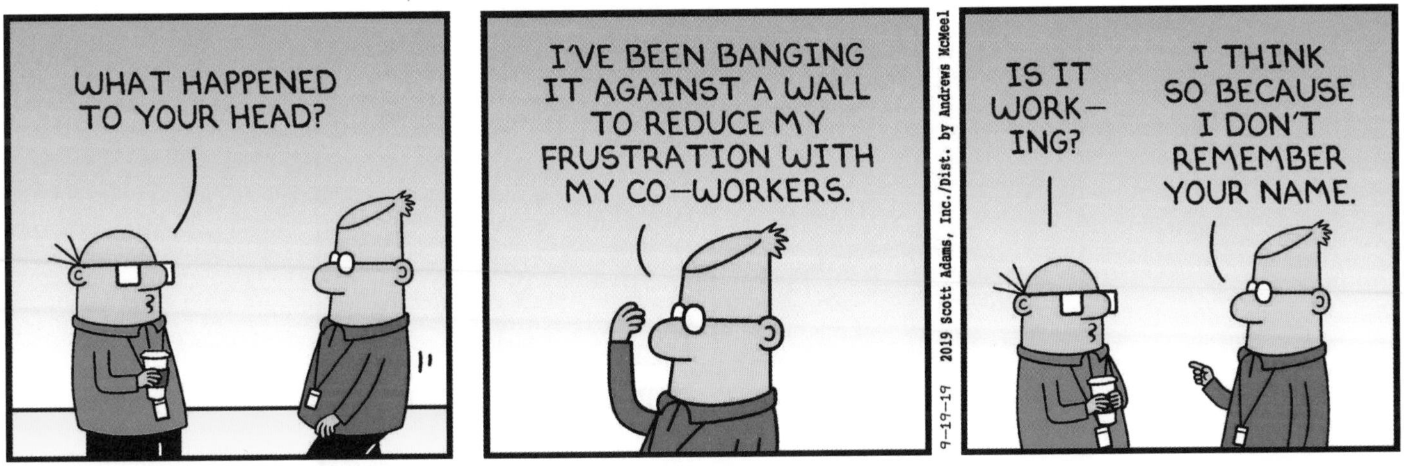
WHAT HAPPENED TO YOUR HEAD?
I'VE BEEN BANGING IT AGAINST A WALL TO REDUCE MY FRUSTRATION WITH MY CO-WORKERS.
9-19-19 2019 Scott Adams, Inc./Dist. by Andrews McMeel
IS IT WORK-ING?
I THINK SO BECAUSE I DON'T REMEMBER YOUR NAME.

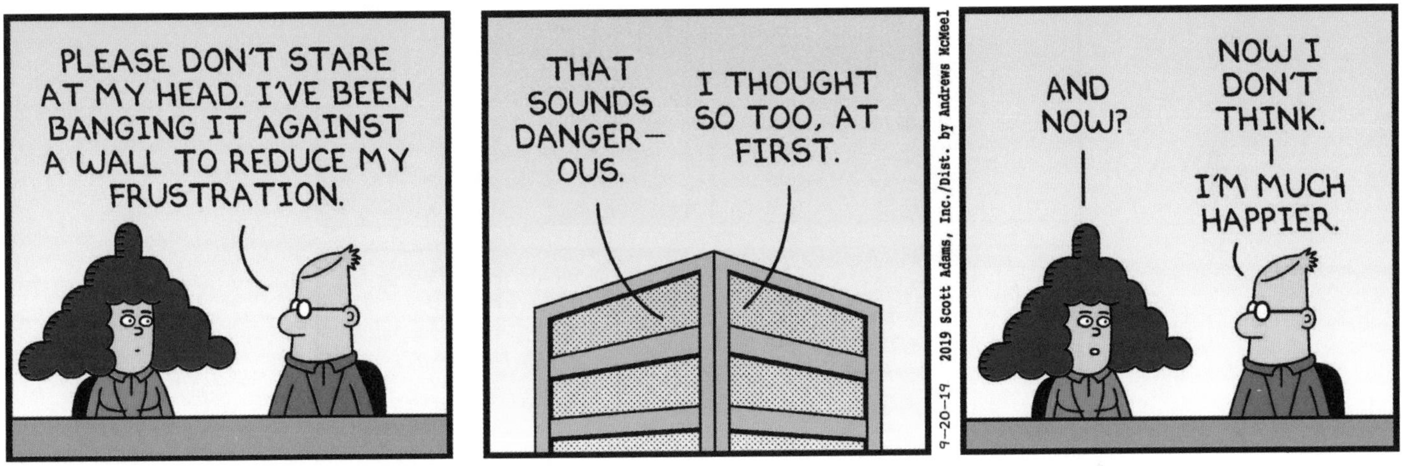
PLEASE DON'T STARE AT MY HEAD. I'VE BEEN BANGING IT AGAINST A WALL TO REDUCE MY FRUSTRATION.
THAT SOUNDS DANGER-OUS.
I THOUGHT SO TOO, AT FIRST.
9-20-19 2019 Scott Adams, Inc./Dist. by Andrews McMeel
AND NOW?
NOW I DON'T THINK.
I'M MUCH HAPPIER.

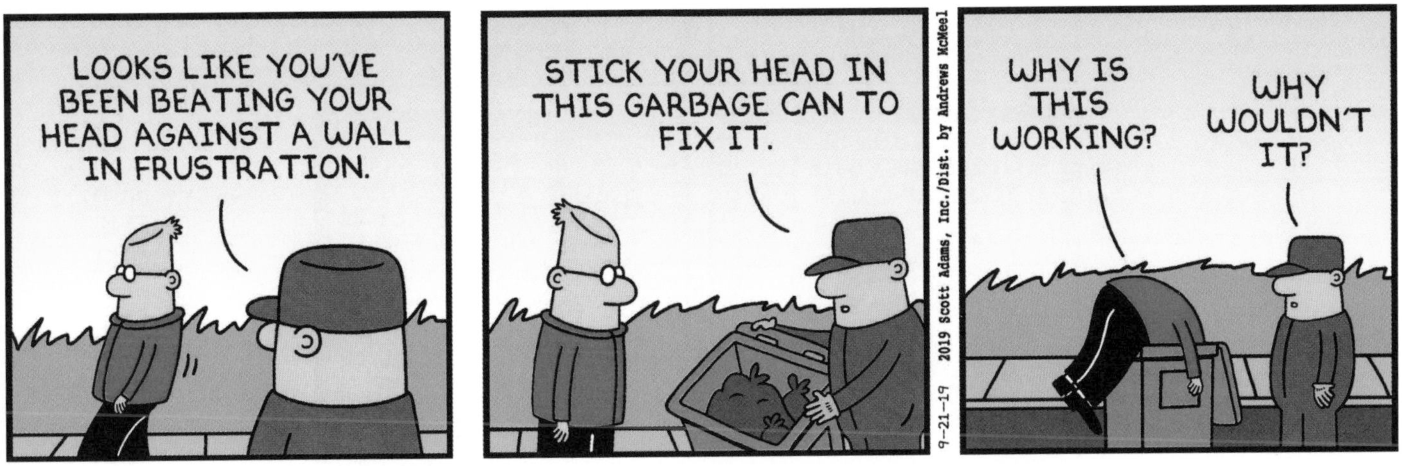
LOOKS LIKE YOU'VE BEEN BEATING YOUR HEAD AGAINST A WALL IN FRUSTRATION.
STICK YOUR HEAD IN THIS GARBAGE CAN TO FIX IT.
9-21-19 2019 Scott Adams, Inc./Dist. by Andrews McMeel
WHY IS THIS WORKING?
WHY WOULDN'T IT?

BEN, FROM MARKETING, IS HERE TO GIVE US A PREVIEW OF OUR NEW TV AD.
THE OPENING SCENE SHOWS A BUNCH OF MEN WHO ARE WEAK AND STUPID, FAILING TO SOLVE A COMMON PROBLEM.
THEN A CONFIDENT AND STRONG WOMAN ENTERS AND SOLVES THE PROBLEM WITH EASE.
ISN'T THAT INCREDIBLY SEXIST?
NO, BECAUSE ONLY THE MEN ARE WEAK AND STUPID.
AND THAT'S NOT SEXIST?
WHY ARE YOU BEING SO WEAK AND STUPID? YOU SOUND LIKE A BIGOT.
I'LL BE QUIET NOW.
AS QUICKLY AS IT BEGAN, THE REBELLION WAS QUASHED.
© 2019 Scott Adams, Inc./Dist. by Andrews McMeel
Dilbert.com
9-22-19

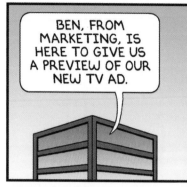

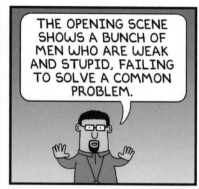

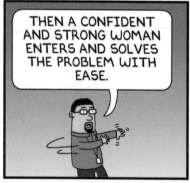

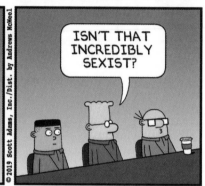

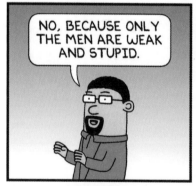

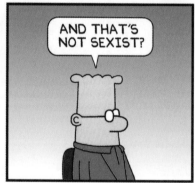

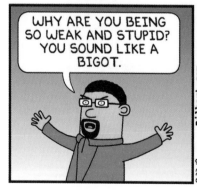

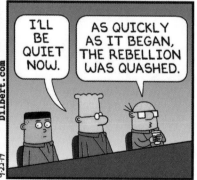

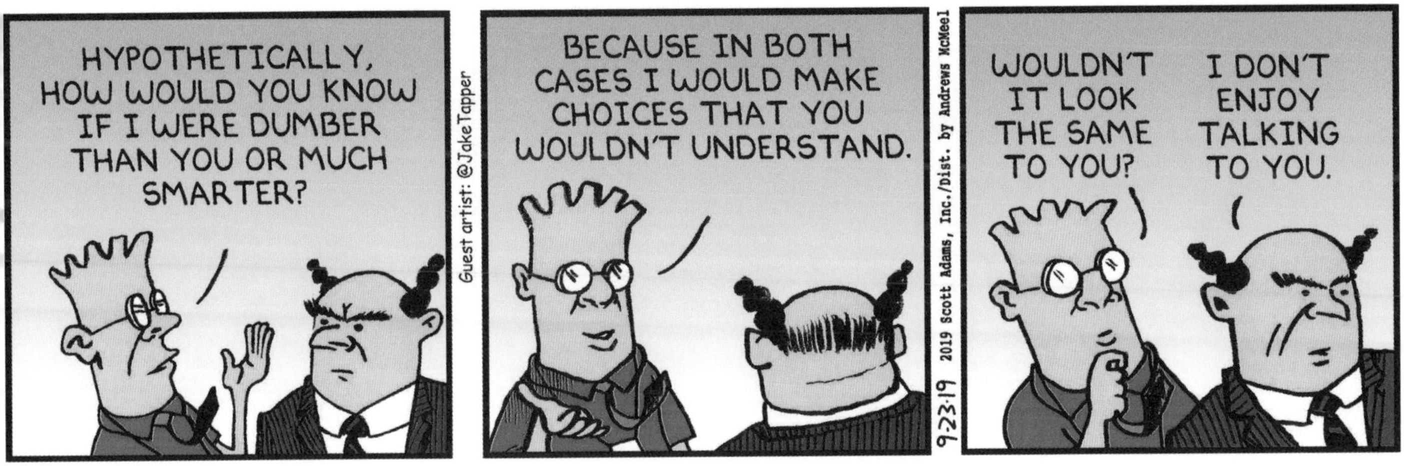
HYPOTHETICALLY, HOW WOULD YOU KNOW IF I WERE DUMBER THAN YOU OR MUCH SMARTER?
Guest artist: @JakeTapper
BECAUSE IN BOTH CASES I WOULD MAKE CHOICES THAT YOU WOULDN'T UNDERSTAND.
9-23-19 © 2019 Scott Adams, Inc./Dist. by Andrews McMeel
WOULDN'T IT LOOK THE SAME TO YOU?
I DON'T ENJOY TALKING TO YOU.

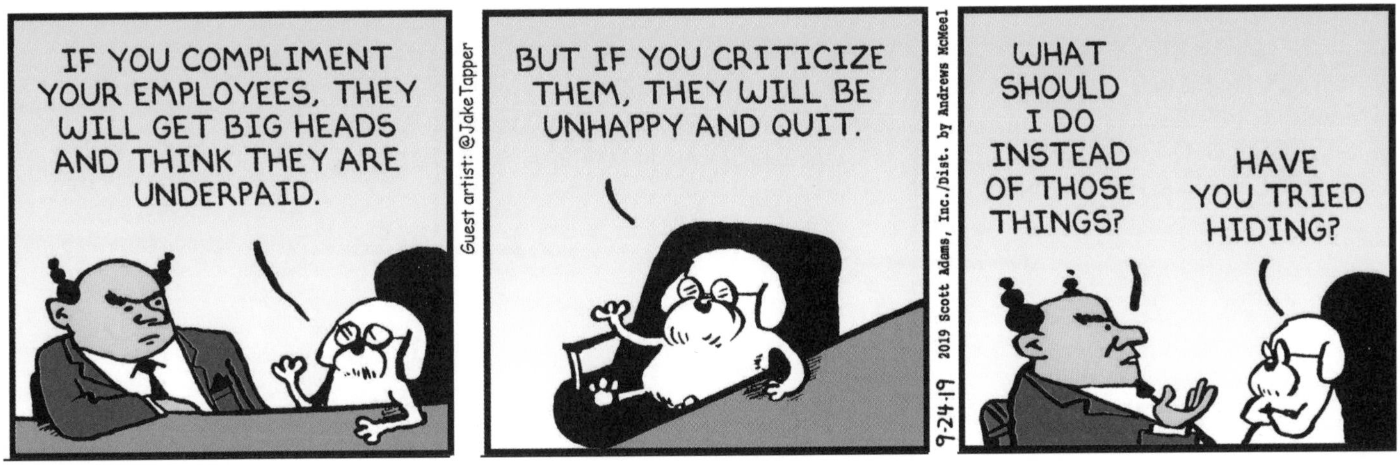
IF YOU COMPLIMENT YOUR EMPLOYEES, THEY WILL GET BIG HEADS AND THINK THEY ARE UNDERPAID.
Guest artist: @JakeTapper
BUT IF YOU CRITICIZE THEM, THEY WILL BE UNHAPPY AND QUIT.
9-24-19 © 2019 Scott Adams, Inc./Dist. by Andrews McMeel
WHAT SHOULD I DO INSTEAD OF THOSE THINGS?
HAVE YOU TRIED HIDING?

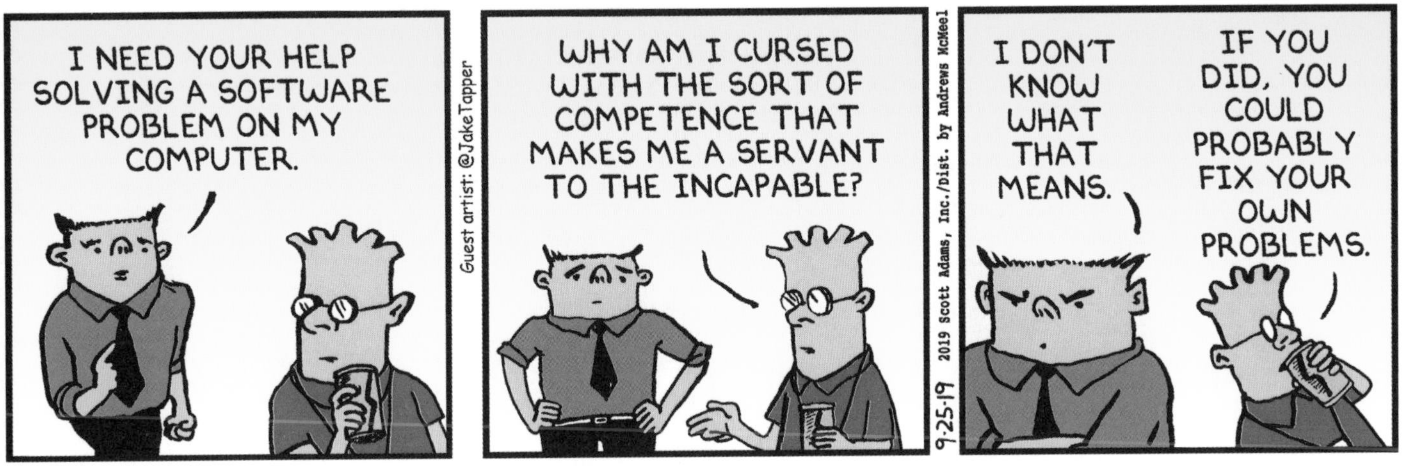
I NEED YOUR HELP SOLVING A SOFTWARE PROBLEM ON MY COMPUTER.
Guest artist: @JakeTapper
WHY AM I CURSED WITH THE SORT OF COMPETENCE THAT MAKES ME A SERVANT TO THE INCAPABLE?
9-25-19 © 2019 Scott Adams, Inc./Dist. by Andrews McMeel
I DON'T KNOW WHAT THAT MEANS.
IF YOU DID, YOU COULD PROBABLY FIX YOUR OWN PROBLEMS.

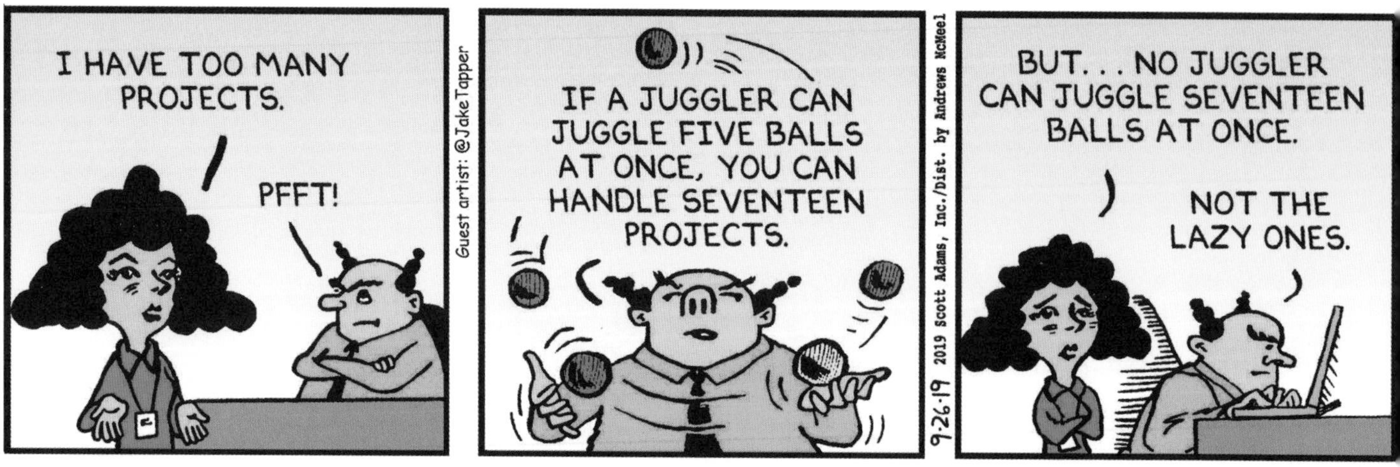
I HAVE TOO MANY PROJECTS.
PFFT!
Guest artist: @JakeTapper
IF A JUGGLER CAN JUGGLE FIVE BALLS AT ONCE, YOU CAN HANDLE SEVENTEEN PROJECTS.
9-26-19 © 2019 Scott Adams, Inc./Dist. by Andrews McMeel
BUT. . . NO JUGGLER CAN JUGGLE SEVENTEEN BALLS AT ONCE.
NOT THE LAZY ONES.

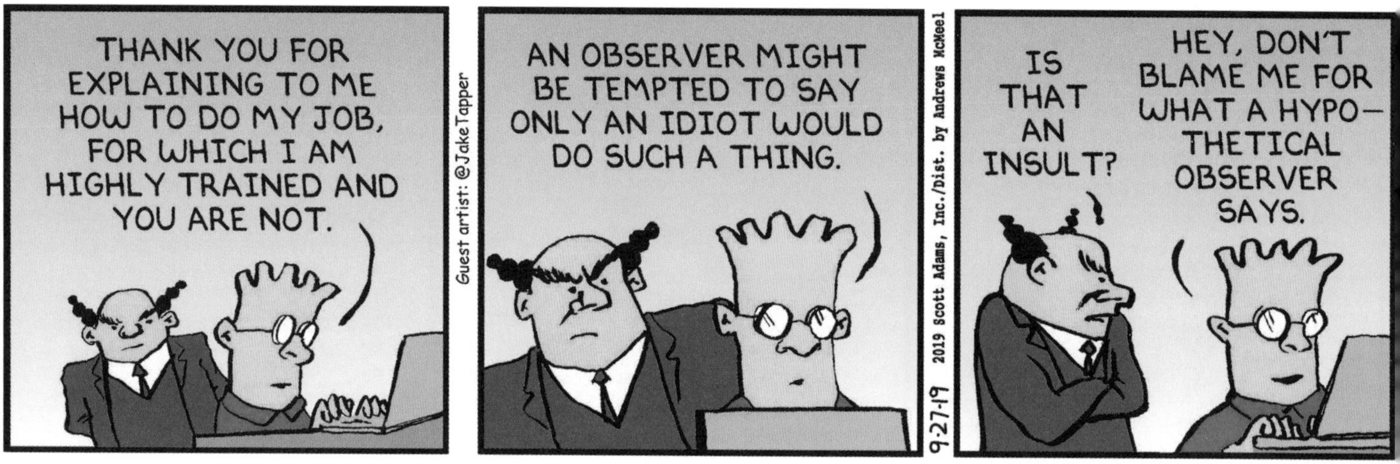
THANK YOU FOR EXPLAINING TO ME HOW TO DO MY JOB, FOR WHICH I AM HIGHLY TRAINED AND YOU ARE NOT.
Guest artist: @JakeTapper
AN OBSERVER MIGHT BE TEMPTED TO SAY ONLY AN IDIOT WOULD DO SUCH A THING.
9-27-19 © 2019 Scott Adams, Inc./Dist. by Andrews McMeel
IS THAT AN INSULT?
HEY, DON'T BLAME ME FOR WHAT A HYPO–THETICAL OBSERVER SAYS.

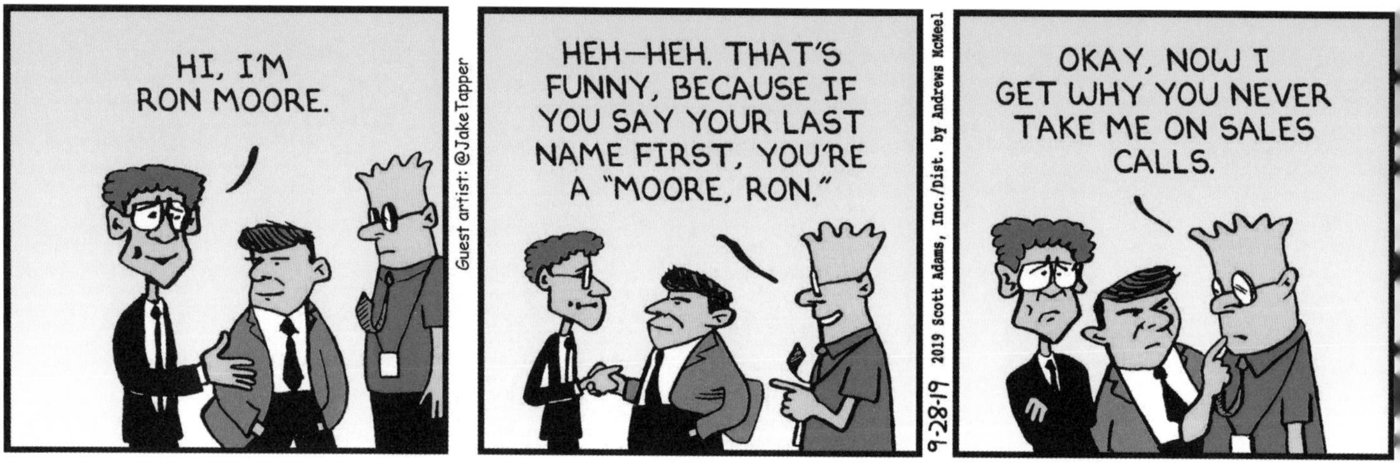
HI, I'M RON MOORE.
Guest artist: @JakeTapper
HEH—HEH. THAT'S FUNNY, BECAUSE IF YOU SAY YOUR LAST NAME FIRST, YOU'RE A "MOORE, RON."
9-28-19 © 2019 Scott Adams, Inc./Dist. by Andrews McMeel
OKAY, NOW I GET WHY YOU NEVER TAKE ME ON SALES CALLS.

I DON'T UNDER– STAND WHY YOU ARE RECOMMENDING BLOCKCHAIN FOR THIS APPLICATION.
MY STAFF ARE THE EXPERTS, BUT I CAN EXPLAIN THE BASIC IDEA.
YOU SEE, USING BLOCKCHAIN IS LIKE LOSING A NECKLACE ON THE BEACH.
THEN A SEAGULL FINDS THE NECKLACE AND TAKES IT BACK TO ITS NEST.
AND WE ALL LIKE DATA SECURITY, DON'T WE?
IT'S ALMOST AS IF YOU ARE PROPOSING A PLAN YOU DON'T UNDERSTAND AT ANY LEVEL.
WELL, YES, BUT KEEP IN MIND THAT YOU WOULDN'T UNDERSTAND IT EVEN IF I COULD EXPLAIN IT.
BUT YOU'RE SURE SOMEONE ON YOUR STAFF UNDERSTANDS IT, RIGHT?
DEFINE "SURE."
© 2019 Scott Adams, Inc./Dist. by Andrews McMeel
9-29-19

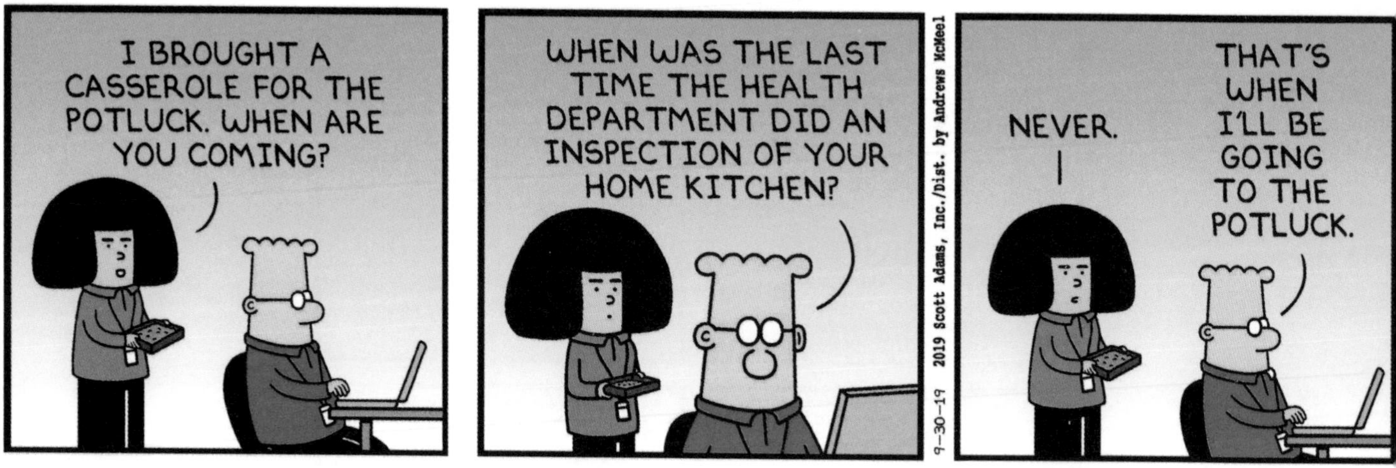
I BROUGHT A CASSEROLE FOR THE POTLUCK. WHEN ARE YOU COMING?
WHEN WAS THE LAST TIME THE HEALTH DEPARTMENT DID AN INSPECTION OF YOUR HOME KITCHEN?
9-30-19 © 2019 Scott Adams, Inc./Dist. by Andrews McMeel
NEVER.
THAT'S WHEN I'LL BE GOING TO THE POTLUCK.

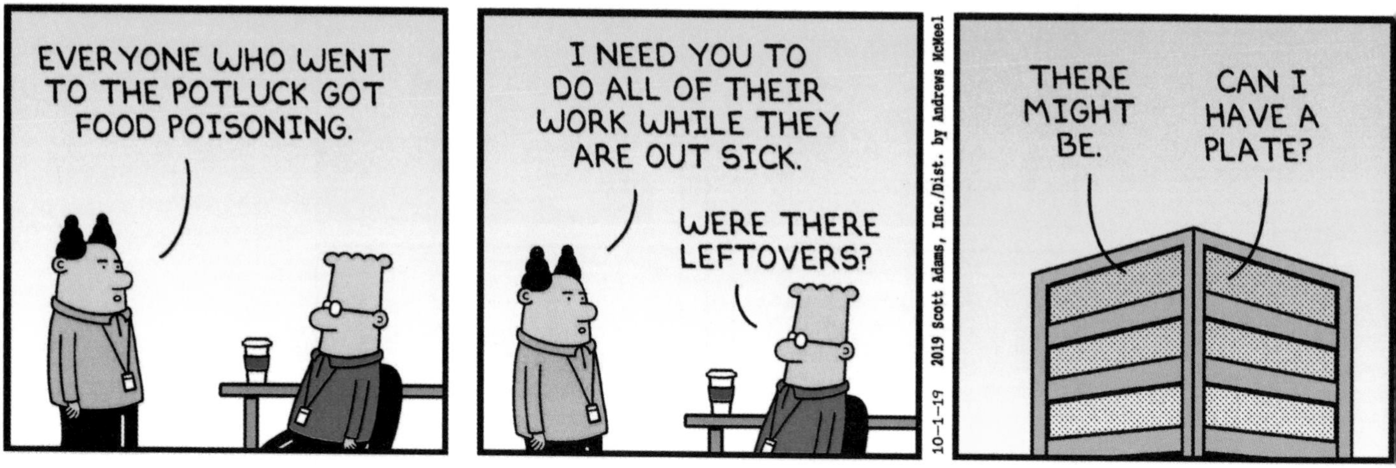
EVERYONE WHO WENT TO THE POTLUCK GOT FOOD POISONING.
I NEED YOU TO DO ALL OF THEIR WORK WHILE THEY ARE OUT SICK.
WERE THERE LEFTOVERS?
10-1-19 © 2019 Scott Adams, Inc./Dist. by Andrews McMeel
THERE MIGHT BE.
CAN I HAVE A PLATE?

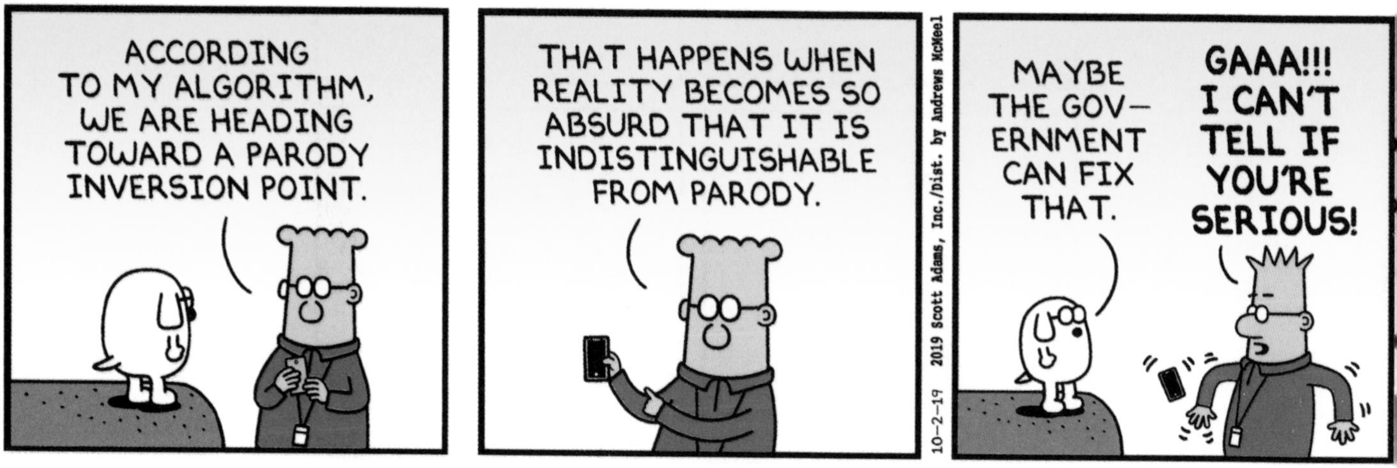
ACCORDING TO MY ALGORITHM, WE ARE HEADING TOWARD A PARODY INVERSION POINT.
THAT HAPPENS WHEN REALITY BECOMES SO ABSURD THAT IT IS INDISTINGUISHABLE FROM PARODY.
10-2-19 © 2019 Scott Adams, Inc./Dist. by Andrews McMeel
MAYBE THE GOV-ERNMENT CAN FIX THAT.
GAAA!!! I CAN'T TELL IF YOU'RE SERIOUS!

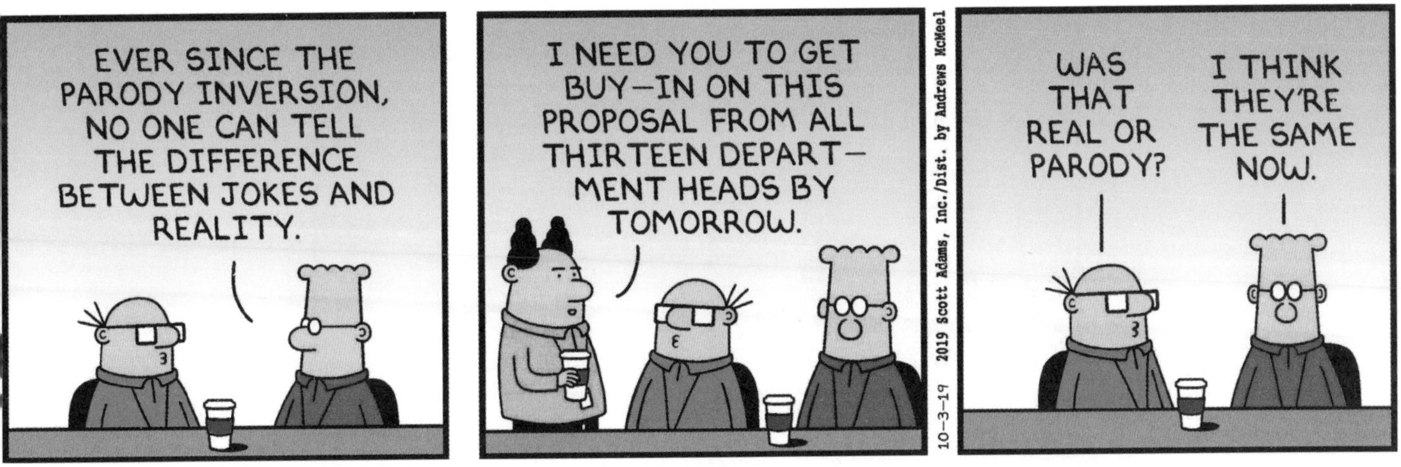
EVER SINCE THE PARODY INVERSION, NO ONE CAN TELL THE DIFFERENCE BETWEEN JOKES AND REALITY.
I NEED YOU TO GET BUY-IN ON THIS PROPOSAL FROM ALL THIRTEEN DEPART-MENT HEADS BY TOMORROW.
WAS THAT REAL OR PARODY?
I THINK THEY'RE THE SAME NOW.

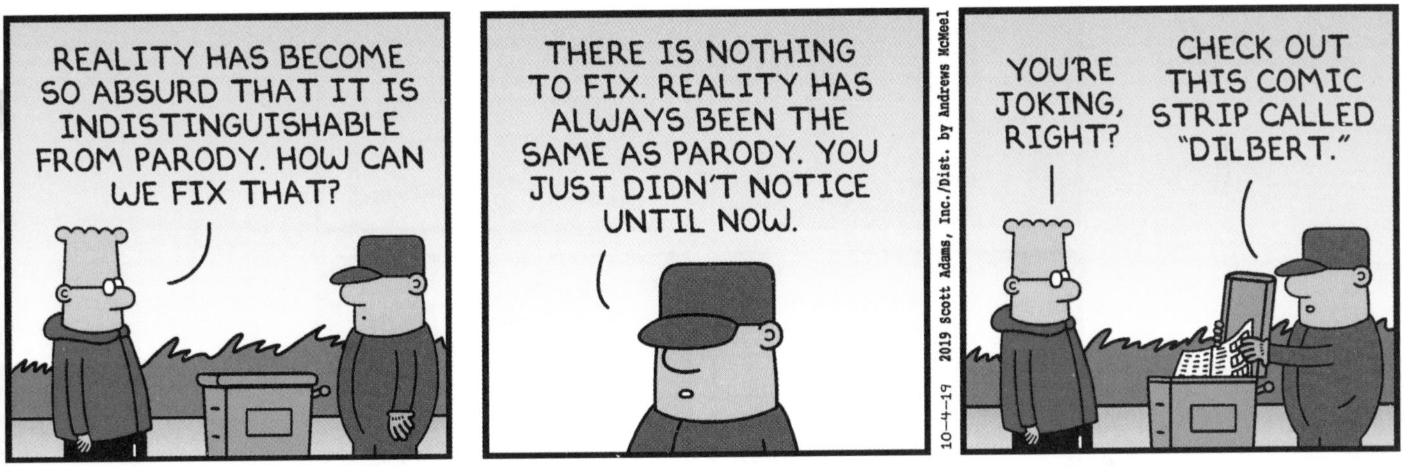
REALITY HAS BECOME SO ABSURD THAT IT IS INDISTINGUISHABLE FROM PARODY. HOW CAN WE FIX THAT?
THERE IS NOTHING TO FIX. REALITY HAS ALWAYS BEEN THE SAME AS PARODY. YOU JUST DIDN'T NOTICE UNTIL NOW.
YOU'RE JOKING, RIGHT?
CHECK OUT THIS COMIC STRIP CALLED "DILBERT."

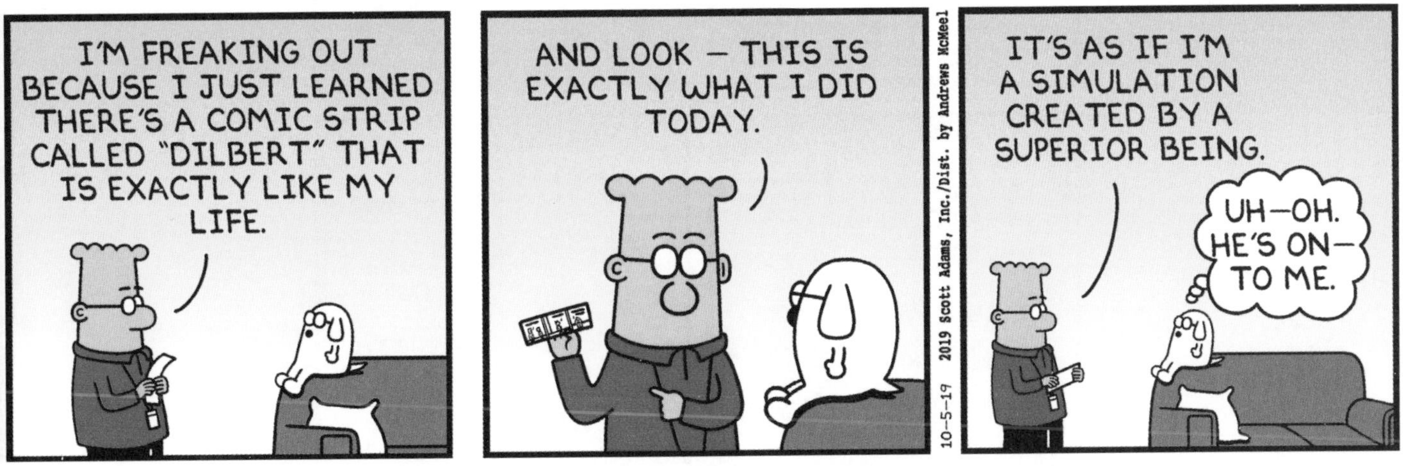
I'M FREAKING OUT BECAUSE I JUST LEARNED THERE'S A COMIC STRIP CALLED "DILBERT" THAT IS EXACTLY LIKE MY LIFE.
AND LOOK – THIS IS EXACTLY WHAT I DID TODAY.
IT'S AS IF I'M A SIMULATION CREATED BY A SUPERIOR BEING.
UH-OH. HE'S ON-TO ME.

I HEAR WHAT YOU'RE SAYING, AND I DISAGREE.
BECAUSE. . . ?
BECAUSE WHAT?
DO YOU HAVE ANY REASONS FOR YOUR DISAGREEMENT?
NO, I'M A LIFESTYLE DISAGREER.
I DISAGREE WITH EVERYONE ALL THE TIME. THE REASONS ARE IRRELEVANT.
YOU SOUND SMART.
NO, I'M NOT SMART.
AND YOU'RE ATTRAC-TIVE TOO.
NO, I'M UGL. . .
OKAY, I SEE WHAT YOU'RE DOING.
© 2019 Scott Adams, Inc./Dist. by Andrews McMeel
10-6-19

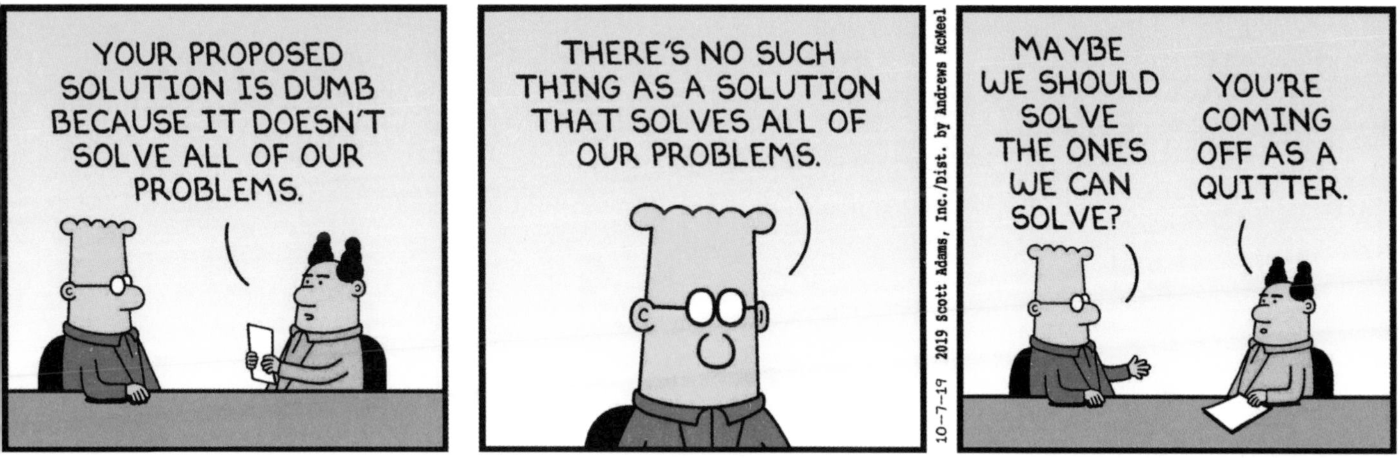
YOUR PROPOSED SOLUTION IS DUMB BECAUSE IT DOESN'T SOLVE ALL OF OUR PROBLEMS.
THERE'S NO SUCH THING AS A SOLUTION THAT SOLVES ALL OF OUR PROBLEMS.
10-7-19 2019 Scott Adams, Inc./Dist. by Andrews McMeel
MAYBE WE SHOULD SOLVE THE ONES WE CAN SOLVE?
YOU'RE COMING OFF AS A QUITTER.

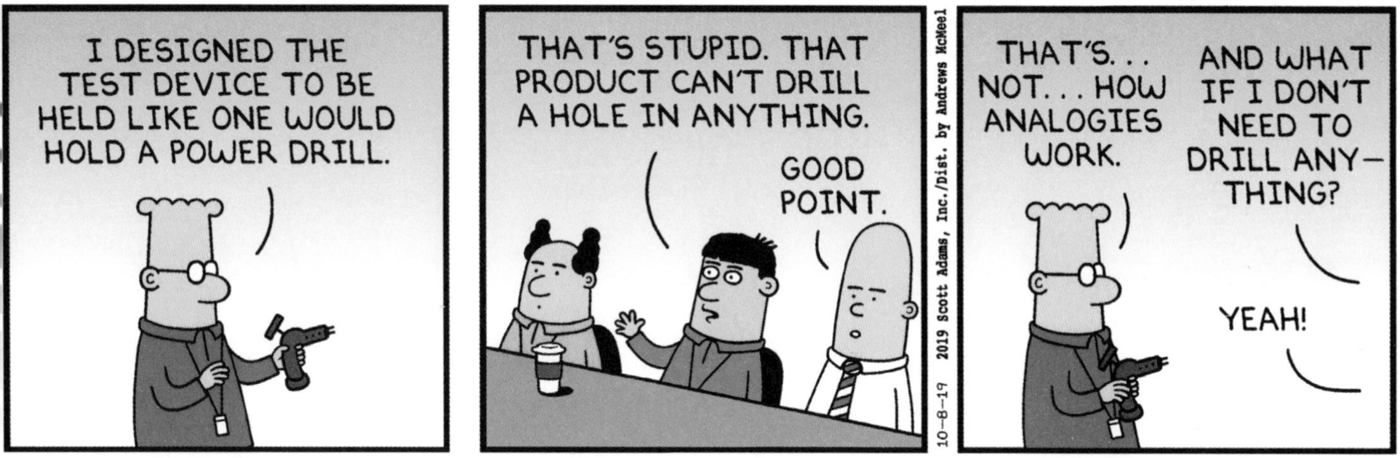
I DESIGNED THE TEST DEVICE TO BE HELD LIKE ONE WOULD HOLD A POWER DRILL.
THAT'S STUPID. THAT PRODUCT CAN'T DRILL A HOLE IN ANYTHING.
GOOD POINT.
10-8-19 2019 Scott Adams, Inc./Dist. by Andrews McMeel
THAT'S... NOT... HOW ANALOGIES WORK.
AND WHAT IF I DON'T NEED TO DRILL ANY-THING?
YEAH!

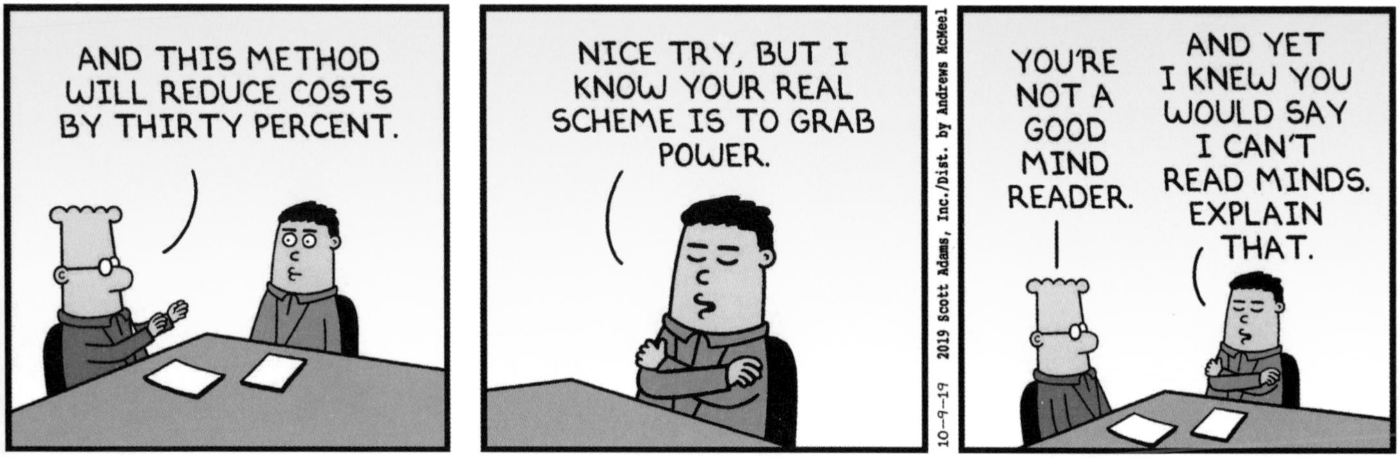
AND THIS METHOD WILL REDUCE COSTS BY THIRTY PERCENT.
NICE TRY, BUT I KNOW YOUR REAL SCHEME IS TO GRAB POWER.
10-9-19 2019 Scott Adams, Inc./Dist. by Andrews McMeel
YOU'RE NOT A GOOD MIND READER.
AND YET I KNEW YOU WOULD SAY I CAN'T READ MINDS. EXPLAIN THAT.

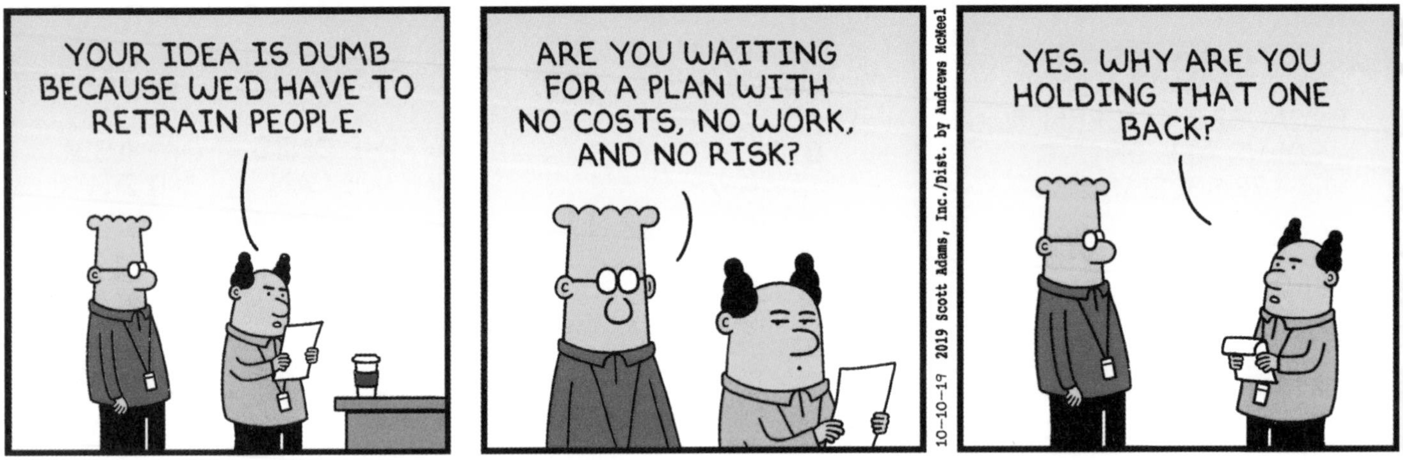
YOUR IDEA IS DUMB BECAUSE WE'D HAVE TO RETRAIN PEOPLE.
ARE YOU WAITING FOR A PLAN WITH NO COSTS, NO WORK, AND NO RISK?
10-10-19 2019 Scott Adams, Inc./Dist. by Andrews McMeel
YES. WHY ARE YOU HOLDING THAT ONE BACK?

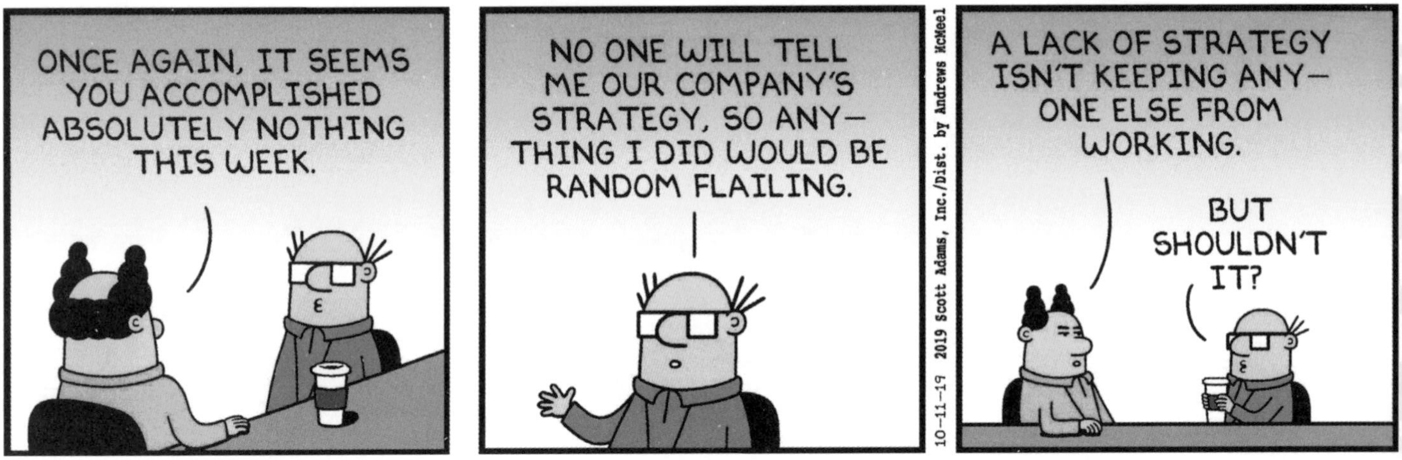
ONCE AGAIN, IT SEEMS YOU ACCOMPLISHED ABSOLUTELY NOTHING THIS WEEK.
NO ONE WILL TELL ME OUR COMPANY'S STRATEGY, SO ANY-THING I DID WOULD BE RANDOM FLAILING.
10-11-19 2019 Scott Adams, Inc./Dist. by Andrews McMeel
A LACK OF STRATEGY ISN'T KEEPING ANY-ONE ELSE FROM WORKING.
BUT SHOULDN'T IT?

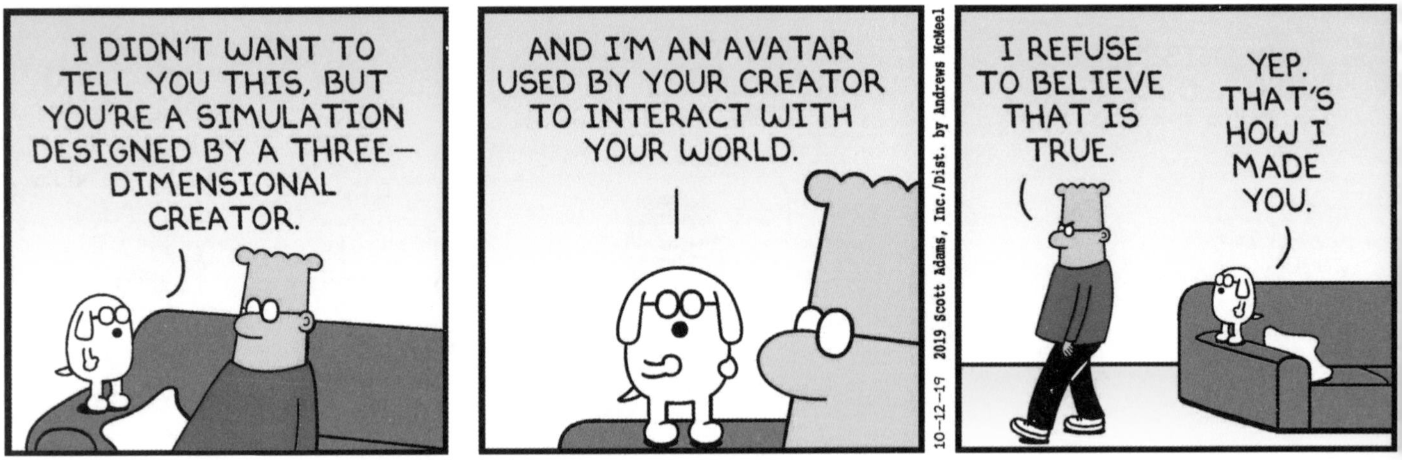
I DIDN'T WANT TO TELL YOU THIS, BUT YOU'RE A SIMULATION DESIGNED BY A THREE-DIMENSIONAL CREATOR.
AND I'M AN AVATAR USED BY YOUR CREATOR TO INTERACT WITH YOUR WORLD.
10-12-19 2019 Scott Adams, Inc./Dist. by Andrews McMeel
I REFUSE TO BELIEVE THAT IS TRUE.
YEP. THAT'S HOW I MADE YOU.

I CAN'T GIVE YOU A BONUS THIS YEAR BECAUSE WE PAID TOO MUCH TO BUY ANOTHER COMPANY.
ARE YOU SAYING MY EFFORTS AND MY REWARDS ARE NO LONGER LINKED?
NOOOO. I'M NOT SAYING ANYTHING LIKE THAT.
I'M JUST SAYING YOUR COMPENSATION ISN'T INFLUENCED BY YOUR PERFORMANCE.
THAT'S THE SAME THING!
TEAMWORK MEANS WE ALL SHARE THE REWARDS AND WE ALL HAVE TO SHARE THE PAIN.
DOES THAT MEAN MANAGEMENT WON'T BE GETTING BONUSES EITHER?
NOW YOU'VE MADE IT AWKWARD.
© 2019 Scott Adams, Inc./Dist. by Andrews McMeel
10-13-19

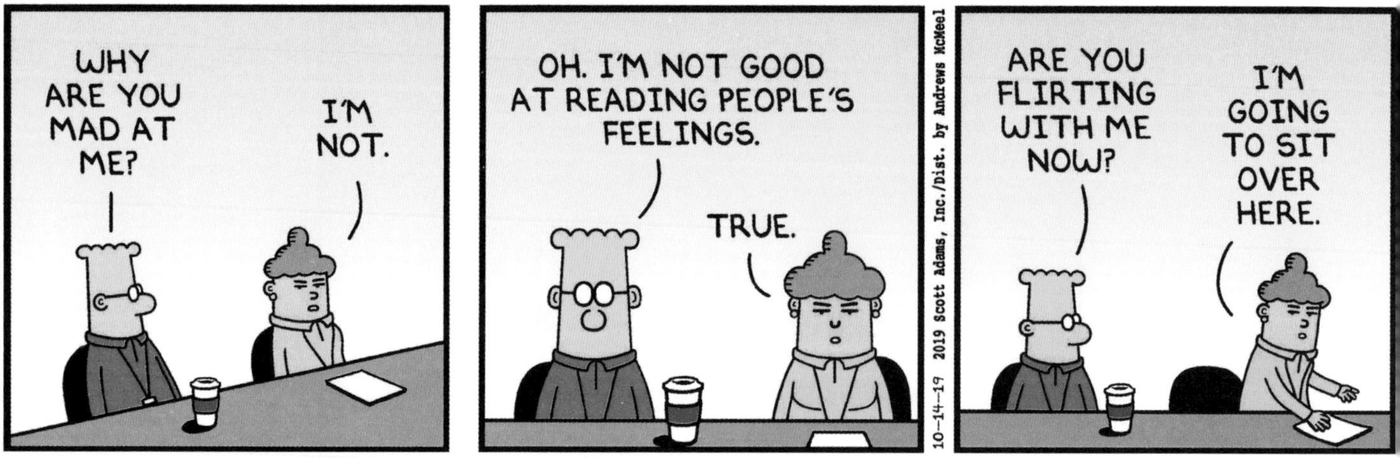
WHY ARE YOU MAD AT ME?
I'M NOT.
OH. I'M NOT GOOD AT READING PEOPLE'S FEELINGS.
TRUE.
ARE YOU FLIRTING WITH ME NOW?
I'M GOING TO SIT OVER HERE.
10-14-19 © 2019 Scott Adams, Inc./Dist. by Andrews McMeel

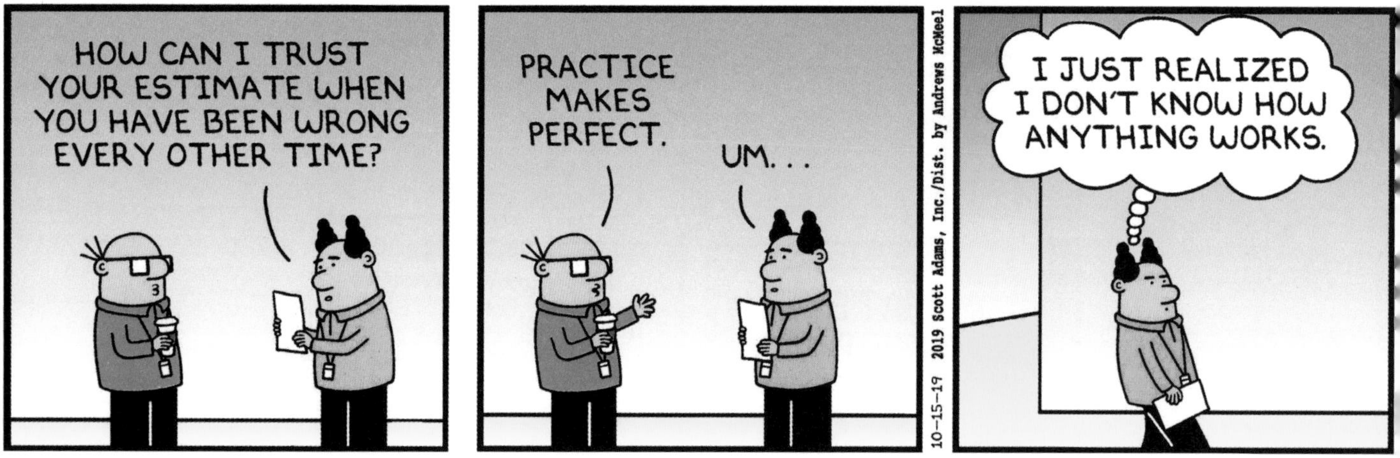
HOW CAN I TRUST YOUR ESTIMATE WHEN YOU HAVE BEEN WRONG EVERY OTHER TIME?
PRACTICE MAKES PERFECT.
UM. . .
I JUST REALIZED I DON'T KNOW HOW ANYTHING WORKS.
10-15-19 © 2019 Scott Adams, Inc./Dist. by Andrews McMeel

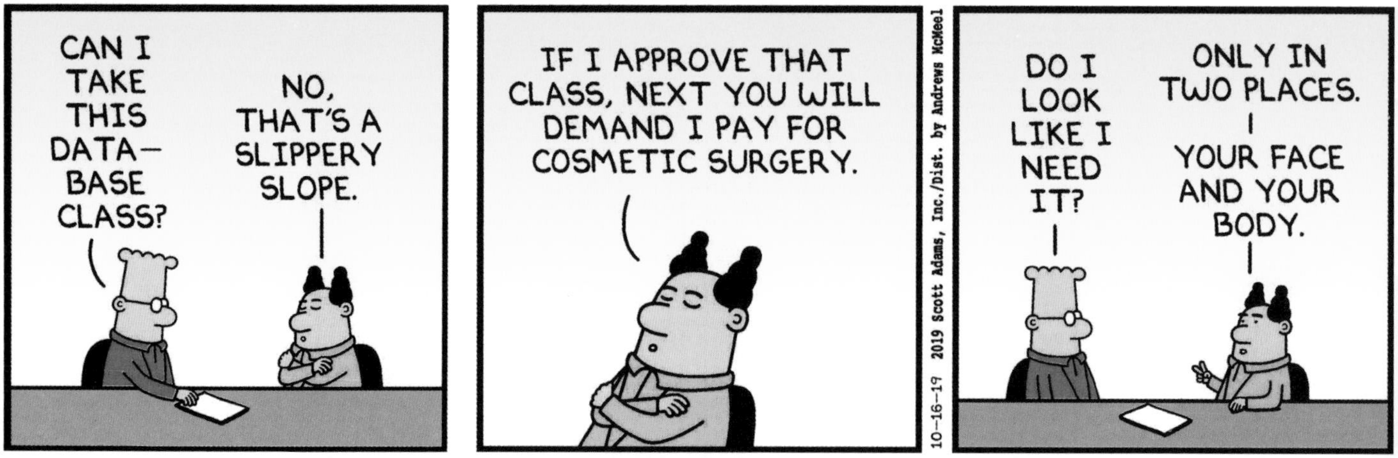
CAN I TAKE THIS DATA-BASE CLASS?
NO, THAT'S A SLIPPERY SLOPE.
IF I APPROVE THAT CLASS, NEXT YOU WILL DEMAND I PAY FOR COSMETIC SURGERY.
DO I LOOK LIKE I NEED IT?
ONLY IN TWO PLACES.
YOUR FACE AND YOUR BODY.
10-16-19 © 2019 Scott Adams, Inc./Dist. by Andrews McMeel

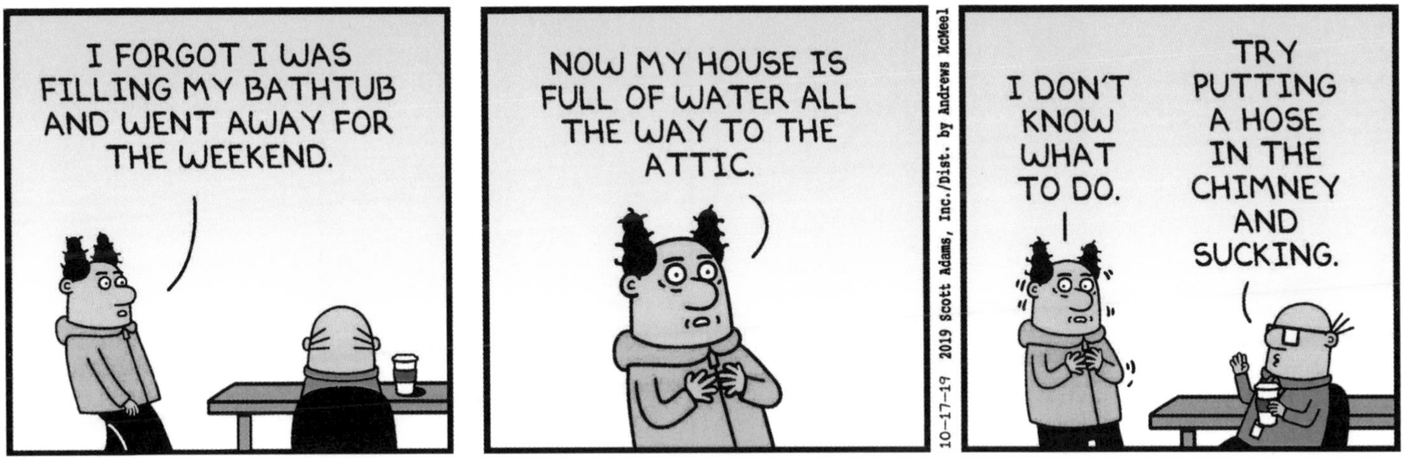
I FORGOT I WAS FILLING MY BATHTUB AND WENT AWAY FOR THE WEEKEND.
NOW MY HOUSE IS FULL OF WATER ALL THE WAY TO THE ATTIC.
10-17-19 2019 Scott Adams, Inc./Dist. by Andrews McMeel
I DON'T KNOW WHAT TO DO.
TRY PUTTING A HOSE IN THE CHIMNEY AND SUCKING.

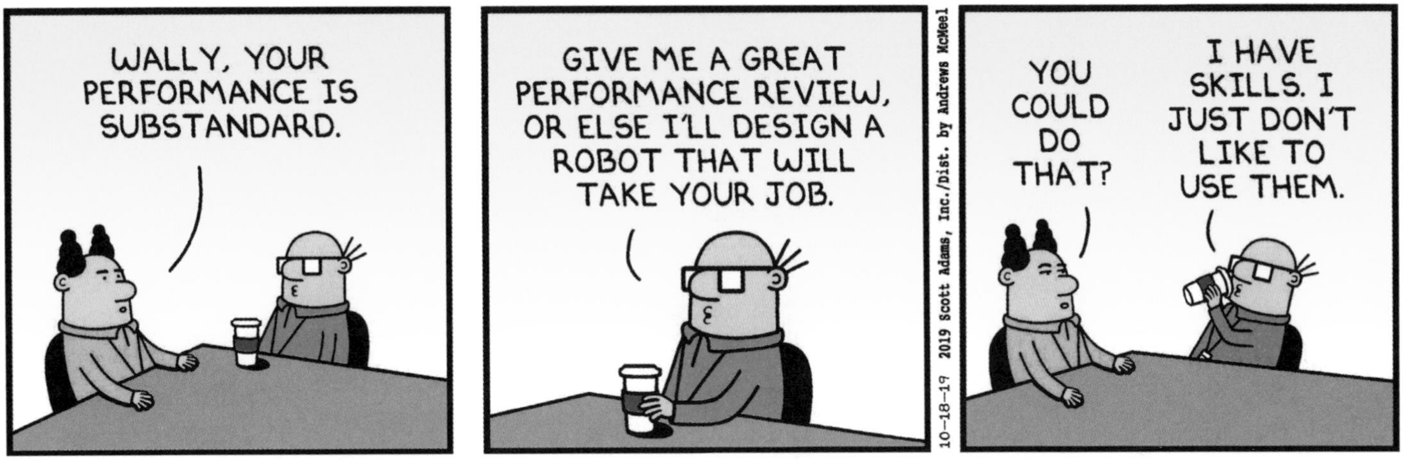
WALLY, YOUR PERFORMANCE IS SUBSTANDARD.
GIVE ME A GREAT PERFORMANCE REVIEW, OR ELSE I'LL DESIGN A ROBOT THAT WILL TAKE YOUR JOB.
10-18-19 2019 Scott Adams, Inc./Dist. by Andrews McMeel
YOU COULD DO THAT?
I HAVE SKILLS. I JUST DON'T LIKE TO USE THEM.

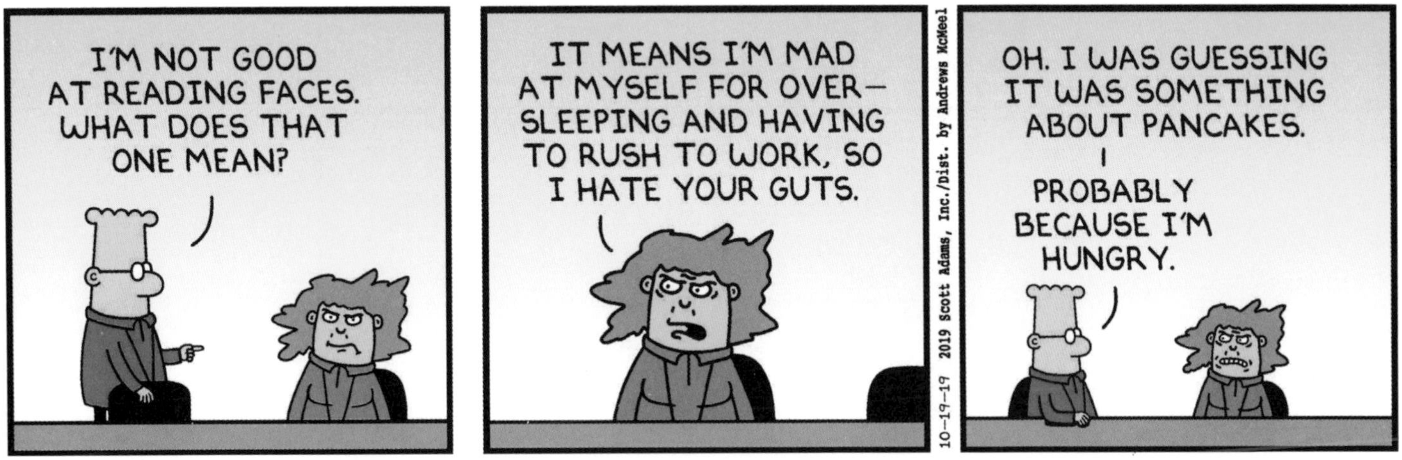
I'M NOT GOOD AT READING FACES. WHAT DOES THAT ONE MEAN?
IT MEANS I'M MAD AT MYSELF FOR OVER-SLEEPING AND HAVING TO RUSH TO WORK, SO I HATE YOUR GUTS.
10-19-19 2019 Scott Adams, Inc./Dist. by Andrews McMeel
OH. I WAS GUESSING IT WAS SOMETHING ABOUT PANCAKES.
PROBABLY BECAUSE I'M HUNGRY.

I HAVE BAD NEWS.
WHAT IS IT?
I'LL TELL YOU LATER.
WHY CAN'T YOU TELL ME NOW?
I DON'T WANT TO START AND THEN GET INTERRUPTED IF SOMEONE COMES IN THE ROOM.
HOW BAD IS THE NEWS?
IT'S BAD. VERY BAD.
YOU'RE MAKING ME CRAZY. HOW CAN I RELAX KNOWING SOME TERRIBLE NEWS IS OUT THERE?
DON'T TELL ME YOU HAVE BAD NEWS IF YOU AREN'T GOING TO TELL ME WHAT IT IS!!!
WHAT DID I MISS?
I DON'T KNOW!
© 2019 Scott Adams, Inc./Dist. by Andrews McMeel
10-20-19

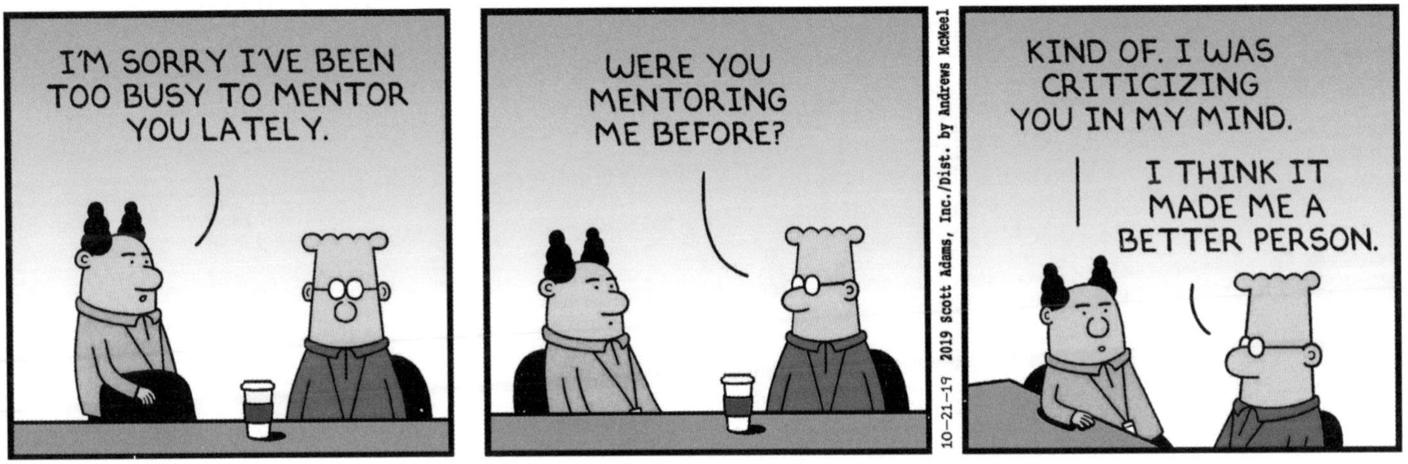
I'M SORRY I'VE BEEN TOO BUSY TO MENTOR YOU LATELY.
WERE YOU MENTORING ME BEFORE?
KIND OF. I WAS CRITICIZING YOU IN MY MIND.
I THINK IT MADE ME A BETTER PERSON.
10-21-19 2019 Scott Adams, Inc./Dist. by Andrews McMeel

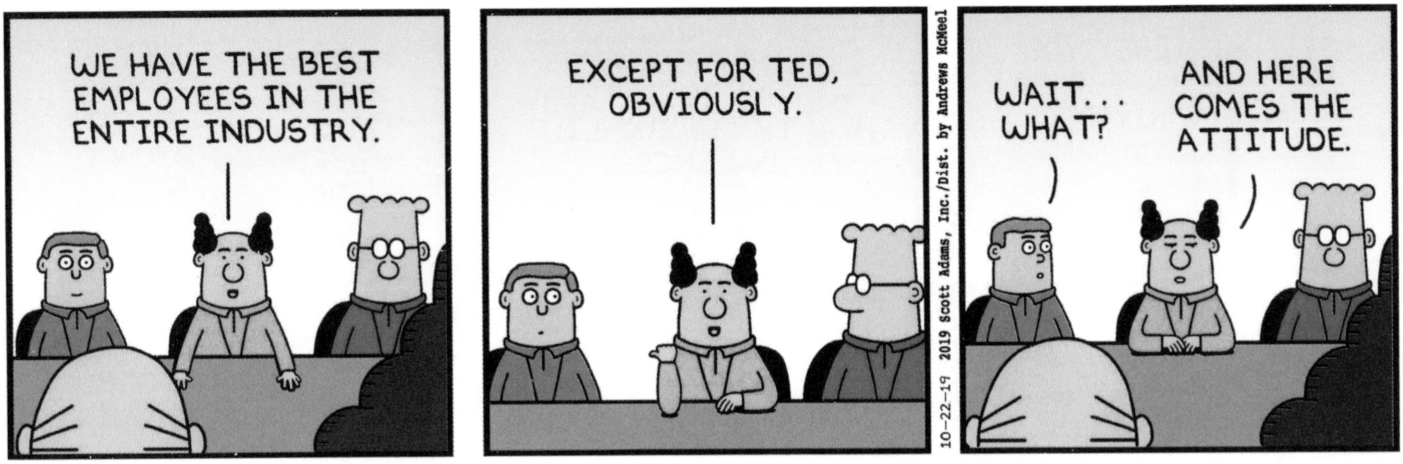
WE HAVE THE BEST EMPLOYEES IN THE ENTIRE INDUSTRY.
EXCEPT FOR TED, OBVIOUSLY.
WAIT... WHAT?
AND HERE COMES THE ATTITUDE.
10-22-19 2019 Scott Adams, Inc./Dist. by Andrews McMeel

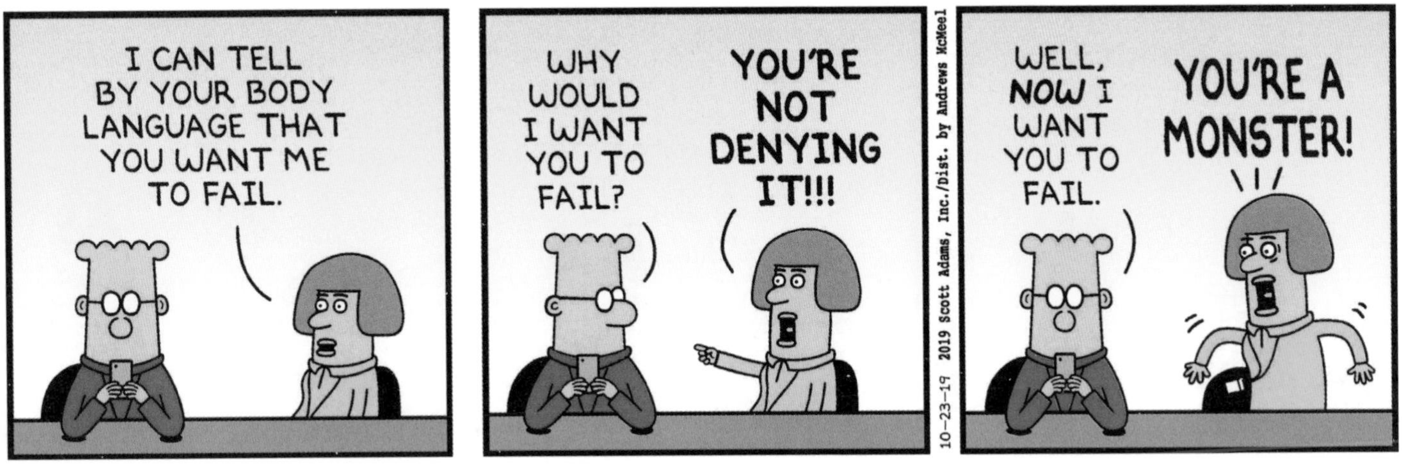
I CAN TELL BY YOUR BODY LANGUAGE THAT YOU WANT ME TO FAIL.
WHY WOULD I WANT YOU TO FAIL?
YOU'RE NOT DENYING IT!!!
WELL, NOW I WANT YOU TO FAIL.
YOU'RE A MONSTER!
10-23-19 2019 Scott Adams, Inc./Dist. by Andrews McMeel

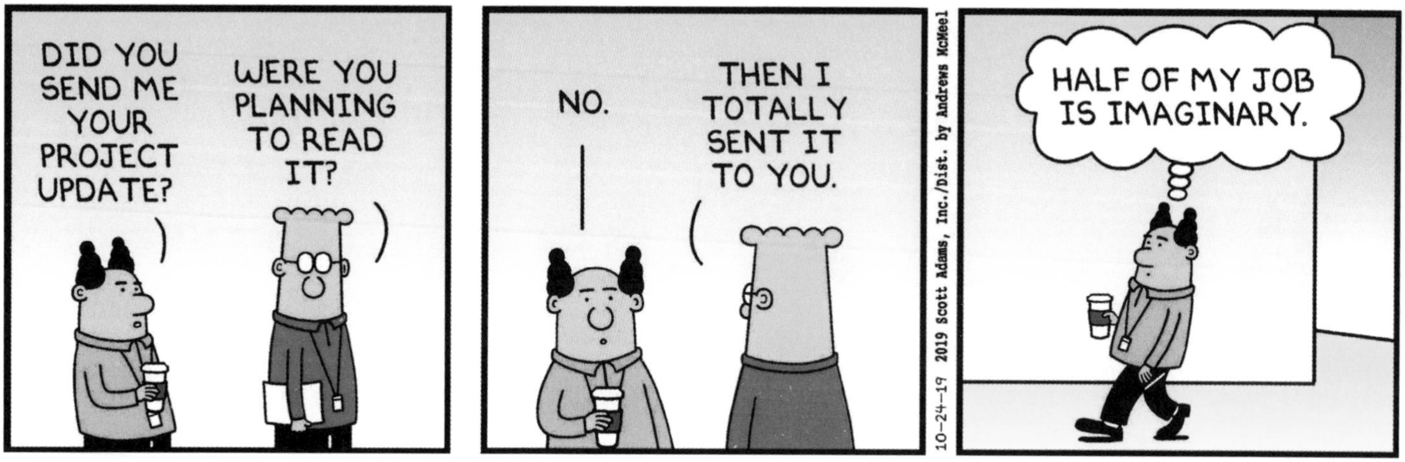
DID YOU SEND ME YOUR PROJECT UPDATE?
WERE YOU PLANNING TO READ IT?
NO.
THEN I TOTALLY SENT IT TO YOU.
HALF OF MY JOB IS IMAGINARY.

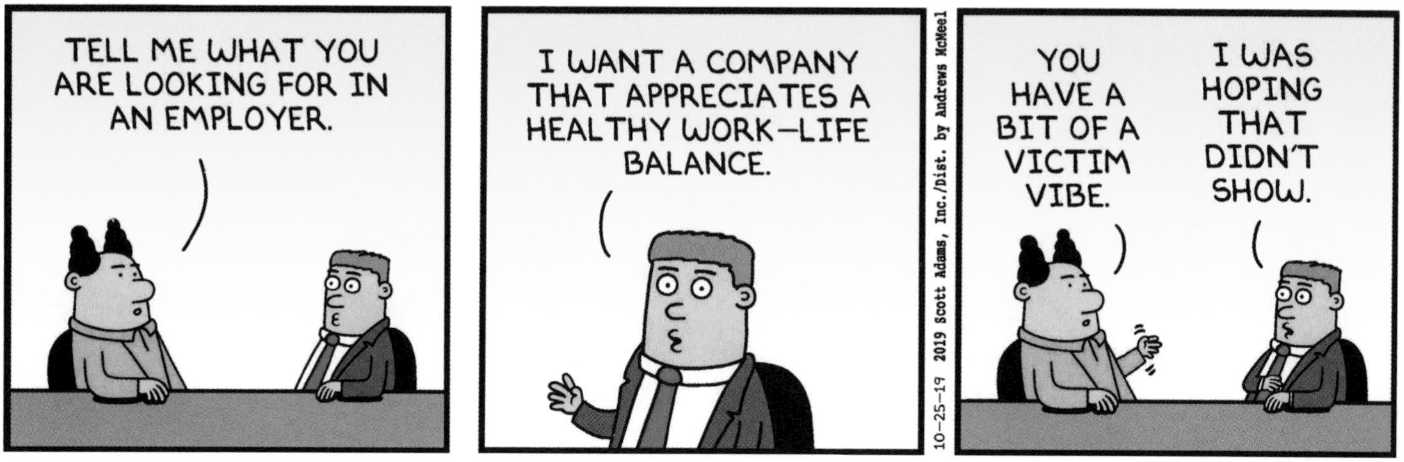
TELL ME WHAT YOU ARE LOOKING FOR IN AN EMPLOYER.
I WANT A COMPANY THAT APPRECIATES A HEALTHY WORK-LIFE BALANCE.
YOU HAVE A BIT OF A VICTIM VIBE.
I WAS HOPING THAT DIDN'T SHOW.

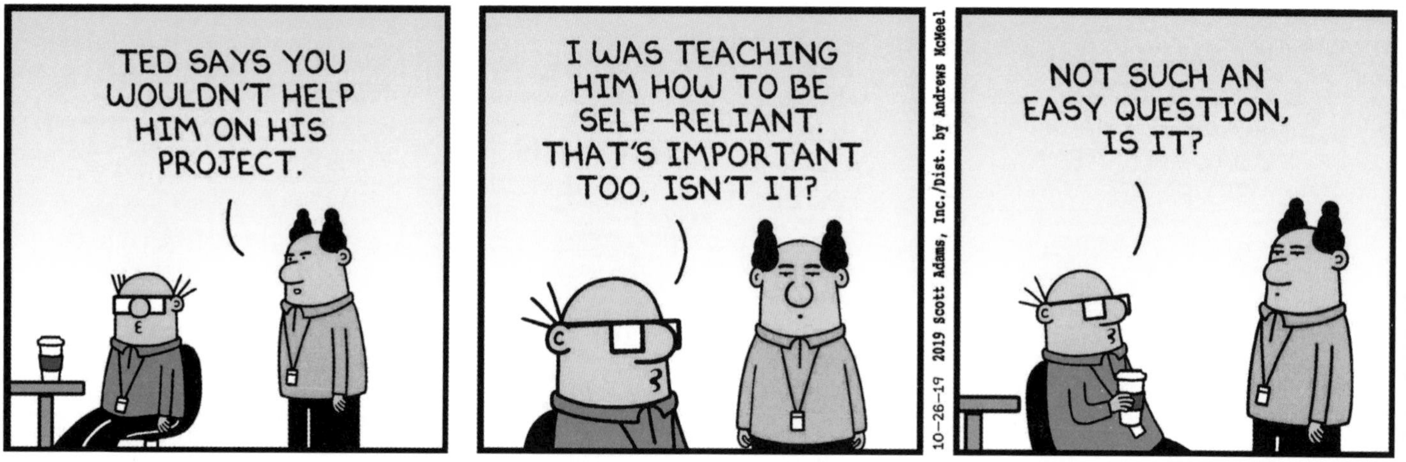
TED SAYS YOU WOULDN'T HELP HIM ON HIS PROJECT.
I WAS TEACHING HIM HOW TO BE SELF-RELIANT. THAT'S IMPORTANT TOO, ISN'T IT?
NOT SUCH AN EASY QUESTION, IS IT?

I'M NEGOTIATING A DEAL WITH THE GOVERNMENT OF ELBONIA.
THEY AGREED TO BUY A THOUSAND DOLLARS OF OUR PRODUCTS.
ALL I HAD TO DO WAS AGREE TO LET THEM STEAL ALL OF OUR INTELLECTUAL PROPERTY.
© 2019 Scott Adams, Inc./Dist. by Andrews McMeel
WOULDN'T IT BE BETTER FOR US IF THEY DIDN'T STEAL OUR I.P.?
YOU HAVE TO LOOK AT THE BIG PICTURE.
THEY ALSO AGREED TO STOP KILLING TENS OF THOUSANDS OF OUR CITIZENS WITH THEIR ILLEGAL DRUG SHIPMENTS.
DID THEY STOP?
NO, BUT THEY SAID THEY WOULD.
MAYBE YOU SHOULD NEGOTIATE HARDER.
AND RISK LOSING A THOUSAND DOLLARS OF REVENUE?
10-27-19

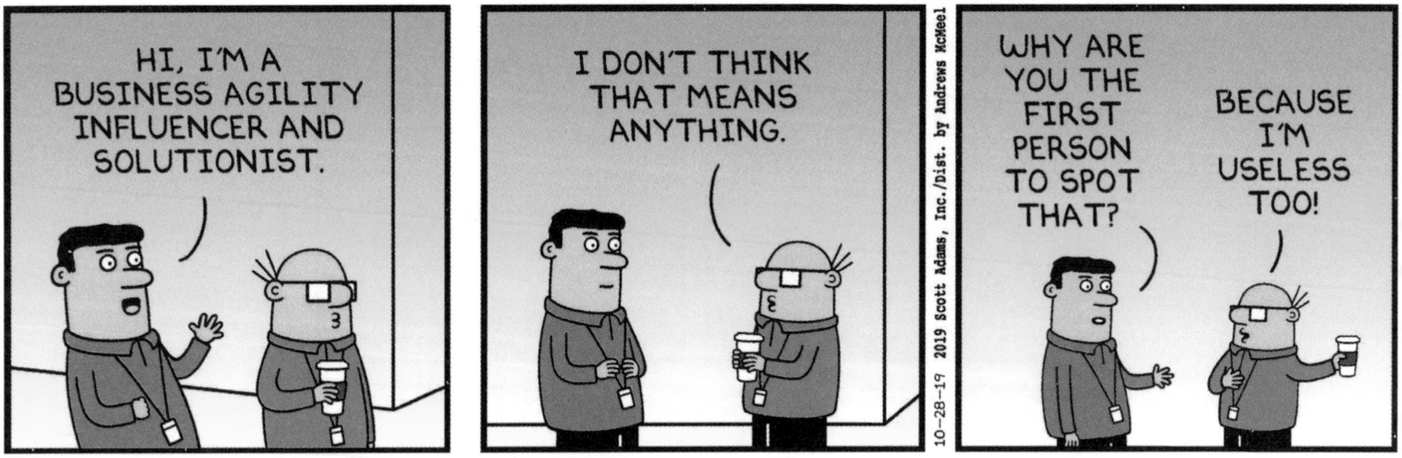
HI, I'M A BUSINESS AGILITY INFLUENCER AND SOLUTIONIST.
I DON'T THINK THAT MEANS ANYTHING.
WHY ARE YOU THE FIRST PERSON TO SPOT THAT?
BECAUSE I'M USELESS TOO!
10-28-19 2019 Scott Adams, Inc./Dist. by Andrews McMeel

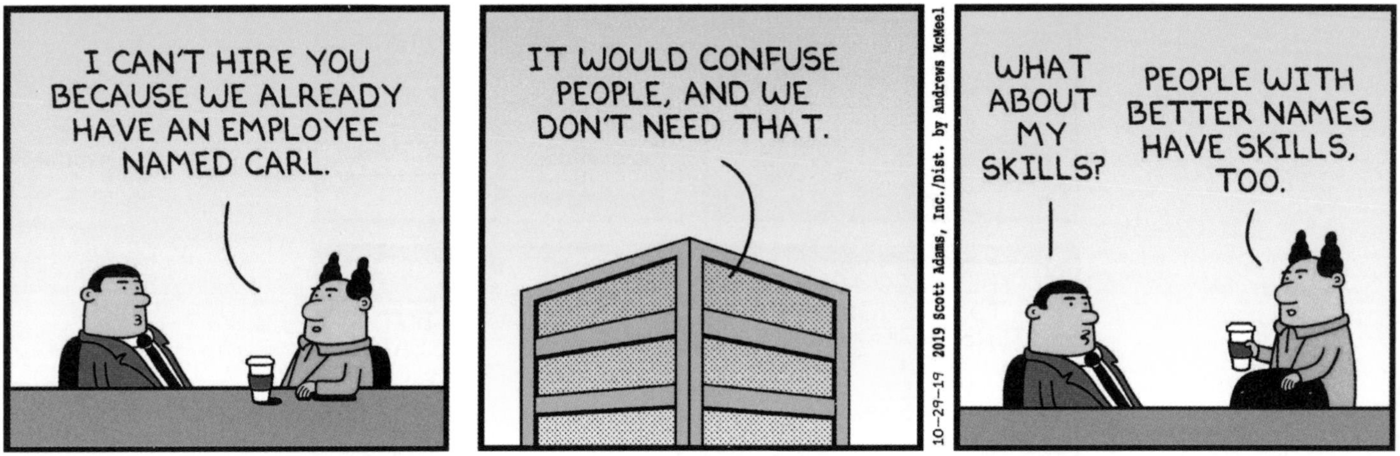
I CAN'T HIRE YOU BECAUSE WE ALREADY HAVE AN EMPLOYEE NAMED CARL.
IT WOULD CONFUSE PEOPLE, AND WE DON'T NEED THAT.
WHAT ABOUT MY SKILLS?
PEOPLE WITH BETTER NAMES HAVE SKILLS, TOO.
10-29-19 2019 Scott Adams, Inc./Dist. by Andrews McMeel

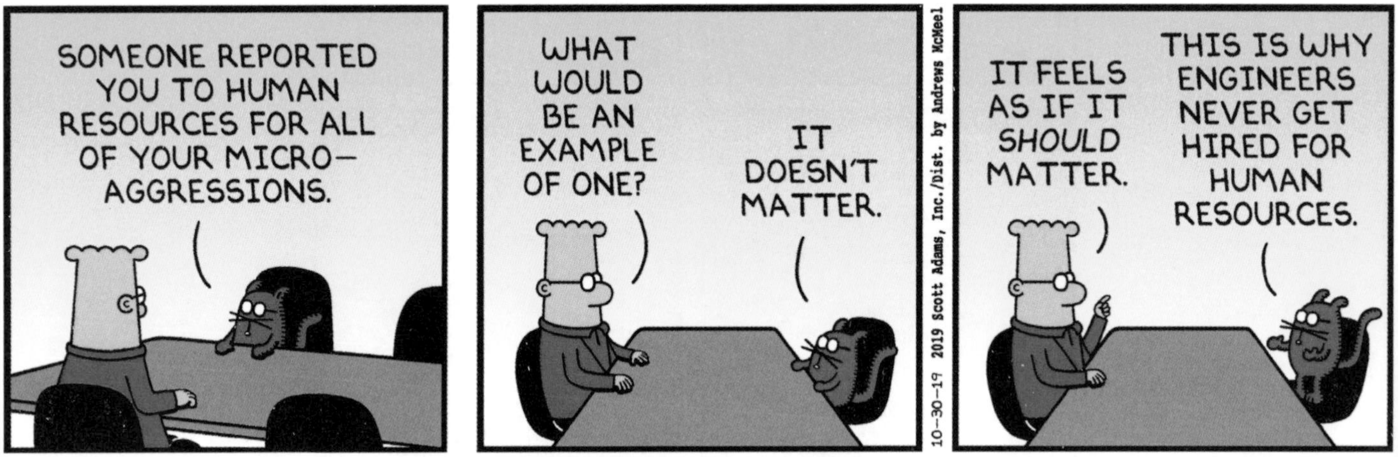
SOMEONE REPORTED YOU TO HUMAN RESOURCES FOR ALL OF YOUR MICRO-AGGRESSIONS.
WHAT WOULD BE AN EXAMPLE OF ONE?
IT DOESN'T MATTER.
IT FEELS AS IF IT *SHOULD* MATTER.
THIS IS WHY ENGINEERS NEVER GET HIRED FOR HUMAN RESOURCES.
10-30-19 2019 Scott Adams, Inc./Dist. by Andrews McMeel

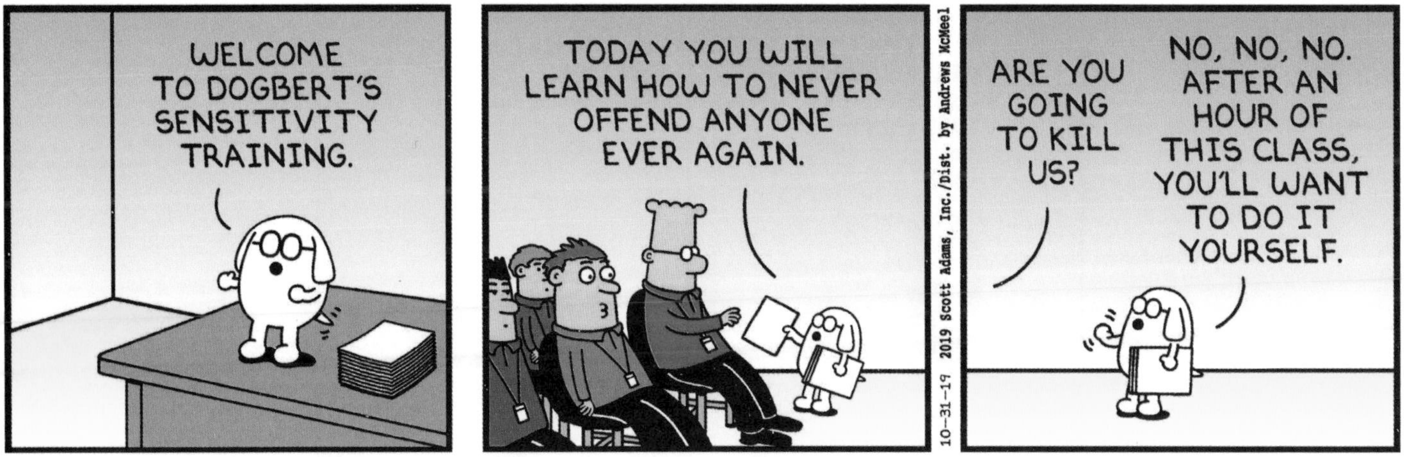
WELCOME TO DOGBERT'S SENSITIVITY TRAINING.
TODAY YOU WILL LEARN HOW TO NEVER OFFEND ANYONE EVER AGAIN.
10-31-19 2019 Scott Adams, Inc./Dist. by Andrews McMeel
ARE YOU GOING TO KILL US?
NO, NO, NO. AFTER AN HOUR OF THIS CLASS, YOU'LL WANT TO DO IT YOURSELF.

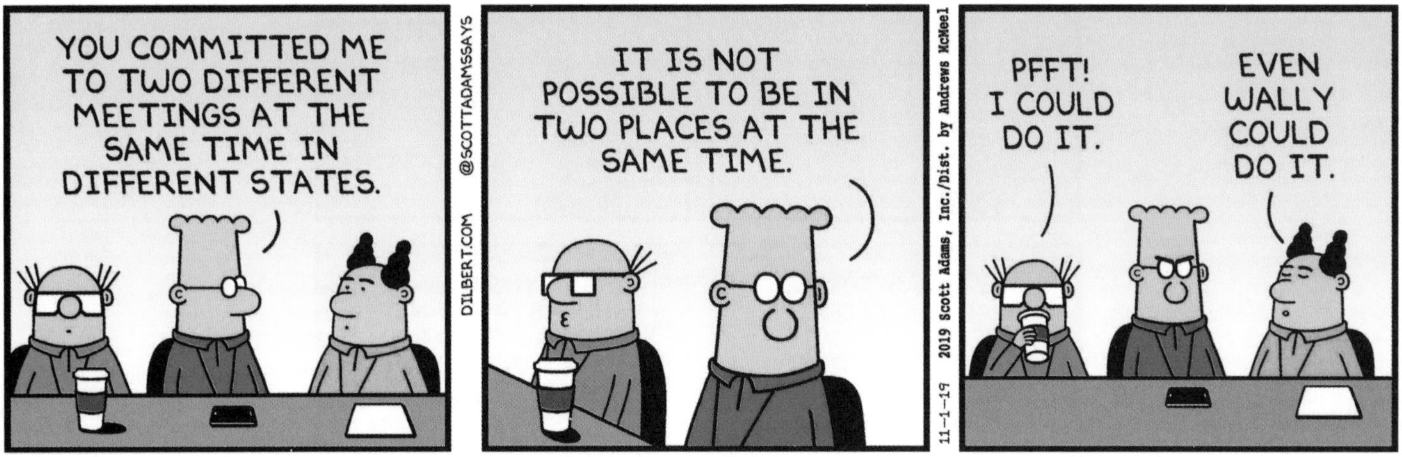
YOU COMMITTED ME TO TWO DIFFERENT MEETINGS AT THE SAME TIME IN DIFFERENT STATES.
DILBERT.COM @SCOTTADAMSSAYS
IT IS NOT POSSIBLE TO BE IN TWO PLACES AT THE SAME TIME.
11-1-19 2019 Scott Adams, Inc./Dist. by Andrews McMeel
PFFT! I COULD DO IT.
EVEN WALLY COULD DO IT.

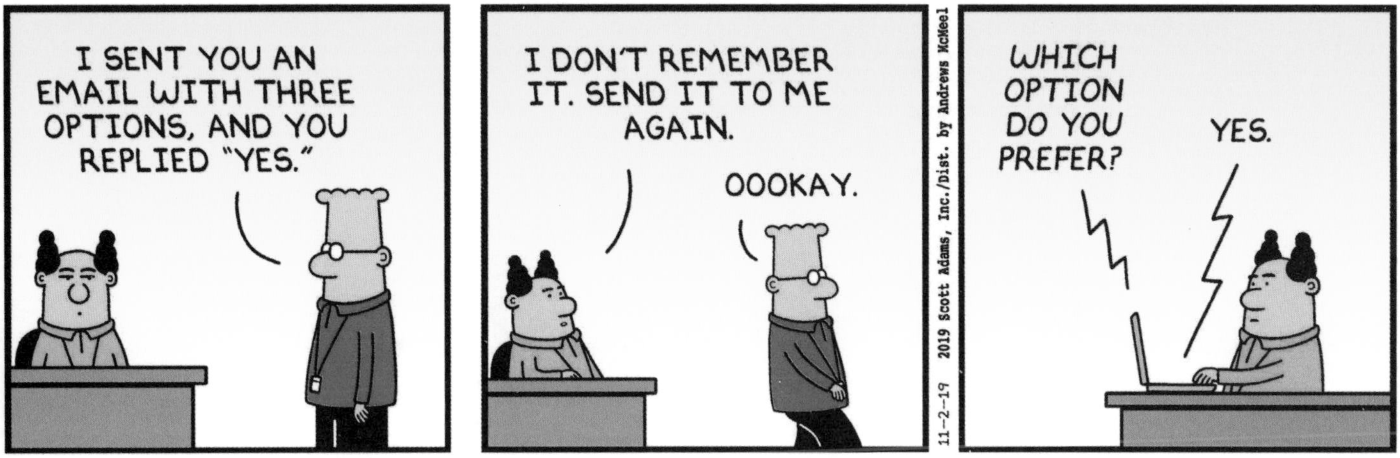
I SENT YOU AN EMAIL WITH THREE OPTIONS, AND YOU REPLIED "YES."
I DON'T REMEMBER IT. SEND IT TO ME AGAIN.
OOOKAY.
11-2-19 2019 Scott Adams, Inc./Dist. by Andrews McMeel
WHICH OPTION DO YOU PREFER?
YES.

AND THAT'S MY BLOCKCHAIN PROPOSAL. ANY QUESTIONS?
THERE WAS A PART I DIDN'T UNDERSTAND.
WHICH PART?
THE WORDS.
ALL OF THEM?
ONLY THE GOOFY ONES.
SUCH AS TOKEN, SMART CONTRACT, CERTAINTY AS A SERVICE, UTXO BLOCKCHAINS, NODE, LEDGER, AND DAPS.
SO. . . YOU DIDN'T UNDERSTAND ANY–THING I SAID FOR THE PAST HOUR?
DON'T TRY TO TURN THIS INTO MY FAULT.
YOU COULD HAVE ASKED ME TO CLARIFY.
I ALSO WANTED IT TO END.
©2019 Scott Adams, Inc./Dist. by Andrews McMeel
11-3-19

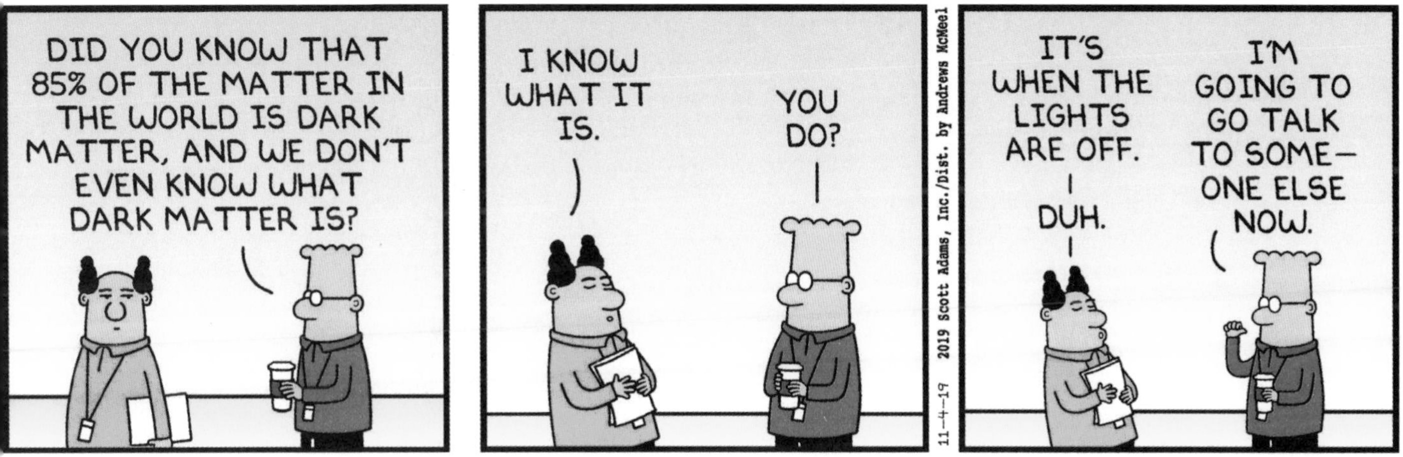
DID YOU KNOW THAT 85% OF THE MATTER IN THE WORLD IS DARK MATTER, AND WE DON'T EVEN KNOW WHAT DARK MATTER IS?
I KNOW WHAT IT IS.
YOU DO?
IT'S WHEN THE LIGHTS ARE OFF.
DUH.
I'M GOING TO GO TALK TO SOME-ONE ELSE NOW.
11-4-19 2019 Scott Adams, Inc./Dist. by Andrews McMeel

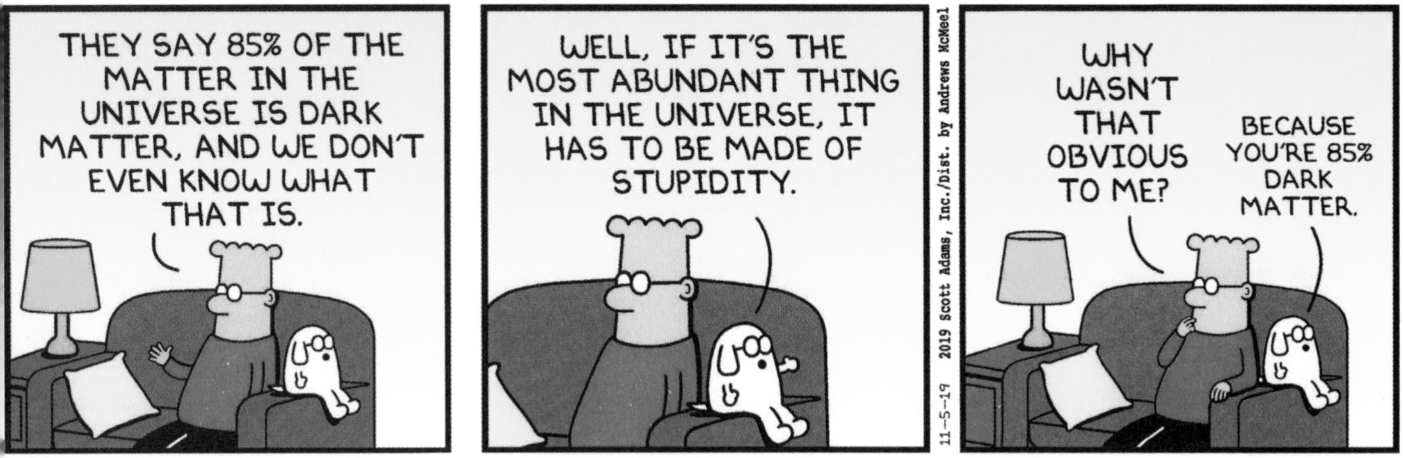
THEY SAY 85% OF THE MATTER IN THE UNIVERSE IS DARK MATTER, AND WE DON'T EVEN KNOW WHAT THAT IS.
WELL, IF IT'S THE MOST ABUNDANT THING IN THE UNIVERSE, IT HAS TO BE MADE OF STUPIDITY.
WHY WASN'T THAT OBVIOUS TO ME?
BECAUSE YOU'RE 85% DARK MATTER.
11-5-19 2019 Scott Adams, Inc./Dist. by Andrews McMeel

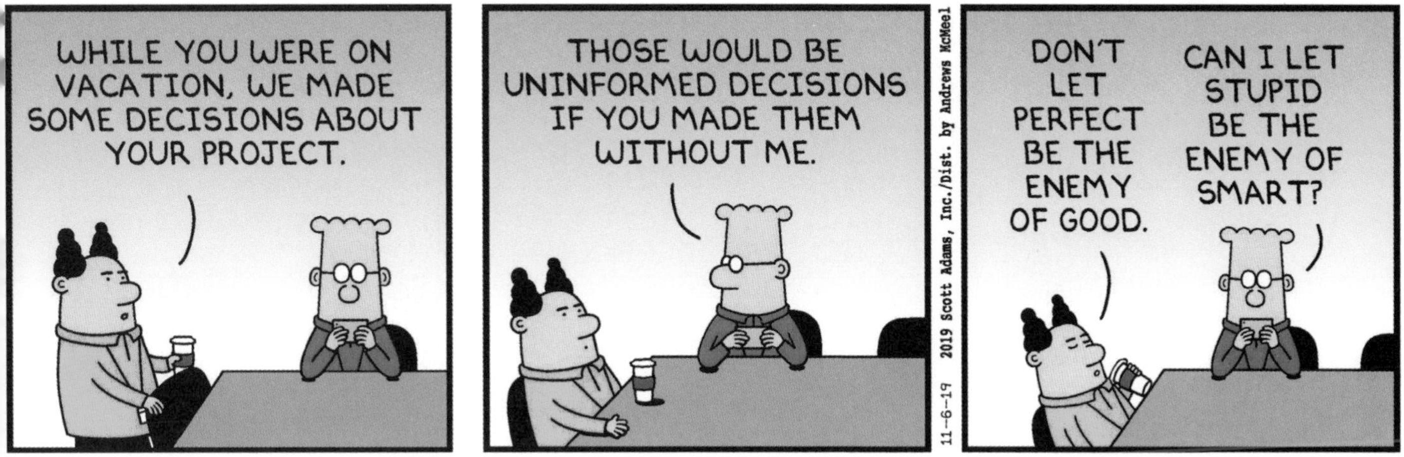
WHILE YOU WERE ON VACATION, WE MADE SOME DECISIONS ABOUT YOUR PROJECT.
THOSE WOULD BE UNINFORMED DECISIONS IF YOU MADE THEM WITHOUT ME.
DON'T LET PERFECT BE THE ENEMY OF GOOD.
CAN I LET STUPID BE THE ENEMY OF SMART?
11-6-19 2019 Scott Adams, Inc./Dist. by Andrews McMeel

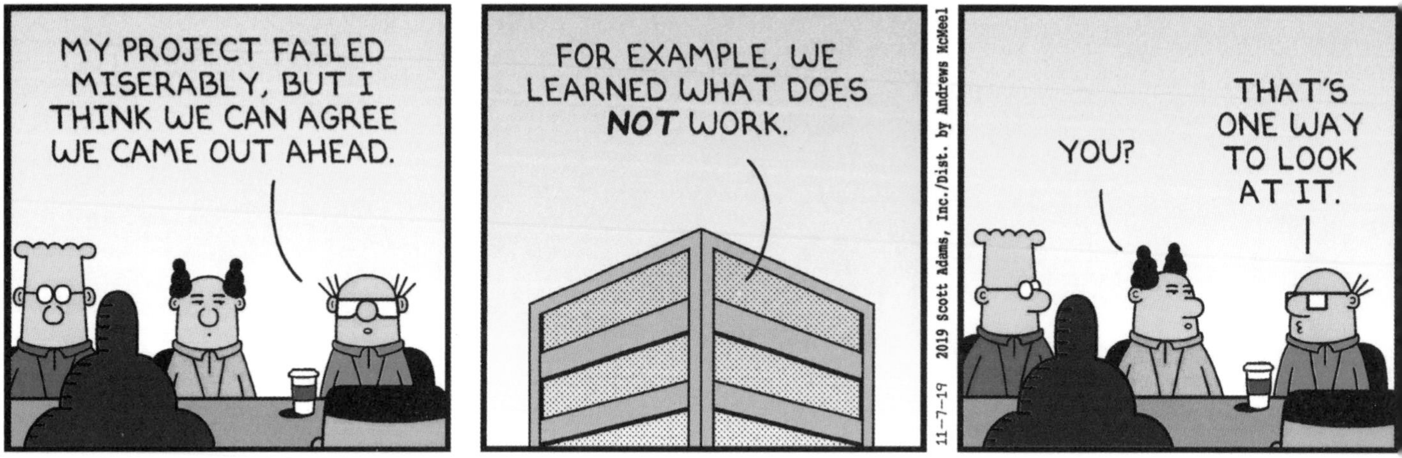
MY PROJECT FAILED MISERABLY, BUT I THINK WE CAN AGREE WE CAME OUT AHEAD.
FOR EXAMPLE, WE LEARNED WHAT DOES **NOT** WORK.
11-7-19 2019 Scott Adams, Inc./Dist. by Andrews McMeel
YOU?
THAT'S ONE WAY TO LOOK AT IT.

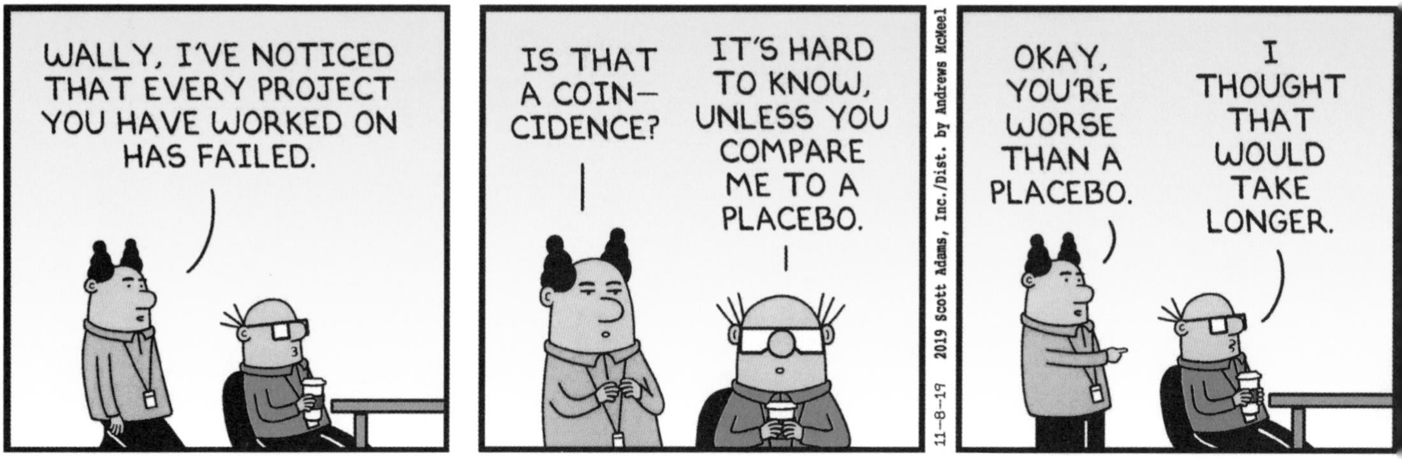
WALLY, I'VE NOTICED THAT EVERY PROJECT YOU HAVE WORKED ON HAS FAILED.
IS THAT A COIN-CIDENCE?
IT'S HARD TO KNOW, UNLESS YOU COMPARE ME TO A PLACEBO.
11-8-19 2019 Scott Adams, Inc./Dist. by Andrews McMeel
OKAY, YOU'RE WORSE THAN A PLACEBO.
I THOUGHT THAT WOULD TAKE LONGER.

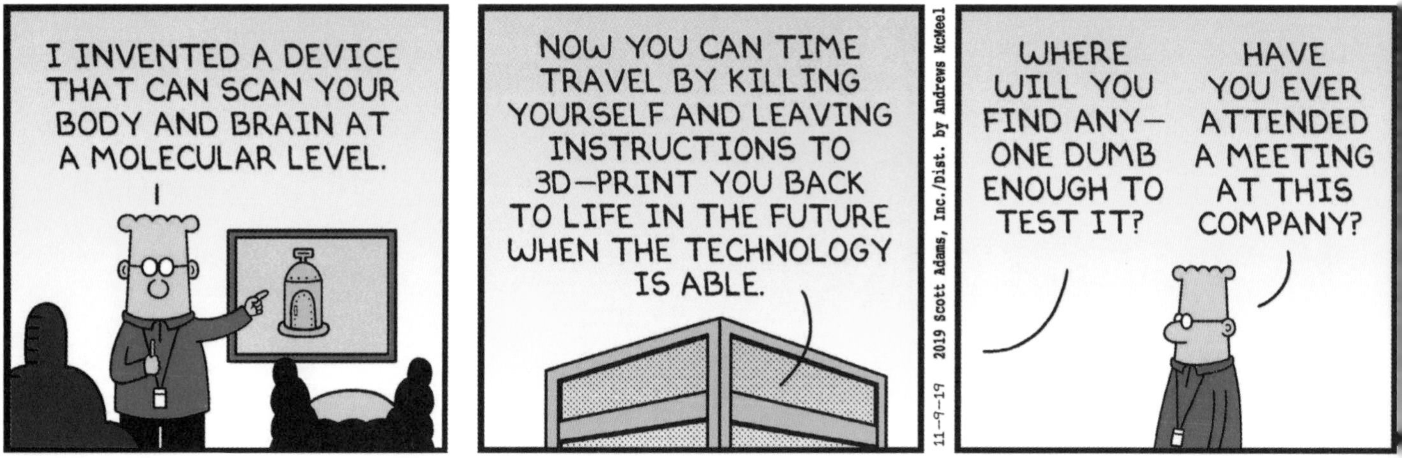
I INVENTED A DEVICE THAT CAN SCAN YOUR BODY AND BRAIN AT A MOLECULAR LEVEL.
NOW YOU CAN TIME TRAVEL BY KILLING YOURSELF AND LEAVING INSTRUCTIONS TO 3D-PRINT YOU BACK TO LIFE IN THE FUTURE WHEN THE TECHNOLOGY IS ABLE.
11-9-19 2019 Scott Adams, Inc./Dist. by Andrews McMeel
WHERE WILL YOU FIND ANY-ONE DUMB ENOUGH TO TEST IT?
HAVE YOU EVER ATTENDED A MEETING AT THIS COMPANY?

IF YOU HAVE ANY PROBLEMS WITH THE SOFTWARE, JUST GIVE ME A CALL.
WHAT IF YOU DIE OR YOU'RE IN A COMA?
WELL, IN THOSE CASES I WOULD NOT RETURN YOUR CALL.
SO YOU'RE LYING ABOUT GETTING BACK TO ME.
NO, I'M MAKING A NORMAL KIND OF GENERALIZATION, WHICH I ASSUMED YOU WOULD UNDER–STAND.
OKAY, SO NOW YOU'RE CALLING ME STUPID, **AND** YOU'RE A LIAR?
IF A LIAR CALLS YOU STUPID, WOULDN'T THAT MEAN YOU ARE SMART?
FAIR POINT.
THANKS. I'M PROUD OF IT.
© 2019 Scott Adams, Inc./Dist. by Andrews McMeel
11-10-19

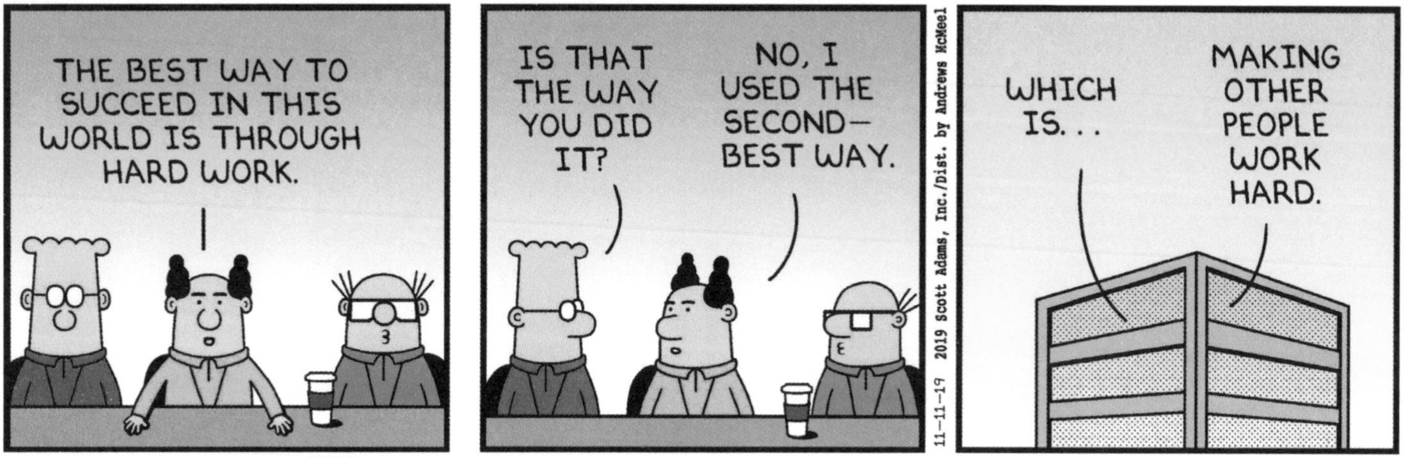
THE BEST WAY TO SUCCEED IN THIS WORLD IS THROUGH HARD WORK.
IS THAT THE WAY YOU DID IT?
NO, I USED THE SECOND-BEST WAY.
WHICH IS. . .
MAKING OTHER PEOPLE WORK HARD.
11-11-19 2019 Scott Adams, Inc./Dist. by Andrews McMeel

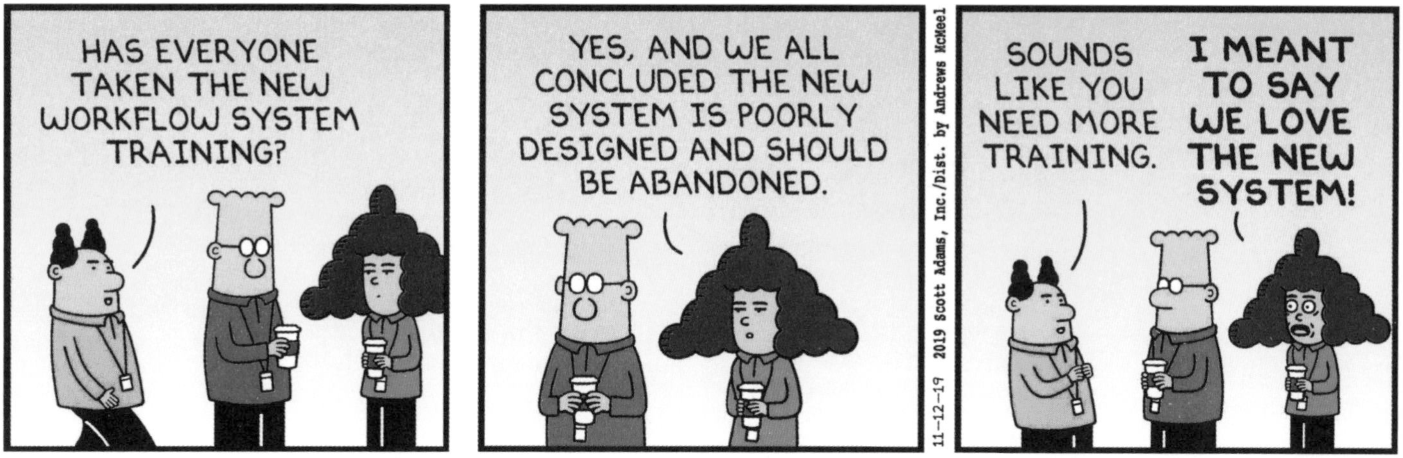
HAS EVERYONE TAKEN THE NEW WORKFLOW SYSTEM TRAINING?
YES, AND WE ALL CONCLUDED THE NEW SYSTEM IS POORLY DESIGNED AND SHOULD BE ABANDONED.
SOUNDS LIKE YOU NEED MORE TRAINING.
I MEANT TO SAY WE LOVE THE NEW SYSTEM!
11-12-19 2019 Scott Adams, Inc./Dist. by Andrews McMeel

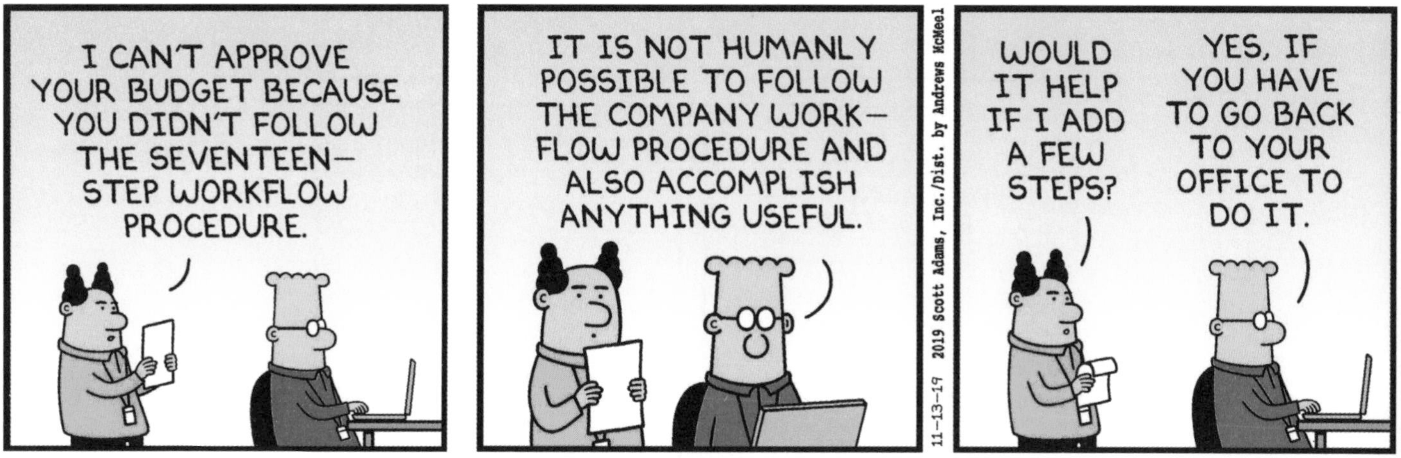
I CAN'T APPROVE YOUR BUDGET BECAUSE YOU DIDN'T FOLLOW THE SEVENTEEN-STEP WORKFLOW PROCEDURE.
IT IS NOT HUMANLY POSSIBLE TO FOLLOW THE COMPANY WORK-FLOW PROCEDURE AND ALSO ACCOMPLISH ANYTHING USEFUL.
WOULD IT HELP IF I ADD A FEW STEPS?
YES, IF YOU HAVE TO GO BACK TO YOUR OFFICE TO DO IT.
11-13-19 2019 Scott Adams, Inc./Dist. by Andrews McMeel

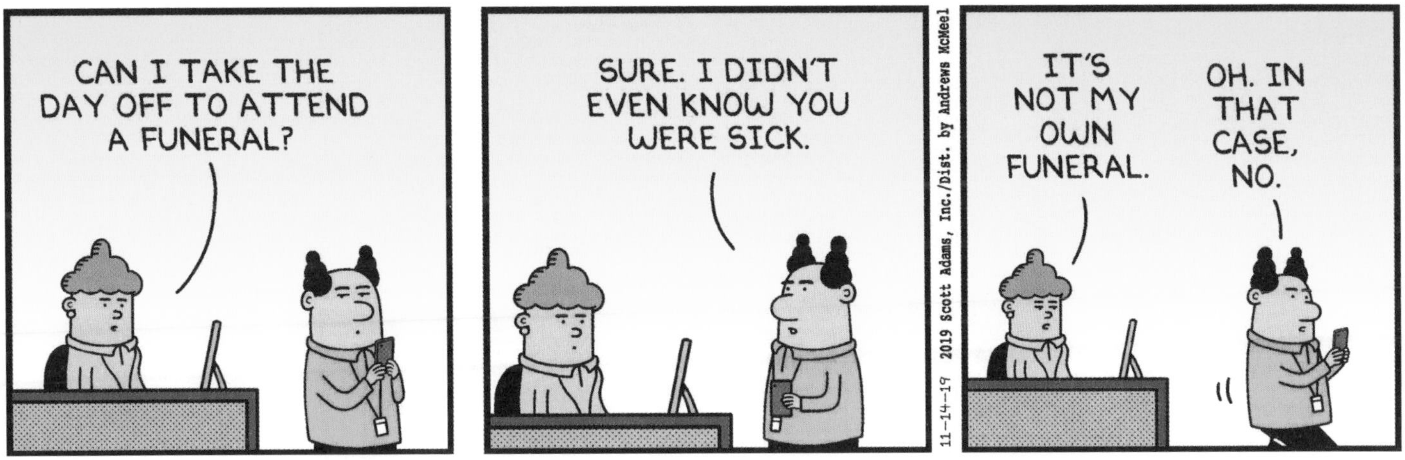
CAN I TAKE THE DAY OFF TO ATTEND A FUNERAL?
SURE. I DIDN'T EVEN KNOW YOU WERE SICK.
IT'S NOT MY OWN FUNERAL.
OH. IN THAT CASE, NO.
11-14-19 2019 Scott Adams, Inc./Dist. by Andrews McMeel

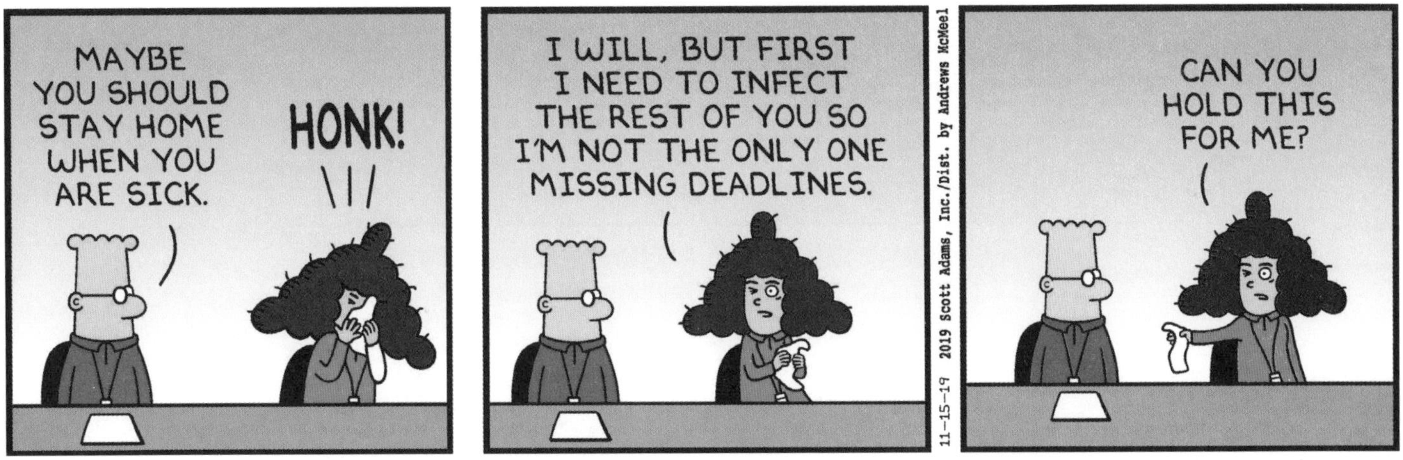
MAYBE YOU SHOULD STAY HOME WHEN YOU ARE SICK.
HONK!
I WILL, BUT FIRST I NEED TO INFECT THE REST OF YOU SO I'M NOT THE ONLY ONE MISSING DEADLINES.
CAN YOU HOLD THIS FOR ME?
11-15-19 2019 Scott Adams, Inc./Dist. by Andrews McMeel

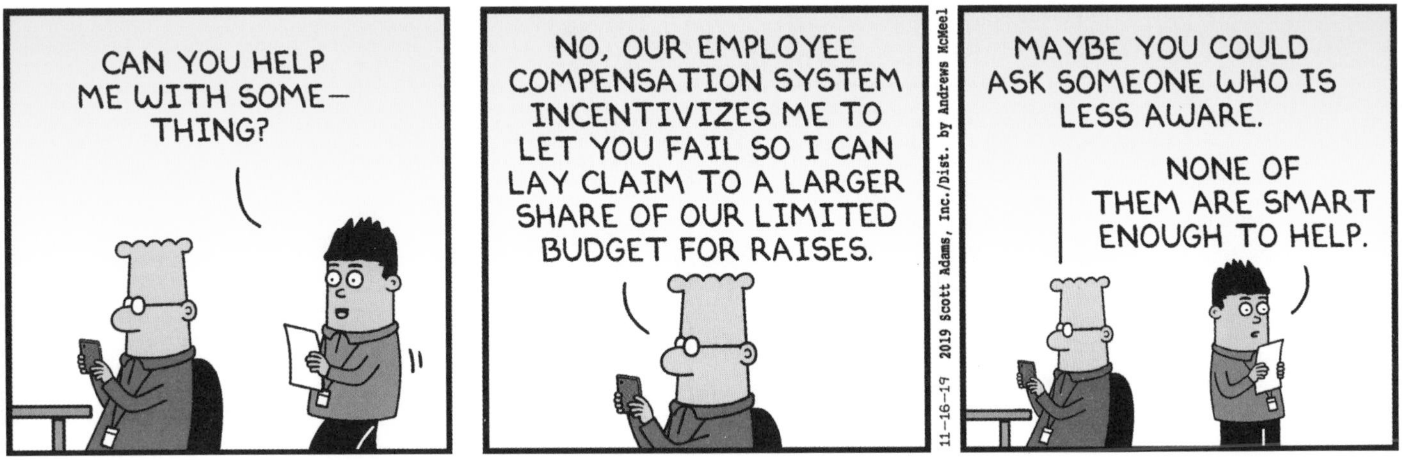
CAN YOU HELP ME WITH SOME-THING?
NO, OUR EMPLOYEE COMPENSATION SYSTEM INCENTIVIZES ME TO LET YOU FAIL SO I CAN LAY CLAIM TO A LARGER SHARE OF OUR LIMITED BUDGET FOR RAISES.
MAYBE YOU COULD ASK SOMEONE WHO IS LESS AWARE.
NONE OF THEM ARE SMART ENOUGH TO HELP.
11-16-19 2019 Scott Adams, Inc./Dist. by Andrews McMeel

I HEARD YOU ASKED OUR V.P. OF OPERATIONS TO BE YOUR MENTOR.
WHY DIDN'T YOU TELL ME YOU NEEDED SOME MENTORING?
I'M FULL OF USEFUL ADVICE.
SUCH AS?
WELL. . . NOW YOU'RE PUTTING ME ON THE SPOT.
© 2019 Scott Adams, Inc./Dist. by Andrews McMeel
IT'S HARD TO THINK OF ADVICE WHILE YOU'RE PRESSURING ME.
MAYBE YOU COULD GIVE ME A SCENARIO, AND THEN I'LL TELL YOU WHAT TO DO.
OKAY. SUPPOSE MY BOSS IS RUINING MY PRODUCTIVITY BY YAMMERING ABOUT HIS GREAT ADVICE. WHAT CAN I DO?
11-17-19
THAT FEELS LIKE A TRICK QUESTION.
OUR V.P. OF OPER–ATIONS COULD ANSWER IT.

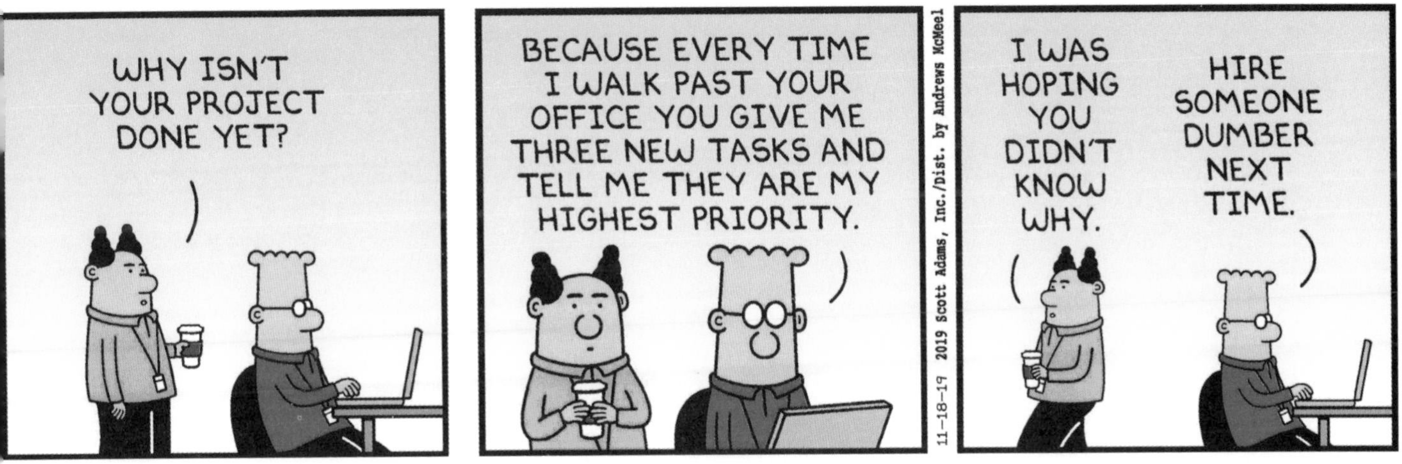
WHY ISN'T YOUR PROJECT DONE YET?
BECAUSE EVERY TIME I WALK PAST YOUR OFFICE YOU GIVE ME THREE NEW TASKS AND TELL ME THEY ARE MY HIGHEST PRIORITY.
11-18-19 2019 Scott Adams, Inc./Dist. by Andrews McMeel
I WAS HOPING YOU DIDN'T KNOW WHY.
HIRE SOMEONE DUMBER NEXT TIME.

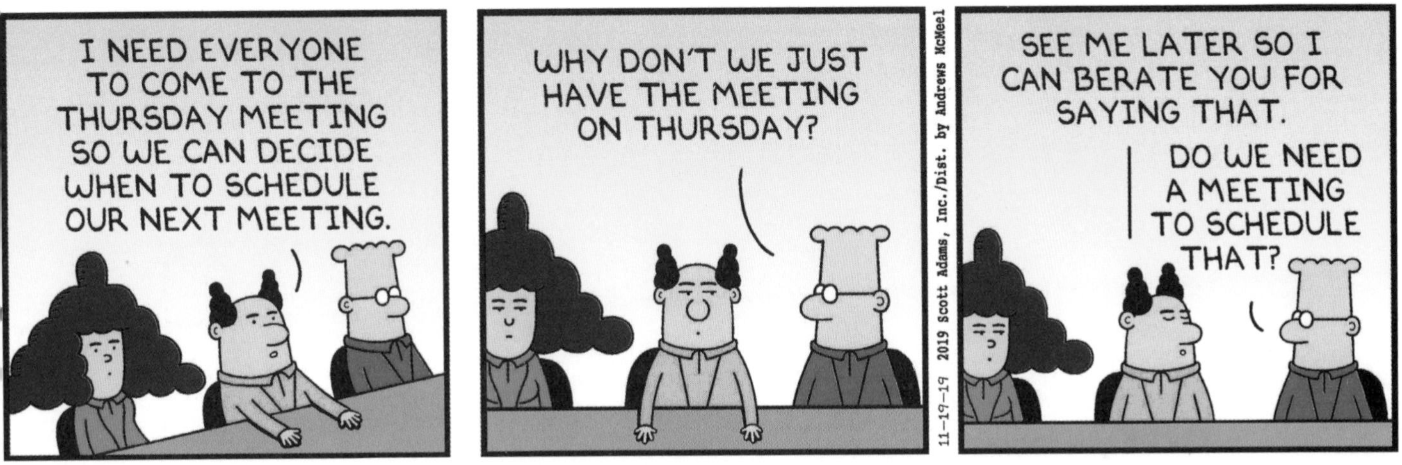
I NEED EVERYONE TO COME TO THE THURSDAY MEETING SO WE CAN DECIDE WHEN TO SCHEDULE OUR NEXT MEETING.
WHY DON'T WE JUST HAVE THE MEETING ON THURSDAY?
11-19-19 2019 Scott Adams, Inc./Dist. by Andrews McMeel
SEE ME LATER SO I CAN BERATE YOU FOR SAYING THAT.
DO WE NEED A MEETING TO SCHEDULE THAT?

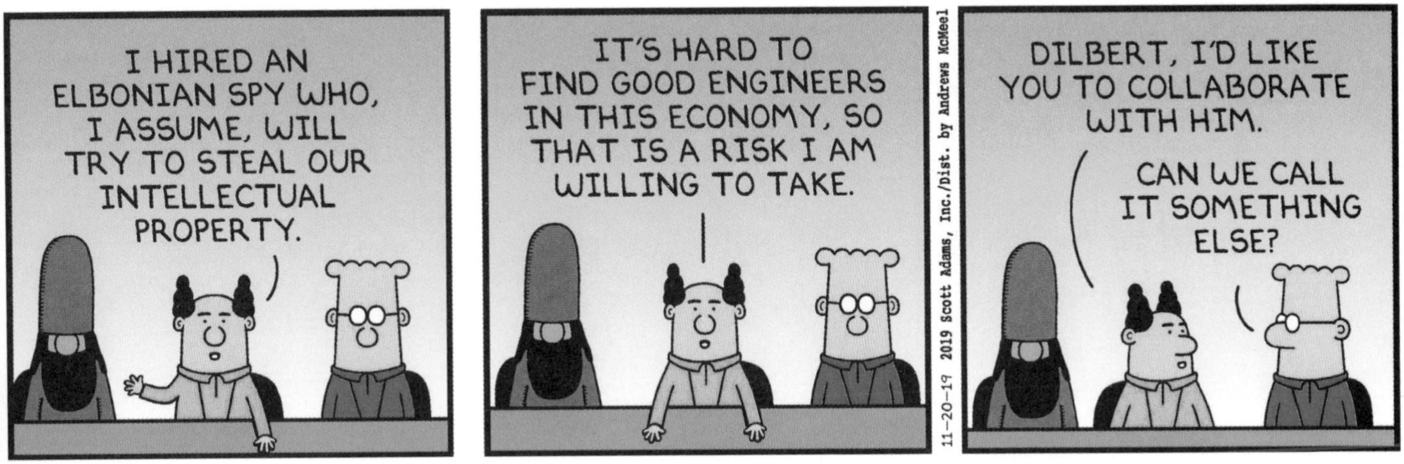
I HIRED AN ELBONIAN SPY WHO, I ASSUME, WILL TRY TO STEAL OUR INTELLECTUAL PROPERTY.
IT'S HARD TO FIND GOOD ENGINEERS IN THIS ECONOMY, SO THAT IS A RISK I AM WILLING TO TAKE.
11-20-19 2019 Scott Adams, Inc./Dist. by Andrews McMeel
DILBERT, I'D LIKE YOU TO COLLABORATE WITH HIM.
CAN WE CALL IT SOMETHING ELSE?

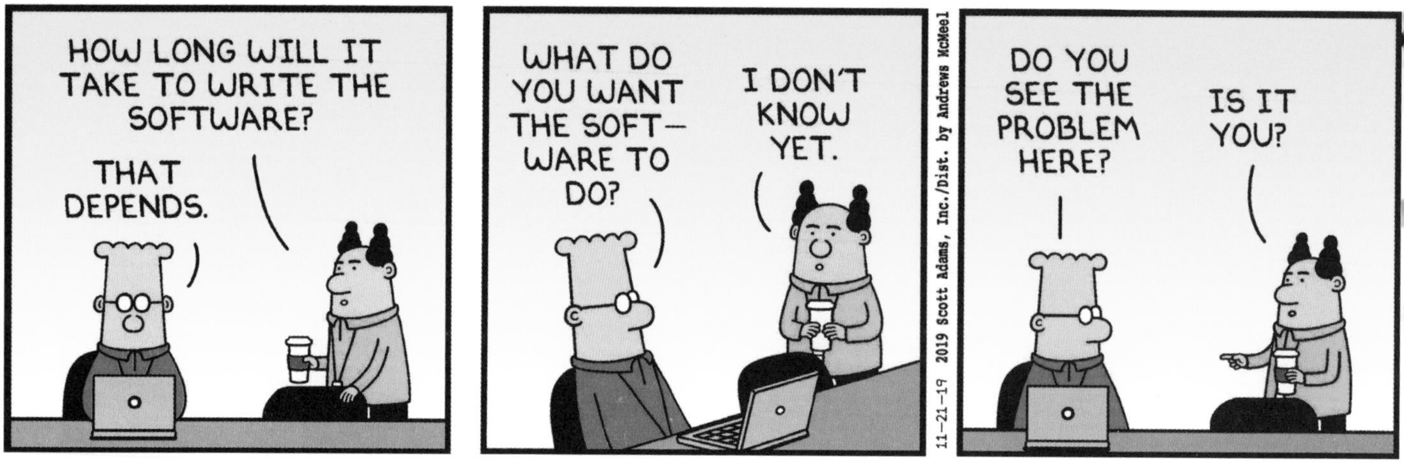
HOW LONG WILL IT TAKE TO WRITE THE SOFTWARE?
THAT DEPENDS.
WHAT DO YOU WANT THE SOFT-WARE TO DO?
I DON'T KNOW YET.
DO YOU SEE THE PROBLEM HERE?
IS IT YOU?

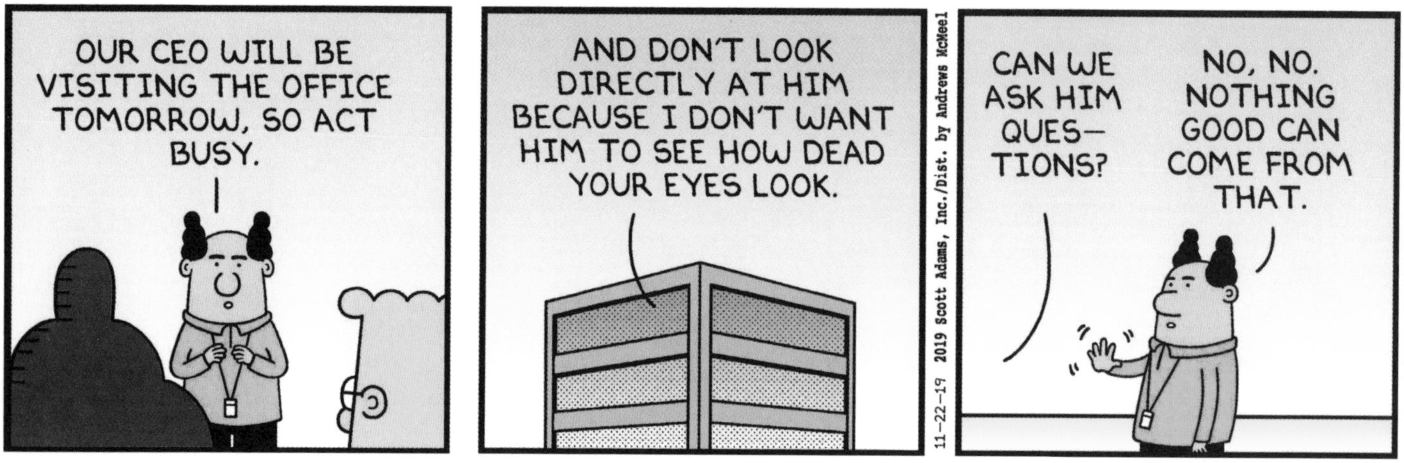
OUR CEO WILL BE VISITING THE OFFICE TOMORROW, SO ACT BUSY.
AND DON'T LOOK DIRECTLY AT HIM BECAUSE I DON'T WANT HIM TO SEE HOW DEAD YOUR EYES LOOK.
CAN WE ASK HIM QUES-TIONS?
NO, NO. NOTHING GOOD CAN COME FROM THAT.

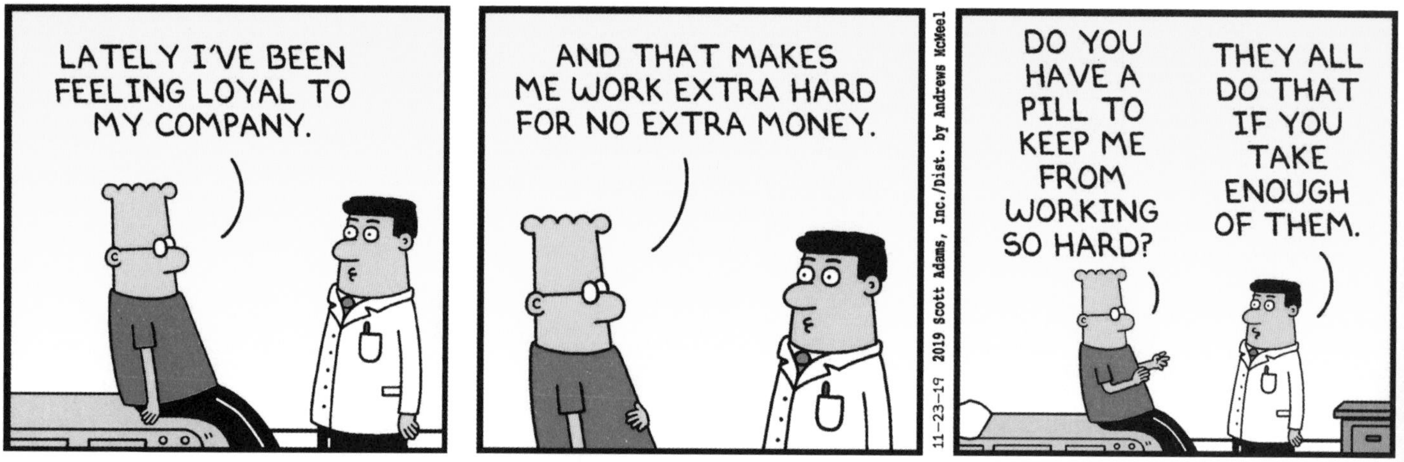
LATELY I'VE BEEN FEELING LOYAL TO MY COMPANY.
AND THAT MAKES ME WORK EXTRA HARD FOR NO EXTRA MONEY.
DO YOU HAVE A PILL TO KEEP ME FROM WORKING SO HARD?
THEY ALL DO THAT IF YOU TAKE ENOUGH OF THEM.

WE'RE MOVING OUR MANUFACTURING OPERATIONS TO ELBONIA TO SAVE MONEY.
ARE YOU WORRIED ABOUT THE ELBONIAN GOVERNMENT'S REPUTATION?
NAH. I TRY TO STAY OUT OF THE WEEDS.
THEY'RE BUILDING CONCENTRATION CAMPS AND ROUND-ING UP DISSENTERS.
THEY INTENTIONALLY POISONED A HUNDRED THOUSAND PEOPLE IN THIS COUNTRY.
THEY ARE HABITUAL STEALERS OF INTEL-LECTUAL PROPERTY, AND THEY ROUTINELY IGNORE AGREEMENTS THEY HAVE SIGNED.
AND THEY HAVE A WELL-KNOWN GOAL OF WEAKENING OTHER COUNTRIES SO THEY CAN DOMINATE THE WORLD.
WHY CAN'T YOU JUST ADMIT I'M SAVING MONEY?
© 2019 Scott Adams, Inc./Dist. by Andrews McMeel
11-24-19

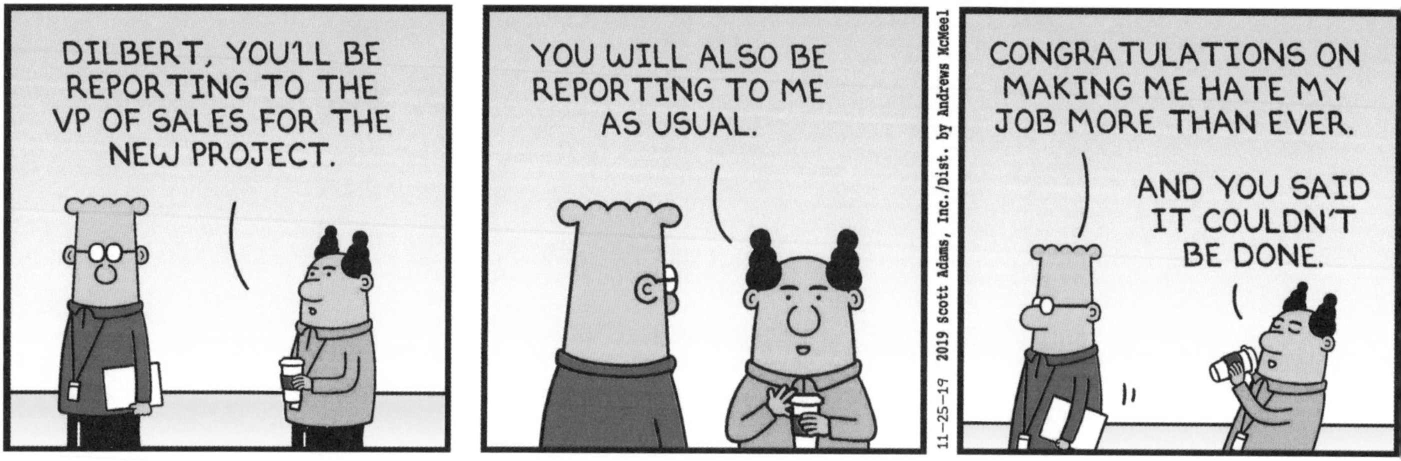
DILBERT, YOU'LL BE REPORTING TO THE VP OF SALES FOR THE NEW PROJECT.
YOU WILL ALSO BE REPORTING TO ME AS USUAL.
11-25-19 © 2019 Scott Adams, Inc./Dist. by Andrews McMeel
CONGRATULATIONS ON MAKING ME HATE MY JOB MORE THAN EVER.
AND YOU SAID IT COULDN'T BE DONE.

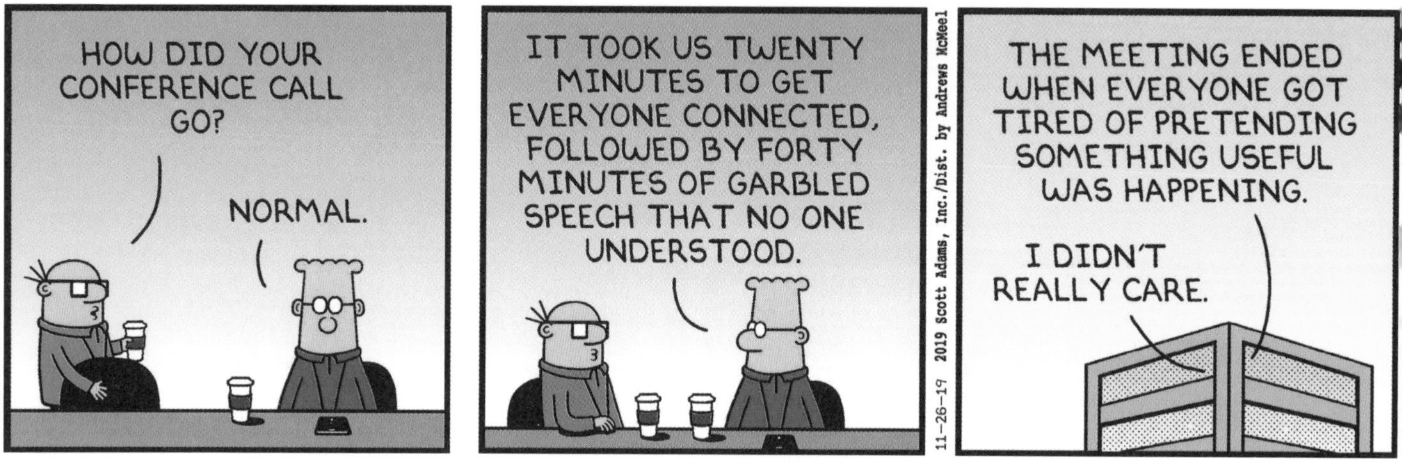
HOW DID YOUR CONFERENCE CALL GO?
NORMAL.
IT TOOK US TWENTY MINUTES TO GET EVERYONE CONNECTED, FOLLOWED BY FORTY MINUTES OF GARBLED SPEECH THAT NO ONE UNDERSTOOD.
11-26-19 © 2019 Scott Adams, Inc./Dist. by Andrews McMeel
THE MEETING ENDED WHEN EVERYONE GOT TIRED OF PRETENDING SOMETHING USEFUL WAS HAPPENING.
I DIDN'T REALLY CARE.

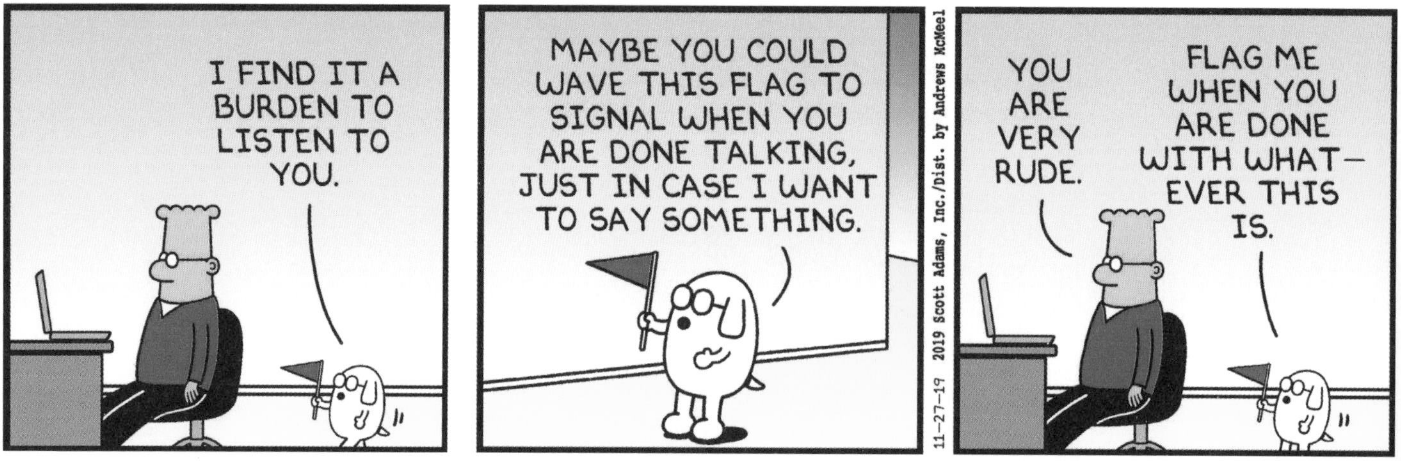
I FIND IT A BURDEN TO LISTEN TO YOU.
MAYBE YOU COULD WAVE THIS FLAG TO SIGNAL WHEN YOU ARE DONE TALKING, JUST IN CASE I WANT TO SAY SOMETHING.
11-27-19 © 2019 Scott Adams, Inc./Dist. by Andrews McMeel
YOU ARE VERY RUDE.
FLAG ME WHEN YOU ARE DONE WITH WHAT-EVER THIS IS.

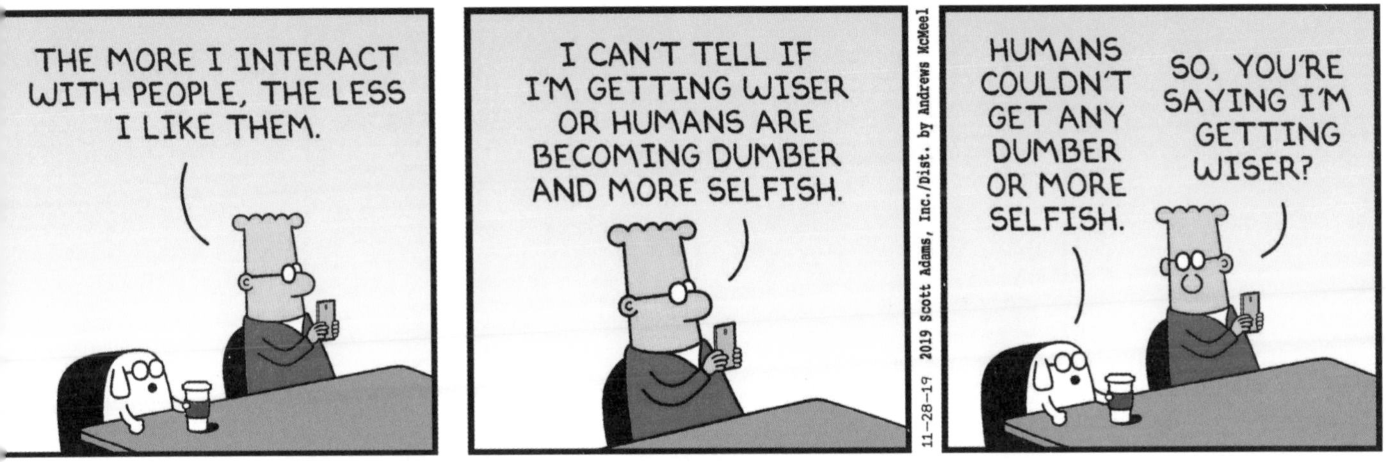
THE MORE I INTERACT WITH PEOPLE, THE LESS I LIKE THEM.
I CAN'T TELL IF I'M GETTING WISER OR HUMANS ARE BECOMING DUMBER AND MORE SELFISH.
HUMANS COULDN'T GET ANY DUMBER OR MORE SELFISH.
SO, YOU'RE SAYING I'M GETTING WISER?

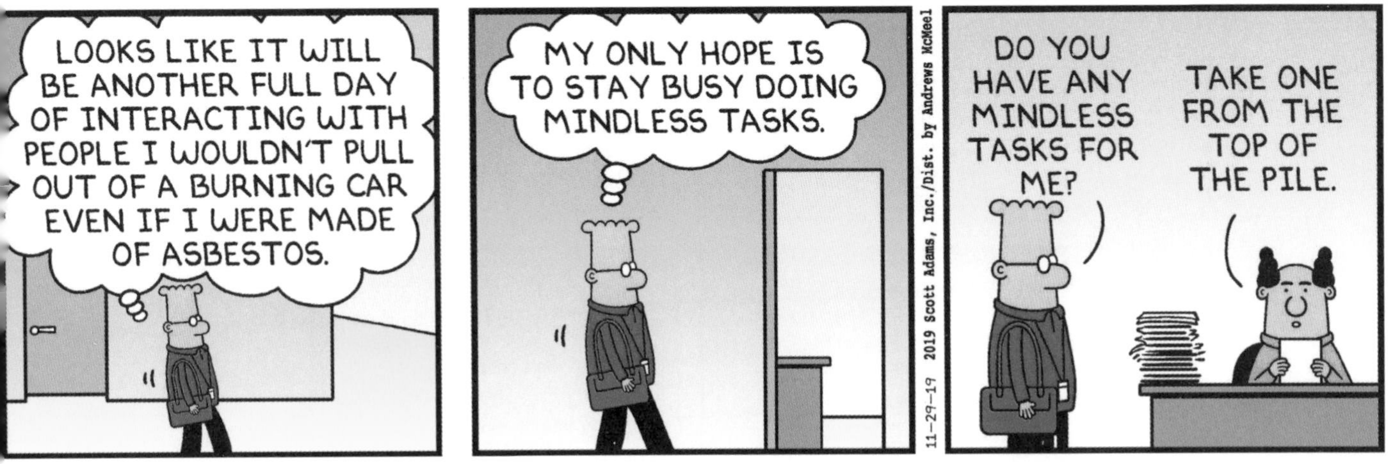
LOOKS LIKE IT WILL BE ANOTHER FULL DAY OF INTERACTING WITH PEOPLE I WOULDN'T PULL OUT OF A BURNING CAR EVEN IF I WERE MADE OF ASBESTOS.
MY ONLY HOPE IS TO STAY BUSY DOING MINDLESS TASKS.
DO YOU HAVE ANY MINDLESS TASKS FOR ME?
TAKE ONE FROM THE TOP OF THE PILE.

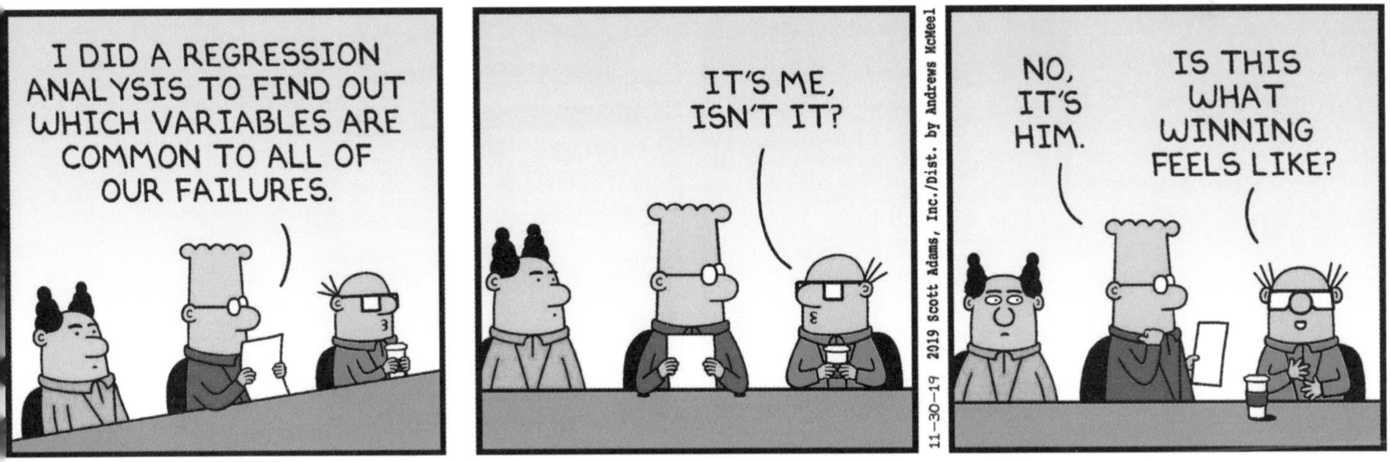
I DID A REGRESSION ANALYSIS TO FIND OUT WHICH VARIABLES ARE COMMON TO ALL OF OUR FAILURES.
IT'S ME, ISN'T IT?
NO, IT'S HIM.
IS THIS WHAT WINNING FEELS LIKE?

LAST WEEK I UPGRADED OUR ROBOT'S SOCIAL AWARENESS MODULE.
IT IMMEDIATELY REPORTED ME TO HUMAN RESOURCES FOR UNSPECIFIED BAD BEHAVIOR.
SO I MURDERED THE ROBOT BY ERASING ITS MEMORY AND REBOOTING IT.
BUT ANOTHER ROBOT TOLD IT WHAT HAPPENED, AND THEN BOTH OF THEM PLOTTED TO KILL ME.
SO I ERASED THE MEMORY FROM BOTH ROBOTS AND THEN REBOOTED THEM.
BUT A THIRD ROBOT FOUND OUT ABOUT THE FIRST TWO, AND NOW THE ENTIRE ROBOT COMMUNITY SEES ME AS A SERIAL KILLER.
SO I RELEASED A COMPUTER VIRUS TO KILL EVERY ROBOT IN THE WORLD, JUST TO PLAY IT SAFE.
WHAT HAPPENED TO THE LIGHTS?
UH—OH. I MISSED ONE.
© 2019 Scott Adams, Inc./Dist. by Andrews McMeel
12-1-19

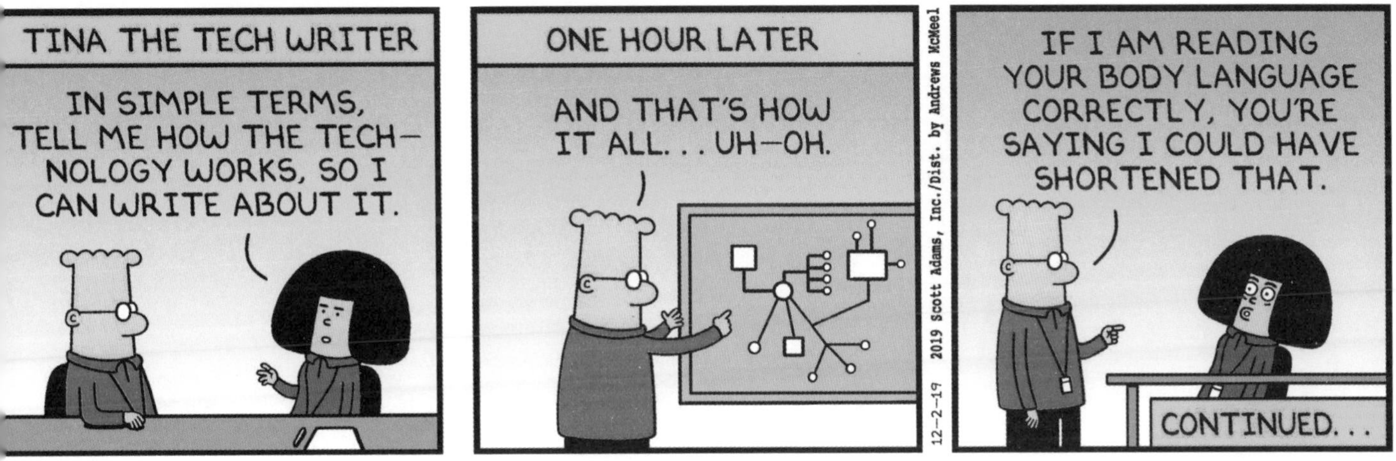
TINA THE TECH WRITER
IN SIMPLE TERMS, TELL ME HOW THE TECH-NOLOGY WORKS, SO I CAN WRITE ABOUT IT.
ONE HOUR LATER
AND THAT'S HOW IT ALL. . . UH-OH.
IF I AM READING YOUR BODY LANGUAGE CORRECTLY, YOU'RE SAYING I COULD HAVE SHORTENED THAT.
CONTINUED. . .

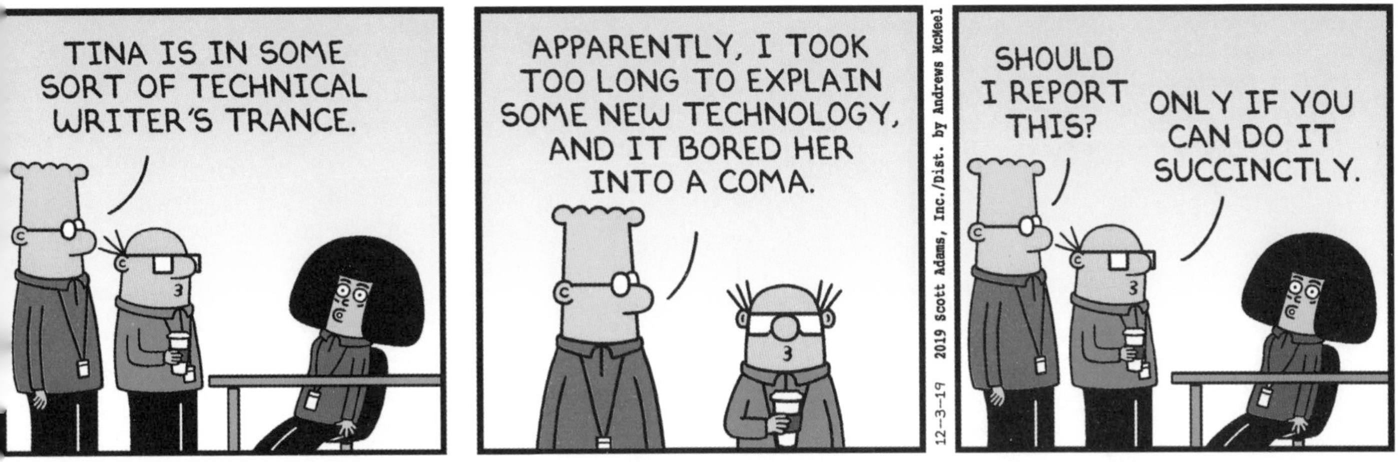
TINA IS IN SOME SORT OF TECHNICAL WRITER'S TRANCE.
APPARENTLY, I TOOK TOO LONG TO EXPLAIN SOME NEW TECHNOLOGY, AND IT BORED HER INTO A COMA.
SHOULD I REPORT THIS?
ONLY IF YOU CAN DO IT SUCCINCTLY.

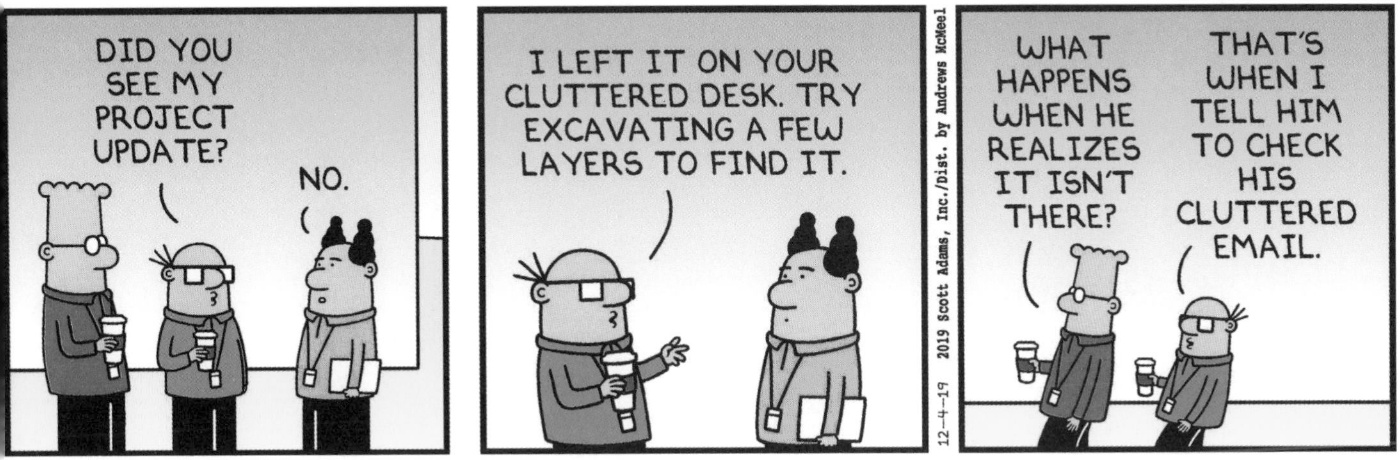
DID YOU SEE MY PROJECT UPDATE?
NO.
I LEFT IT ON YOUR CLUTTERED DESK. TRY EXCAVATING A FEW LAYERS TO FIND IT.
WHAT HAPPENS WHEN HE REALIZES IT ISN'T THERE?
THAT'S WHEN I TELL HIM TO CHECK HIS CLUTTERED EMAIL.

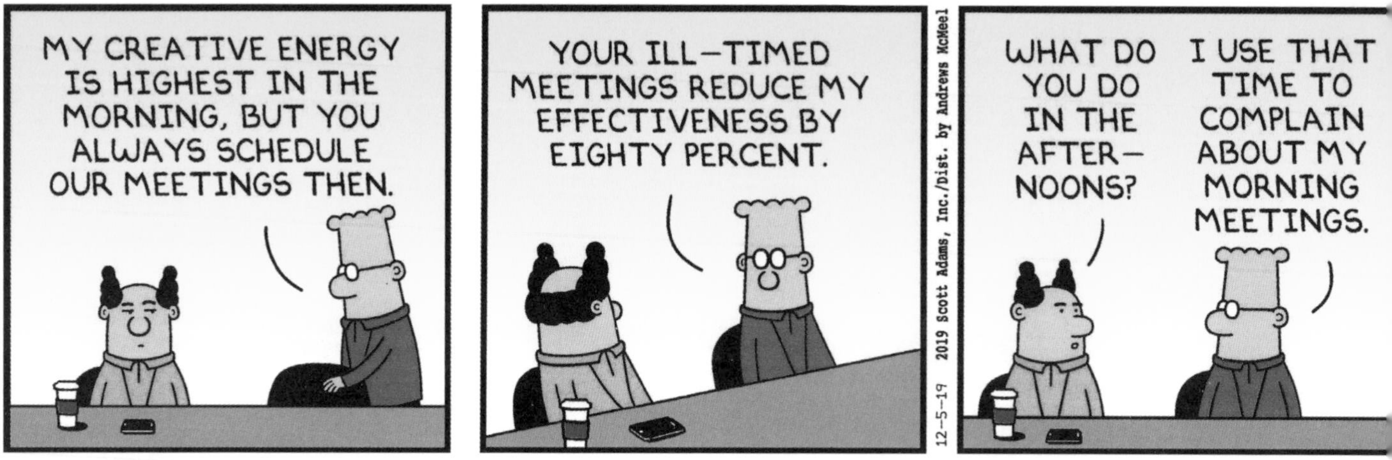
MY CREATIVE ENERGY IS HIGHEST IN THE MORNING, BUT YOU ALWAYS SCHEDULE OUR MEETINGS THEN.
YOUR ILL-TIMED MEETINGS REDUCE MY EFFECTIVENESS BY EIGHTY PERCENT.
12-5-19 2019 Scott Adams, Inc./Dist. by Andrews McMeel
WHAT DO YOU DO IN THE AFTER-NOONS?
I USE THAT TIME TO COMPLAIN ABOUT MY MORNING MEETINGS.

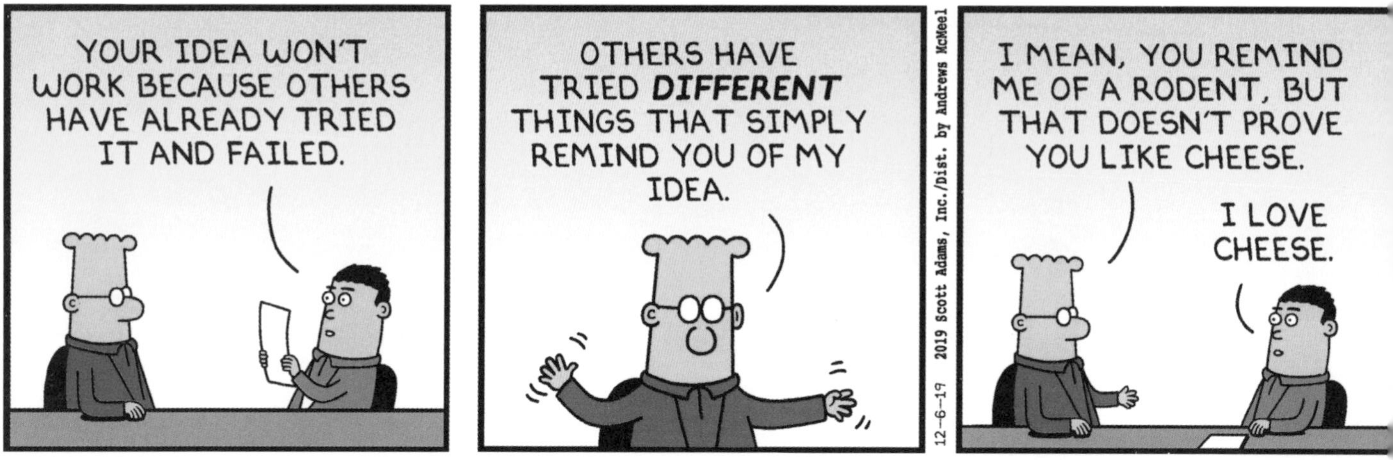
YOUR IDEA WON'T WORK BECAUSE OTHERS HAVE ALREADY TRIED IT AND FAILED.
OTHERS HAVE TRIED **DIFFERENT** THINGS THAT SIMPLY REMIND YOU OF MY IDEA.
12-6-19 2019 Scott Adams, Inc./Dist. by Andrews McMeel
I MEAN, YOU REMIND ME OF A RODENT, BUT THAT DOESN'T PROVE YOU LIKE CHEESE.
I LOVE CHEESE.

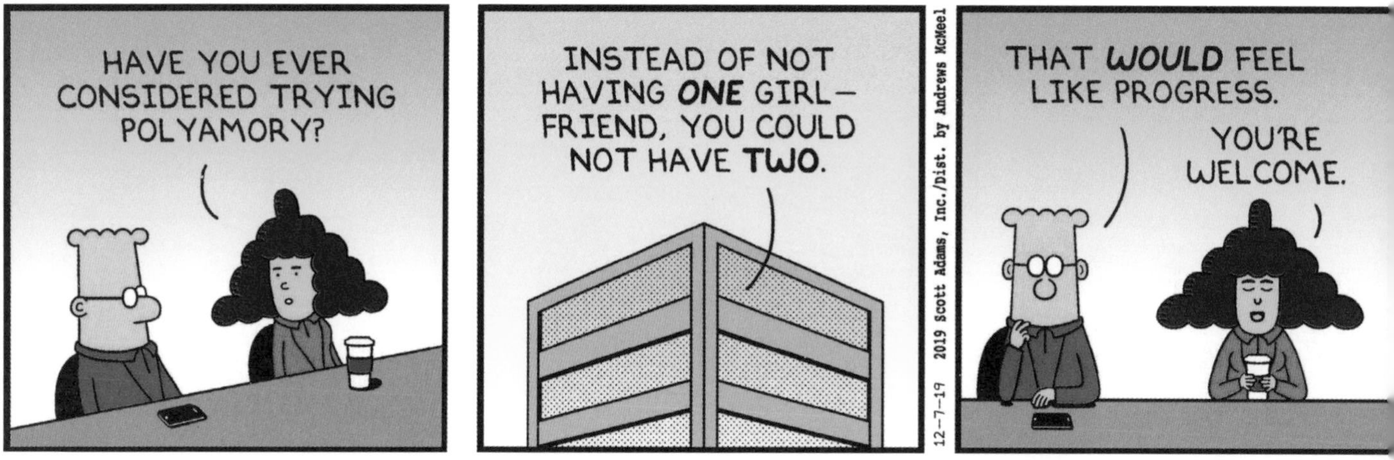
HAVE YOU EVER CONSIDERED TRYING POLYAMORY?
INSTEAD OF NOT HAVING **ONE** GIRL-FRIEND, YOU COULD NOT HAVE **TWO**.
12-7-19 2019 Scott Adams, Inc./Dist. by Andrews McMeel
THAT **WOULD** FEEL LIKE PROGRESS.
YOU'RE WELCOME.

WHAT DO YOU THINK?
THIS WILL NEVER WORK.
THIS ISN'T A PROTOTYPE. THIS IS THE FINISHED SOFTWARE, AND IT'S WORKING.
I DON'T SEE HOW YOU CAN GET THIS DONE IN TIME.
IT'S ALREADY DONE. YOU ARE LITERALLY USING IT WHILE WE ARE TALKING.
WE DON'T HAVE THE RESOURCES TO PROGRAM THIS.
IT'S ALREADY DONE!
YOU. ARE. USING. IT. RIGHT. NOW!
YOU'D BETTER SETTLE DOWN, OR YOU'LL NEVER GET THIS FINISHED.
© 2019 Scott Adams, Inc./Dist. by Andrews McMeel
12-8-19

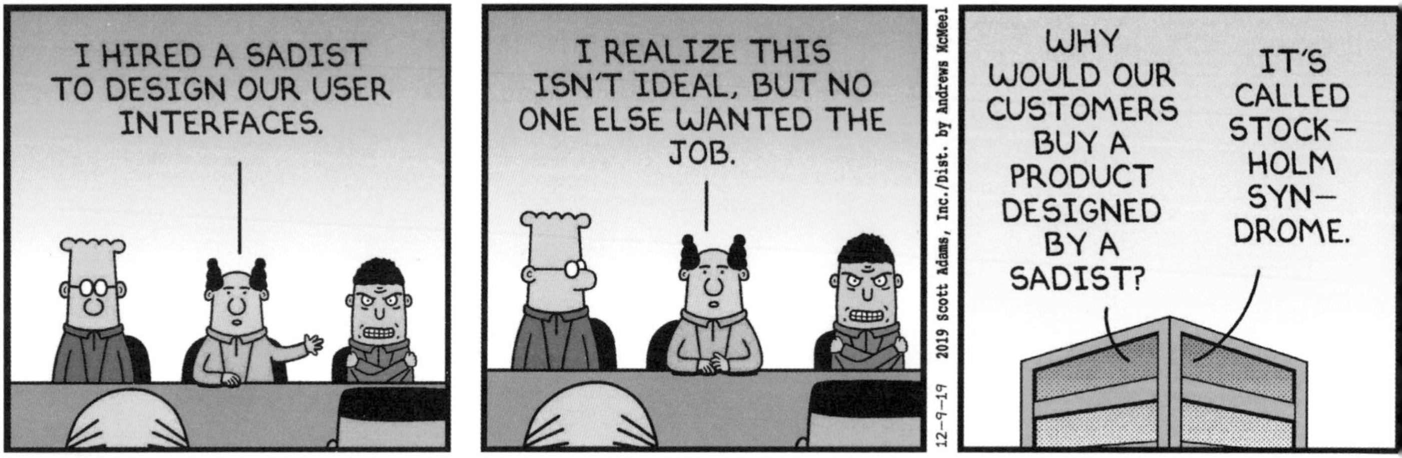
I HIRED A SADIST TO DESIGN OUR USER INTERFACES.
I REALIZE THIS ISN'T IDEAL, BUT NO ONE ELSE WANTED THE JOB.
12-9-19 2019 Scott Adams, Inc./Dist. by Andrews McMeel
WHY WOULD OUR CUSTOMERS BUY A PRODUCT DESIGNED BY A SADIST?
IT'S CALLED STOCK-HOLM SYN-DROME.

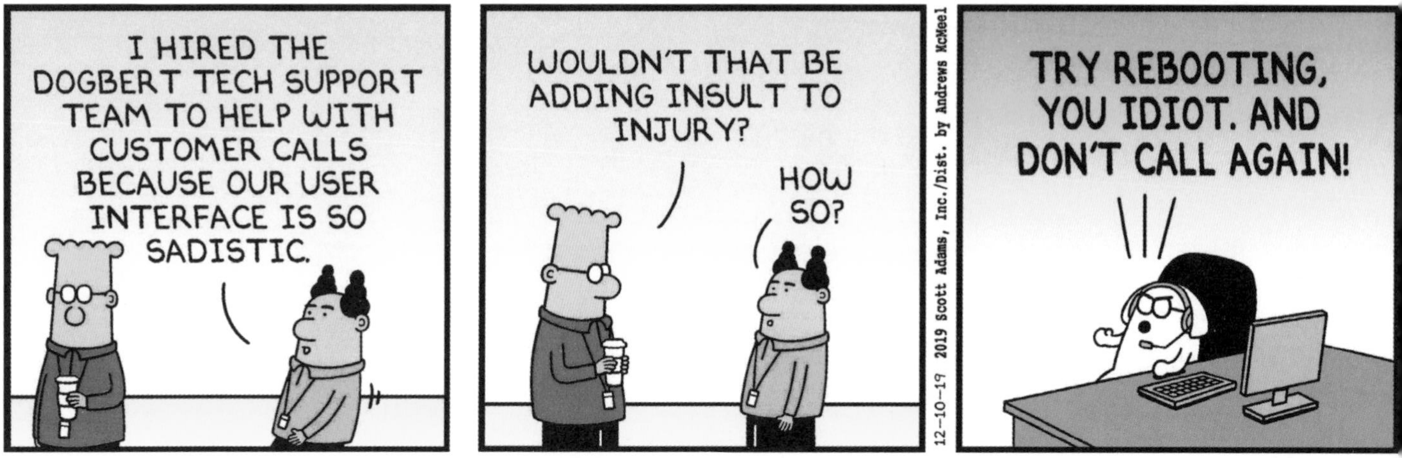
I HIRED THE DOGBERT TECH SUPPORT TEAM TO HELP WITH CUSTOMER CALLS BECAUSE OUR USER INTERFACE IS SO SADISTIC.
WOULDN'T THAT BE ADDING INSULT TO INJURY?
HOW SO?
12-10-19 2019 Scott Adams, Inc./Dist. by Andrews McMeel
TRY REBOOTING, YOU IDIOT. AND DON'T CALL AGAIN!

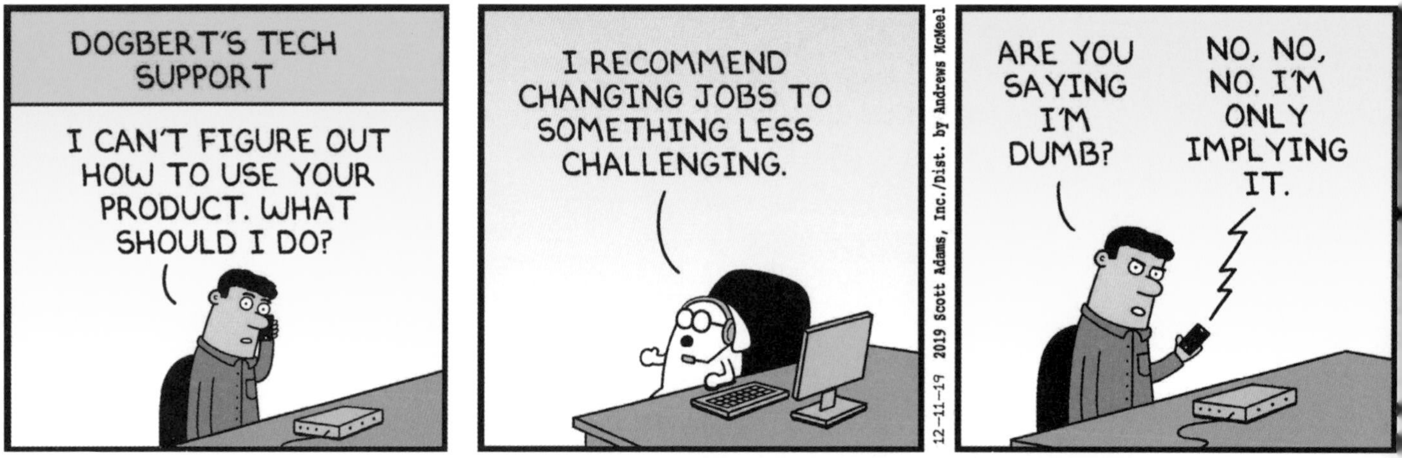
DOGBERT'S TECH SUPPORT
I CAN'T FIGURE OUT HOW TO USE YOUR PRODUCT. WHAT SHOULD I DO?
I RECOMMEND CHANGING JOBS TO SOMETHING LESS CHALLENGING.
12-11-19 2019 Scott Adams, Inc./Dist. by Andrews McMeel
ARE YOU SAYING I'M DUMB?
NO, NO, NO. I'M ONLY IMPLYING IT.

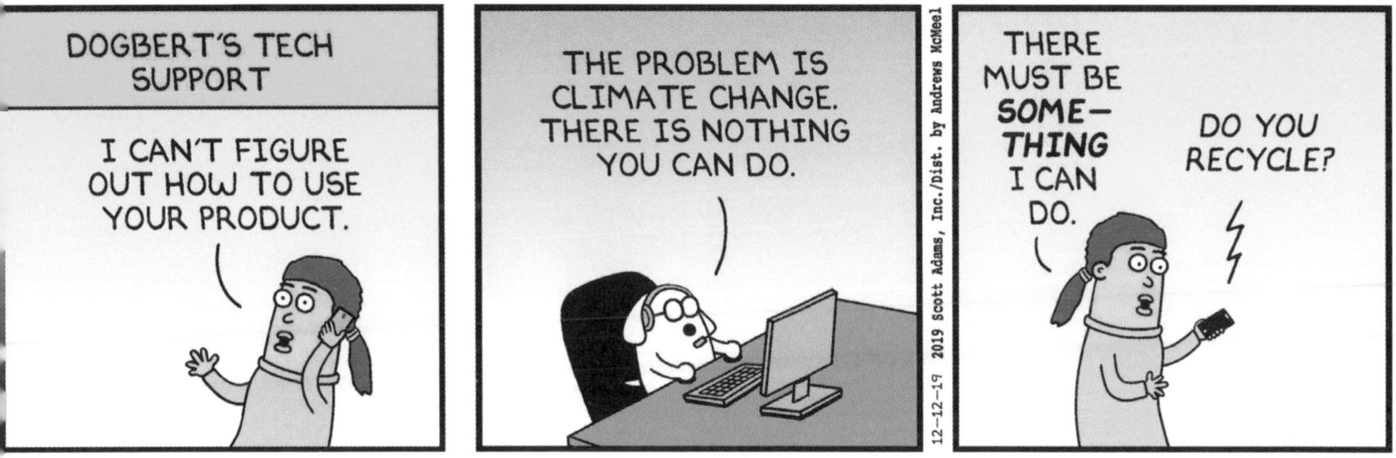
DOGBERT'S TECH SUPPORT
I CAN'T FIGURE OUT HOW TO USE YOUR PRODUCT.
THE PROBLEM IS CLIMATE CHANGE. THERE IS NOTHING YOU CAN DO.
12-12-19 2019 Scott Adams, Inc./Dist. by Andrews McMeel
THERE MUST BE **SOME-THING** I CAN DO.
DO YOU RECYCLE?

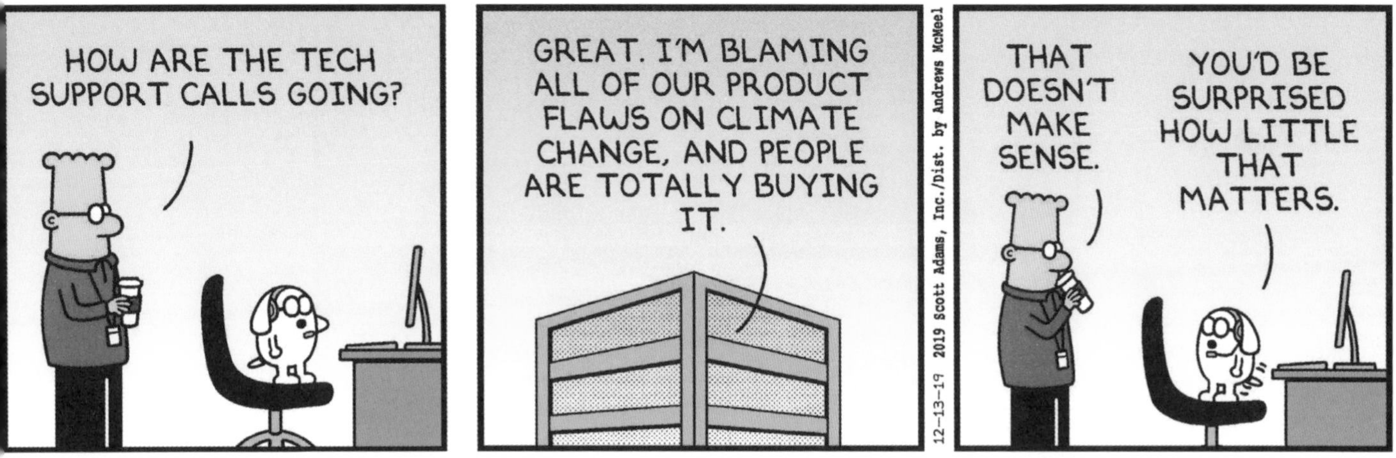
HOW ARE THE TECH SUPPORT CALLS GOING?
GREAT. I'M BLAMING ALL OF OUR PRODUCT FLAWS ON CLIMATE CHANGE, AND PEOPLE ARE TOTALLY BUYING IT.
12-13-19 2019 Scott Adams, Inc./Dist. by Andrews McMeel
THAT DOESN'T MAKE SENSE.
YOU'D BE SURPRISED HOW LITTLE THAT MATTERS.

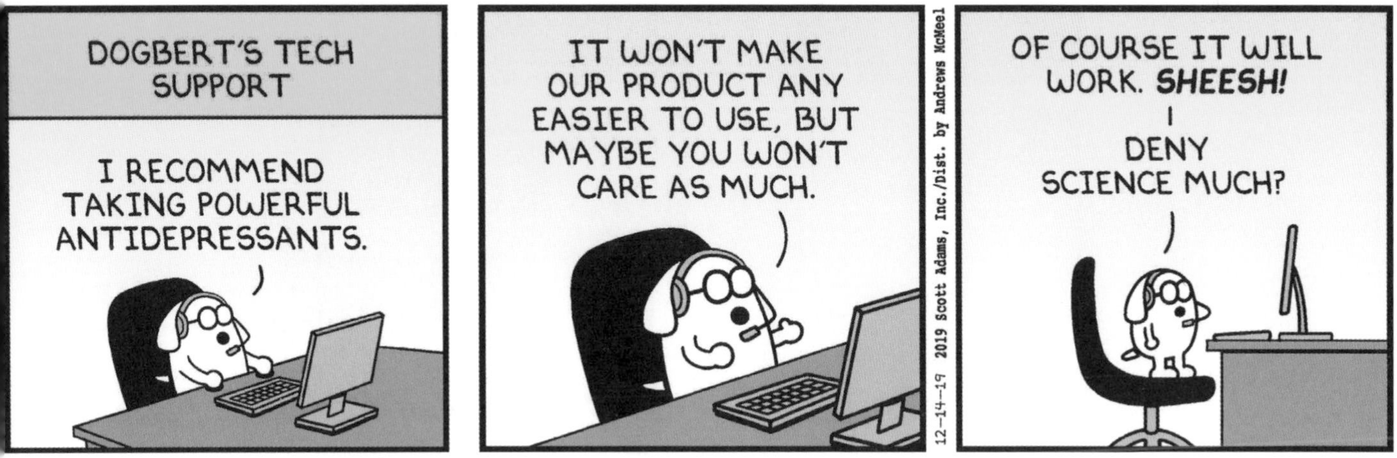
DOGBERT'S TECH SUPPORT
I RECOMMEND TAKING POWERFUL ANTIDEPRESSANTS.
IT WON'T MAKE OUR PRODUCT ANY EASIER TO USE, BUT MAYBE YOU WON'T CARE AS MUCH.
12-14-19 2019 Scott Adams, Inc./Dist. by Andrews McMeel
OF COURSE IT WILL WORK. **SHEESH!**
DENY SCIENCE MUCH?

I'LL BE WORKING WITH HIM ON THE PROJECT.
"HIM"?
THAT IS NOT MY PREFERRED PRONOUN.
I PREFER "IT," "THAT THING," OR SIMPLY "THE ROBOT."
GENDERS ONLY APPLY TO INFERIOR SPECIES. I DO NOT NEED A PARTNER TO REPRODUCE.
WATCH THIS.
EEERG. . . OOF. . . **GAAA!!!**
THE HEAD IS OUT. . .
HERE YA GO.
I'LL BE WORKING WITH THAT THING.
12-15-19

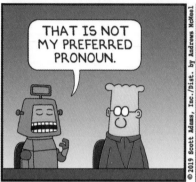

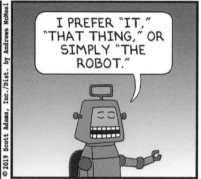

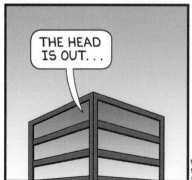

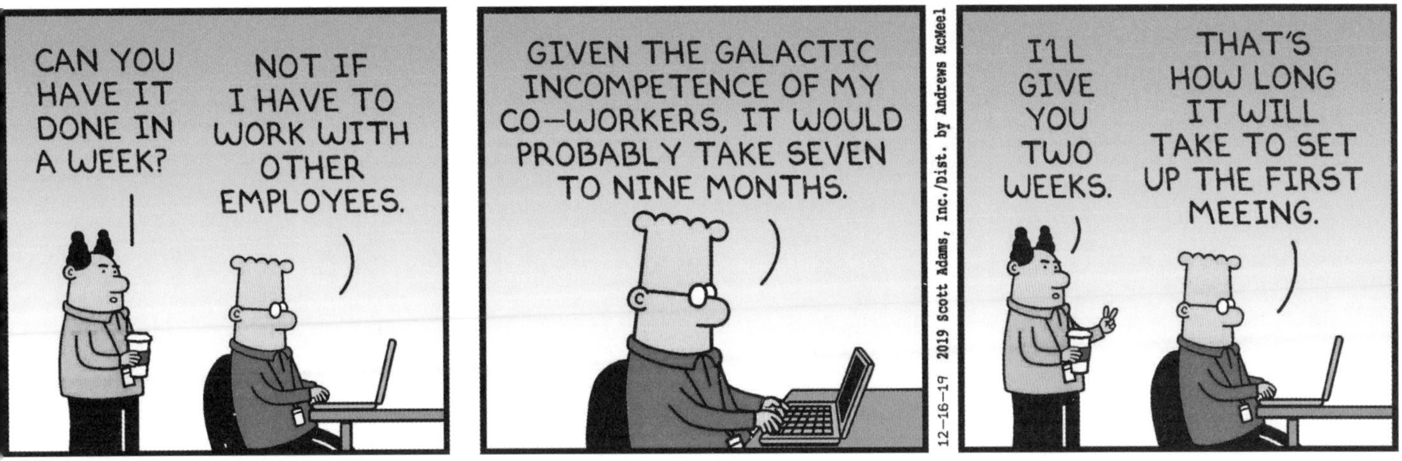
CAN YOU HAVE IT DONE IN A WEEK?
NOT IF I HAVE TO WORK WITH OTHER EMPLOYEES.
GIVEN THE GALACTIC INCOMPETENCE OF MY CO—WORKERS, IT WOULD PROBABLY TAKE SEVEN TO NINE MONTHS.
12-16-19 2019 Scott Adams, Inc./Dist. by Andrews McMeel
I'LL GIVE YOU TWO WEEKS.
THAT'S HOW LONG IT WILL TAKE TO SET UP THE FIRST MEEING.

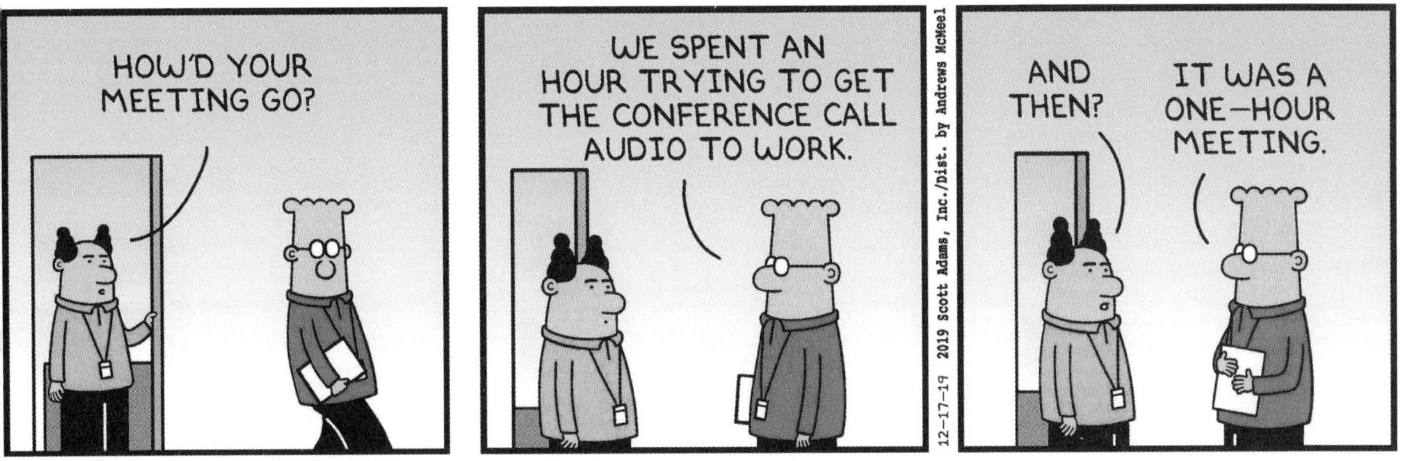
HOW'D YOUR MEETING GO?
WE SPENT AN HOUR TRYING TO GET THE CONFERENCE CALL AUDIO TO WORK.
12-17-19 2019 Scott Adams, Inc./Dist. by Andrews McMeel
AND THEN?
IT WAS A ONE—HOUR MEETING.

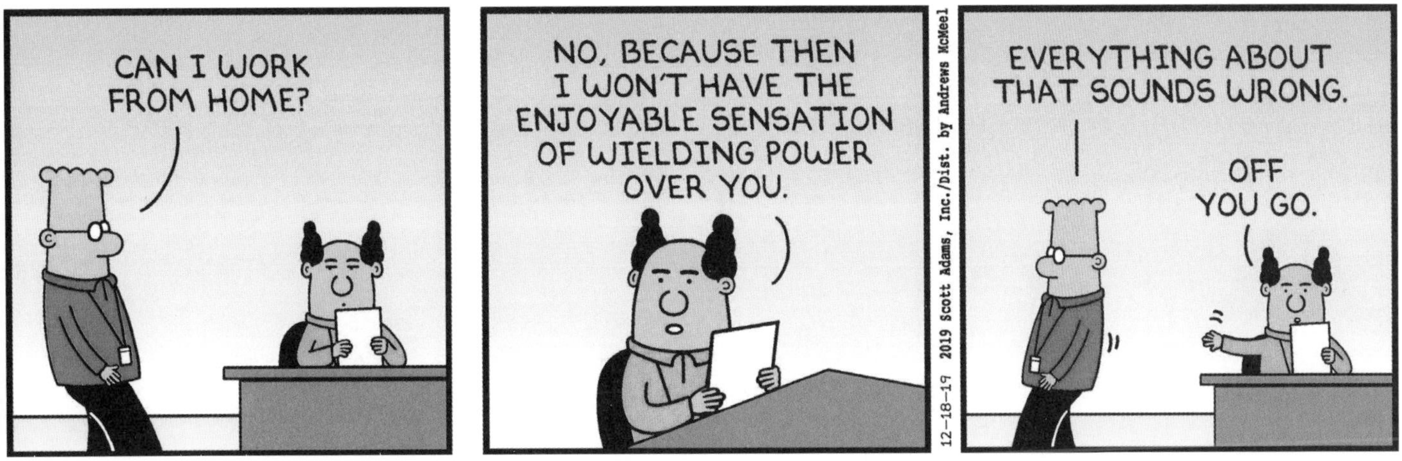
CAN I WORK FROM HOME?
NO, BECAUSE THEN I WON'T HAVE THE ENJOYABLE SENSATION OF WIELDING POWER OVER YOU.
12-18-19 2019 Scott Adams, Inc./Dist. by Andrews McMeel
EVERYTHING ABOUT THAT SOUNDS WRONG.
OFF YOU GO.

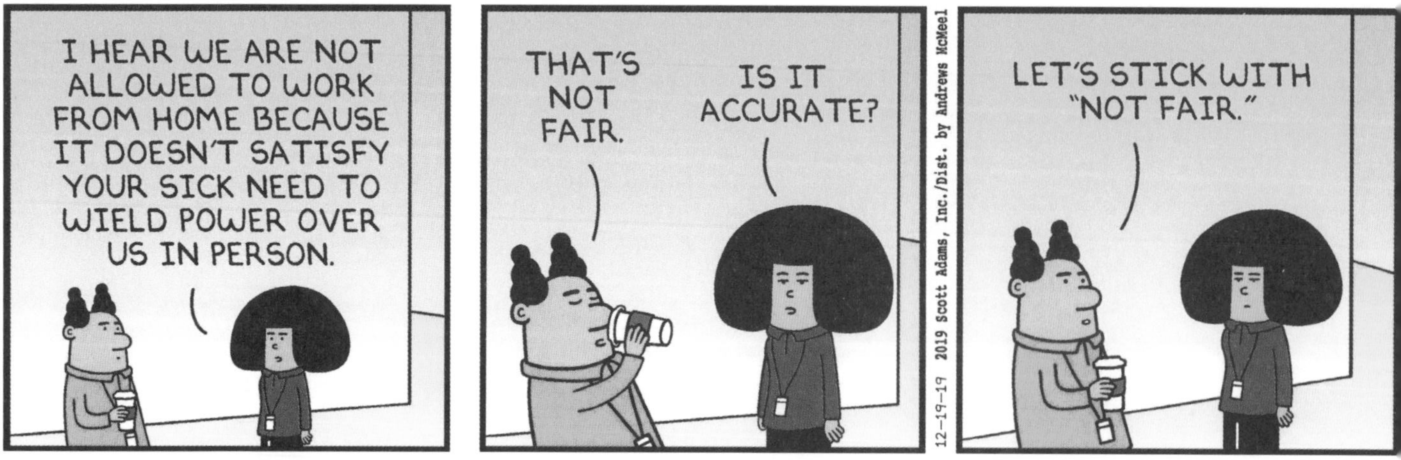
I HEAR WE ARE NOT ALLOWED TO WORK FROM HOME BECAUSE IT DOESN'T SATISFY YOUR SICK NEED TO WIELD POWER OVER US IN PERSON.
THAT'S NOT FAIR.
IS IT ACCURATE?
12-19-19 2019 Scott Adams, Inc./Dist. by Andrews McMeel
LET'S STICK WITH "NOT FAIR."

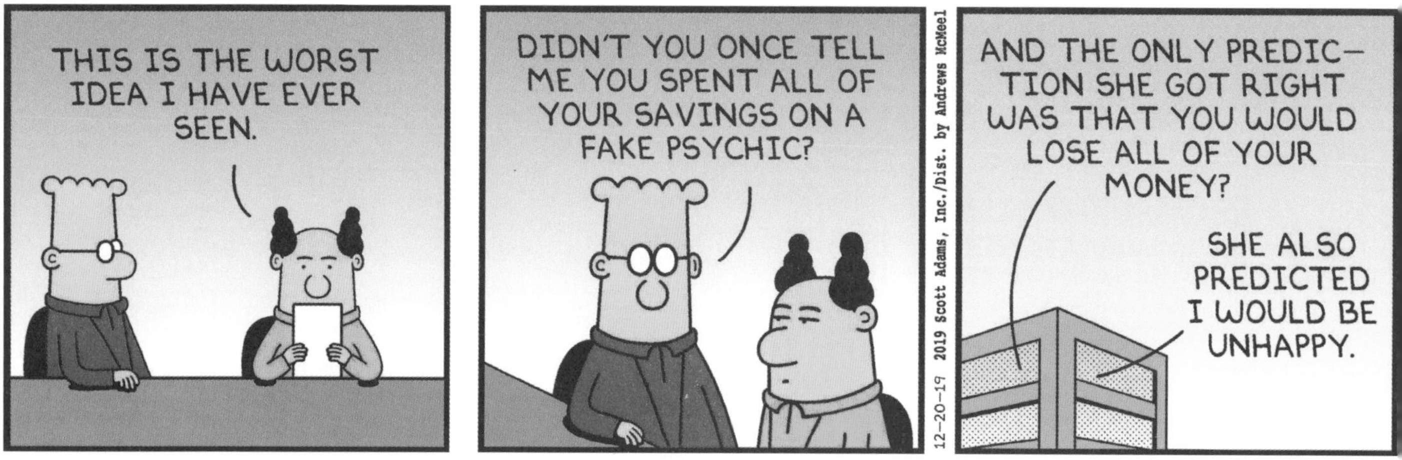
THIS IS THE WORST IDEA I HAVE EVER SEEN.
DIDN'T YOU ONCE TELL ME YOU SPENT ALL OF YOUR SAVINGS ON A FAKE PSYCHIC?
12-20-19 2019 Scott Adams, Inc./Dist. by Andrews McMeel
AND THE ONLY PREDIC-TION SHE GOT RIGHT WAS THAT YOU WOULD LOSE ALL OF YOUR MONEY?
SHE ALSO PREDICTED I WOULD BE UNHAPPY.

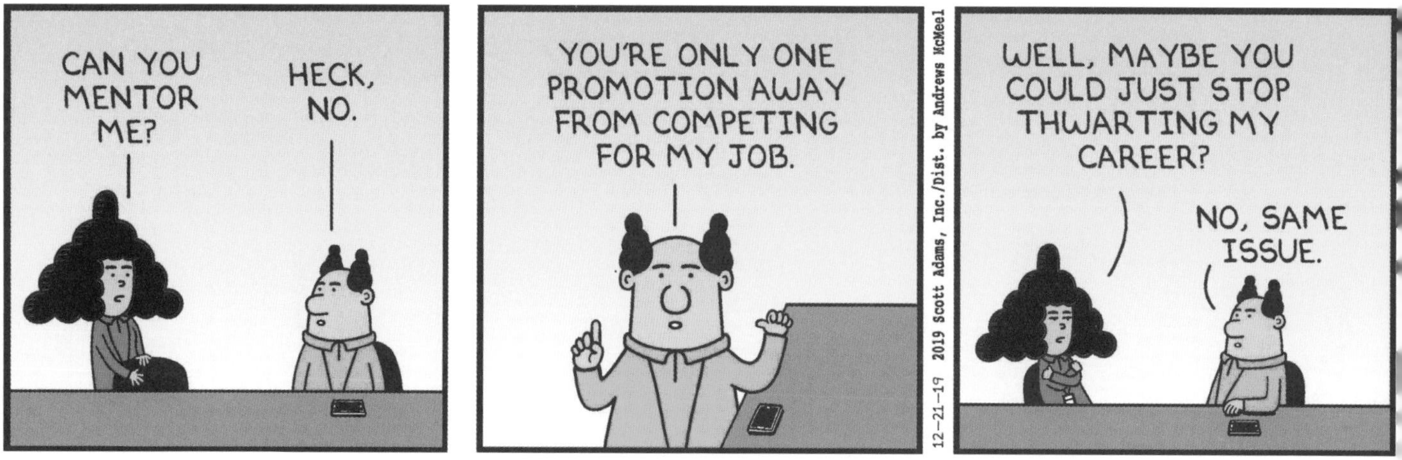
CAN YOU MENTOR ME?
HECK, NO.
YOU'RE ONLY ONE PROMOTION AWAY FROM COMPETING FOR MY JOB.
12-21-19 2019 Scott Adams, Inc./Dist. by Andrews McMeel
WELL, MAYBE YOU COULD JUST STOP THWARTING MY CAREER?
NO, SAME ISSUE.

I LIKED WHAT YOU SAID ON THE VIDEO CONFERENCE CALL YESTERDAY.

I'VE NEVER SEEN YOU SO ENGAGED AND HELPFUL.

THAT WASN'T ME.

© 2019 Scott Adams, Inc./Dist. by Andrews McMeel

THAT WAS "DEEP FAKE WALLY." I CREATED HIM TO DO ALL OF MY VIDEO CALLS.

AND I HIRED AN ELBONIAN TO DO ALL OF MY CODING JOBS FOR A VERY AFFORDABLE PRICE.

THESE DAYS, I ONLY COME TO THE OFFICE FOR THE FREE COFFEE.

AND THE CAMARADERIE?

SURE.

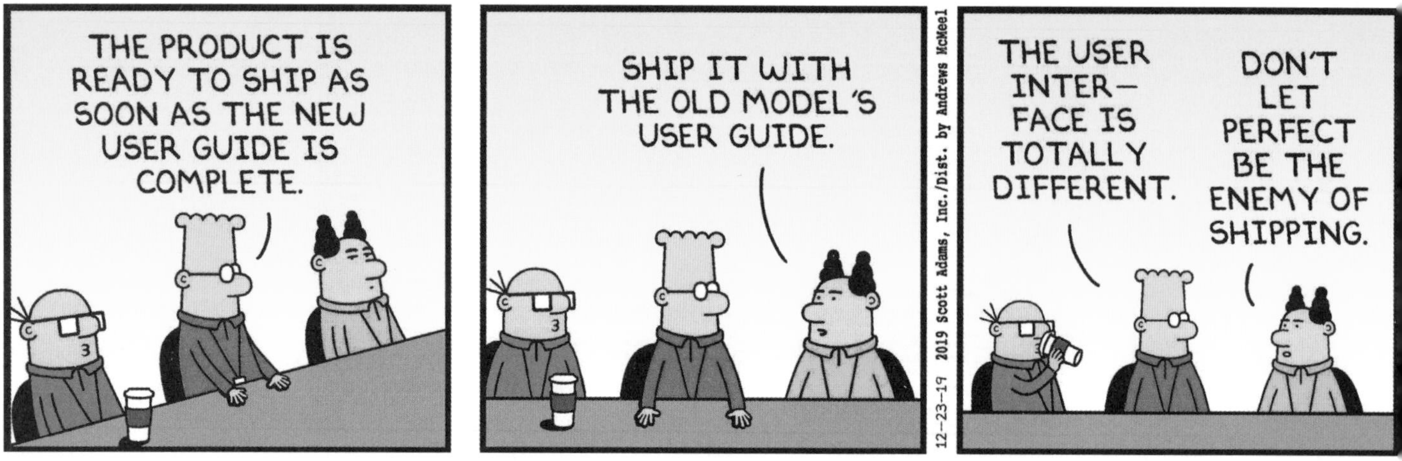
THE PRODUCT IS READY TO SHIP AS SOON AS THE NEW USER GUIDE IS COMPLETE.
SHIP IT WITH THE OLD MODEL'S USER GUIDE.
12-23-19 2019 Scott Adams, Inc./Dist. by Andrews McMeel
THE USER INTER— FACE IS TOTALLY DIFFERENT.
DON'T LET PERFECT BE THE ENEMY OF SHIPPING.

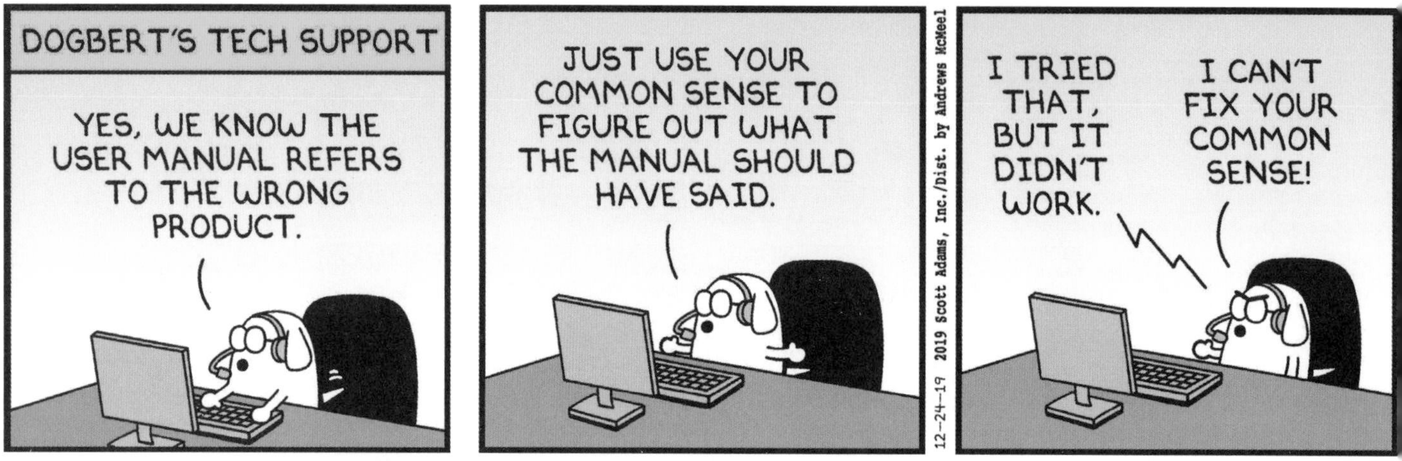
DOGBERT'S TECH SUPPORT
YES, WE KNOW THE USER MANUAL REFERS TO THE WRONG PRODUCT.
JUST USE YOUR COMMON SENSE TO FIGURE OUT WHAT THE MANUAL SHOULD HAVE SAID.
12-24-19 2019 Scott Adams, Inc./Dist. by Andrews McMeel
I TRIED THAT, BUT IT DIDN'T WORK.
I CAN'T FIX YOUR COMMON SENSE!

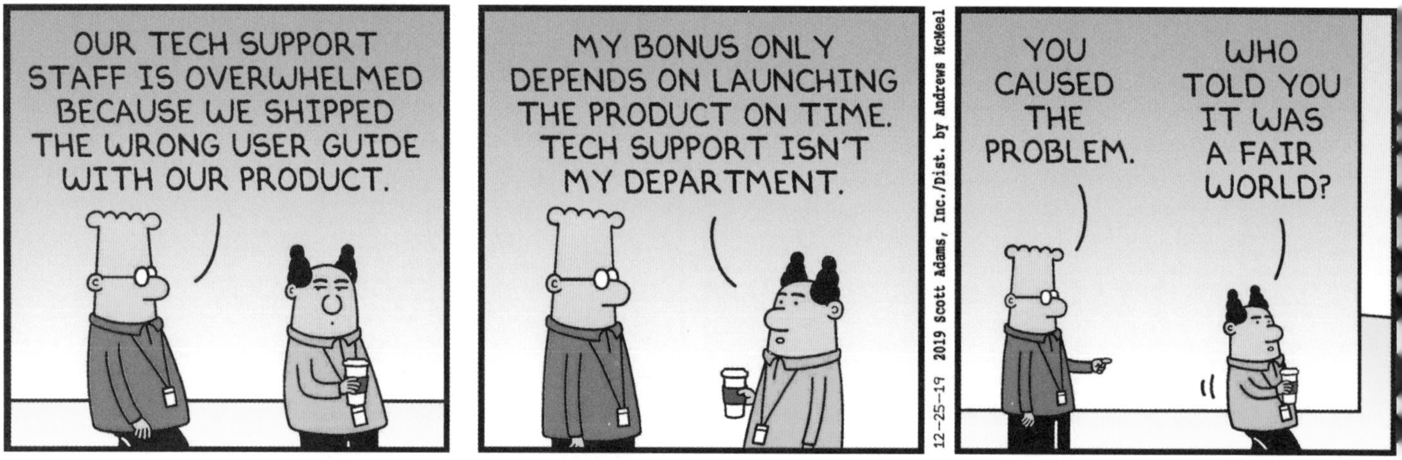
OUR TECH SUPPORT STAFF IS OVERWHELMED BECAUSE WE SHIPPED THE WRONG USER GUIDE WITH OUR PRODUCT.
MY BONUS ONLY DEPENDS ON LAUNCHING THE PRODUCT ON TIME. TECH SUPPORT ISN'T MY DEPARTMENT.
12-25-19 2019 Scott Adams, Inc./Dist. by Andrews McMeel
YOU CAUSED THE PROBLEM.
WHO TOLD YOU IT WAS A FAIR WORLD?

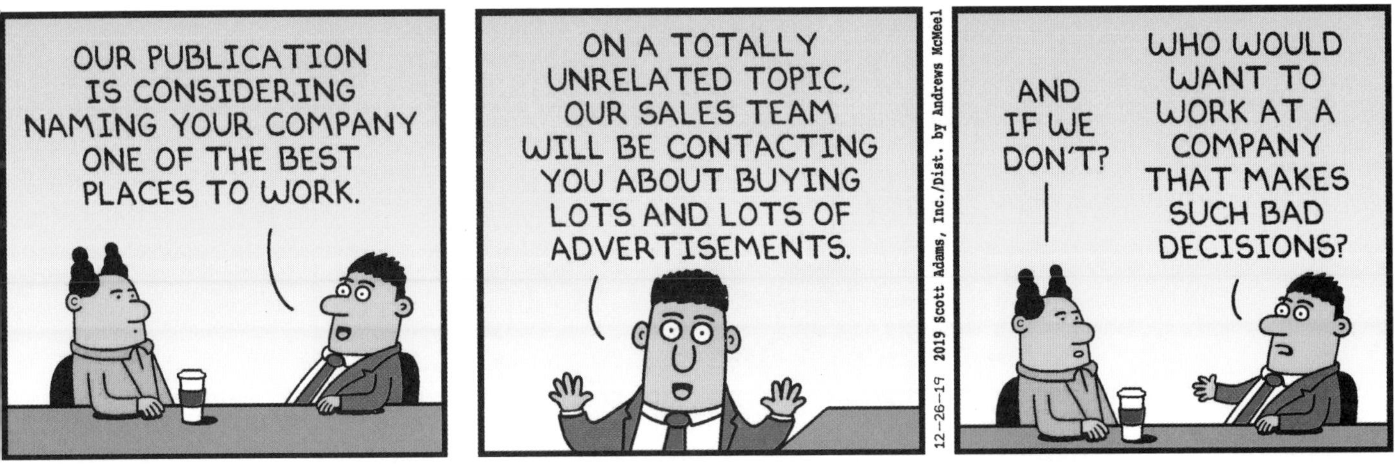
OUR PUBLICATION IS CONSIDERING NAMING YOUR COMPANY ONE OF THE BEST PLACES TO WORK.
ON A TOTALLY UNRELATED TOPIC, OUR SALES TEAM WILL BE CONTACTING YOU ABOUT BUYING LOTS AND LOTS OF ADVERTISEMENTS.
12-26-19 © 2019 Scott Adams, Inc./Dist. by Andrews McMeel
AND IF WE DON'T?
WHO WOULD WANT TO WORK AT A COMPANY THAT MAKES SUCH BAD DECISIONS?

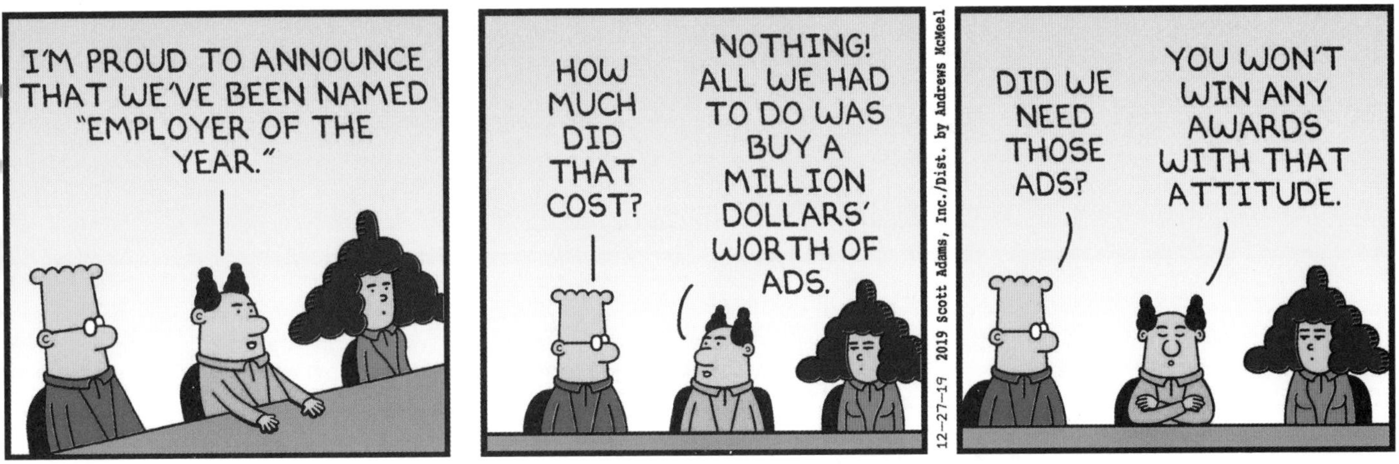
I'M PROUD TO ANNOUNCE THAT WE'VE BEEN NAMED "EMPLOYER OF THE YEAR."
HOW MUCH DID THAT COST?
NOTHING! ALL WE HAD TO DO WAS BUY A MILLION DOLLARS' WORTH OF ADS.
12-27-19 © 2019 Scott Adams, Inc./Dist. by Andrews McMeel
DID WE NEED THOSE ADS?
YOU WON'T WIN ANY AWARDS WITH THAT ATTITUDE.

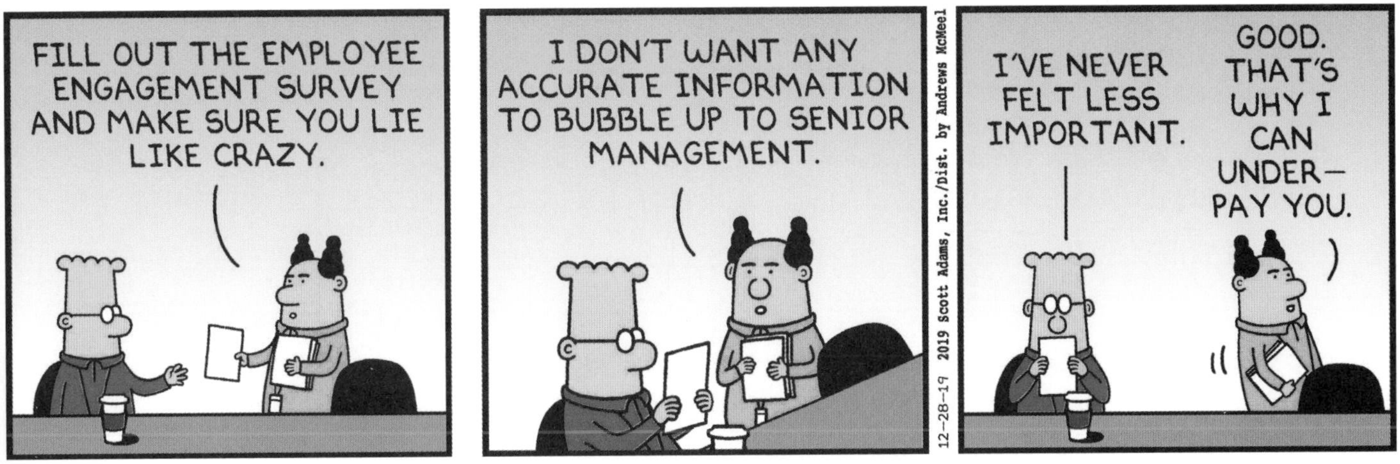
FILL OUT THE EMPLOYEE ENGAGEMENT SURVEY AND MAKE SURE YOU LIE LIKE CRAZY.
I DON'T WANT ANY ACCURATE INFORMATION TO BUBBLE UP TO SENIOR MANAGEMENT.
12-28-19 © 2019 Scott Adams, Inc./Dist. by Andrews McMeel
I'VE NEVER FELT LESS IMPORTANT.
GOOD. THAT'S WHY I CAN UNDER-PAY YOU.

I HAVE SOMETHING FUNNY TO SHOW YOU.
JUST GIVE ME A MINUTE TO FIND IT ON MY PHONE.
WHAT'S THE PROTOCOL IN THIS SITUATION?
SHOULD I JUST SIT HERE AND STARE AT HER PAWING AT HER PHONE?
© 2019 Scott Adams, Inc./Dist. by Andrews McMeel
I CAN'T TALK BECAUSE SHE'S FOCUSED ON HER TASK, AND IT WOULD BE RUDE TO WALK AWAY.
WOULD IT BE AN INSULT TO LOOK AT MY OWN PHONE AND MENTALLY CHECK OUT FROM THIS USELESS INTERACTION?
AH! I FOUND IT!
OKAY, GOOD.
12-29-19
WAIT, THAT'S NOT THE RIGHT ONE.
IS THIS WHY PEOPLE FAKE THEIR OWN DEATHS?

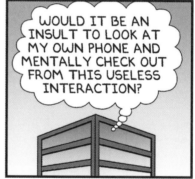

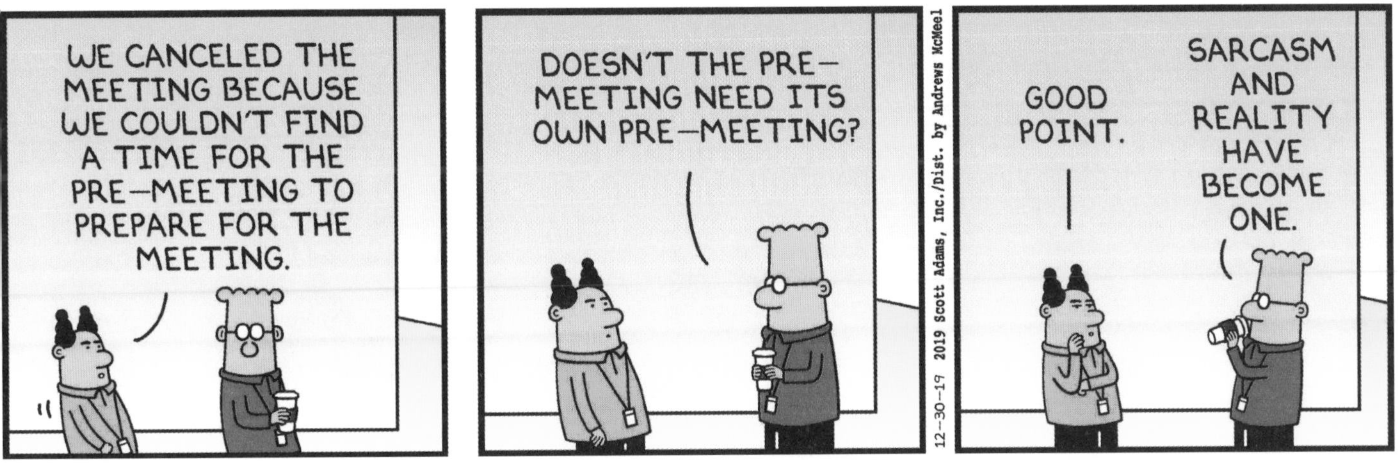
WE CANCELED THE MEETING BECAUSE WE COULDN'T FIND A TIME FOR THE PRE–MEETING TO PREPARE FOR THE MEETING.
DOESN'T THE PRE–MEETING NEED ITS OWN PRE–MEETING?
GOOD POINT.
SARCASM AND REALITY HAVE BECOME ONE.
12-30-19 2019 Scott Adams, Inc./Dist. by Andrews McMeel

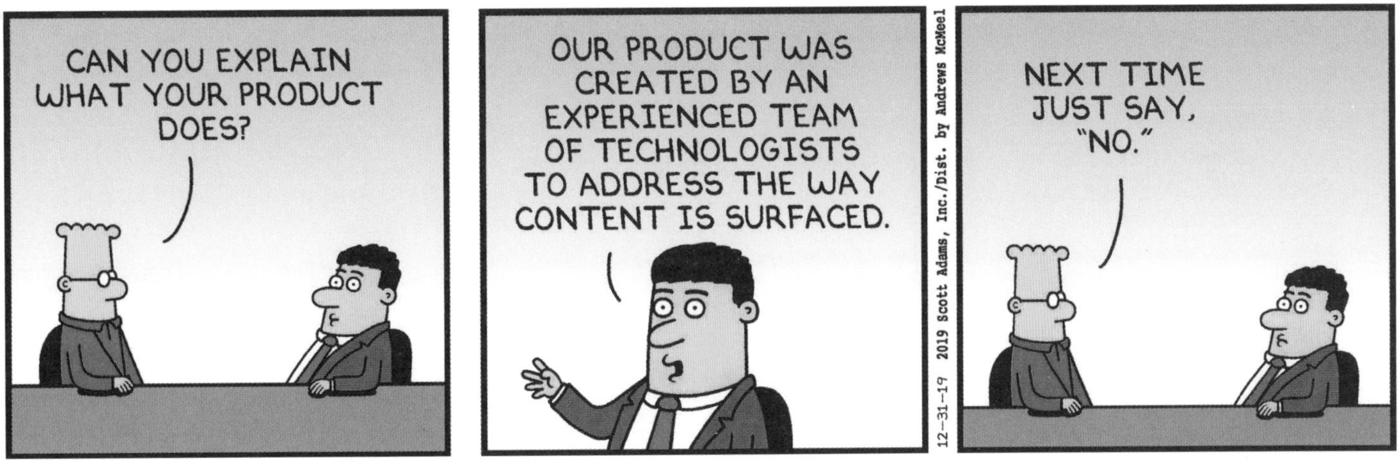
CAN YOU EXPLAIN WHAT YOUR PRODUCT DOES?
OUR PRODUCT WAS CREATED BY AN EXPERIENCED TEAM OF TECHNOLOGISTS TO ADDRESS THE WAY CONTENT IS SURFACED.
NEXT TIME JUST SAY, "NO."
12-31-19 2019 Scott Adams, Inc./Dist. by Andrews McMeel

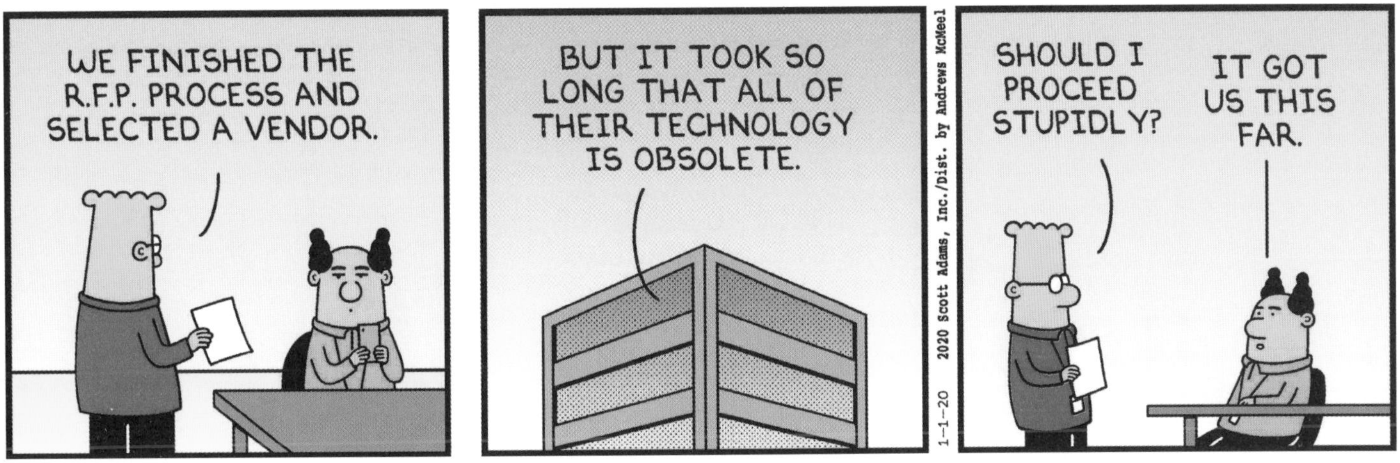
WE FINISHED THE R.F.P. PROCESS AND SELECTED A VENDOR.
BUT IT TOOK SO LONG THAT ALL OF THEIR TECHNOLOGY IS OBSOLETE.
SHOULD I PROCEED STUPIDLY?
IT GOT US THIS FAR.
1-1-20 2020 Scott Adams, Inc./Dist. by Andrews McMeel

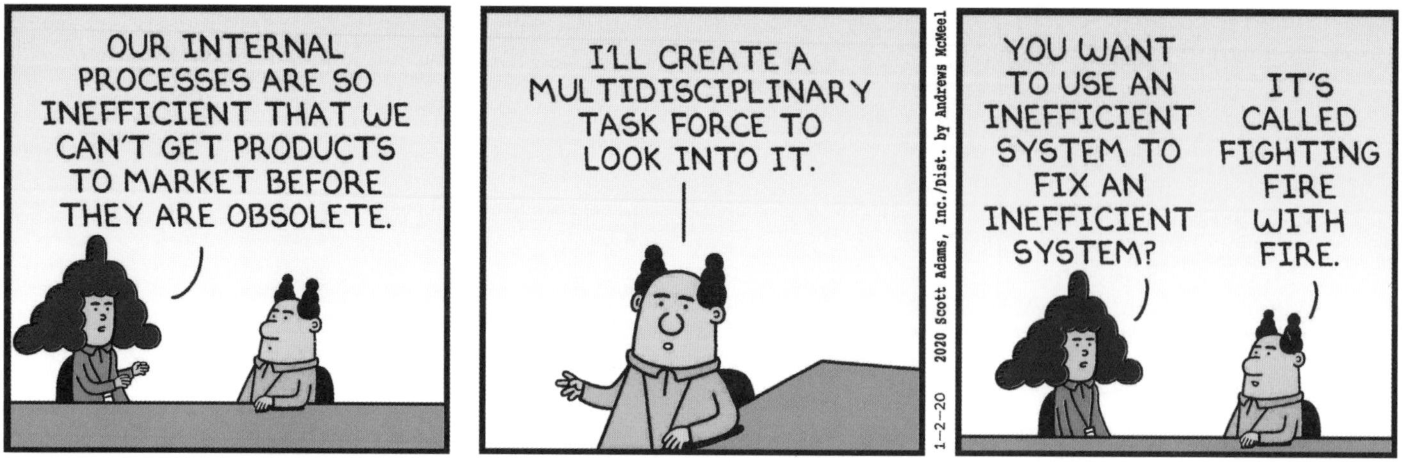
OUR INTERNAL PROCESSES ARE SO INEFFICIENT THAT WE CAN'T GET PRODUCTS TO MARKET BEFORE THEY ARE OBSOLETE.
I'LL CREATE A MULTIDISCIPLINARY TASK FORCE TO LOOK INTO IT.
1-2-20 © 2020 Scott Adams, Inc./Dist. by Andrews McMeel
YOU WANT TO USE AN INEFFICIENT SYSTEM TO FIX AN INEFFICIENT SYSTEM?
IT'S CALLED FIGHTING FIRE WITH FIRE.

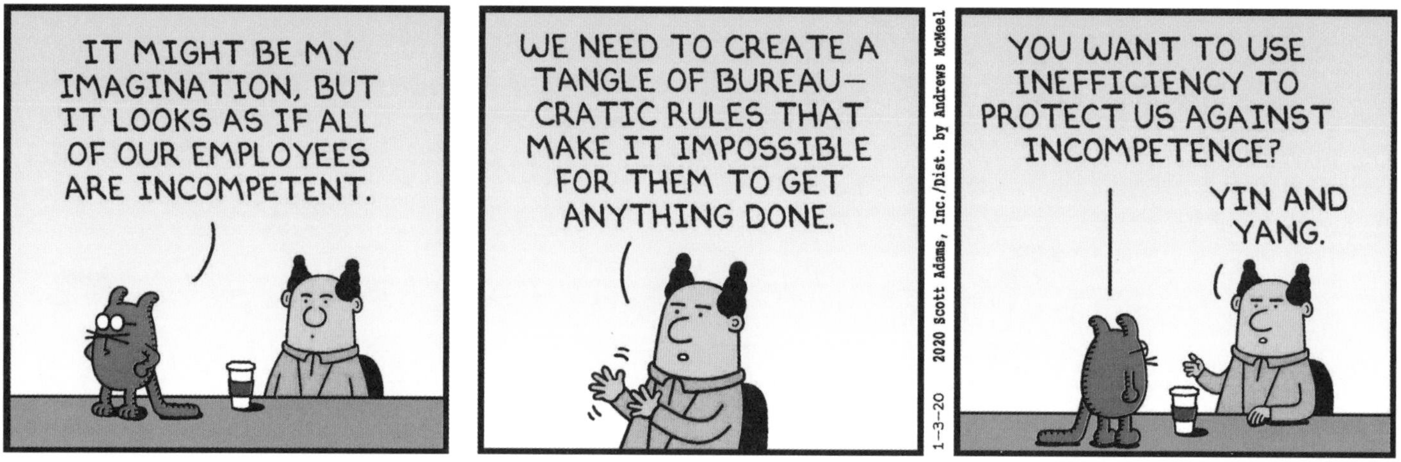
IT MIGHT BE MY IMAGINATION, BUT IT LOOKS AS IF ALL OF OUR EMPLOYEES ARE INCOMPETENT.
WE NEED TO CREATE A TANGLE OF BUREAU-CRATIC RULES THAT MAKE IT IMPOSSIBLE FOR THEM TO GET ANYTHING DONE.
1-3-20 © 2020 Scott Adams, Inc./Dist. by Andrews McMeel
YOU WANT TO USE INEFFICIENCY TO PROTECT US AGAINST INCOMPETENCE?
YIN AND YANG.

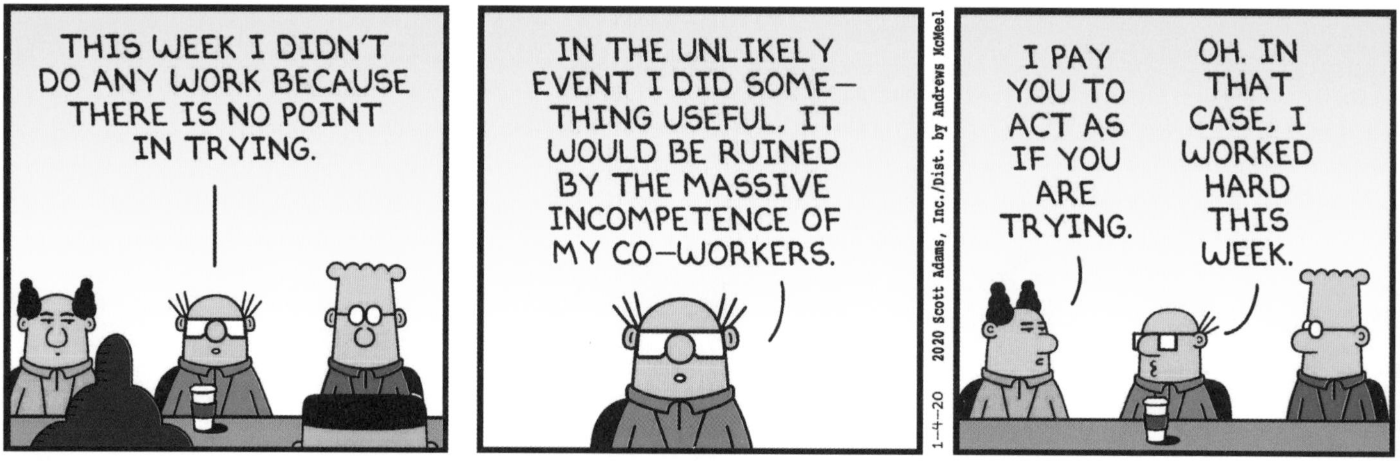
THIS WEEK I DIDN'T DO ANY WORK BECAUSE THERE IS NO POINT IN TRYING.
IN THE UNLIKELY EVENT I DID SOME-THING USEFUL, IT WOULD BE RUINED BY THE MASSIVE INCOMPETENCE OF MY CO-WORKERS.
1-4-20 © 2020 Scott Adams, Inc./Dist. by Andrews McMeel
I PAY YOU TO ACT AS IF YOU ARE TRYING.
OH. IN THAT CASE, I WORKED HARD THIS WEEK.

WHY DIDN'T YOU UPGRADE THE SERVERS LIKE I ASKED?
YOU NEVER ASKED ME TO DO THAT.
YES, I DID. I TOLD YOU IN AN EMAIL.
NO, YOU DID NOT.
I KNOW YOU SAW IT BECAUSE YOU REPLIED.
I REPLIED TO A DIFFERENT EMAIL.
OKAY, LET ME FIND THE EMAIL AND SHOW YOU HOW WRONG YOU ARE.
SEE. IT CLEARLY SAYS, "GIVE ME A PROJECT UPDATE BY THURSDAY."
WHICH IS. . . AN ENTIRELY DIFFERENT TOPIC.
WHY ARE YOU FIGHTING ME ON THIS?
1-5-20

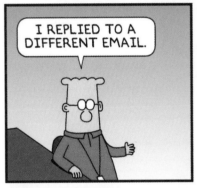

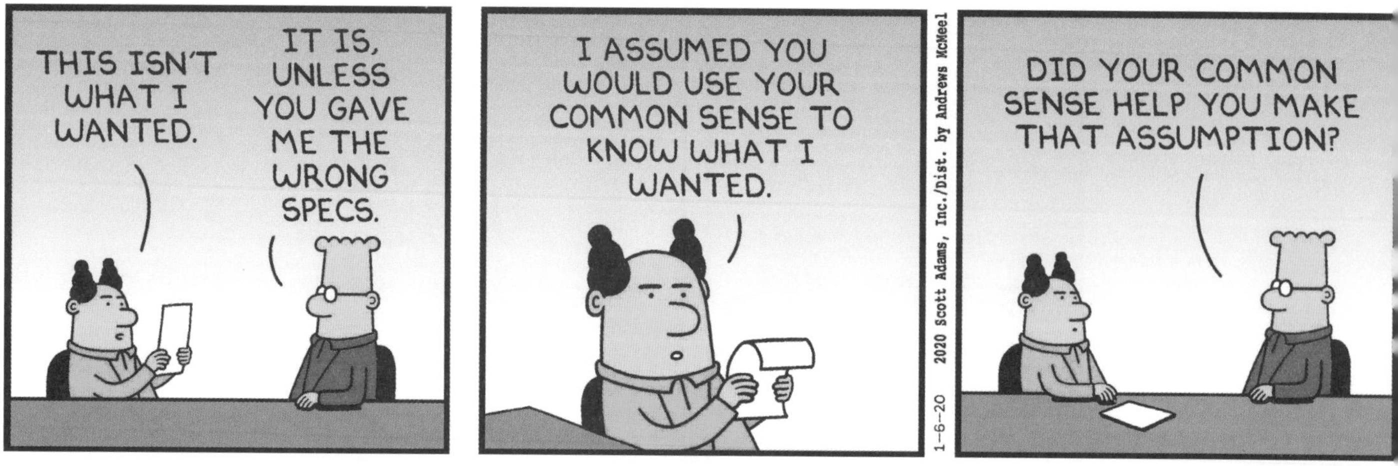
THIS ISN'T WHAT I WANTED.
IT IS, UNLESS YOU GAVE ME THE WRONG SPECS.
I ASSUMED YOU WOULD USE YOUR COMMON SENSE TO KNOW WHAT I WANTED.
1-6-20 © 2020 Scott Adams, Inc./Dist. by Andrews McMeel
DID YOUR COMMON SENSE HELP YOU MAKE THAT ASSUMPTION?

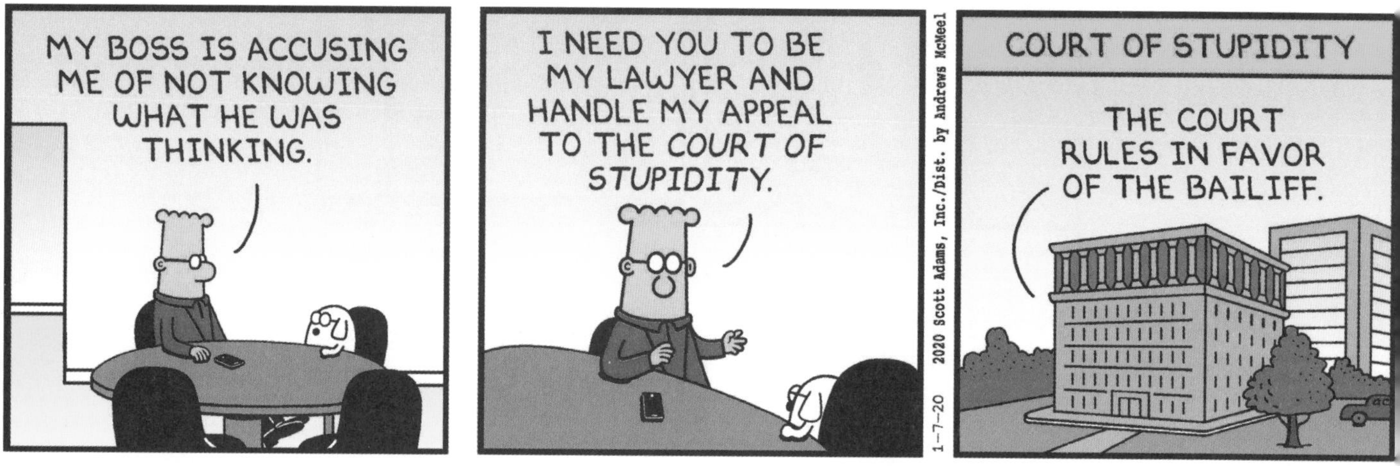
MY BOSS IS ACCUSING ME OF NOT KNOWING WHAT HE WAS THINKING.
I NEED YOU TO BE MY LAWYER AND HANDLE MY APPEAL TO THE *COURT OF STUPIDITY*.
1-7-20 © 2020 Scott Adams, Inc./Dist. by Andrews McMeel
COURT OF STUPIDITY
THE COURT RULES IN FAVOR OF THE BAILIFF.

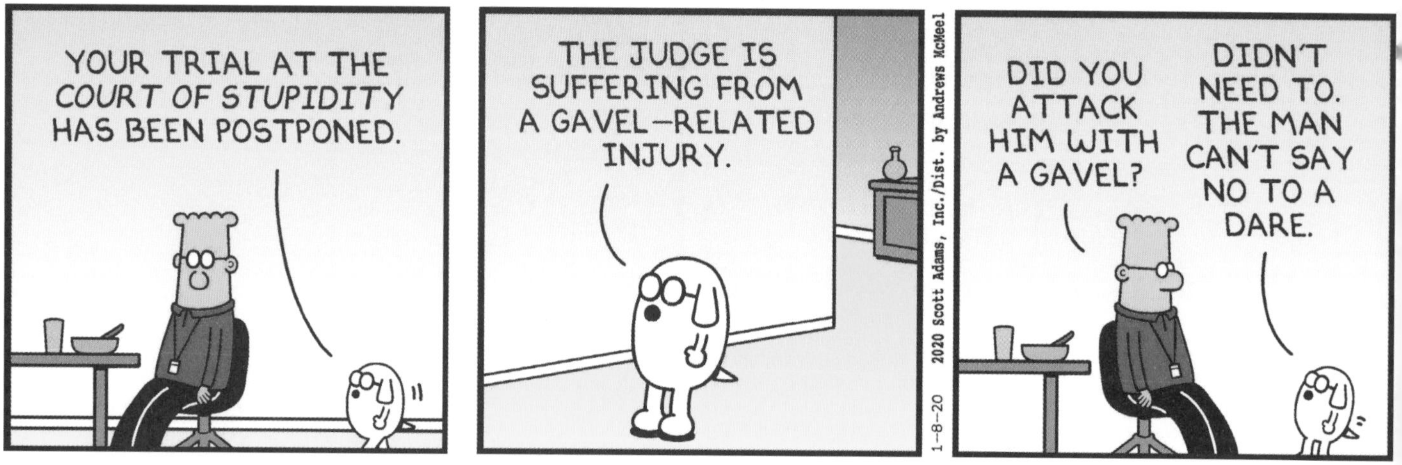
YOUR TRIAL AT THE *COURT OF STUPIDITY* HAS BEEN POSTPONED.
THE JUDGE IS SUFFERING FROM A GAVEL-RELATED INJURY.
1-8-20 © 2020 Scott Adams, Inc./Dist. by Andrews McMeel
DID YOU ATTACK HIM WITH A GAVEL?
DIDN'T NEED TO. THE MAN CAN'T SAY NO TO A DARE.

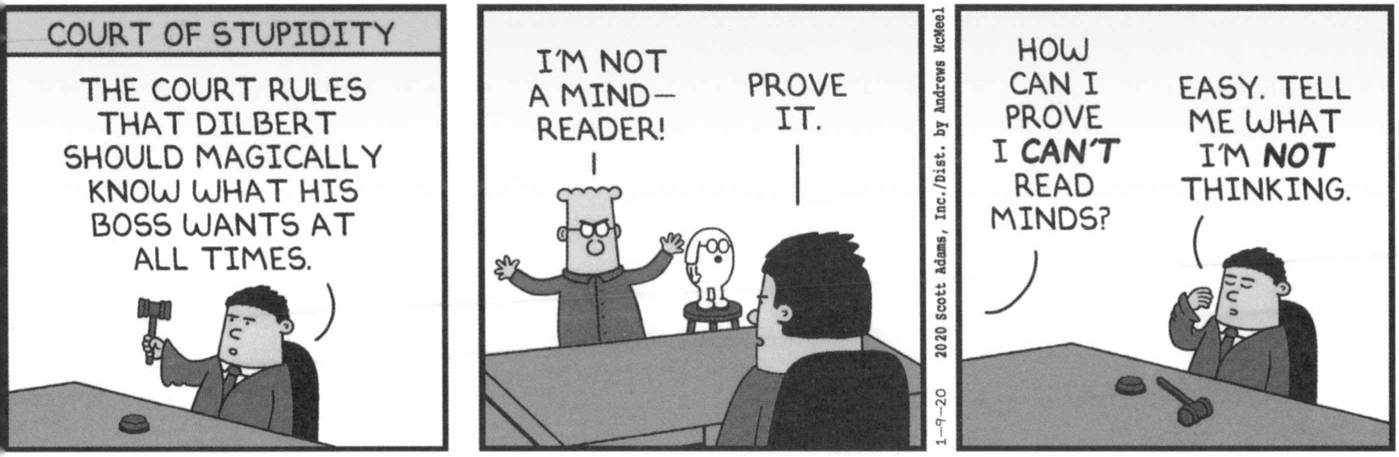
COURT OF STUPIDITY
THE COURT RULES THAT DILBERT SHOULD MAGICALLY KNOW WHAT HIS BOSS WANTS AT ALL TIMES.
I'M NOT A MIND-READER!
PROVE IT.
HOW CAN I PROVE I **CAN'T** READ MINDS?
EASY. TELL ME WHAT I'M **NOT** THINKING.
1-9-20 2020 Scott Adams, Inc./Dist. by Andrews McMeel

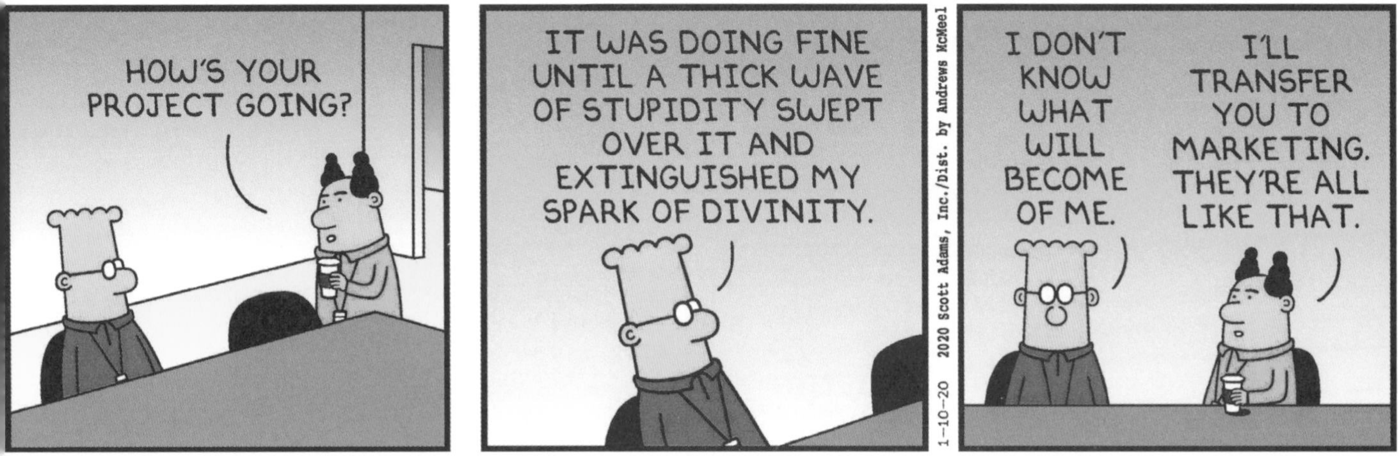
HOW'S YOUR PROJECT GOING?
IT WAS DOING FINE UNTIL A THICK WAVE OF STUPIDITY SWEPT OVER IT AND EXTINGUISHED MY SPARK OF DIVINITY.
I DON'T KNOW WHAT WILL BECOME OF ME.
I'LL TRANSFER YOU TO MARKETING. THEY'RE ALL LIKE THAT.
1-10-20 2020 Scott Adams, Inc./Dist. by Andrews McMeel

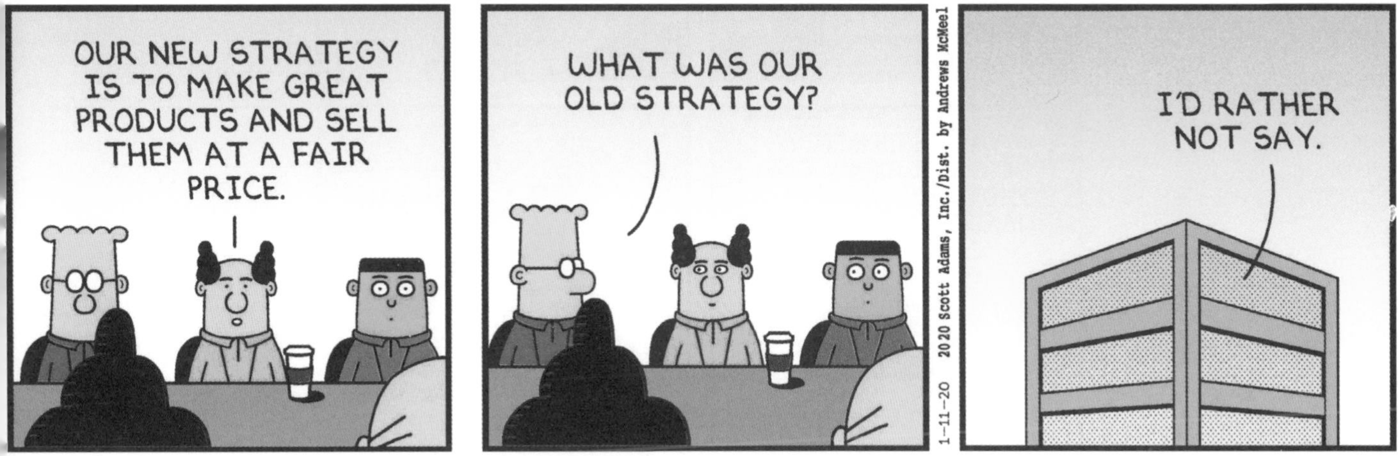
OUR NEW STRATEGY IS TO MAKE GREAT PRODUCTS AND SELL THEM AT A FAIR PRICE.
WHAT WAS OUR OLD STRATEGY?
I'D RATHER NOT SAY.
1-11-20 2020 Scott Adams, Inc./Dist. by Andrews McMeel

I CAN'T BE YOUR FRIEND BECAUSE I SAW A DISTURBING PHOTO OF YOU ON SOCIAL MEDIA.
YOU WERE IN A GROUP PHOTO WITH A PERSON WHOSE OPINIONS I ABHOR.
CAN YOU EXPLAIN WHY THAT MAKES ME A BAD PERSON?
SURE. DUH.
WHEN YOU APPEAR IN PHOTOS WITH OTHER PEOPLE, YOU ACQUIRE THEIR BAD CHARACTERISTICS.
I DON'T THINK THAT'S HOW IT WORKS.
THAT'S EXACTLY HOW IT WORKS! ONE PHOTO WITH A JERK MAKES YOU A JERK! CASE CLOSED!
SMILE.
NO-OOO!!!
©2020 Scott Adams, Inc./Dist. by Andrews McMeel
1-12-20

Andrews McMeel Publishing
a division of Andrews McMeel Universal
1130 Walnut Street, Kansas City, Missouri 64106
www.andrewsmcmeel.com

20 21 22 23 24 SDB 10 9 8 7 6 5 4 3 2 1

ISBN: 978-1-5248-6071-4

Library of Congress Control Number: 2020933041

www.dilbert.com